SENTENCE SKILLS

A Workbook for Writers

SIXTH EDITION

FORM A

SENTENCE SKILLS
A Workbook for Writers

SIXTH EDITION

FORM A

JOHN LANGAN

Atlantic Community College

McGraw
Hill

Boston, Massachusetts   Burr Ridge, Illinois   Dubuque, Iowa
Madison, Wisconsin   New York, New York   San Francisco, California   St. Louis, Missouri

McGraw-Hill

A Division of The **McGraw·Hill** *Companies*

SENTENCE SKILLS: A WORKBOOK FOR WRITERS, FORM A,

This book is printed on acid-free paper.

1 2 3 4 5 6 7 8 9 0 DOC/DOC 9 0 9 8 7

ISBN 0-07-036672-1

Editorial director: *Phillip Butcher*
Sponsoring editor: *Tim Julet/Peggy Rehberger*
Marketing manager: *Lesley Denton*
Project manager: *Pat Frederickson*
Production supervisor: *Louise A. Karam*
Designer: *Matthew Baldwin/Rafael Hernandez*
Cover designer: *AM Design/John Hite*
Cover illustrator: *Tina Hill*
Compositor: *Electronic Publishing Services, Inc.*
Typeface: *11/13 Times Roman*
Printer: *R. R. Donnelley & Sons Company*

http://www.mhcollege.com

About
The Author

John Langan has taught reading and writing at Atlantic Community College near Atlantic City, New Jersey, for over twenty years. The author of a popular series of college textbooks on both subjects, he enjoys the challenge of developing materials that teach skills in an especially clear and lively way. Before teaching, he earned advanced degrees in writing at Rutgers University and in reading at Glassboro State College. He also spent a year writing fiction that, he says, "is now at the back of a drawer waiting to be discovered and acclaimed posthumously." While in school, he supported himself by working as a truck driver, machinist, battery assembler, hospital attendant, and apple packer. He presently lives with his wife, Judith Nadell, near Philadelphia. Among his everyday pleasures are running, working on his Macintosh computer, and watching Philadelphia sports teams on TV. He also loves to read: newspapers at breakfast, magazines at lunch, and a chapter or two of a recent book ("preferably an autobiography") at night.

Contents

APPENDIXES

To the Instructor

Sentence Skills will help students learn to write effectively. It includes a basic rhetoric as well as full attention to grammar, punctuation, mechanics, and usage skills.

The book contains nine distinctive features to aid instructors and their students:

1   ***Coverage of basic writing skills is exceptionally thorough.*** The book pays special attention to fragments, run-ons, verbs, and other areas where students have serious problems. At the same time, a glance at the table of contents shows that the book treats skills (such as dictionary use and spelling improvement) not found in other texts. In addition, parts of the book are devoted to the basics of effective writing, to practice in editing and proofreading, and to achieving variety in sentence writing.

2   ***The book has a clear and flexible format.*** It is organized in four easy-to-use parts. Part One is a guide to the goals of effective writing followed by a series of activities to help students practice and master those goals. Part Two is a comprehensive treatment of the rules of grammar, mechanics, punctuation, and usage needed for clear writing. Part Three provides a series of mastery, proofreading, and editing tests to reinforce the sentence skills presented in Part Two. Part Four describes methods for writing varied and interesting sentences.

Since parts, sections, and chapters are self-contained, instructors can move easily from, for instance, a rhetorical principle or writing assignment in Part One to a grammar rule in Part Two to a mastery test in Part Three to a combining activity in Part Four.

3   ***Students learn sentence skills within a writing context.*** Researchers of writing have shown that students learn grammar and mechanics skills best within the context of actual writing assignments. Part One of the book therefore begins with the basic principles of paragraph and essay writing and provides a series of topics for writing. The remaining parts of the book present sentence skills as customs or conventions of English that students should master to help them better express their ideas.

4 **Practice activities are numerous.** Most skills are reinforced by activities, review tests, and mastery tests, as well as tests in the *Instructor's Manual.* For many of the skills in the book, there are over one hundred practice sentences.

5 **Practice materials are varied and lively.** In many basic writing texts, exercises are monotonous and dry, causing students to lose interest in the skills presented. In *Sentence Skills,* many exercises involve students in various ways. An inductive opening project allows students to see what they already know about a given skill. Within chapters, students may be asked to underline answers, add words, generate their own sentences, or edit passages. And the lively and engaging practice materials and readings in the book both maintain interest and help students appreciate the value of vigorous details in writing.

6 **Terminology is kept to a minimum.** In general, rules are explained using words students already know. A clause is a *word group;* a coordinating conjunction is a *joining word;* a nonrestrictive element is an *interrupter.* At the same time, traditional grammatical terms are mentioned briefly for students who learned them somewhere in the past and are comfortable seeing them again.

7 **Self-teaching is encouraged.** Students may check their answers to the introductory projects and the practice activities in Part Two by referring to the answers in Appendix B. In this way, they are given the responsibility for teaching themselves. At the same time, to ensure that the answer key is used as a learning tool only, answers are *not* given for the review tests in Part Two or for any of the reinforcement tests in Part Three. These answers appear in the *Annotated Instructor's Edition* and the *Instructor's Manual;* they can be copied and handed out to students at the discretion of the instructor.

8 **Diagnostic and achievement tests are provided.** These tests appear in Appendix A of the book. Each test may be given in two parts, the second of which provides instructors with a particularly detailed picture of a student's skill level.

9 **Valuable learning aids accompany the book.** The *Annotated Instructor's Edition* includes answers for all the activities and tests. The comprehensive *Instructor's Manual* contains (1) a complete set of additional mastery tests, (2) a model syllabus along with suggestions for teaching the course, and (3) an answer key. The manual is 8½ by 11 inches, so that the answer pages and the added mastery tests can be conveniently reproduced on copying machines. Another learning aid is a software disk to help students review and practice many of the skills in the text. Finally, instructors have at their disposal McGraw-Hill's *Allwrite!*—a high-interest, interactive grammar tutorial program on CD-ROM.

CHANGES IN THE NEW EDITION

The helpful comments of writing instructors who have used previous versions of *Sentence Skills* have prompted a major change in the new edition. The book now begins with a guide to the basic principles of writing, followed by a series of activities to help students practice and master those goals. Here are features of this new part of the book:

- ● *Attention to attitude.* In its opening pages, the book helps students recognize and deal with their attitude about writing. Attitude is shown to be an important part of learning to write well.
- ● *Focus on four basic goals in writing.* After looking at an effective model paper, students learn the four basic steps they should take to write effectively.
- ● *Emphasis on process.* Students are then shown that writing is a process, and that a paper typically begins with one or more prewriting strategies and proceeds through an outline and a series of drafts and revisions that continue up to a final proofreading.
- ● *Treatment of both the paragraph and the essay.* A model paragraph is expanded into an essay as part of helping students learn the basics of both paragraph and essay writing.
- ● *A sequence of learning activities.* The second chapter in Part One contains a carefully designed sequence of interesting activities that help students learn and master the principles of effective writing, one step at a time.
- ● *Spotlight on specific details.* In particular, the activities will help students understand the nature of specific details and how to generate those details. As writing instructors well know, learning how to write concretely is a key stage for students to master in becoming effective writers.

Along with the new Part One, changes in other parts of the text include an updating and upgrading of practice materials. In particular, a number of multicultural names have been added to better represent the diversity of students using the book. Moreover, a guide to how students can work with and learn from each other in a collaborative way has been added to the introduction to the book.

ACKNOWLEDGMENTS

Reviewers who have provided assistance include Carlo Annese, Bergen Community College; Matthew Corcoran, York College; Marlys Cordoba, College of the Siskiyous; Judy Covington, Trident Technical Community College; John J. Covolo, Lakeland Community College; Dr. Miriam Dick, Mercy College; Toni Empringhan, El Camino Community College; Jeanne Gilligan, Delaware Technical and Community College; Roland Gosselin, CUNY—Bronx Community College; Marjorie B. Green, Caldwell Community College; Pamela Hudson, Hawaii Community College; Howard Irby, CUNY—Bronx Community College; Mary Likely, Nassau Community College; Orlandus Moss, Adirondack Community College; Michael Orlando, Bergen Community College; Charles Piltch, CUNY— John Jay College; Cheryl Roberts, Tarrant County Junior College; Sam Rogal, Illinois Valley Community College; Madeline Seltzer, Manor Jr. College; Linda Tappmeyer, Southwest Baptist University; Edna Troiano, Charles County Community College; and Miriam Wasserman, CUNY—New York City Technical College. I am also grateful for the help provided by Janet M. Goldstein as I worked on this revision of the book.

John Langan

Introduction: Learning Sentence Skills

WHY LEARN SENTENCE SKILLS?

Why should someone planning a career as a nurse have to learn sentence skills? Why should an accounting major have to pass a competency test in grammar as part of a college education? Why should a potential physical therapist or graphic artist or computer programmer have to spend hours learning the rules of English? Perhaps you asked questions like these when you found yourself in a class with this book. On the other hand, perhaps you *know* you need to strengthen basic writing skills, even though you may be unclear about the specific ways the skills will be of use to you. Whatever your views, you should understand why sentence skills—all the rules that make up standard English—are so important.

Clear Communication

Standard English, or "language by the book," is needed to communicate your thoughts to others with a minimal amount of distortion and misinterpretation. Knowing the traditional rules of grammar, punctuation, and usage will help you write clear sentences when communicating with others. You may have heard of the party game in which one person whispers a message to the next person; the message is passed, in turn, along a line of several other people. By the time the last person in line is asked to give the message aloud, it is usually so garbled and inaccurate that it barely resembles the original. Written communication in some form of English other than standard English carries the same potential for disaster.

To see how important standard English is to written communication, examine the pairs of sentences on the following pages and answer the questions in each case.

1. Which sentence indicates that there might be a plot against Ted?
    a. We should leave Ted. These fumes might be poisonous.
    b. We should leave, Ted. These fumes might be poisonous.
2. Which sentence encourages self-mutilation?
    a. Leave your paper and hand in the dissecting kit.
    b. Leave your paper, and hand in the dissecting kit.
3. Which sentence indicates that the writer has a weak grasp of geography?
    a. As a child, I lived in Lake Worth, which is close to Palm Beach and Alaska.
    b. As a child, I lived in Lake Worth, which is close to Palm Beach, and Alaska.
4. In which sentence does the dog warden seem dangerous?
    a. Foaming at the mouth, the dog warden picked up the stray.
    b. Foaming at the mouth, the stray was picked up by the dog warden.
5. Which announcer was probably fired from the job?
    a. Outside the Academy Awards theater, the announcer called the guests names as they arrived.
    b. Outside the Academy Awards theater, the announcer called the guests' names as they arrived.
6. On the basis of the opening lines below of two students' exam essays, which student seems likely to earn a higher grade?
    a. Defense mechanisms is the way people hides their inner feelings and deals with stress. There is several types that we use to be protecting our true feelings.
    b. Defense mechanisms are the methods people use to cope with stress. Using a defense mechanism allows a person to hide his or her real desires and goals.
7. On the basis of the following lines taken from two English papers, which student seems likely to earn a higher grade?
    a. A big problem on this campus is apathy, students don't participate in college activities. Such as clubs, student government, and plays.
    b. The most pressing problem on campus is the disgraceful state of the student lounge area. The floor is dirty, the chairs are torn, and the ceiling leaks.

8. On the basis of the following sentences taken from two employees' reports, which worker is more likely to be promoted?
    a. The spring line failed by 20 percent in the meeting of projected profit expectations. Which were issued in January of this year.
    b. Profits from our spring line were disappointing. They fell 20 percent short of January's predictions.
9. On the basis of the following paragraphs taken from two job application letters, which job prospect would you favor?
    a. Let me say in closing that their are an array of personal qualities I have presented in this letter, together, these make me hopeful of being interviewed for this attraktive position.

        sincerly yours'

        Brian Davis

    b. I feel I have the qualifications needed to do an excellent job as assistant manager of the jewelry department at Horton's. I look forward to discussing the position further at a personal interview.

        Sincerely yours,

        Richard O'Keeney

In each case, the first choice (*a*) contains sentence-skills mistakes. These mistakes range from missing or misplaced commas to misspellings to wordy or pretentious language. As a result of these mistakes, clear communication cannot occur—and misunderstandings, lower grades, and missed job opportunities are probable results. The point, then, is that all the rules that make up standard written English should be a priority if you want your writing to be clear and effective.

Success in College

Standard English is essential if you want to succeed in college. Any report, paper, review, essay exam, or assignment you are responsible for should be written in the best standard English you can produce. If not, it won't matter how fine your ideas are or how hard you worked—most likely, you will receive a lower grade than you would otherwise deserve. In addition, because standard English requires you to express your thoughts in precise, clear sentences, training yourself to follow the rules can help you think more logically. And the basic logic you learn to practice at the sentence level will help as you work to produce well-reasoned papers in all your subjects.

Success at Work

Knowing standard English will also help you achieve success on the job. Studies have shown repeatedly that skillful communication, more than any other factor, is the key to job satisfaction and steady career progress. A solid understanding of standard English is a basic part of this vital communication ability. Moreover, most experts agree that we are now living in an "age of information"—a time when people who use language skillfully have a great advantage over those who do not. Fewer of us will be working in factories or at other types of manual labor. Many more of us will be working with information in various forms—accumulating it, processing it, analyzing it. No matter what kind of job you are preparing yourself for, technical or not, you will need to know standard English to keep pace with this new age. Otherwise, you are likely to be left behind, limited to low-paying jobs that offer few challenges or financial rewards.

Success in Everyday Life

Standard English will help you succeed not just at school and work but in everyday life as well. It will help you feel more comfortable, for example, in writing letters to friends and relatives. It will enable you to write effective notes to your children's schools. It will help command attention to a letter of complaint that you write to a company about a product. It will allow you to write letters of inquiry about bills—hospital, medical, utility, or legal—or about any kind of service. To put it simply, in our daily lives, those who can use and write standard English have more power than those who cannot.

HOW THIS BOOK IS ORGANIZED

- A good way to get a quick sense of any book is to turn to the table of contents. By referring to pages vii–x, you will see that the book is organized into four basic parts. What are they?

  _____

  _____

  _____

  _____

- Part One is an introduction to _____

- Part Two deals with sentence skills. How many skills areas (sections) are covered in all? (Count them.) _____

- Part Three reinforces the skills presented in Part Two. What are the four kinds of reinforcement activities in Part Three?

  _____

  _____

  _____

  _____

- Turn to the introduction to Part Four to learn the purpose of that part of the book and write the purpose here: _____

  _____

- Helpful charts in the book include (*fill in the missing words*) the _____

  _____ on the inside front cover, the _____ charts in

  Appendix C, and the _____ of sentence skills on the inside

  back cover.

- Finally, three appendixes at the end of the book contain:

  _____

  _____

  _____

HOW TO USE THIS BOOK

Here is a way to use *Sentence Skills*. First, read and work through Part One, Effective Writing—a guide to the goals of effective writing followed by a series of activities to help you practice and master those goals. Your instructor may direct you to certain activities, depending on your needs. In addition, the paragraph and essay writing assignments on pages 73–80 should not be done all at once but should be spread out over the course of the semester.

Second, take the diagnostic test on pages 505–515. By analyzing which sections of the test give you trouble, you will discover which skills you need to concentrate on. When you turn to an individual skill in Part Two, begin by reading and thinking about the introductory project. Often, you will be pleasantly surprised to find that you know more about this area of English than you thought you did. After all, you have probably been speaking English with fluency and ease for many years; you have an instinctive knowledge of how the language works. This knowledge gives you a solid base for refining your skills.

Your third step is to work on the skills in Part Two by reading the explanations and completing the practices. You can check your answers to each practice activity in this part by turning to the answer key at the back of the book (Appendix B). Try to figure out *why* you got some answers wrong—you want to uncover any weak spots in your understanding.

Your next step is to use the review tests at the ends of chapters in Part Two to evaluate your understanding of a skill in its entirety. Your instructor may also ask you to take the mastery tests or other reinforcement tests in Part Three of the book. To help ensure that you take the time needed to learn each skill thoroughly, the answers to these test are *not* in the answer key.

While you are working through individual skills, you should also take time for the sentence-combining activities in Part Four.

WORKING WITH OTHERS

In addition to working on your own or with your instructor (or both), you will benefit by working with other students. Here is a specific way to proceed.

- Work with one other student (as a pair) or with two or three other students (as a small group). Sit together so you can talk easily with one another.

- Suppose that you are studying "Fragments," an early chapter in Part Two. Take turns reading aloud the "Introductory Project" and make sure you agree with one another on your answers to the four fill-in items. Then turn to the back of the book to check your answers. If you have any questions about the material, share them with your partner or partners. Also, be ready to help explain anything about the material that may seem unclear to your partner or partners. In a nutshell, interact with one another and help one another.

- Continue through the chapter, reading aloud each explanation and then taking turns doing the practice materials. No one person should do all the reading or answering; you should share the work. Make sure you agree before going from one explanation or activity to the next.

- You will find that working as part of a pair or small group will energize and motivate you and help you teach one another. Talking and interacting with your peers can, indeed, help learning. Whenever you have a question or problem that your team cannot deal with, use your instructor as a resource.

- When you and other groups get to the end of a chapter, your instructor may give you an answer key so that you can check all of your answers. Alternatively, your instructor may work together with the whole class, quickly reviewing the material.

AS YOU BEGIN

The emphasis in this book is on writing clear, error-free sentences as well as on composition. And the heart of the book is the practice materials that help reinforce the sentence skills you learn. A great deal of effort has been taken to make the practices lively and engaging and to avoid the dull, repetitive skills work that has given grammar books such a bad reputation. This text will help you stay interested as you work on the rules of English that you need to learn. The rest is a matter of your personal determination and hard work. If you decide—and only you can decide—that effective writing is important to your school and career goals and that you want to learn the basic skills needed to write clearly and effectively, this book will help you reach those goals.

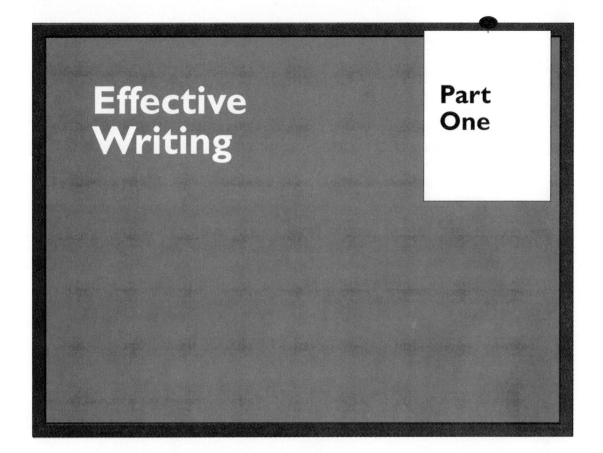

Effective Writing

Part One

INTRODUCTION

Part One is a guide to the goals of effective writing followed by a series of activities to help you practice and master those goals. Read the first chapter carefully. Then work through the series of activities in the second chapter. Your instructor may direct you to certain exercises, depending on your needs. After completing the activities, begin work on the paragraph and essay writing assignments at the end of the chapter.

At the same time that you are writing papers, start working through the sentence skills in Parts Two, Three, and Four of the book. You want to practice the sentence skills in the context of actual writing assignments. That is the surest way to master the rules of grammar, mechanics, punctuation, and usage.

Note: Your goal should be to check each of your papers carefully, doing your best to apply the sentence skills you have learned. To help you achieve such a transfer, your instructor may ask you to rewrite a paper as many times as necessary to correct sentence-skills mistakes. A writing progress chart on pages 537–538 (in Appendix C) will help you track your performance.

A Brief Guide to Effective Writing

This part of the book will show you how to write effective paragraphs and essays. The following questions will be answered in turn:

1 Why does your attitude about writing matter?
2 What is a paragraph?
3 What are the goals of effective writing?
4 How do you reach the goals of effective writing?
5 What is an essay?
6 What are the parts of an essay?

WHY DOES YOUR ATTITUDE ABOUT WRITING MATTER?

Your attitude about writing is an important part of learning to write well. To get a sense of just how you feel about writing, read the following statements. Put a check beside those statements with which you agree. (This activity is not a test, so try to be as honest as possible.)

_____ 1. A good writer should be able to sit down and write a paper straight through without stopping.

_____ 2. Writing is a skill that anyone can learn with practice.

_____ 3. I'll never be good at writing because I make too many mistakes in spelling, grammar, and punctuation.

_____ 4. Because I dislike writing, I always start a paper at the last possible minute.

_____ 5. I've always done poorly in English, and I don't expect that to change.

Now read the following comments about these five statements. The comments will help you see if your attitude is hurting or helping your efforts to become a better writer.

1 *A good writer should be able to sit down and write a paper straight through without stopping.*

The statement is *false*. Writing is, in fact, a process. It is done not in one easy step but in a series of steps, and seldom at one sitting. If you cannot do a paper all at once, that simply means you are like most of the other people on the planet. It is harmful to carry around the false idea that writing should be an easy matter.

2 *Writing is a skill that anyone can learn with practice.*

This statement is *absolutely true*. Writing is a skill, like driving or word processing, that you can master with hard work. If you want to learn to write, you can. It is as simple as that. If you believe this, you are ready to learn how to become a competent writer.

Some people hold the false belief that writing is a natural gift, which some have and others do not. Because of this belief, they never make a truly honest effort to learn to write—and so they never learn.

3 *I'll never be good at writing because I make too many mistakes in spelling, grammar, and punctuation.*

The first concern in good writing should be *content*—what you have to say. Your ideas and feelings are what matter most. You should not worry about spelling, grammar, and punctuation while working on content.

Unfortunately, some people are so self-conscious about making mistakes that they do not focus on what they want to say. They need to realize that a paper is best done in stages and that the rules can and should wait until a later stage in the writing process. Through review and practice, you will eventually learn how to follow the rules with confidence.

4 *Because I dislike writing, I always start a paper at the last possible minute.*

This is all too common. You feel you are *going to* do poorly and then behave in a way to ensure you *will* do poorly! Your attitude is so negative that you defeat yourself—not even allowing enough time to really try.

Again, what you need to realize is that writing is a process. Because it is done in steps, you don't have to get it right all at once. Just get started well in advance. If you allow yourself enough time, you'll find a way to make a paper come together.

5   *I've done poorly in English in the past, and I don't expect that to change now.*

How you may have performed in the *past* does not control how you can perform in the *present*. Even if you did poorly in English in high school, it is in your power to make this one of your best subjects in college. If you believe writing can be learned, and if you work hard at it, you *will* become a better writer.

In brief, your attitude is crucial. If you believe you are a poor writer and always will be, chances are you will not improve. If you realize you can become a better writer, chances are you will improve. Depending on how you allow yourself to think, you can be your own best friend or your own worst enemy.

WHAT IS A PARAGRAPH?

A *paragraph* is a series of sentences about one main idea, or *point*. A paragraph typically starts with a point, and the rest of the paragraph provides specific details to support and develop that point.

Consider the following paragraph, written by a student named Gary Callahan.

Returning to School

Starting college at the age of twenty-nine was not easy for me. For one thing, I did not have much support from my parents or friends. My father asked, "Didn't you get dumped on enough in high school? Why go back for more?" My mother worried, "Where's the money going to come from?" My friends seemed threatened. "Hey, there's the college man," they would say when I approached. Another reason that starting college was difficult was that I had bad memories of school. I had spent years of my life sitting in classrooms completely bored, watching clocks tick ever so slowly toward the final bell. When I was not bored, I was afraid of being embarrassed. Once a teacher called on me and then said, "Ah, forget it, Callahan," when he realized I did not know that answer. Finally, I soon learned that college would give me little time with my family. After work every day, I have just an hour and ten minutes to eat and spend time with my wife and daughter before going off to class. When I get back, my daughter is in bed, and my wife and I have only a little time together. Then the time on weekends goes by quickly, with all the homework I have to do. But I am going to persist because I believe a better life awaits me with a college degree.

The above paragraph, like many effective paragraphs, starts by stating a main idea, or point. In this case, the point is that starting college at age twenty-nine was not easy. A *point* is a general idea that contains an opinion.

In our everyday lives, we constantly make points about all kinds of matters. We express all kinds of opinions: "That was a terrible movie." "My psychology instructor is the best teacher I have ever had." "My sister is a generous person." "Eating at that restaurant was a mistake." "That team should win the playoff game." "Waitressing is the worst job I ever had." "Our state should allow the death penalty." "Cigarette smoking should be banned everywhere." In *talking* to people, we don't always give the reasons for our opinions. But in *writing,* we *must* provide reasons to support our ideas. Only by supplying solid evidence for any point that we make can we communicate effectively with readers.

An effective paragraph, then, not only must make a point but must support it with *specific evidence*—reasons, examples, and other details. Such specifics help prove to readers that the point is a reasonable one. Even if readers do not agree with the writer, at least they have in front of them the evidence on which the writer has based his or her opinion. Readers are like juries; they want to see the evidence so that they can make their own judgments.

Take a moment now to examine the evidence that Gary has provided to back up his point about starting college at twenty-nine. Complete the following outline of Gary's paragraph by summarizing in a few words his reasons and the details that develop them. The first reason and its supporting details are summarized for you as an example.

Point: Starting college at the age of twenty-nine was not easy.

Reason 1: Little support from parents and friends

Details that develop reason 1: Father asked why I wanted to be dumped on again, mother worried about tuition money, friends seemed threatened

Reason 2: I had bad memory of school.

Details that develop reason 2: being bored, and afraid of being embarrassed by teacher

Reason 3: College will give me little time to spend with my family

Details that develop reason 3: after work there would be little time to eat and spend with them also my weekeen would be full time

As the outline makes clear, Gary provides three reasons to support his point about starting college at twenty-nine: (1) he had little support from his friends or parents, (2) he had bad memories of school, and (3) college left him little time with

of homework.

his family. Gary also provides vivid details to back up each of his three reasons. His reasons and descriptive details enable readers to see why he feels that starting college at twenty-nine was not easy.

To write an effective paragraph, then, aim to do what Gary has done: begin by making a point, and then go on to support that point with specific evidence. Finally, like Gary, end your paper with a sentence that rounds off the paragraph and provides a sense of completion.

WHAT ARE THE GOALS OF EFFECTIVE WRITING?

Now that you have considered an effective student paragraph, it is time to look at four goals of effective writing:

Goal 1: Make a Point

It is often best to state your point in the first sentence of your paper, just as Gary does in his paragraph about returning to school. The sentence that expresses the main idea, or point, of a paragraph is called the *topic sentence.* Activities on pages 40–43 in the next chapter of this book will help you learn how to write a topic sentence.

Goal 2: Support the Point

To support your point, you need to provide specific reasons, examples, and other details that explain and develop it. The more precise and particular your supporting details are, the better your readers can "see," "hear," and "feel" them. Activities on pages 35–40 and 44–56 in the next chapter will help you learn how to be specific in your writing.

Goal 3: Organize the Support

You will find it helpful to learn two common ways of organizing the support in a paragraph—*listing order* and *time order.* You should also learn the signal words, known as *transitions,* that increase the effectiveness of each method.

Listing Order: The writer organizes the supporting evidence in a paper by providing a list of two or more reasons, examples, or details. Often the most important or interesting item is saved for last because the reader is most likely to remember the last thing read.

Transition words that indicate listing order include the following:

one	second	also	next	last of all
for one thing	third	another	moreover	finally
first of all	next	in addition	furthermore	

The paragraph about starting college uses a listing order: it lists three reasons why starting college at twenty-nine is not easy, and each of those three reasons is introduced by one of the above transitions. In the spaces below, write in the three transitions:

For one thing   *Another reason*   *Finally.*

The first reason in the paragraph about starting college is introduced with *for one thing,* the second reason by *another,* and the third reason by *finally.*

Time Order: Supporting details are presented in the order in which they occurred. *First* this happened; *next* this; *after* that, this; and so on. Many paragraphs, especially paragraphs that tell a story or give a series of directions, are organized in a time order.

Transition words that show time relationships include the following:

transition words

first	before	after	when	then
next	during	now	while	until
as	soon	later	often	finally

Read the paragraph below, which is organized in time order. See if you can underline the six transition words that show the time relationships.

Della had a sad experience while driving home last night. She traveled along the dark, winding road that led toward her home. She was only two miles from her house when she noticed a glimmer of light in the road. The next thing she knew, she heard a sickening thud and realized she had struck an animal. The light, she realized, had been its eyes reflected in her car's headlights. Della stopped the car and ran back to see what she had hit. It was a handsome cocker spaniel, with blond fur and long ears. As she bent over the still form, she realized there was nothing to be done. The dog was dead. Della searched the dog for a collar and tags. There was nothing. <u>Before</u> leaving, she walked to several nearby houses, asking if anyone knew who owned the dog. No one did. <u>Finally</u> Della gave up and drove on. She was sad to leave someone's pet lying there alone.

The main point of the paragraph is stated in its first sentence: "Della had a sad experience while driving home last night." The support for this point is all the details of Della's experience. Those details are presented in the order in which they occurred. The time relationships are highlighted by these transitions: *while, when, next, as, before,* and *finally.*

More about Transitions: Transitions are words and phrases that indicate relationships between ideas. They are like signposts that guide travelers, showing them how to move smoothly from one place to the next. Be sure to take advantage of transitions. They will help organize and connect your ideas, and they will help your readers follow the direction of your thoughts.

To see how transitions help, put a check beside the item in each pair that is easier to read and understand.

Pair A

_____ One way to stay in shape is to eat low-calorie, low-fat foods. A good strategy is to walk or jog at least twenty minutes four times a week.

 One way to stay in shape is to eat low-calorie, low-fat foods. Another good strategy is to walk or jog at least twenty minutes four times a week.

Pair B

_____ I begin each study session by going to a quiet place and setting out my textbook, pen, and notebook. I check my assignment book to see what I have to read.

_____ I begin each study session by going to a quiet place and setting out my textbook, pen, and notebook. Then I check my assignment book to see what I have to read.

In each pair, the second item is easier to read and understand. In pair A, the listing word *another* makes it clear that the writer is going on to a second way to stay in shape. In pair B, the time word *then* makes the relationship between the sentences clear. The writer first sets out the textbook and a pen and notebook and *then* checks an assignment book to see what to do.

Activities on pages 56–60 will give you practice in the use of listing order and time order, as well as transitions, to organize the supporting details of a paragraph.

Goal 4: Write Error-Free Sentences

If you use correct spelling and follow the rules of grammar, punctuation, and usage, your sentences will be clear and well written. But by no means must you have all that information in your head. Even the best of writers need to use reference materials to be sure their writing is correct. So when you write your papers, keep a good dictionary and grammar handbook nearby.

In general, however, save them for after you've gotten your ideas firmly down in writing. You'll see in the next part of this guide that Gary made a number of sentence errors as he worked on his paragraph. But he simply ignored them until he got to a later draft of his paper, when there would be time enough to make the needed corrections.

HOW DO YOU REACH THE GOALS OF EFFECTIVE WRITING?

Even professional writers do not sit down and write a paper automatically, in one draft. Instead, they have to work on it a step at a time. Writing a paper is a process that can be divided into the following steps:

- *Step 1:* Getting Started through Prewriting
- *Step 2:* Preparing a Scratch Outline
- *Step 3:* Writing the First Draft
- *Step 4:* Revising
- *Step 5:* Proofreading

These steps are described on the following pages.

Step 1: Getting Started through Prewriting

What you need to learn first are strategies for working on a paper. These strategies will help you do the thinking needed to figure out both the point you want to make and the support you have for that point.

There are several *prewriting strategies*—strategies you use before writing the first draft of your paper:

- Freewriting
- Questioning
- Clustering
- Making a list

Freewriting: *Freewriting* is just sitting down and writing whatever comes into your mind about a topic. Do this for ten minutes or so. Write without stopping and without worrying at all about spelling, grammar, or the like. Simply get down on paper all the information about the topic that occurs to you.

Here is the freewriting Gary did on his problems with returning to school. Gary had been given the assignment "Write about a problem you are facing at the present time." Gary felt right away that he would write about his college situation. He began prewriting as a way to explore and generate details on his topic.

Example of Freewriting

One thing I want to write about is going back to school. At age twenty-nine. A lot to deal with. I sometimes wonder if Im nuts to try to do this or just stupid. I had to deal with my folks when I decided. My dad hated school. He knew when to quit, I'll say that for him. But he doesn't understand Im different. I have a right to my own life. And I want to better myself. He teases me alot. Says things like didnt you get dumped on enough in high school, why go back for more. My mom doesnt understand either. Just keeps worring about where the money was coming from. Then my friends. They make fun of me. Also my wife has to do more of the heavy house stuff because I'm out so much. Getting back to my friends, they say dumb things to get my goat. Like calling me the college man or saying ooh, we'd better watch our grammer. Sometimes I think my dads right, school was no fun for me. Spent years just sitting in class waiting for final bell so I could escape. Teachers didnt help me or take an intrest, some of them made me feel like a real loser. Now things are different and I like most of my instructors. I can talk to the instructor after class or to ask questions if I'm confused. But I really need more time to spend with family, I hardly see them any more. What I am doing is hard all round for them and me.

Notice that there are problems with spelling, grammar, and punctuation in Gary's freewriting. Gary is not worried about such matters, nor should he be. He is just concentrating on getting ideas and details down on paper. He knows that it is best to focus on one thing at a time. At this stage, he just wants to write out thoughts as they come to him, to do some thinking on paper.

You should take the same approach when freewriting: explore your topic without worrying at all about being "correct." Figuring out what you want to say should have all your attention in this early stage of the writing process.

Questioning: *Questioning* means that you think about your topic by writing down a series of questions and answers about it. Your questions can start with words like *what, when, where, why,* and *how.*

Here are some questions that Gary might have asked while developing his paper, as well as some answers to those questions:

Example of Questioning

Why do I have a problem with returning to school? My parents and friends don't support me.
How do they not support me? Dad asks why I want to be dumped on more. Mom is upset
because college costs lots of money. Friends tease me about being a college man.
When do they not support me? When I go to my parents' home for Friday night visits, when
my friends see me walking toward them.
Where do I have this problem? At home, where I barely see my wife and daughter before
having to go to class, and where I have to let my wife do house things on weekends while
I'm studying.
Why else do I have this problem? High school was bad experience.
What details back up the idea that high school was bad experience? Sat in class bored,
couldn't wait to get out, teachers didn't help me. One embarrassed me when I didn't
know the answer.

Clustering: Clustering is another prewriting strategy that can be used to generate
material for a paper. It is helpful for people who like to do their thinking in a visual
way.

In *clustering,* you begin by stating your subject in a few words in the center of
a blank sheet of paper. Then as ideas come to you, put them in ovals, boxes, or
circles about the subject, and draw lines to connect them to the subject. Put minor
ideas or details in smaller boxes or circles, and also use connecting lines to show
how they relate.

Keep in mind that there is no right or wrong way of clustering. It is a way to
think on paper about how various ideas and details relate to one another. Below is
an example of clustering that Gary might have done to develop his idea.

Example of Clustering

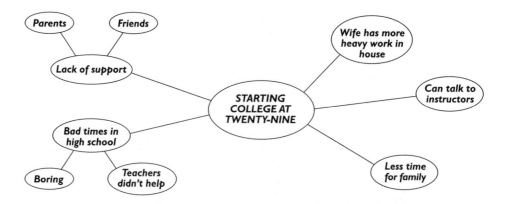

Making a List: In *making a list*—a prewriting strategy also known as *listing, list making,* and *brainstorming*—you make a list of ideas and details that could go into your paper. Simply pile these items up, one after another, without worrying about putting them in any special order. Try to accumulate as many details as you can think of.

After Gary did his freewriting about returning to school, he made up the list of details shown below.

Example of Listing

parents give me hard time when they see me
Dad hated school
Dad quit school after eighth grade
Dad says I was dumped on enough in high school
Dad asks why I want to go back for more
Mom also doesnt understand
keeps asking how Ill pay for it
friends give me a hard time too
friends call me college man
say they have to watch their grammar
my wife has more heavy work around the house
also high school had been no fun for me
just sat in class after class
couldnt wait for final bell to ring
wanted to escape
teachers didn't help me
teachers didn't take an interest in me
one called on me, then told me to forget it
I felt like a real loser
I didn't want to go back to his class
now I'm more sure of myself
OK not to know an answer
talk to instructors after class
job plus schoolwork take all my time
get home late, then rush through dinner
then spend evening studying
even have to do homework on weekends

One detail led to another as Gary expanded his list. Slowly but surely, more supporting material emerged that he could use in developing his paper. By the time he had finished his list, he was ready to plan an outline of this paragraph and to write his first draft.

Notice that in making a list, as in freewriting, details are included that will not actually end up in the final paragraph. Gary decided later not to develop the idea that his wife now has more heavy work to do in the house. And he realized that several of his details were about why school is easier in college ("now I'm more sure of myself," "OK not to know an answer," and "talk to instructors after class"); such details were not relevant to his point.

It is natural for a number of such extra or unrelated details to appear as part of the prewriting process. The goal of prewriting is to get a lot of information down on paper. You can then add to, shape, and subtract from your raw material as you take your paper through the series of writing drafts.

Important Points about Prewriting Strategies: Some writers may use only one of the prewriting strategies described here. Others may use bits and pieces of all four strategies. Any one strategy can lead to another. Freewriting may lead to questioning or clustering, which may then lead to a list. Or a writer may start with a list and then use freewriting or questioning to develop items on the list. During this early stage of the writing process, as you do your thinking on paper, anything goes. You should not expect a straight-line progression from the beginning to the end of your paper. Instead, there probably will be a constant moving back and forth as you work to discover your point and decide just how you will develop it.

Keep in mind that prewriting can also help you choose from among several topics. Gary might not have been so sure about which problem to write about. Then he could have made a list of possible topics—areas in his life in which he has had problems. After selecting two or three topics from the list, he could have done some prewriting on each to see which seemed most promising. After finding a likely topic, Gary would have continued with his prewriting activities until he had a solid main point and plenty of support.

Finally, remember that you are not ready to begin writing a paper until you know your main point and many of the details that can be used to support it. Don't rush through prewriting. It's better to spend more time on this stage than to waste time writing a paragraph for which you have no solid point and not enough interesting support.

Step 2: Preparing a Scratch Outline

A *scratch outline* is a brief plan for a paragraph. It shows at a glance the point of the paragraph and the main support for that point. It is the logical backbone on which the paper is built.

This rough outline often follows freewriting, questioning, clustering, or listing—or all four. Or it may gradually emerge in the midst of these strategies. In fact, trying to outline is a good way to see if you need to do more prewriting. If a solid outline does not emerge, then you know you need to do more prewriting to clarify your main point or its support. Once you have a workable outline, you may realize, for instance, that you want to do more listing to develop one of the supporting details in the outline.

In Gary's case, as he was working on his list of details, he suddenly discovered what the plan of his paragraph could be. He went back to the list, crossed out items that he now realized did not fit, and added the following comments.

Examples of List with Comments

Starting college at twenty-nine isn't easy—three reasons

parents give me hard time when they see me
Dad hated school
Dad quit school after eighth grade
Dad says I was dumped on enough in high school
Dad asks why I want to go back for more
Mom also doesnt understand   *Parents and friends*
keeps asking how Ill pay for it   *don't support me*
friends give me a hard time too
friends call me college man
say they have to watch their grammar
~~my wife has more heavy work around the house~~
also high school had been no fun for me
just sat in class after class
couldnt wait for final bell to ring
wanted to escape
teachers didn't help me   *Bad school memories*
teachers didn't take an interest in me
one called on me, then told me to forget it
I felt like a real loser
I didn't want to go back to his class
~~now I'm more sure of myself~~
~~OK not to know an answer~~
~~talk to instructors after class~~
job plus schoolwork take all my time   *Not enough time*
get home late, then rush through dinner   *with family*
then spend evening studying
even have to do homework on weekends

Under the list, Gary was now able to prepare his scratch outline.

Example of Scratch Outline

Starting college at age twenty-nine isn't easy.

(1)   Little support from parents or friends

(2)   Bad memories of high school

(3)   Not enough time to spend with family.

After all his preliminary writing, Gary sat back, pleased. He knew he had a promising paper—one with a clear point and solid support. Gary was now ready to write the first draft of his paper, using his outline as a guide.

Step 3: Writing the First Draft

When you write your first draft, be prepared to put in additional thoughts and details that didn't emerge in your prewriting. And don't worry if you hit a snag. Just leave a blank space or add a comment such as "Do later" and press on to finish the paper. Also, don't worry yet about grammar, punctuation, or spelling. You don't want to take time correcting words or sentences that you may decide to remove later. Instead, make it your goal to develop the content of your paper with plenty of specific details.

Here is Gary's first draft:

First Draft

Last fall, I finaly realized that I was stuck in a dead-end job. I wasnt making enough money and I was bored to tears. I figured I had to get some new skills which meant going back to school. Begining college at age twenty-nine turned out to be much tougher than I thought it would be. My father didnt understand, he hated school. That's why he quit after eighth grade. He would ask, Didnt you get dumped on enough in high school? Then wondered why I wanted to go back for more of the same thing. My mother was worried about where the money was comming from and said so. When my freinds saw me coming down the st. They would make fun of me with remarks like Hey there's the college man. They may have a point. School never was much fun for me. I spent years just siting in class waiting for the final bell to ring. So I could escape. The teachers werent much help to me. One time, a teacher called on me then told me to forget it. I felt like a real loser and didnt want to go back to his class. College takes time away from my family. ADD MORE DETAILS LATER. All this makes it very hard for me.

After Gary finished the draft, he was able to put it aside until the next day. You will benefit as well if you can allow some time between finishing a draft and starting to revise.

Step 4: Revising

Revising is as much a stage in the writing process as prewriting, outlining, and writing a first draft. *Revising* means that you rewrite a paper, building on what has been done, to make it stronger and better. One writer has said about revision, "It's like cleaning house—getting rid of all the junk and putting things in the right order." A typical revision means writing at least one or two more drafts.

Here is Gary's second draft.

Second Draft

> Starting college at age twenty-nine turned out to be much tougher than I thought. For one thing I did not have much support. My father hated school, so he asked, Didnt you get dumped on enough in high school? Also he asked why I wanted to go back for more. My mother worried about where the money was coming from. My friends would make fun of me. Hey there's the college man, they would say as soon as they saw me. Another reason why starting college was hard for me was what happened to me in high school. I spent years just sitting in class waiting for the final bell to ring. I was really bored. Also the teachers like to embaras me. One teacher called on me and then said forget it. He must of relized I didn't know the answer. I felt like a real loser and didnt want to go back in his class for weeks. Finally I've learned that college takes time away from my family. I have to go to work every day. I have a little over one hour to eat dinner and spend time with my wife and daughter. Then I have to go off to class and when I get back my daughter is in bed asleep. My wife and I have only a little time together. On weekends I have lots of homework to do, so the time goes by very fast. College is hard for me, but I am going to stay there so I can have a better life.

Notice that in redoing the draft, Gary started by clearly stating the point of his paragraph. Also, he inserted clear transitions to set off the three reasons why starting college at twenty-nine was difficult for him. He decided to omit the detail about his father quitting school to keep the focus of the paragraph more firmly on his own difficulties. He added more details so that he would have enough support for each of his three reasons. He also began to correct some of his spelling mistakes and added a final sentence to round off the paragraph.

Gary then went on to revise the second draft. Since he was doing his paper on a word processor, he was able to print it out quickly. He double-spaced the lines, allowing room for revisions, which he added in longhand during his third draft. (Note that if you are not using a word processor, you may want to do each draft on every other line of a page, so that there is room to revise. Also, write on only one side of a page, so that you see your entire paper at one time.) Shown below are some of the changes that Gary made in longhand as he worked on his third draft.

Part of Third Draft

Starting college at ~~the~~ age ~~of~~ twenty-nine ~~turned out to be much tougher than I thought.~~ *was not easy for me.* For one thing, I did not have much support *from my parents and friends.* My father ~~hated school, so he~~ asked, ~~"Didnt~~ *"Didn't* you get dumped on enough in high school? ~~Also he asked why I wanted to go back for more.~~ *Why go back for more?"* My mother worried, ~~about where~~ *"Where's* the money ~~was coming from.~~ *going to come from?"* My friends ~~would make fun of me. Hey~~ *seemed threatened. "Hey,* there's the college man," they would say ~~as soon as they saw me.~~ *when I approached.* Another reason ~~why~~ *that* starting college was ~~hard for me~~ *difficult*. . . .

After writing out these and other changes, Gary typed them into his word processor and printed out the almost-final draft of his paper. He was now ready to do careful proofreading.

Step 5: Proofreading

Proofreading, the final stage in the writing process, means checking a paper carefully for spelling, grammar, punctuation, and other errors. You are ready for this stage when you are satisfied with your choice of supporting details, the order in which they are presented, and the way they and your topic sentence are worded.

At this point in his work, Gary used his dictionary to do final checks on his spelling. He used a grammar handbook (such as the one in Part Two of this text) to be sure about grammar, punctuation, and usage. Gary also read through his paper carefully, looking for typing errors, omitted words, and any other errors he may have missed before. Proofreading is often hard to do—students have spent so much time with their work, or so little, that they want to avoid it. But if it is done carefully, this important final step will ensure that your paper looks as good as possible.

Hints for Proofreading

1   One helpful trick at this stage is to read your paper out loud. You will probably hear awkward wordings and become aware of spots where the punctuation needs to be improved. Make the changes needed for your sentences to read smoothly and clearly.

2   Another helpful technique is to take a sheet of paper and cover your paragraph so that you can expose just one line at a time and check it carefully.

3   A third strategy is to read your paper backward, from the last sentence to the first. This helps keep you from getting caught up in the flow of the paper and missing small mistakes—which is easy to do, since you're so familiar with what you mean to say.

WHAT IS AN ESSAY?

An essay does the same thing a paragraph does: it starts with a point, and the rest of it provides specific details to support and develop that point. However, a paragraph is a series of *sentences* about one main idea or point, while an *essay* is a series of *paragraphs* about one main idea or point—called the *central idea*. Since an essay is much longer than one paragraph, it allows a writer to develop a topic in more detail. Despite the greater length of an essay, the process of writing it is the same as that for writing a paragraph: prewriting, preparing a scratch outline, writing and revising drafts, and proofreading.

Here are the major differences between a paragraph and an essay:

Paragraph	Essay
Made up of sentences	Made up of paragraphs.
Starts with a sentence containing the main point (topic sentence).	Starts with an introductory paragraph containing the central idea, expressed in a sentence called the *thesis statement* (or *thesis sentence*).
Body of paragraph contains specific details that support and develop the topic sentence.	Body of essay contains paragraphs that support and develop the central idea. Each of these paragraphs has its own main supporting point, stated in a topic sentence.
Paragraph often ends with a closing sentence that rounds it off.	Essay ends with a concluding paragraph that rounds it off.

Later in his writing course, Gary was asked to expand his paragraph into an essay. Here is the essay that resulted:

For a typical college freshman, entering college is fun, and an exciting time of life. It is a time not just to explore new ideas in classes but to lounge out on the grass chatting with new friends, to sit having soda and pizza in the cafeteria, or to listen to music and play cards in the student lounge. I see the crowds of eighteen-year-olds enjoying all that college has to offer, and I sometimes envy them their freedom. Instead of being a typical freshman, I am twenty-nine years old, and beginning college has been a difficult experience for me. I have had to deal with lack of support, bad memories of past school experiences, and too little time for my family.

Few people in my life support my decision to enter college. My father is especially bewildered by the choice I have made. He himself quit school after finishing eighth grade, and he assumes that I should hate school as much as he did. "Didn't you get dumped on enough in high school?" he asks me. "Why go back for more?" My mother is a little more understanding of my desire for an education, but the cost of college terrifies her. She has always believed that college was a privilege only the rich could afford. "Where in the world will all that money come from?" she says. And my friends seem threatened by my decision. They make fun of me, suggesting that I'm going to think I'm too good to hang around with the likes of them. "Ooooh, here comes the college man," they say when they see me approach. "We'd better watch our grammar."

I have had to deal not only with family and friends but with unhappy memories of my earlier school career. I attended an enormous high school where I was just one more faceless kid in the crowd. My classes seemed meaningless to me. I can remember almost none of them in any detail. What I do remember about high school was just sitting, bored, until I felt nearly brain-dead, watching the clock hands move ever so slowly toward dismissal time. Such periods of boredom were occasionally interrupted by moments of acute embarrassment. Once an algebra teacher called on me and then said, "Oh, forget it, Callahan," in disgusted tones when he realized I didn't know the answer. My response, of course, was to shrink down in my chair and try to become invisible for the rest of the semester.

Furthermore, my decision to enter college has meant I have much less time to spend with my family. I work eight hours a day. Then I rush home and have all of an hour and ten minutes to eat dinner and spend time with my wife and daughter before I rush off again, this time to class. When I return from class, I am dead tired. My little girl is already asleep. My wife and I have only a little time to talk together before I collapse into bed. Weekends are a little better, but not much. That's when I try to get my papers written and catch up on a few chores around the house. My wife tries to be understanding, but it's hard on her to have so little support from me these days. And I'm missing out on a lot of special times in my daughter's life. For instance, I didn't realize she had begun to walk until three days after it happened.

So why do I put myself and my family through all these difficulties? Sometimes I'm not sure myself. But then I look at my little girl sleeping, and I think about the kind of life I am going to be able to give her. My college degree may make it possible for me to get a job that is more rewarding, both financially and emotionally. I believe I will be a better provider for my family, as well as a more well-rounded human being. I hope that the rewards of a college degree will eventually outweigh the problems I am experiencing now.

WHAT ARE THE PARTS OF AN ESSAY?

When Gary decided to expand his paragraph into an essay, he knew he would need to write an introductory paragraph, several supporting paragraphs, and a concluding paragraph.

Each of these parts of the essay is explained below.

Introductory Paragraph

What an Introductory Paragraph Does: A well-written introductory paragraph will often do the following.

1   *Gain the reader's interest.*   On pages 30–31 are several time-tested methods used to draw the reader into an essay.

2 *Present the thesis statement.* The thesis statement expresses the central idea of an essay, just as a topic sentence states the main idea of a paragraph. Here's an example of a thesis statement.

A vacation at home can be wonderful.

An essay with this thesis statement would go on to explain some positive things about vacationing at home.

What is the thesis statement in Gary's essay? Find that statement on page 27 and write it here:

_____

_____

You should have written down the next-to-last sentence in the introductory paragraph of Gary's essay.

3 *Lay out a plan of development.* A *plan of development* is a brief statement of the main supporting details for the central idea. These supporting details should be presented in the order in which they will be discussed in the essay. The plan of development can be blended into the thesis statement or presented separately.

Blended into a thesis statement: A vacation at home can be wonderful because you can avoid the hassles of travel, make use of your knowledge of the area, and indulge in special activities.

Presented separately: A vacation at home can be wonderful. At home you can avoid the hassles of travel, make use of your knowledge of the area, and indulge in special activities.

Note that some essays lend themselves better than others to a plan of development. At the least, your introductory paragraph should gain the reader's interest and present the thesis statement.

What is the plan of development in Gary's essay? Find the sentence on page 27 that states Gary's plan of development and write it here:

_____

_____

_____

You should have written down the last sentence in the introductory paragraph of Gary's essay.

Four Common Methods of Introduction

1 ***Begin with a broad statement and narrow it down to your thesis statement.*** Broad statements can capture your reader's interest while introducing your general topic. They may provide useful background material as well. The writer of the introductory paragraph below begins with a broad statement about her possessions. She then narrows the focus down to the three possessions that are the specific topic of the paper.

> I have many possessions that I would be sad to lose. Because I love to cook, I would miss several kitchen appliances that provide me with so many happy cooking adventures. I would also miss the wonderful electronic equipment that entertains me every day, including my large-screen television set and my VCR. I would miss the two telephones on which I have spent many interesting hours chatting in every part of my apartment, including the bathtub. But if my apartment were burning down, I would most want to rescue three things that are irreplaceable and hold great meaning for me—the silverware set that belonged to my grandmother, my mother's wedding gown, and my giant photo album.

2 ***Present an idea or situation that is the opposite of what you will be writing about.*** One way to gain the reader's interest is to show the difference between your opening idea or situation and the one to be discussed in the essay.

> The role of computers in schools is constantly growing. Such growth is based on a widespread faith that computers can answer many of the learning needs of our students. Many people believe that it is just a matter of time before computers do all but take the place of human teachers. However, educators should be cautious about introducing computers into curriculums. Computers may interfere with the learning of critical language skills, they may move too fast for students to digest new concepts, and they are poor substitutes for certain real-world experiences.

3 ***Tell a brief story.*** An interesting incident or anecdote is hard for a reader to resist. In an introduction, a story should be no more than a few sentences, and it should relate meaningfully to—and so lead the reader toward—your central idea. The story you tell can be an experience of your own, of someone you know, or of someone you have read about. For instance, in the following introduction, the author tells a simple personal story that serves as background for his central idea.

I remember the September morning that I first laid eyes on Jill. I'd been calling clients at my desk at work when I heard a warm, musical laugh. There was something so attractive about the sound that I got up to get a cup of coffee and to find the source of that laugh. I discovered the voice to be that of a young, auburn-haired woman we had just hired from a temporary agency. Soon after, Jill and I began going out, and we spent the next two years together. Only recently have we decided to break up because of disagreements about finances, about children, and about our relationship with her family.

4   *Ask one or more questions.* The questions may be those you intend to answer in your essay, or they may show that your topic relates directly to readers. In the following example, the questions are designed to gain readers' interest and convince them that the essay applies to them.

Does your will to study collapse when someone suggests getting a pizza? Does your social life compete with your class attendance? Is there a huge gap between your intentions and your actions? If the answers to these questions are yes, yes, and yes, read on. You can benefit from some powerful ways to motivate yourself: setting goals and consciously working to reach them, using rational thinking, and developing a positive personality.

Which of these four methods of introduction does Gary use in his essay?

_____

Gary begins with an idea that is the opposite of what he is writing about. His essay is about his difficulties with college life, but he begins with the idea that college "is fun, and an exciting time" for some students.

Supporting Paragraphs

The traditional college essay has three supporting paragraphs. But some essays will have two supporting paragraphs, and others will have four or more. Each supporting paragraph should have its own topic sentence, stating the point to be developed in that paragraph.

Notice that each of the supporting paragraphs in Gary's essay has its own topic sentence. For example, the topic sentence of his first supporting paragraph is "Few people in my life are supportive of my decision to enter college."

What is the topic sentence of Gary's second supporting paragraph?

_____

What is the topic sentence for Gary's third supporting paragraph?

_____

In each case, Gary's topic sentence is the first sentence of the paragraph.

Concluding Paragraph

An essay that ended with its final supporting paragraph would probably leave the reader wondering if the author was really done. A concluding paragraph is needed for a sense of completion. Here are two common methods of conclusion.

Two Common Methods of Conclusion

1   ***Provide a summary and a final thought.***   Using wording that is different from your introduction, restate your thesis and main supporting points. This review gives readers an overview of your essay and helps them remember what they've read. A final thought signals the end of the paper, as in the following concluding paragraph from an essay about personal possessions.

> If my home ever really did burn down, I would hope to be able to rescue some of the physical things that so meaningfully represent my past. My grandmother's silver set is a reminder of the grandparents who enriched my childhood, my mother's wedding gown is a glamorous souvenir of two important weddings, and my photo album is a rich storage bin of family and personal history. I would hate to lose them. However, if I did, I would take comfort in the fact that the most important storage place for family and personal memories is my own mind.

2   ***Focus on the future.***   A focus on the future often involves a prediction or a recommendation. This method of conclusion may refer in a general way to the central idea, or it may include a summary. The following conclusion from an essay about self-motivation combines a summary with a prediction. The prediction adds further support for the central idea.

> So get your willpower in gear, and use the three keys to self-motivation—set goals and work to reach them, think rationally, and develop a positive personality. You will find that a firm commitment to this approach becomes easier and easier. Progress will come more often and more readily, strengthening your resolve even further.

What kind of conclusion does Gary use in his essay?

_____

In his conclusion, Gary refers to his central idea in the context of the future. He makes hopeful points about what his and his family's life will be like after he gets a college degree.

CHAPTER REVIEW

Answer each of the following questions by filling in the blank or circling the answer you think is correct.

1. *True or false?* ___/___ Writing is a skill that anyone can learn with practice.
2. An effective paragraph or essay is one that
   a. makes a point.
   b. provides specific support.
   c. makes a point and provides specific support.
   d. none of the above.

3. The sentence that states the main idea of a paragraph is known as the _____

   sentence; the sentence that states the central idea of an essay is known as the

   _____ statement.
4. Prewriting can help a writer find
   a. a good topic to write about.
   b. a good main point to make about the topic.
   c. enough details to support the main point.
   d. all of the above.

5. *True or false?* _____ During the freewriting process, you should not concern yourself with spelling, punctuation, or grammar.

6. One step that everyone should use at some stage of the writing process is to

   prepare a plan for the paragraph or essay known as a(n) _____

   _____ .
7. When you start writing, your first concern should be
   a. spelling.
   b. content.
   c. grammar.
   d. punctuation.

8. Two common ways of organizing a paragraph are _____ order and

   _____ order.
9. The words *first, next, then, also, another,* and *finally* are examples of signal

   words, commonly known as _____ .
10. A thesis statement
   a. is generally part of an essay's introduction.
   b. states the central idea of the essay.
   c. can be followed by the essay's plan of development.
   d. all of the above.

PREVIEW: A LOOK AHEAD

The next chapter provides a series of activities to help you master three of the four goals of effective writing: (1) making a point, (2) supporting the point with specific details, and (3) organizing the support. Part Two of this book and a dictionary will help you with the fourth goal—writing error-free sentences. Part Three of the book presents tests to help you master the skills in Part Two.

Practice in Effective Writing

The following series of activities will strengthen your understanding of the writing guidelines presented in the preceding chapter. Through practice, you will gain a better sense of the goals of effective writing and how to reach those goals. You will also help prepare yourself for the writing assignments that follow the activities.

Your instructor may ask you to do the entire series of activities or may select the activities that are most suited to your particular needs.

I UNDERSTANDING GENERAL VERSUS SPECIFIC IDEAS

A paragraph is made up of a main idea, which is general, and the specific ideas that support it. So to write well, you must understand the difference between general and specific ideas.

It is helpful to realize that you use general and specific ideas all the time in your everyday life. For example, in choosing a video to rent, you may think, "Which kind of video should I rent—an action movie, a comedy, or a romance?" In such a case, *video* is the general idea, and *action movie, comedy,* and *romance* are the specific ideas.

Or you may decide to begin an exercise program. In that case, you might consider walking, jumping rope, or lifting weights. In this case, *exercise* is the general idea, and *walking, jumping rope,* and *lifting weights* are the specific ideas.

Or if you are talking to a friend about a date that didn't work out well, you may say, "The dinner was terrible, the car broke down, and we had little to say to each other." In this case, the general idea is *the date didn't work out well,* and the specific ideas are the three reasons you named.

The four activities here will give you experience in recognizing the relationship between *general* and *specific* ideas. They will also provide a helpful background for all the information and activities that follow.

Activity 1

Each group of words consists of one general idea and four specific ideas. The general idea includes all the specific ideas. Underline the general idea in each group.

Example   jeep   van   truck   <u>vehicle</u>   sedan

1. salty   bitter   <u>flavor</u>   sweet   sour
2. <u>jewelry</u>   necklace   ring   earrings   bracelet
3. dime   nickel   <u>coin</u>   quarter   half-dollar
4. fax machine   copier   computer   calculator   <u>office machine</u>
5. theft   murder   rape   <u>crime</u>   holdup
6. cracker   <u>snack</u>   carrot stick   cookie   popcorn
7. mascara   <u>cosmetic</u>   foundation   lipstick   eye shadow
8. yes   no   I don't know   <u>answer</u>   maybe
9. <u>yard work</u>   mowing   planting   trimming hedges   feeding plants
10. job interviews   wedding   car accidents   being fired   <u>stressful times</u>

Activity 2

In each item below, one idea is general and the others are specific. The general idea includes the specific ones. In the spaces provided, write in two more specific ideas that are covered by the general idea.

Example   *General:* exercises
                 Specific: chin-ups, jumping jacks,   <u>*sit-ups*</u> ,   <u>*push-ups*</u>

1. *General:* pizza toppings
   Specific: sausage, mushrooms,   _____ , _____
2. *General:* furniture
   Specific: rocking chair, coffee table,   _____ , _____
3. *General:* magazines
   Specific: *Reader's Digest, Newsweek,*   _____ , _____
4. *General:* Birds
   Specific: eagle, pigeon,   _____ , _____
5. *General:* types of music
   Specific: jazz, classical,   _____ , _____

6. *General:* cold symptoms
    Specific: aching muscles, watery eyes,   _____ , _____
7. *General:* children's games
    Specific: hopscotch, dodgeball,   _____ , _____
8. *General:* transportation
    Specific: plane, motorcycle,   _____ , _____
9. *General:* city problems
    Specific: overcrowding, pollution,   _____ , _____
10. *General:* types of TV shows
    Specific: cartoons, situation comedies,   _____ , _____

Activity 3

Read each group of specific ideas below. Then circle the letter of the general idea that tells what the specific ideas have in common. Note that the general idea should not be too broad or too narrow. Begin by trying the example item, and then read the explanation that follows.

Example   *Specific ideas:* peeling potatoes, washing dishes, cracking eggs, cleaning out refrigerator

The general idea is

a.   household jobs.
b.   kitchen tasks.
c.   steps in making dinner.

Explanation: It is true that the specific ideas are all household jobs, but they have in common something even more specific—they are all tasks done in the kitchen. Therefore answer *a* is too broad, and the correct answer is *b*. Answer *c* is too narrow because it doesn't cover all the specific ideas. While two of them could be steps in making a dinner ("peeling potatoes" and "cracking eggs"), two have nothing to do with making dinner.

1. *Specific ideas:* crowded office, rude coworkers, demanding boss, unreasonable deadlines

    The general idea is

    a.   problems.
    b.   work problems.
    c.   problems with work schedules.

2. *Specific ideas:* cactus, rosebush, fern, daisy

   The general idea is
   a. plants.
   b. plants that have thorns.
   c. plants that grow in the desert.

3. *Specific ideas:* Band-Aids, gauze, smelling salts, aspirin

   The general idea is
   a. supplies.
   b. first-aid supplies.
   c. supplies for treating a headache.

4. *Specific ideas:* trout, whales, salmon, frogs

   The general idea is
   a. animals.
   b. fish.
   c. creatures living in water.

5. *Specific ideas:* Hershey bar, lollipop, mints, fudge

   The general idea is
   a. food.
   b. candy.
   c. chocolate.

6. *Specific ideas:* "Go to bed," "Pick up that trash," "Run twenty laps," "Type this letter"

   The general idea is
   a. remarks.
   b. orders.
   c. the boss's orders.

7. *Specific ideas:* "I had no time to study," "The questions were unfair," "I had a headache," "The instructor didn't give us enough time"

   The general idea is
   a. statements.
   b. excuses for being late.
   c. excuses for not doing well on a test.

8. *Specific ideas:* candle, sun, headlight, flashlight

The general idea is
a. things that are very hot.
b. light sources for a home.
c. sources of light.

9. *Specific ideas:* driving with expired license plates, driving over the speed limit, parking without putting money in the meter, driving without a license

The general idea is
a. ways to cause a traffic accident.
b. traffic problems.
c. ways to get a ticket.

10. *Specific ideas:* "Do you come here often?" "Would you like to dance?" "Let me buy you a drink," "What's your zodiac sign?"

The general idea is
a. things that people say to one another.
b. things people commonly say to one another at a wedding.
c. things people say in a singles bar.

Activity 4

In the following items, the specific ideas are given but the general ideas are unstated. Fill in the blanks with the unstated general ideas.

Example   *General idea:* _____ car problems _____
       Specific ideas: flat tire   dented bumper
                        cracked windshield   dirty oil filter

1. *General idea:* _____ relatives _____
   Specific ideas: nephew   grandmother
                     aunt   cousin

2. *General idea:* _____ Shoes _____
   Specific ideas: boots   sneakers
                     moccasins   slippers

3. *General idea:* _____ Outside Hobies. _____
   Specific ideas: camping   hiking
                     fishing   hunting

4. *General idea:* _____
   Specific ideas: broom   sponge
                        mop   glass cleaner

5. *General idea:* _____
   Specific ideas: cloudy   sunny
                        snowy   rainy

6. *General idea:* _____
   Specific ideas: Spread mustard on slice of bread
                        Add turkey and cheese
                        Put lettuce on top of cheese
                        Cover with another slice of bread

7. *General idea:* _____
   Specific ideas: thermos of lemonade   insect repellent
                        basket of food   blanket

8. *General idea:* _____
   Specific ideas: fleas in carpeting   loud barking
                        tangled fur   veterinary bills

9. *General idea:* _____
   Specific ideas: diabetes   cancer
                        appendicitis   broken leg

10. *General idea:* _____
    Specific ideas: flooded basements   wet streets
                        rainbow   overflowing rivers

2 UNDERSTANDING THE PARAGRAPH

A *paragraph* is made up of a main idea and a group of related sentences that develop the main idea. The main idea often appears in a sentence known as the *topic sentence.*

It is helpful to remember that a topic sentence is a *general* statement. The other sentences provide specific support for the general statement.

Activity

Each group of sentences below could be written as a short paragraph. Circle the letter of the topic sentence in each case. To find the topic sentence, ask yourself, "Which is a general statement supported by the specific details in the other three statements?"

Begin by trying the example item below. First circle the letter of the sentence you think expresses the main idea. Then read the explanation.

Example   a.   Newspapers are a good source of local, national, and world news.
b.   The cartoons and crossword puzzles in newspapers are entertaining.
c.   Newspapers have a lot to offer.
d.   Newspapers often include coupons worth far more than the cost of the paper.

Explanation: Sentence *a* explains one important benefit of newspapers. Sentences *b* and *d* provide other specific advantages of newspapers. In sentence *c,* however, no one specific benefit is explained. Instead, the words "a lot to offer" refer only generally to such benefits. Therefore sentence *c* is the topic sentence; it expresses the main idea. The other sentences support that idea by providing examples.

1. a.   Even when Food City is crowded, there are only two cash registers open.
b.   The frozen foods are often partially thawed.
c.   I will never shop at Food City again.
d.   The market is usually out of sale items within a few hours.

2. a.   Buy only clothes that will match what's already in your closet.
b.   To be sure you're getting the best price, shop in a number of stores before buying.
c.   Avoid trendy clothes; buy basic pieces that never go out of style.
d.   By following a few simple rules, you can have nice clothes without spending a fortune.

3. a.   Once my son said a vase jumped off the shelf by itself.
b.   When my son breaks something, he always has an excuse.
c.   He claimed that my three-month-old daughter climbed out of her crib and knocked a glass over.
d.   Another time, he said an earthquake must have caused a mirror to crack.

4. a.   Mars should be the first planet explored by astronauts.
b.   Astronauts could mine Mars for aluminum, magnesium, and iron.
c.   The huge volcano on Mars would be fascinating to study.
d.   Since Mars is close to Earth, we might want to have colonies there one day.

5. a.   Instead of talking on the telephone, we leave messages on answering machines.
b.   People rarely talk to one another these days.
c.   Rather than talking with family members, we sit silently in front of our TV sets all evening.
d.   In cars, we ignore our traveling companions to listen to the radio.

3   UNDERSTANDING THE TOPIC SENTENCE

As already explained, most paragraphs center on a main idea, which is often expressed in a topic sentence. An effective topic sentence does two things. First, it presents the topic of the paragraph. Second, it expresses the writer's attitude or opinion or idea about the topic. For example, look at the following topic sentence:

Professional athletes are overpaid.

In the topic sentence, the topic is *professional athletes;* the writer's idea about the topic is that professional athletes *are overpaid.*

Activity

For each topic sentence below, underline the topic and double-underline the point of view that the writer takes toward the topic.

Examples   Living in a small town has many advantages.

Car phones should be banned.

1. The apartments on Walnut Avenue are a fire hazard.
2. Losing my job turned out to have benefits.
3. Blues is the most interesting form of American music.
4. Our neighbor's backyard is a dangerous place.
5. Paula and Jeff are a practical couple.
6. Snakes do not deserve their bad reputation.
7. Pollution causes many problems in American cities.
8. New fathers should receive "paternity leave."
9. People with low self-esteem often need to criticize others.
10. Learning to write effectively is largely a matter of practice.

4   IDENTIFYING TOPICS, TOPIC SENTENCES, AND SUPPORT

The following activity will sharpen your sense of the differences between topics, topic sentences, and supporting sentences.

Activity

Each group of items below includes one topic, one main idea (expressed in a topic sentence), and two supporting details for that idea. In the space provided, label each item with one of the following:

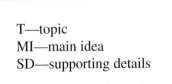

T—topic
MI—main idea
SD—supporting details

1. ____ a. The weather in the summer is often hot and sticky.
   ____ b. Summer can be an unpleasant time of year.
   ____ c. Summer.
   ____ d. Bug bites, poison ivy, and allergies are a big part of summertime.

2. ____ a. The new Ultimate sports car is bound to be very popular.
   ____ b. The company has promised to provide any repairs needed during the first three years at no charge.
   ____ c. Because it get thirty miles per gallon of gas, it offers real savings on fuel costs.
   ____ d. The new Ultimate sports car.

3. ____ a. Decorating an apartment doesn't need to be expensive.
   ____ b. A few plants add a touch of color without costing a lot of money.
   ____ c. Inexpensive braided rugs can be bought to match nearly any furniture.
   ____ d. Decorating an apartment.

4. ____ a. Long practice sessions and busy game schedules take too much time away from schoolwork.
   ____ b. High school sports.
   ____ c. The competition between schools may become so intense that, depending on the outcome of one game, athletes are either adored or scorned.
   ____ d. High school sports put too much pressure on young athletes.

5. ____ a. After mapping out the best route to your destination, phone ahead for motel reservations.
   ____ b. A long car trip.
   ____ c. Following a few guidelines before a long car trip can help you avoid potential problems.
   ____ d. Have your car's engine tuned as well, and have the tires, brakes, and exhaust system inspected.

5   RECOGNIZING SPECIFIC DETAILS I

Specific details are examples, reasons, particulars, and facts. Such details are needed to effectively support and explain a topic sentence. They provide the evidence needed for us to understand, as well as to feel and experience, a writer's point.

Below is a topic sentence followed by two sets of supporting sentences. Put a check by the set that provides sharp, specific details.

Topic sentence: Ticket sales for a recent Rolling Stones concert proved that the classic rock band is still very popular.

_____   a.   Fans came from everywhere to buy tickets to the concert. People wanted good seats and were willing to endure a great deal of various kinds of discomfort as they waited in line for many hours. Some people actually waited for days, sleeping at night in uncomfortable circumstances. Good tickets were sold out extremely quickly.

_____   b.   The first person in the long ticket line spent three days standing in the hot sun and three nights sleeping on the concrete without even a pillow. The man behind her waited equally long in his wheelchair. The ticket window opened at 10:00 A.M., and the tickets for the good seats—those in front of the stage—were sold out an hour later.

Explanation: The second set (*b*) provides specific details. Instead of a vague statement about fans who were "willing to endure a great deal of various kinds of discomforts," we get vivid details we can see and picture clearly: "three days standing in the hot sun," "three nights sleeping on the concrete without even a pillow," "The man behind her waited equally long in his wheelchair."

Instead of a vague statement that tickets were "sold out extremely quickly," we get exact and vivid details: "The ticket window opened at 10:00 A.M., and the tickets for the good seats—those in front of the stage—were sold out an hour later."

Specific details are often like a movie script. They provide us with such clear pictures that we could make a film of them if we wanted to. You would know just how to film the information given in the second set of sentences. You would show the fans in line under a hot sun and, later, sleeping on the concrete. The first person in line would be shown sleeping without a pillow under her head. You would show tickets finally being sold, and after an hour, you could show the ticket seller explaining that all of the seats in front of the stage were sold out.

In contrast, the writer of the first set of sentences (*a*) fails to provide the specific information needed. If you were asked to make a film based on set *a,* you would have to figure out on your own just what particulars to show.

When you are working to provide specific supporting information in a paper, if might help to ask yourself, "Could someone easily film this information?" If the answer is yes, your supporting details are specific enough for your readers to visualize.

Activity

Each topic sentence below is followed by two sets of supporting details, Write *S* (for *specific*) in the space next to the set that provides specific support for the point. Write *G* (for *general*) next to the set that offers only vague, general support.

1. *Topic sentence:* The West Side shopping mall is an unpleasant place.

_____ a. The floors are covered with cigarette butts, dirty paper plates, and spilled food. The stores are so crowded I had to wait twenty minutes just to get a dressing room to try on a shirt.

_____ b. It's very dirty, and not enough places are provided for trash. The stores are not equipped to handle the large number of shoppers that often shows up.

Hint: Which set of supporting details could you more readily use in a film?

2. *Topic sentence:* Our golden retriever is a wonderful pet for children.

_____ a. He is gentle, patient, eager to please, and affectionate. Capable of following orders, he is also ready to think for himself and find solutions to a problem. He senses children's moods and goes along with their wishes.

_____ b. He doesn't bite, even when children pull his tail. After learning to catch a ball, he will bring it back again and again, seemingly always ready to play. If the children don't want to play anymore, he will just sit by their side, gazing at them with his faithful eyes.

3. *Topic sentence:* My two-year-old daughter's fearlessness is a constant source of danger to her.

_____ a. She doesn't realize that certain activities are dangerous. Even when I warn her, she will go ahead and do something that could hurt her. I have to constantly be on the lookout for dangerous situations and try to protect her from them.

_____ b. For instance, she loves going to the swimming pool. That's great. But she will jump into water that is way over her head. She likes animals and will run to pet any dog that wanders by, no matter how unfriendly.

4. *Topic sentence:* People's views of scientists are often more fiction than fact.

_____ a.   Scientists are portrayed in movies as crazy guys with long hair, thick glasses, and shabby clothes. Incapable of remembering the time of day, these imaginary scientists skip meals and prefer the company of laboratory animals to that of their own children. In reality, scientists get hungry at mealtime, love their children, and go to work in suits.

_____ b.   People don't know exactly what scientists do and fantasize a lot about their work. Instead of thinking of scientists as real people who do a particular type of work, people think of them as weird, antisocial geniuses whom one could spot a mile away. In reality, most scientists look and act much like their neighbors.

5. *Topic sentence:* Early theories of child raising were very different from today's theories.

_____ a.   The first books on child raising came out hundreds of years ago. The advice they contained was based almost entirely on superstitions and other untrue beliefs. Some of the advice was harmless, but some could lead to long-term effects. They told parents to do things to their children that seem to us to make no sense at all.

_____ b.   One early book, for example, advised mothers not to breast-feed their babies right after feeling anger because the anger would go into the milk and injure the child. Another told parents to begin toilet training their children at the age of three weeks and to tie their babies' arms down for several months to prevent thumb sucking.

6   RECOGNIZING SPECIFIC DETAILS II

Activity

At several points in each of the following paragraphs you are given a choice of two sets of supporting details. Write *S* (for *specific*) in the space next to the set that provides specific support for the point. Write *G* (for *general*) next to the set that offers only vague, general support.

Paragraph 1

My daughter is as shy as I am, and it breaks my heart to see her dealing with the same problems I had to deal with in my childhood because of my shyness. I feel very sad for her when I see the problems she has making friends.

_____ a. It takes her a long time to begin to do the things other children do to make friends, and her feelings get hurt very easily over one thing and another. She is not at all comfortable about making connections with her classmates at school.

_____ b. She usually spends Christmas vacation alone because by that time of year she doesn't have friends yet. Only when her birthday comes in the summer is she confident enough to invite school friends to her party. Once she sends out the invitations, she almost sleeps by the telephone, waiting for the children to respond. If they say they can't come, her eyes fill with tears.

I recognize very well her signs of shyness, which make her look smaller and more fragile than she really is.

_____ c. When she has to talk to someone she doesn't know well, she speaks in a whisper and stares sideways. Pressing her hands together, she lifts her shoulders as though she wished she could hide her head between them.

_____ d. When she is forced to talk to anyone other than her family and her closest friends, the sound of her voice and the position of her head change. Even her posture changes in a way that makes it look as if she's trying make her body disappear.

It is hard for me to watch her passing unnoticed at school.

_____ e. She never gets chosen for a special job or privilege, even though she tries her best, practicing in privacy at home. She just doesn't measure up. Worst of all, even her teacher seems to forget her existence much of the time.

_____ f. Although she rehearses in our basement, she never gets chosen for a good part in a play. Her voice is never loud or clear enough. Worst of all, her teacher doesn't call on her in class for days at a time.

Paragraph 2

It is said that the dog is man's best friend, but I strongly believe that the honor belongs to the telephone directory. A directory can't play ball with me, but it can help me find many ways to entertain myself.

_____ a. If I am bored, tired, or out of ideas, the telephone directory can tell me where to go for dinner, recreation, and entertainment.

_____ b. The other day the directory guided me to a charming restaurant, The China Bowl. I frequently use the directory to find movies, theaters, concerts, and museums.

While the dog is a faithful friend, the telephone directory helps me be a good citizen.

_____ c. I use the phone numbers in the directory's blue pages to learn the guidelines of my town's recycling programs, the rules for garbage disposal, and the procedures of the snow emergency program.

_____ d. The directory's blue pages help me perform my duties as a citizen because they list telephone numbers of agencies and departments in my town and state. I can find out a great deal about a variety of types of rules and guidelines.

A dog might help me meet people I see in the park, but the directory helps me meet other important people.

_____ e. When I need to find someone to provide some sort of service for me, I know that I can find help in the Yellow Pages. Looking at the Yellow Pages, I can find someone to call. The Yellow Pages have been especially helpful when I have moved to a new city.

_____ f. I moved to Chicago two years ago, and the Yellow Pages helped me quickly find Dr. Morris, a very good family physician; Mrs. DeJames, the best hairstylist I've ever used; and Mr. Henderson, a wonderful repairman.

7   PROVIDING SPECIFIC DETAILS

Activity

Each of the following sentences contains a general word or words, set off in *italic* type. Substitute sharp, specific words in each case.

Example   After the parade, the city was littered with *garbage*.

After the parade, the city street was littered with multicolored

confetti, dirty popcorn, and lifeless balloons.

1. If I had the money, I'd visit *several places*.

2. It took her *a long time* to get home.

3. Ron is often stared at because of his *unusual hair color and style.*

_____

_____

4. After you pass *two buildings,* you'll see my house on the left.

_____

_____

5. Amy's purse is crammed with *lots of stuff.*

_____

_____

6. I bought *some junk food* for the long car trip.

_____

_____

7. The floor by the front seat of my car is covered with *things.*

_____

_____

8. When his mother said no to his request for a toy, the child *reacted strongly.*

_____

_____

9. Victor gave his girlfriend *a surprise present* for Valentine's Day.

_____

_____

10. My cat can *do a wonderful trick.*

_____

_____

8 SELECTING DETAILS THAT FIT

The details in your paper must all clearly relate to and support your opening point. If a detail does not support your point, leave it out. Otherwise, your paper will lack unity. For example, see if you can circle the letter of the two sentences that do *not* support the topic sentence below.

Topic sentence: Mario is a very talented person.

a. Mario is always courteous to his professors.
b. He has created beautiful paintings in his art course.
c. Mario is the lead singer in a local band.
d. He won an award in a photography contest.
e. He is hoping to become a professional photographer.

Explanation: Being courteous may be a virtue, but it is not a talent, so sentence *a* does not support the topic sentence. Also, Mario's desire to become a professional photographer tells us nothing about his talent; thus sentence *e* does not support the topic sentence either. The other three statements all clearly back up the topic sentence. Each in some way supports the idea that Mario is talented—in art, as a singer, or as a photographer.

Activity

In each group below, circle the two items that do *not* support the topic sentence.

1. *Topic sentence:* Carla seems attracted only to men who are unavailable.
   a. She once fell in love with a man serving a life sentence in prison.
   b. Her parents worry about her inability to connect with a nice single man.
   c. She wants to get married and have kids before she is thirty.
   d. Her current boyfriend is married.
   e. Recently she had a huge crush on a Catholic priest.

2. *Topic sentence:* Some dog owners have little consideration for other people.
   a. Obedience lessons can be a good experience for both the dog and the owner.
   b. Some dog owners let their dogs leave droppings on the sidewalk or in other people's yards.
   c. They leave the dog home alone for hours, barking and howling and waking the neighbors.
   d. Some people keep very large dogs in small apartments.
   e. Even when small children are playing nearby, they let their bad-tempered dogs run loose.

3. *Topic sentence:* Dr. Eliot is a very poor instructor.
   a. He cancels class frequently with no explanation.
   b. When a student asks a question that he can't answer, he becomes irritated with the student.
   c. He got his Ph.D. at a university in another country.
   d. He's taught at the college for many years and is on a number of faculty committees.
   e. He puts off grading papers until the end of the semester, and then returns them all at once.

4. *Topic sentence:* Some doctors seem to think it is all right to keep patients waiting.
   a. Pharmaceutical sales representatives sometimes must wait hours to see a doctor.
   b. The doctors stand in the hallway chatting with nurses and secretaries even when they have a waiting room full of patients.
   c. Patients sometimes travel long distances to consult with a particular doctor.
   d. When a patient calls before an appointment to see if the doctor is on time, the answer if often yes even when the doctor is two hours behind schedule.
   e. Some doctors schedule appointments in a way that ensures long lines, to make it appear that they are especially skillful.

5. *Topic sentence:* Several factors were responsible for the staggering loss of lives when the *Titanic* sank.
   a. Over 1,500 people died in the *Titanic* disaster; only 711 survived.
   b. Despite warnings about the presence of icebergs, the captain allowed the *Titanic* to continue at high speed.
   c. If the ship had hit the iceberg head-on, its watertight compartments might have kept it from sinking; however, it hit on the side, resulting in a long, jagged gash through which water poured in.
   d. The *Titanic,* equipped with the very best communication systems available in 1912, sent out SOS messages.
   e. When the captain gave orders to abandon the *Titanic,* many passengers refused because they believed the ship was unsinkable, so many lifeboats were only partly filled.

9   PROVIDING DETAILS THAT FIT

Activity 1

Each topic sentence below is followed by one supporting detail. See if you can add a second detail in each case. Make sure your detail supports the topic sentence.

1. *Topic sentence:* There are good reasons why the video store is losing so many customers.
   a.   The store stocks only one copy of every movie, even the most popular titles.

   b.   _____

2. *Topic sentence:* The little boy did some dangerous stunts on his bicycle.
   a.   He rode down a flight of steps at top speed.

   b.   _____

3. *Topic sentence:* Craig has awful table manners.
   a.   He stuffs his mouth with food and then begins a conversation.

   b.   _____

4. *Topic sentence:* There are many advantages to living in the city.
   a.   One can meet many new people with interesting backgrounds.

   b.   _____

5. *Topic sentence:* All high school students should have summer jobs.
   a.   Summer jobs help teens learn to handle a budget.

   b.   _____

Activity 2

See if you can add *two* supporting details for each of the topic sentences below.

1. *Topic sentence:* The managers of this apartment building don't care about their renters.
   a.   Mrs. Harris has been asking them to fix her leaky faucet for two months.

   b.   _____

   c.   _____

2. *Topic sentence:* None of the shirts for sale were satisfactory.
   a.   Some were attractive but too expensive.

   b.   _____

   c.   _____

3. *Topic sentence:* After being married for forty years, Mr. and Mrs. Lambert have grown similar in odd ways.
   a.   They both love to have a cup of warm apple juice just before bed.

   b.   _____

   c.   _____

4. *Topic sentence:* It is a special time for me when my brother is in town.
   a.   We always go bowling together and then stop for pizza.

   b.   _____

   c.   _____

5. *Topic sentence:* Our neighbor's daughter is very spoiled.
   a.   When anyone else in the family has a birthday, she gets several presents too.

   b.   _____

   c.   _____

10   PROVIDING DETAILS IN A PARAGRAPH

Activity

The following paragraph needs specific details to back up its three supporting points. In the spaces provided, write two or three sentences of convincing details for each supporting point.

A Disappointing Concert

Although I had looked forward to seeing my favorite musical group in concert, the experience was disappointing. For one thing, our seats were terrible, in two ways. _____

_____

_____

_____

In addition, the crowd made it hard to enjoy the music. _____

_____

_____

_____

_____

_____

And finally, the band members acted as if they didn't want to be there. _____

_____

_____

_____

_____

II   OMITTING AND GROUPING DETAILS WHEN PLANNING A PAPER

One common way to develop material for a paper is to (1) make up a list of details about your point. The next steps are to (2) omit details that don't truly support your point and (3) group together remaining details in logical ways. Omitting details that don't fit and grouping related details together are part of learning how to write effectively.

See if you can figure out a way to put the following details into three groups. Put *A* in front of the details that go with one group, *B* in front of the details that go with a second group, and *C* in front of the details that make up a third group. Cross out the four details that do not relate to the topic sentence.

Topic sentence: My brother Sean caused our parents lots of headaches when he was a teenager.

_____   In constant trouble at school

_____   While playing a joke on his lab partner, nearly blew up the chemistry lab

_____   Girlfriend was eight years older than he and had been married twice

_____   Girlfriend had a very sweet four-year-old son

_____   Parents worried about people Sean spent his time with

_____   Several signs that he was using drugs

_____   Failed so many courses that he had to go to summer school in order to graduate

_____   Was suspended twice for getting into fights between classes

_____   Our father taught math at the high school we attended

_____   His money just disappeared, and he never had anything to show for it

_____   His best pal had been arrested for armed robbery

_____   Often looked glassy-eyed

_____   Hung around with older kids who had dropped out of school

_____   Until he was in eighth grade, he had always been on the honor roll

_____   No one was allowed in his room, which he kept locked whenever away from home

_____   Has managed to turn his life around now that he's in college

Explanation: After thinking about the list for a while, you probably realized that the details about Sean's trouble at school form one group. He got in trouble at school for nearly blowing up the chemistry lab, failing courses, and fighting between classes. Another group of details has to do with his parents' worrying about the people he spent time with. His parents were worried because he had an older girlfriend, a best friend who was arrested for armed robbery, and older friends who were school dropouts. Finally, there are the details about signs that he was using drugs: his money disappearing, his glassy-eyed appearance, and not allowing others in his room.

The main idea—that, as a teenager, the writer's brother caused their parents lots of headaches—can be supported with three kinds of evidence: the trouble he got into at school, his friends, and the signs indicating he was on drugs. The other four items in the list do not logically go with any of these three types of evidence and so should be omitted.

Activity

This activity will give you practice in omitting and grouping details. See if you can figure out a way to put the following details into three groups. Put _A_ in front of the details that go with one group, _B_ in front of the details that go with a second group, and _C_ in front of the details that make up a third group. Cross out the four details that do not relate to the topic sentence.

Topic sentence: There are interesting and enjoyable ways for children to keep their classroom skills strong over summer vacation.

_____   Kids can help figure out how big a tip to leave in a restaurant.

_____   They can keep their reading skills sharp in various ways.

_____   Summer is a good time for learning to swim.

_____   Reading the newspaper with Mom or Dad will keep kids in touch with challenging reading.

_____   Adults can ask a child to do such tasks as count their change.

_____   Kids can have fun improving their writing skills.

_____ A child might enjoy writing a diary of his or her summer activities.

_____ Weekly visits to the library will keep them in touch with good books.

_____ After returning to school, children can write about their summer vacation.

_____ Kids should also have plenty of physical exercise over the summer.

_____ Arithmetic skills can be polished over the summer.

_____ Parents can encourage kids to write letters to relatives.

_____ Parents should take children to the library during the school year too.

_____ In the grocery store, a child can compare prices and choose the best bargains.

_____ Even the comic strips provide reading practice for a young child.

_____ Getting a pen-pal in another state can give a child an enjoyable reason to write over the summer.

12   USING TRANSITIONS

As already stated, transitions are signal words that help readers follow the direction of the writer's thought. To see the value of transitions, look at the two versions of the short paragraph below. Check the version that is easier to read and understand.

_____ a. Where will you get the material for your writing assignments? There are several good sources. Your own experience is a major resource. For an assignment about childhood, for instance, you can draw on your own numerous memories of childhood. Other people's experience is extremely useful. You may have heard people you know or even people on TV or radio talking about their childhood. Or you can interview people with a specific writing assignment in mind. Books and magazines are a good source of material for assignments. Many experts, for example, have written about various aspects of childhood.

_____ b. Where will you get the material for your writing assignments? There are several good sources. First of all, your own experience is a major resource. For an assignment about childhood, for instance, you can draw on your own numerous memories of childhood. In addition, other people's experiences are extremely useful. You may have heard people you know or even people on TV or radio talking about their childhood. Or you can interview people with a specific writing assignment in mind. Finally, books and magazines are a good source of material for assignments. Many experts, for example, have written about various aspects of childhood.

Explanation: You no doubt chose the second version, *b.* The listing transitions—*first of all, in addition,* and *finally*—make it clear when the author is introducing a new supporting point. The reader of paragraph *b* is better able to follow the author's line of thinking and to note that three main sources of material for assignments are being listed: your own experience, other people's experience, and books and magazines.

Activity

The following paragraphs use listing order or time order. In each case, fill in the blanks with appropriate transitions from the box above the paragraph. Use each transition once.

1.

after	now	first	soon	while

My husband has developed an involving hobby, in which I, unfortunately, am unable to share. He _____ enrolled in ground flight instruction classes at the local community college. The lessons were all about air safety regulations and procedures. _____ passing a difficult exam, he decided to take flying lessons at the city airport. Every Monday he would wake at six o'clock in the morning and drive happily to the airport, eager to see his instructor. _____he was taking lessons, he started to buy airplane magazines and talk about them constantly. "Look at that Cessna 150," he would say. "Isn't she a beauty?" _____, after many lessons, he is flying by himself. _____ he will be able to carry passengers. That is my biggest nightmare. I know he will want me to fly with him, but I am not a lover of heights. I can't understand why someone would leave the safety of the ground to be in the sky, defenseless as a kite.

2.

finally	for one thing	second

The home economics class I took in high school convinced me that home-making would never be my strong point. _____, there was my experience making chocolate cookies. I gathered the ingredients, including a big chunk of semisweet chocolate, and threw them into the mixing bowl. As I started the mixer, there was a terrible grinding sound. Miss Hooley, my teacher, pointed out that I was supposed to *melt* the chocolate before mixing it in.

_____, I didn't do so well making out menus for a week's nutritious meals. Miss Hooley didn't think it was funny that I filled my menu with comments like "Invite Mom over to cook" and "Send out for Chinese food." _____, there was my lack of success in sewing. Actually, I thought sewing was fun. I loved to stomp on the sewing machine's foot pedal and make it roar loudly. I finished sewing my blouse before anyone else in the class. Unfortunately, I had sewed the armholes and neck opening shut.

3.

later	soon	when	then

At the age of thirty-one I finally had the opportunity to see snow for the first time in my life. It was in New York City on a cloudy afternoon in November. My daughter and I had gone to the American Museum of Natural History.

_____ we left the museum, snow was falling gently. I thought that it was so beautiful! It made me remember movies I had seen countless times in my native Brazil. We decided to find a taxi. _____ we were crossing Central Park, snuggled in the cozy cab, watching the snow cover trees, bushes, branches, and grass. We were amazed to see the landscape quickly change from fall to winter. _____ we arrived in front of our hotel, and I still remember stepping on the crisp snow and laughing like a child who is touched by magic. _____ that day, I heard on the radio that a snowstorm was coming. I was naive enough to wait for thunder and the other sounds of a rainstorm. I did not know yet that snow, even a snowstorm, is silent and soft.

4.

last of all	another	first of all	in addition

Public school students who expect to attend school from September to June, and then have a long summer vacation, may be in for a big surprise before long.

For a number of reasons, many schools are switching to a year-round calendar. _____, many educators point out that the traditional school calendar was established years ago when young people had to be available during the summer months to work on farms, but this necessity has long

since passed. _____ reason is that a longer school year accommodates individual learning rates more effectively. That is, fast learners can go into more depth about a subject that interests them, while those who learn at a slower pace have more time to master the essential material.

_____, many communities have gone to year-round school to relieve overcrowding, since students can be put on different schedules through-

out the year. _____, and perhaps most important, educators feel that year-round schools eliminate the loss of learning that many students experience over a long summer break.

13   ORGANIZING DETAILS IN A PARAGRAPH

The supporting details in a paragraph must be organized in a meaningful way. The two most common methods of organizing details are listing order and time order. The activities that follow will give you practice in both methods of organization.

Activity I

Use *listing order* to arrange the scrambled list of sentences below. Number each supporting sentence, 1, 2, 3, . . . so that you go from the least important item to what is presented as the most important item.

Note that transitions will help by making clear the relationships between some of the sentences.

Topic sentence: I am no longer a big fan of professional sports, for a number of reasons.

_____   Basketball and hockey continue well into the baseball season, and football doesn't have its Super Bowl until the middle of winter, when basketball should be at center stage.

_____   In addition, I detest the high fives, taunting, and trash talk that so many professional athletes now indulge in during games.

_____   Second, I am bothered by the length of professional sports seasons.

_____   Also, professional athletes have no loyalty to a team or city as they greedily sell their abilities to the highest bidder.

_____ For one thing, greed is the engine running professional sports.

_____ There are numerous news stories of professional athletes in trouble with the law because of drugs, guns, fights, traffic accidents, or domestic violence.

_____ After a good year, athletes making millions become unhappy if they aren't rewarded with a new contract calling for even more millions.

_____ But the main reason I've become disenchanted with professional sports is the disgusting behavior of so many of its performers.

Activity 2

Use *time order* to arrange the scrambled sentences below. Number the supporting sentences in the order in which they occur in time (1, 2, 3, . . .).

Note that transitions will help by making clear the relationships between sentences.

Topic sentence: If you are a smoker, the following steps should help you quit.

_____ Before your "quit day" arrives, have a medical checkup to make sure it will be all right for you to begin an exercise program.

_____ You should then write down on a card your decision to quit and the date of your "quit day."

_____ When your "quit day" arrives, stop smoking and start your exercise program.

_____ Finally, remind yourself repeatedly how good you will feel when you can confidently tell yourself and others that you are a nonsmoker.

_____ Place the card in a location where you will be sure to see it every day.

_____ When you begin this exercise program, be sure to drink plenty of water every day and to follow a sensible diet.

_____ After making a definite decision to stop smoking, select a specific "quit day."

_____ Eventually, your exercise program should include activities strenuous enough to strengthen your lung capacity and your overall stamina.

14   UNDERSTANDING THE PLAN OF DEVELOPMENT IN AN ESSAY

Activity

Complete each thesis statement below by adding a third supporting idea. Use wording that is parallel to the two supporting ideas already provided.

1. The people who have given me the best advice are my father, my grandmother, and my _____.

2. The qualities I most admire in my best friend are her sense of humor, her loyalty, and her _____.

3. Reading a novel, taking a warm bath, and_____ are excellent ways to relax at the end of a long day.

4. Fights with my wife usually stem from disagreements about money, child raising, and_____.

5. Sticking to a diet, keeping a schedule, and _____ are the most difficult challenges I face.

6. My three favorite possessions are my photograph albums, my letters from friends, and my_____.

7. To find work in a day care center satisfying, a person should enjoy teaching, have lots of patience, and_____.

8. My neighbors are most annoying when they play music late at night, borrow items and never return them, and_____.

9. New college students need advice on managing their time, communicating with their instructors, and_____.

10. Three weeks of vacation, and exercise center, and _____ are among the great benefits I receive at work.

15   RECOGNIZING SPECIFIC DETAILS IN AN ESSAY

Activity

For each supporting paragraph in the essay below, there are two sets of supporting details. Write *S* (for *specific*) in the blank next to the set that provides specific support for the topic sentence. Write *G* (for *general*) in the blank next to the set with only vague, general support.

Introduction

What would you do if one of your friends—a terrific guy who is good-natured, generous, and outgoing—invited you over for dinner? You're probably thinking, "I'd certainly go. Why not?" Would you still go if your friend, a prince of a fellow, was a lousy host? Well, that's the dilemma my old college friend Ben presents. Everybody likes Ben, but nobody wants to be invited to his place for the evening because he doesn't manage his time well, he's an awful cook, and he's messy.

Supporting Paragraph 1

The first problem is that Ben has no sense of how to plan a schedule.

_____ a.   He doesn't seem to think ahead when he invites people over for the evening. When you show up at the time he invited you, you find that he isn't ready for you at all. In fact, he hasn't even begun to prepare dinner. Because he's so busy preparing dinner, he is unable to give his attention to his guests. He expects his guests to take care of themselves or follow him around the kitchen while he prepares dinner. His inability to manage his time can cause his guests a lot of inconvenience and result in a pretty boring evening.

_____ b.   For example, say he invites you over for dinner at six. When you show up at that hour, you will probably meet him just getting home from work. Then you will watch him wander around his kitchen for a while, wondering aloud what to make for dinner. Likely as not, he'll decide to try something that takes a great deal of time, like eggplant Parmesan, leaving you to entertain yourself either watching him prepare dinner or watching TV. By nine o'clock, you'll be begging him for a few carrot sticks, an apple—anything.

Supporting Paragraph 2

Second, Ben is a truly awful cook.

_____ a. If he does manage to come up with something to eat before you die of hunger, it will probably be so terrible it'll make your tongue curl. He has dreamed up such creative dishes as pork chops with lime sauce and potatoes mashed with sardines. After the first bite, most guests try to find a way to hide the rest under their napkin. Once he stood in front of the cupboard for twenty minutes, muttering, "Well, now, let's see what we've got here." Then he fussed like a mad scientist over ingredients he found and came up with something he called "cereal burgers."

_____ b. Although it doesn't seem that hard to find some tasty-sounding recipes and follow them, Ben doesn't seem capable of doing that. In fact, he prefers not to use recipes at all. He likes to make up his own food combinations. This sounds like a good idea, but it rarely turns out well when Ben does it. The main reasons are that he has such bad taste and also he often has very few ingredients in the apartment. He considers it a challenge to come up with an edible meal based on whatever happens to remain on his cupboard shelves. The idea of shopping with guests in mind never enters his mind.

Supporting Paragraph 3

Finally, Ben's apartment is so messy it's unpleasant to spend time there.

_____ a. It is challenging to find a place to sit in his apartment, and you may have something on the floor get on your shoes. Ben doesn't seem to notice that he can't find anything and doesn't have any room to sit down. The truth is, it doesn't bother him to be surrounded by all types of things that most people would have thrown in the garbage can or recycled ages ago. Even people who are not terribly neat themselves are shocked by the jumbled environment in Ben's apartment.

_____ b. When you cross his living room floor, a half-eaten lollipop may stick to the soles of your shoes. When you sit on the sofa, you hear the crunch of hidden crackers. You'd like to move, but all the other seats are buried under mountains of papers, laundry, and pizza boxes. One measure of Ben's messiness is the reaction of our friend Cruz. Cruz's bedroom floor is covered with underwear and empty Chinese food containers. His living room rug, once green, is gray with dust. Last time I spoke to Cruz, he observed, "I had dinner at Ben's last night. Boy, is his apartment a mess."

Conclusion

As I said, Ben is a heck of a guy. He is kind to old people and children. He doesn't have a bad thing to say about anyone. In December, he collects toys for the poor. He tells wonderful jokes and is extremely well read. His friends can't say enough good things about him. They love to spend time with him—anywhere except at his place.

16   PROVIDING DETAILS IN AN ESSAY

Activity

The supporting paragraphs of the following essay need more specific details. In the spaces provided, add a sentence or two of convincing details for each idea.

Introduction

I remember the September morning that I first laid eyes on Jill. I'd been calling clients at my desk at work when I heard a warm, musical laugh. There was something so attractive about the sound that I got up to get a cup of coffee and to find the source of that laugh. I discovered the voice to be that of a young, auburn-haired woman we had just hired from a temporary agency. Soon after, Jill and I began going out, and we spent the next two years together. Only recently have we decided to break up because of disagreements about finances, about children, and about our relationship with her family.

Supporting Paragraph 1

First of all, Jill and I have very different ideas about how to handle money. She likes to spend a lot of money on entertainment, and I don't. _____

_____

_____

_____

_____

In addition, while I think saving for the future is essential, she thinks it's silly.

_____

_____

_____

_____

Also, I feel she uses credit cards too freely. _____

_____

_____

_____

_____

Supporting Paragraph 2

Second, our thoughts about children are quite different. One conflict we had was over whether or not we should have any children. _____

_____

_____

_____

_____

If she did have children, her ideas about how they should be cared for are different from mine. _____

_____

_____

_____

_____

Her ideas about how children should be educated also differ greatly from my own. _____

_____

_____

_____

_____

Supporting Paragraph 3

Finally, we disagreed about how to deal with her family. Jill expected us to spend a lot of time with her parents, a prospect that horrifies me. _____

_____

_____

_____

_____

She also expected us to consult her parents before we made any major deci-sions; I haven't found their advice all that wise. _____

_____

_____

_____

_____

Conclusion

I care a lot about Jill, and I miss having her in my life. But I am convinced that our marriage would have been a mistake because of our conflicting views on finances, children, and family. I have no regrets about the decision to break off our relationship.

17   PROVIDING TRANSITIONS IN AN ESSAY

Activity I

The following essay uses time order. Fill in the blanks with appropriate transitions from the box. Use every transition once. You will probably find it helpful to check off (✓) each transition as you use it.

then	finally	first	as
before	often	soon	when
until	while	next	after

Most mornings at my office pass in a rather typical—and peaceful—fashion. _____, I go over the calendar and write reminders to myself about my day's schedule. I also go through the list of orders that were taken the day before, checking to be sure everything is clear. A series of other tasks follow _____ it's time for lunch. However, life at my office was not so typical this morning because of a black cloud, a loud alarm, and a visitor wearing a "mask."

The surprises began with a mistake made by our office boy. _____ I was working at my computer, I suddenly heard cursing behind me.

_____ trying to replace the toner cartridge in our copying machine, Greg, the office boy, had dropped the cartridge, and a cloud of black toner dust was rising in the air above the copier. _____ the dust could begin to subside, it started to go into an air conditioning duct nearby. Someone ran to turn off the air conditioning, but some dust still got into the duct system. We all became aware of a fine black powder on our bodies and all the surfaces in the office.

The _____ episode of the morning was equally upsetting. Suddenly a very loud clanging filled the offices, as if a giant telephone were ringing. It took us a few seconds to realize that it was the fire alarm. Everyone

_____ herded quickly down the stairs. In short order, there were around two hundred people on the front sidewalk wondering where the smoke and hot flames were. As it turned out, there were none. Someone on another floor had burned some toast in a toaster that he had, against the rules, brought into the building. As a result, he triggered the alarm system. We all returned to our desks, hoping to get some work done.

_____, we had to deal with a third unexpected event and a visitor wearing a "mask." Our office is in the same building as a veterinarian.

We _____ hear the yipping of dogs and the yowling of cats as they are carried in to see the doctor. However, we had never actually had a visitor from the vet's office. But _____ a secretary heard some scratching and opened the office door to check, something large and furry dashed in between her legs. It hid under a desk where we couldn't really get a good look at it, but we could hear it snarling and spitting at us. Fortunately,

it was _____ followed by its owner, who told us the angry animal was a raccoon. "Don't worry," he assured us. "We're almost sure it doesn't have rabies, but we're just having it tested to be certain."

_____ his announcement, the office once again cleared out very quickly.

After the black cloud, the false alarm, and the surprise visitor, I decided I had had enough for one day. I've been home all afternoon with a cold cloth on my forehead, and I'm hoping for a boring day tomorrow.

Activity 2

The following essay uses listing order. Fill in the blanks with appropriate transitions from the box. Use every transition once. You will probably find it helpful to check off (✓) each transition as you use it.

other	another	one	also
furthermore	third	moreover	

Does your will to study collapse when someone suggests getting a pizza? Does your social life compete with your class attendance? Is there a huge gap between your intentions and your actions? If the answers to these questions are yes, yes, and yes, read on. You can benefit from three powerful ways to motivate yourself: setting goals and working consciously to reach them, using rational thinking, and developing a positive personality.

_____ key to self-motivation is deciding on your goals—both long- and short-term—and then really working to reach them. Do you want to be an accountant or a nurse in a few years? Do you want to raise your grade point average this semester? Do you want to get at least a B on a paper this week? Whatever your goal, keep it in mind; it is the future you're working

toward. _____ keep in mind that the great majority of students who can be classified as failures have no goals. Once you've got some goals firmly in mind, decide how to reach them. Perhaps you'll need to study for at least two hours a day. Then think about the reward you'll give yourself for reaching a goal. Maybe for every hour of study, you'll eat a special snack

or listen to your favorite music. _____ rewards for achieving short-term goals might be going to the park, seeing a movie, calling a friend on the phone, and taking a nap.

Along with setting goals, _____ key to self-motivation is learning to think rationally. Instead of seeking shortcuts, do things right. If you're not sure about an important point on an assignment, ask instead of guessing. Don't rationalize about why you don't need to study for a math quiz. Instead, remind yourself that you need a passing grade in math to graduate. Also, rationally examine the benefits of good study habits. When you develop good study habits, studying takes less time and you get more out of it.

_____, as your studying becomes more and more productive, your self-image improves.

A _____ key to self-motivation is developing a positive personality. A positive personality includes attitudes that bring success. For instance, a positive person is enthusiastic, dependable, and supportive of others.

_____, a positive student has an upbeat, can-do self-image. "I can't," "It's too tough," and "Why bother?" aren't in this student's vocabulary.

So get your willpower in gear and use the three keys to self-motivation— set goals and work to reach them, think rationally, and develop a positive personality. You will find that a firm commitment to this approach becomes easier and easier. Progress will come more often and more readily, strengthening your resolve even further.

18 INTRODUCTORY AND CONCLUDING PARAGRAPHS

Activity 1

Four common methods of introducing an essay are as follows:

a Begin with a broad statement and narrow it down to your thesis statement.
b Present an idea or situation that is the opposite of the one you will develop.
c Tell a brief story.
d Ask one or more questions.

Following are four introductions. In the space provided, write the letter of the method of introduction used in each case.

_____ 1. One morning twenty-nine years ago, my father backed out of his parking space, smashed into the Cadillac parked across the street, put the gear into forward, and kept going. "Take it easy, Floyd," yelled Mom. "Better to be late than to die!" But that didn't keep him from accelerating, weaving in and out of traffic, and running into a telephone booth. As a result, I was born in my parents' old green-and-white Chevy instead of at Bradley Hospital. Perhaps it's no surprise, then, that my own car was the location of other key events in my life—an accident that almost killed me, the place where I made a crucial job decision, and my proposal to my wife.

_____ 2. I have had a lot of interesting teachers through the years. Some have taught me useful and interesting facts. Even better, some have shown me how to learn. Some have even inspired me. But of all the wonderful teachers I've had, my favorite is Mrs. Rogers, who taught me how to write, showed me the pleasures of reading, and most important, helped me realize I could do just about anything I put my mind to.

_____ 3. Most mornings at my office pass in a rather typical—and peaceful—fashion. First, I go over the calendar and write reminders to myself about my day's schedule. I also go through the list of orders that were taken the day before, checking to be sure everything is clear. A series of other tasks follows until it's time for lunch. However, life at my office was not so typical this morning because of a black cloud, a loud alarm, and a visitor wearing a "mask."

_____ 4. Does your will to study collapse when someone suggests getting a pizza? Does your social life compete with your class attendance? Is there a huge gap between your intentions and your actions? If the answers to these questions are yes, yes, and yes, read on. You can benefit from some powerful ways to motivate yourself: setting goals and working consciously to reach them, using rational thinking, and developing a positive personality.

Activity 2

Two common methods of concluding an essay are as follows:

a Provide a summary and a final thought.
b Focus on the future.

Following are two conclusions. In the space provided, write the letter of the method of conclusion used in each case.

_____ 1. I care a lot about Jill, and I miss having her in my life. But I am convinced that our marriage would have been a mistake because of our conflicting views on finances, children, and family. I have had no regrets about the decision to break off our relationship.

_____ 2. So get your willpower in gear, and use the three keys to self-motivation—set goals and work to reach them, think rationally, and develop a positive personality. You will find that a firm commitment to this approach becomes easier and easier. Progress will come more often and more readily, strengthening your resolve even further.

19 PREWRITING

These activities will give you practice in some of the prewriting strategies you can use to generate material for a paper. While the focus here is on writing a paragraph, the strategies apply to writing an essay as well. See if you can do two or more of the prewriting activities.

Activity 1: Freewriting

On a sheet of paper, freewrite for several minutes about the best or most disappointing friend you ever had. Don't worry about grammar, punctuation, or spelling. Try to write, without stopping, about whatever comes into your head concerning your best or most disappointing friend.

Activity 2: Questioning

On another sheet of paper, answer the following questions about the friend you've started to write about.

1. When did this friendship take place?
2. Where did it take place?
3. What is one reason you liked or were disappointed in this friend? Give one quality, action, comment, etc. Also, give some details to illustrate this quality.
4. What is another reason that you liked or were disappointed in your friend? What are some details that support the second reason?
5. Can you think of a third thing about your friend that you liked or were disappointed in? What are some details that support the third reason?

Activity 3: Clustering

In the center of a blank sheet of paper, write and circle the words *best friend* or *most disappointing friend.* Then, around the circle, add reasons and details about the friend. Use a series of boxes, circles, or other shapes, along with connecting lines, to set off the reasons and details. In other words, try to think about and explore your topic in a very visual way.

Activity 4: Making a List

On separate paper, make a list of details about the friend. Don't worry about putting them in a certain order. Just get down as many details about the friend as occur to you. The list can include specific reasons you liked or were disappointed in the person and specific details supporting those reasons.

20   OUTLINING, DRAFTING, AND REVISING

Here you will get practice in the writing steps that follow prewriting: outlining, drafting, and revising.

Activity 1: Scratch Outline

On the basis of your prewriting, see if you can prepare a scratch outline made up of your main idea and the three main reasons you liked or were disappointed in your friend. Use the form below:

_____ was my best *or* most disappointing friend.

*Reason 1:*_____

*Reason 2:*_____

*Reason 3:*_____

Activity 2: First Draft

Now write a first draft of your paper. Begin with your topic sentence, stating that a certain friend was the best or most disappointing one you ever had. Then state the first reason to support your main idea, followed by specific details supporting that reason. Next, state the second reason, followed by specific details supporting that reason. Finally, state the third reason, followed by support.

Don't worry about grammar, punctuation, or spelling. Just concentrate on getting down on paper the details about the job.

Activity 3: Revising the Draft

Ideally, you will have a chance to put your paper aside for a while before writing the second draft. In your second draft, try to do all of the following:

1. Add transition words such as *first of all, another,* and *finally* to introduce each of the three reasons you liked or were disappointed in the friend you're writing about.
2. Omit any details that do not truly support your topic sentence.
3. Add more details as needed, making sure you have plenty of support for each of your three reasons.
4. Check to see that your details are vivid and specific. Can you make a supporting detail more concrete? Are there any persuasive, colorful specifics you can add?
5. Try to eliminate wordiness (see page 323) and clichés (see page 320).

6. In general, improve the flow of your writing.
7. Be sure to include a final sentence that rounds off the paper, bringing it to a close.

Activity 4: Proofreading

When you have your almost-final draft of the paper, proofread it as follows:

1. Using your dictionary, check any words that you think might be misspelled. Or use a spell-check program on your word processor.
2. Using Part Two of this book, check your paper for mistakes in grammar, punctuation, and usage.
3. Read the paper aloud, listening for awkward or unclear spots. Make the changes needed for the paragraph to read smoothly and clearly. Even better, see if you can get another person to read the draft aloud to you. The spots that this person has trouble reading are spots where you may have to do some rewriting.
4. Take a sheet of paper and cover your writing so that you can expose and carefully check one line at a time. Or read your writing backward, from the end of the paragraph to the beginning. Look for typing errors, omitted words, and other remaining errors.

Don't fail to proofread carefully. You may be tired of working on your paper at this point, but you want to give the extra effort needed to make it as good as possible. A final push can mean the difference between a higher and a lower grade.

21   PARAGRAPH AND ESSAY WRITING ASSIGNMENTS

Your instructor may ask you to do some of the following paragraph and essay writing assignments. Be sure to refer to the activities above as you write. Also, check the rules for paper format on page 214.

Five Paragraph Assignments

Paragraph Assignment 1: A Sharp Memory of Your Mother or Father

Think of a particularly clear memory you have of your mother or father. It might be a happy memory that warms your heart. Or it could be humorous, frightening, or enraging. The important thing is that it is a sharp, specific recollection that produces a strong emotional response in you. Then write a paragraph about your memory.

Your goal will be to let the reader see exactly what happened and understand what you felt. To accomplish this, you must provide very specific details. Remember that your reader will have no prior knowledge of your mother or father. You are responsible for painting a "word picture" that will let your reader see your parent the way you saw him or her.

Before you begin writing the paragraph itself, do some prewriting. You might jot down answers to the kind of questions a curious reader would have about your memory. Here are a few such questions: Where did this event take place? When? Who was present? How old was your parent when this occurred? How old were you? What did your parent look like? What did he or she say? How did he or she say it? Why is this memory so vivid for you? The answers to questions like these will provide the kind of concrete detail that will make your paragraph come alive.

Begin your paragraph with a summary statement, such as these:

One of my family's most amusing experiences took place when I found my father sleepwalking in the kitchen.

Seeing my mother trip on the sidewalk was the beginning of a difficult morning for me.

Your paragraph will probably be organized in time order, describing the events that occurred from beginning to end. You can help your reader understand the sequence of events if you use time transitions such as *first, next, then, later,* and *finally.*

If you prefer, write instead about a memory of another relative.

Paragraph Assignment 2: A Disagreeable Characteristic

Even the most saintly person has one or more unpleasant traits. Write a paragraph about a particularly disagreeable characteristic of someone you know. Your topic sentence will be a general statement about that person and the quality you've chosen to write about. For example, if you decide to write about your own extreme impatience, your topic sentence might be:

When I let my impatience get out of hand, I often damage my relationships with others.

A paragraph with this topic sentence might list two or three experiences supporting that main idea. Here are two other examples of topic sentences for this paper:

Our neighbor Mr. Nagle is a cruel person.

While my minister is basically a kind man, he much prefers hearing his own voice to anyone else's.

Paragraph Assignment 3: A Special Goal

We all have goals, long-term and short-term. Write a paragraph about one of your important goals. It might be something you hope to achieve over the next few months or the next few years.

Perhaps you plan to overcome a bad habit or get a better job. Begin your paragraph with a topic sentence that clearly states the goal and when you expect to reach it, such as "I hope to have quit smoking by the end of this year" or "After I graduate, I hope to get a nursing job at a local hospital." Then go on to list and explain two or three reasons you wish to reach the goal. To generate some reasons, make a list, and then choose the three you feel are the strongest. Save the most important reason for last.

Paragraph Assignment 4: In Praise of Something

We all are fans of something that we feel greatly enriches our life, such as a pet, basketball, or chocolate. Write a paragraph in which your supporting details show the benefits or virtues of something you adore. For instance, you could write about the advantages of having a dog around the house. Use whatever prewriting strategy you choose to help you come up with more benefits or virtues than you need. Then choose two or three you feel you can explain in colorful detail.

One benefit you might list, for instance, is that a dog makes one feel loved. You could illustrate this benefit by describing an experience such as the following:

> A week ago, I spilled hot coffee on a customer's lap. He was not amused. After the customer left—without leaving a tip, of course—the manager walked past me and said quietly, "Strike one!" When I got home that day and collapsed on a chair, my friend Goldie, a cocker spaniel, hopped onto my lap and licked my face with his broad, warm tongue. I could feel the knot in my stomach loosening.

Here's a sample scratch outline for this assignment.

Topic sentence: Having a dog around the house is one of life's rich pleasures.

(1) A dog is entertaining.

(2) A dog brings out the best in a person.

(3) A dog makes a person feel loved.

Paragraph Assignment 5: A Popular Saying

It seems there are sayings to cover every type of experience, from our sleeping habits ("Early to bed, early to rise, makes a man healthy, wealthy, and wise") to our expectations ("Hope for the best but expect the worst"). Write a paragraph in which you demonstrate through an experience you have had that a particular saying is either true or false.

Begin your paragraph with a clear statement supporting or opposing the saying, such as "When I painted my house last summer, I learned the truth of the saying 'Haste makes waste'" or "When it comes to escaping a fire, the saying 'Haste makes waste' doesn't apply." Then go on to tell your experience in vivid detail. To help your reader follow the sequence of events involved, use a few time transitions (*before, then, during, now,* and so on). Below are some other popular sayings you might wish to consider using in your paper—or use some other popular saying.

Here today, gone tomorrow.

If you don't help yourself, nobody will.

A penny saved is a penny earned.

The early bird catches the worm.

Curiosity killed the cat.

You get what you pay for.

A rolling stone gathers no moss.

Don't count your chickens before they're hatched.

An ounce of prevention is worth a pound of cure.

A journey of a thousand miles must begin with a single step.

Whatever can go wrong, will go wrong.

Don't judge someone until you've walked a mile in his shoes.

Five Essay Assignments

Essay Assignment 1: The Place Where You Live

Write an essay about the best or worst features of your apartment or house. In your introduction, you might begin with a general description of where you live. Then end the paragraph with your thesis statement and plan of development.

Here are some thesis statements that may help you think about and develop your own paper.

Thesis statement: I love my apartment because of its wonderful location, its great kitchen, and my terrific neighbors.

(A supporting paragraph on the apartment's location, for example, might focus on the fact that it's in the middle of a lively, interesting neighborhood with a good supermarket, a drugstore, a variety of restaurants, and so on.)

Thesis statement: My house has three key advantages: a wonderful landlord, a beautiful yard, and housemates that are like family.

(A supporting paragraph about the landlord might explain how he or she fixes things promptly and once, in a special circumstance, allowed you to pay your rent late.)

Thesis statement: A tiny kitchen, dismal decor, and noisy neighbors are the three main disadvantages to my apartment.

(A supporting paragraph on the apartment's dismal decoration could begin with this topic sentence: "The dark and poorly kept walls and floorings are ugly and, even worse, gloomy." Such a sentence might then be followed by some very carefully worded, concrete specifics and perhaps a revealing anecdote.)

Note that listing transitions such as *first of all, second, another, also, in addition, finally,* and so on may help you introduce your supporting paragraphs as well as set off different supporting details within those paragraphs.

● Essay Assignment 2: What Children Really Need

There are many theories about what children need from the adults in their lives. Give some thought to your own childhood, your own children, or your observations of children you know. Decide on three things that *you* believe are essential to a child's growth and development. Then write a five-paragraph essay on those three qualities.

Your introductory paragraph should arouse your readers' interest. For instance, you might explain how important a person's childhood is to the rest of his or her life. The introductory paragraph should also include a thesis statement made up of your central idea and the three necessities you think are so important. For instance, one student's thesis was this: "I feel that three things all children need are love, approval, and a sense of belonging."

Devote each one of the following three supporting paragraphs to one of those important things. Begin each paragraph with a clearly stated topic sentence, and use concrete examples to show how adults can provide each quality to children. Be equally specific in showing what you believe happens when children are not provided with these things. To help your reader make the transition from paragraph to paragraph, use such words as *another thing, in addition,* and *a final quality.* You may wish to consider writing about some of the following things many people feel children need for healthy growth and development.

Unconditional love
Approval
Sense of belonging
Opportunities to experiment
Feeling of safety
Clearly defined limits to behavior
Sense of responsibility

In a concluding paragraph, provide a summary of the points in your paper as well as a final thought to round off your discussion.

Essay Assignment 3: Something Special

Imagine that your apartment or house is burning down. Of course, the best strategy would be to get yourself and others out of the building as quickly as possible. But suppose you knew for sure that you had time to rescue three of your possessions. Which three would you choose? Write an essay in which you discuss the three things in your home that you would most want to save from a fire.

Begin by doing some prewriting to find the items you want to write about. You could, for instance, try making a list and then choosing several of the most likely candidates. Then you could freewrite about each of those candidates. In this way, you are likely to find three possessions that will make strong subjects for this essay. Each will be the basis of a supporting paragraph. Each supporting paragraph will focus on why the object being discussed is so important to you. Make your support as specific and colorful as possible, perhaps using detailed descriptions, anecdotes, or quotations to reveal the importance of each object.

In planning your introduction, consider beginning with a broad, general idea and then narrowing it down to your thesis statement. Here, for example, is one such introduction for this paper:

> I have many possessions that I would be sad to lose. Because I love to cook, I would miss various kitchen appliances that provide me with so many happy cooking adventures. I would also miss the wonderful electronic equipment that entertains me every day, including my large-screen television set and my VCR. I would miss the various telephones on which I have spent many interesting hours chatting in every part of my apartment, including the bathtub. But if my apartment were burning down, I would most want to rescue three things that are irreplaceable and hold great meaning for me—the silverware set that belonged to my grandmother, my mother's wedding gown, and my giant photo album.

Essay Assignment 4: Teaching the Basics

What are you experienced in? Fixing cars? Growing flowers? Baking? Waiting on customers? Giving children's birthday parties? Write an essay teaching readers the basics of an activity in which you have some experience. If you're not sure about which activity to choose, use prewriting to help you find a topic you can support strongly. Once you've chosen your topic, continue to prewrite as a way to find your key points and organize them into three supporting paragraphs. The key details of waiting on customers in a diner, for instance, might be divided according to time order, as seen in the following topic sentences.

> *Topic sentence for supporting paragraph 1:* Greeting customers and taking their orders should not be done carelessly.
>
> *Topic sentence for supporting paragraph 2:* There are right and wrong ways to bring customers their food and to keep track of them during their meal.
>
> *Topic sentence for supporting paragraph 3:* The final interaction with customers may be brief, but it is important.

To make your points clear, be sure to use detailed descriptions and concrete examples throughout your essay. Also, you may want to use transitional words such as *first, then, also, another, when, after, while,* and *finally* to help organize your details.

Essay Assignment 5:
Advantages or Disadvantages of Single Life

More and more people are remaining single longer, and almost half of the people who marry eventually divorce and become single again. Write an essay on the advantages or disadvantages of single life. Each of your three supporting paragraphs will focus on one advantage or one disadvantage. To decide which approach to take, begin by making two lists. A list of advantages might include:

> More freedom of choice
> Lower expenses
> Fewer responsibilities
> Dating opportunities

A list of disadvantages could include:

> Loneliness
> Depression at holidays
> Lack of support in everyday decisions
> Disapproval of parents and family

Go on to list as many specific details as you can think of to support your advantages and disadvantages. Those details will help you decide whether you want your thesis to focus on benefits or drawbacks. Then create a scratch outline made up of your thesis statement and each of your main supporting points. Put the most important or most dramatic supporting point last.

In your introduction, you might gain your reader's interest by asking several questions or by telling a brief, revealing story about single life. As you develop your supporting paragraphs, make sure that each begins with a topic sentence and focuses on one advantage or disadvantage of single life. While writing the essay, continue developing details that vividly support each of your points.

In a concluding paragraph, provide a summary of the points in your paper as well as a final thought to round off your discussion. Your final thought might be in the form of a prediction or a recommendation.

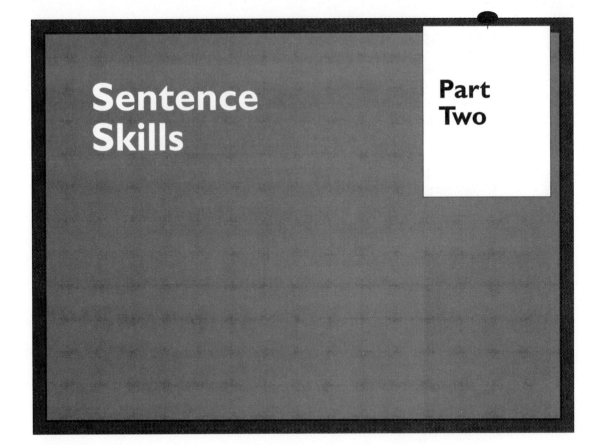

Sentence Skills

Part Two

INTRODUCTION

Part Two explains the basic skills needed to write clear, error-free sentences. While the skills are presented within four traditional categories (grammar, mechanics, punctuation, and word use), each section is self-contained so that you can go directly to the skills you need to work on. Note, however, that you may find it helpful to cover "Subjects and Verbs" before turning to other skills. Typically, the main features of a skill are presented on the first pages of a section; secondary points are developed later. Numerous activities are provided so that you can practice skills enough to make them habits. The activities are varied and range from underlining answers to writing complete sentences involving the skill in question. One or more review tests at the end of each section offer additional practice activities.

Section 1: Grammar

Subjects and Verbs

INTRODUCTORY PROJECT

Understanding subjects and verbs is a big step toward mastering many sentence skills. As a speaker of English, you already have an instinctive feel for these basic building blocks of English sentences. See if you can insert an appropriate word in each space below. The answer will be a subject.

1. The _____ will soon be over.

2. _____ cannot be trusted.

3. A strange _____ appeared in my backyard.

4. _____ is one of my favorite activities.

Now insert an appropriate word in the following spaces. Each answer will be a verb.

5. The prisoner _____ at the judge.

6. My sister _____ much harder than I do.

7. The players _____ in the locker room.

8. Rob and Marilyn _____ with the instructor.

Finally, insert appropriate words in the following spaces. Your answers will be a subject and a verb.

9. The _____ almost _____ out of the tree.

10. Many _____ today _____ sex and violence.

11. The _____ carefully _____ the patient.

12. A _____ quickly _____ the ball.

The basic building blocks of English sentences are subjects and verbs. Understanding them is an important first step toward mastering a number of sentence skills.

Every sentence has a subject and a verb. Who or what the sentence speaks about is called the *subject;* what the sentence says about the subject is called the *verb.* In the following sentences, the subject is underlined once and the verb twice:

People gossip.
The truck belched fumes.
He waved at me.
Alaska contains the largest wilderness area in America.
That woman is a millionaire.
The pants feel itchy.

A SIMPLE WAY TO FIND A SUBJECT

To find a subject, ask *who* or *what* the sentence is about. As shown below, your answer is the subject.

Who is the first sentence about? People
What is the second sentence about? The truck
Who is the third sentence about? He
What is the fourth sentence about? Alaska
Who is the fifth sentence about? That woman
What is the sixth sentence about? The pants

It helps to remember that the subject of a sentence is always a *noun* (any person, place, or thing) or a pronoun. A *pronoun* is simply a word like *he, she, it, you,* or *they* used in place of a noun. In the preceding sentences, the subjects are persons (*People, He, woman*), a place (*Alaska*), and things (*truck, pants*). And note that one pronoun (*He*) is used as a subject.

A SIMPLE WAY TO FIND A VERB

To find a verb, ask what the sentence *says about* the subject. As shown below, your answer is the verb.

What does the first sentence *say about* people? They gossip.
What does the second sentence *say about* the truck? It belched (fumes).

What does the third sentence *say about* him? He <u>waved</u> (at me).

What does the fourth sentence *say about* Alaska? It <u>contains</u> (the largest wilderness area in America).

What does the fifth sentence *say about* that woman? She <u>is</u> (a millionaire).

What does the sixth sentence *say about* the pants? They <u>feel</u> (itchy).

A second way to find the verb is to put *I, you, he, she, it,* or *they* in front of the word you think is a verb. If the result makes sense, you have a verb. For example, you could put *they* in front of *gossip* in the first sentence above, with the result, *they gossip,* making sense. Therefore, you know that *gossip* is a verb. You could use the same test with the other verbs as well.

Finally, it helps to remember that most verbs show action. In "People gossip," the action is gossiping. In "The truck belched fumes," the action is belching. In "He waved at me," the action is waving. In "Alaska contains the largest wilderness area in America," the action is containing.

Certain other verbs, known as *linking verbs,* do not show action. They do, however, give information about the subject of the sentence. In "That woman is a millionaire," the linking verb *is* tells us that the woman is a millionaire. In "The pants feel itchy," the linking verb *feel* gives us the information that the pants are itchy.

Practice 1

In each of the following sentences, draw one line under the subject and two lines under the verb.

Ask *who* or *what* the sentence is about to find the subject. Then ask what the sentence *says about* the subject to find the verb.

1. I ate an entire pizza by myself.
2. Barracuda swim in that lake.
3. Sally failed the test.
4. The television movie ended suddenly.
5. Kerry borrowed change for the pay telephone.
6. The children stared in wide-eyed wonderment at the Thanksgiving Day floats.
7. An old newspaper tumbled down the dirty street.
8. Lola starts every morning with a series of yoga exercises.
9. My part-time job limits my study time.
10. The windstorm blew over the storage shed in the backyard.

Practice 2

Follow the directions given for Practice 1. Note that all of the verbs here are linking verbs.

1. My sister is a terrible speller.
2. Potato chips are Ramon's favorite snack.
3. The defendant appeared very nervous on the witness stand.
4. Art became a father at the age of twenty.
5. The ride going somewhere always seems longer than the ride coming back.
6. That apartment building was an abandoned factory two years ago.
7. My first two weeks on the sales job were the worst ones of my life.
8. The plastic banana split and Styrofoam birthday cake in the bakery window look like real desserts.
9. Jane always feels energized after a cup of coffee.
10. Rooms with white walls seem larger than those with dark-colored walls.

Practice 3

Follow the directions given for Practice 1.

1. That clock runs about five minutes fast.
2. The new player on the team is much too sure of himself.
3. Late-afternoon shoppers filled the aisles of the supermarket.
4. Garbage trucks rumbled down my street on their way to the dump.
5. The children drew pictures on the steamed window.
6. The picture fell suddenly to the floor.
7. Chipmunks live in the woodpile behind my house.
8. Our loud uncle monopolized the conversation at the dinner table.
9. The tomatoes were soft to the touch.
10. The insurance company canceled my policy because of a speeding ticket.

MORE ABOUT
SUBJECTS AND VERBS

Distinguishing Subjects
from Prepositional Phrases

The subject of a sentence never appears within a prepositional phrase. A *prepositional phrase* is simply a group of words beginning with a preposition and ending with the answer to the question *what* or *when*. Here is a list of common prepositions.

about	before	by	in, into	through
above	behind	down	inside	to
across	below	during	of	toward
among	beneath	except	off	under
around	beside	for	on, onto	up
at	between	from	over	with

Cross out prepositional phrases when looking for the subject of a sentence.

~~In the middle of the night~~, we heard footsteps ~~on the roof~~.
The magazines ~~on the table~~ belong ~~in the garage~~.
~~Before the opening kickoff~~, a brass band marched ~~onto the field~~.
The hardware store ~~across the street~~ went ~~out of business~~.
~~In spite of our advice~~, Sally quit her job ~~at Burger King~~.

Practice

Cross out prepositional phrases. Then draw a single line under subjects and a double line under verbs.

1. For that course, you need three different books.
2. The key to the front door slipped from my hand into a puddle.
3. The checkout lines at the supermarket moved very slowly.
4. With his son, Jamal walked to the playground.
5. No quarrel between good friends lasts for a very long time.
6. In one weekend, Martha planted a large vegetable garden in her backyard.

7. Either of my brothers is a reliable worker.

8. The drawer of the bureau sticks on rainy days.

9. During the movie, several people walked out in protest.

10. At a single sitting, my brother reads five or more comic books.

Verbs of More Than One Word

Many verbs consist of more than one word. Here, for example, are some of the many forms of the verb *help:*

helps	should have been helping	will have helped
helped	can help	would have been helped
is helping	would have been helping	has been helped
was helping	will be helping	had been helped
may help	had been helping	must have helped
should help	helped	having helped
will help	have helped	should have been helped
does help	has helped	had helped

Below are sentences that contain verbs of more than one word:

Diane is not working overtime this week.

Another book has been written about the Kennedy family.

We should have stopped for gas at the last station.

The game has just been canceled.

Notes

1   Words like *not, just, never, only,* and *always* are not part of the verb although they may appear within the verb.

The oven is not heating properly.
The boys should just not have stayed out so late.
The game has always been played regardless of the weather.

2   No verb preceded by *to* is ever the verb of a sentence.

Sue wants to go with us.
The newly married couple decided to rent a house for a year.
The store needs extra people to help out at Christmas.

3   No *-ing* word by itself is ever the verb of a sentence. (It may be part of the verb, but it must have a helping verb in front of it.)

We planning the trip for months. (This is not a sentence because the verb is not complete.)
We were planning the trip for months. (This is a complete sentence.)

Practice

Draw a single line under subjects and a double line under verbs. Be sure to include all parts of the verb.

1. He has been sleeping all day.
2. The wood foundations of the shed were attacked by termites.
3. I have not washed my car for several months.
4. The instructor had not warned us about the quiz.
5. The bus will be leaving shortly.
6. You should not try to pet that temperamental hamster.
7. They have just been married by a justice of the peace.
8. He could make a living with his wood carvings.
9. Kim has decided to ask her boss for a raise.
10. The company should have purchased word processors rather than electric typewriters.

Compound Subjects and Verbs

A sentence may have more than one verb:

The dancer stumbled and fell.
Lola washed her hair, blew it dry, and parted it in the middle.

A sentence may have more than one subject:

Cats and dogs are sometimes the best of friends.
The striking workers and their bosses could not come to an agreement.

A sentence may have several subjects and several verbs:

Holly and I read the book and reported on it to the class.
Pete, Nick, and Fran caught the fish in the morning, cleaned them in the afternoon, and ate them that night.

Practice

Draw a single line under subjects and a double line under verbs. Be sure to mark *all* the subjects and verbs.

1. The hypnotist locked his assistant in a box and sawed her in half.
2. Connie began her paper at 7:30 and finished it at midnight.
3. On the shipping pier, the Nissans, Toyotas, and Hondas glittered in the sun.
4. Tony added the column of figures three times and got three different totals.
5. The car sputtered, stalled, and then started again.
6. Whiteflies, mites, and aphids infected my houseplants.
7. Ruth disconnected the computers and carried them to her car.
8. We walked over to the corner deli and bought extra cheese for the party.
9. At the new shopping mall, Tony and Lola looked in windows for two hours and then bought one pair of tube socks.
10. My aunt and uncle married in their twenties, divorced in their thirties, and then remarried in their forties.

Review Test 1

Draw one line under the subjects and two lines under the verbs. As necessary, cross out prepositional phrases to help find subjects. Underline all the parts of a verb. And remember that you may find more than one subject and verb in a sentence.

1. I had not heard about the cancellation of the class.
2. James should have gotten an estimate from the plumber.
3. The family played badminton and volleyball at the picnic.
4. A solution to the problem popped suddenly into my head.
5. My roommate and I will have to study all night for the test.
6. Chang has not been eating in the cafeteria this semester.
7. The white moon hung above the castle like a grinning skull.
8. Len and Marie drove all night and arrived at their vacation cottage early Saturday morning.
9. The game has been postponed because of bad weather and will be rescheduled for later in the season.
10. The sun reflected sharply off the lake and forced me to wear sunglasses.

 Review Test 2

Follow the directions given for Review Test 1.

1. The doctors were speaking gently to the parents of the little girl.
2. A rumor has been spreading about the possible closing of the plant.
3. Diesel trucks with heavy exhaust fumes should be banned from the road.
4. The dental assistant should have warned me about the pain.
5. With their fingers, the children started to draw pictures on the steamed window.
6. Three buildings down the street from my house have been demolished.
7. Rats, squirrels, and bats lived in the attic of the abandoned house.
8. Jack and Bob will be anchoring the long-distance team in the track meet.
9. Reluctantly, I crawled from my bed and stumbled to the bathroom.
10. Tiddledywinks, pick-up sticks, and hearts were our favorite childhood games.

Fragments

WHAT SENTENCE FRAGMENTS ARE

Every sentence must have a subject and a verb and must express a complete thought. A word group that lacks a subject or a verb and that does not express a complete thought is a *fragment*. Following are the most common types of fragments that people write:

1 Dependent-word fragments
2 *-ing* and *to* fragments
3 Added-detail fragments
4 Missing-subject fragments

Once you understand the specific kind or kinds of fragments that you may write, you should be able to eliminate them from your writing. The following pages explain all four fragment types.

1 DEPENDENT-WORD FRAGMENTS

Some word groups that begin with a dependent word are fragments. Here is a list of common dependent words:

Dependent Words

after	if, even if	when, whenever
although, though	in order that	where, wherever
as	since	whether
because	that, so that	which, whichever
before	unless	while
even though	until	who
how	what, whatever	whose

Whenever you start a sentence with one of these words, you must be careful that a fragment does not result. The word group beginning with the dependent word *After* in the selection below is a fragment.

<u>After I stopped drinking coffee.</u> I began sleeping better at night.

A *dependent statement*—one starting with a dependent word like *After*—cannot stand alone. It depends on another statement to complete the thought. "After I stopped drinking coffee" is a dependent statement. It leaves us hanging. We expect in the same sentence to find out *what happened after* the writer stopped drinking coffee. When a writer does not follow through and complete a thought, a fragment results.

To correct the fragment, simply follow through and complete the thought:

After I stopped drinking coffee, I began sleeping better at night.

Remember, then, that *dependent statements by themselves* are fragments. They must be attached to a statement that makes sense standing alone.[*]

Here are two other selections with dependent-word fragments.

Brian sat nervously in the dental clinic. While waiting to have his wisdom tooth pulled.
Maria decided to throw away the boxes. That had accumulated for years in the basement.

"While waiting to have his wisdom tooth pulled" is a fragment; it does not make sense standing by itself. We want to know in the same statement *what Brian did* while waiting to have his tooth pulled. The writer must complete the thought. Likewise, "That had accumulated for years in the basement" is not in itself a complete thought. We want to know in the same statement what *that* refers to.

How to Correct Dependent-Word Fragments

In most cases, you can correct a dependent-word fragment by attaching it to the sentence that comes after it or the sentence that comes before it:

After I stopped drinking coffee, I began sleeping better at night.
(The fragment has been attached to the sentence that comes after it.)
Brian sat nervously in the dental clinic while waiting to have his wisdom tooth pulled.
(The fragment has been attached to the sentence that comes before it.)

---

[*]Some instructors refer to a dependent-word fragment as a *dependent clause*. A *clause* is simply a group of words having a subject and a verb. A clause may be *independent* (expressing a complete thought and able to stand alone) or *dependent* (not expressing a complete thought and not able to stand alone). A dependent clause by itself is a fragment. It can be corrected simply by adding an independent clause.

Maria decided to throw away the boxes that had accumulated for years in the basement.

(The fragment has been attached to the sentence that comes before it.)

Another way of correcting a dependent-word fragment is to eliminate the dependent word and make a new sentence:

I stopped drinking coffee.
He was waiting to have his wisdom tooth pulled.
They had accumulated for years in the basement.

Do not use this second method of correction too frequently, however, for it may cut down on interest and variety in your writing style.

Notes

I   Use a comma if a dependent-word group comes at the *beginning* of a sentence (see also pages 258–259):

After I stopped drinking coffee, I began sleeping better at night.

However, do not generally use a comma if the dependent-word group comes at the end of a sentence:

Brian sat nervously in the dental clinic while waiting to have his wisdom tooth pulled.
Maria decided to throw away the boxes that had accumulated for years in the basement.

2   Sometimes the dependent word *who, that, which,* or *where* appears not at the very start but *near* the start of a word group. A fragment often results.

Today I visited Hilda Cooper. A friend who is in the hospital. I was frightened by her loss of weight.

"A friend who is in the hospital" is not in itself a complete thought. We want to know in the same statement *who* the friend is. The fragment can be corrected by attaching it to the sentence that comes before it.

Today I visited Hilda Cooper, a friend who is in the hospital.

(Here a comma is used to set off "a friend who is in the hospital," which is extra material placed at the end of the sentence.)

Practice 1

Turn each of the dependent-word groups into a sentence by adding a complete thought. Put a comma after the dependent-word group if a dependent word starts the sentence.

Examples   After I got out of high school

After I got out of high school, I spent a year traveling.

The watch that I got fixed

The watch that I got fixed has just stopped working again.

1. After I finished work on Friday

    _____

    _____

2. Because the class was canceled

    _____

    _____

3. When my car stalled on the highway

    _____

    _____

4. The supermarket that I went to

    _____

    _____

5. Before I left the house

    _____

    _____

Practice 2

Underline the dependent-word fragment (or fragments) in each selection. Then correct each fragment by attaching it to the sentence that comes before or the sentence that comes after—whichever sounds more natural. Put a comma after the dependent-word group if it starts the sentence.

1. Although the air conditioner was working. I still felt warm in the room. I wondered if I had a fever.

   _____

   _____

   _____

2. When Tony got into his car this morning. He discovered that he had left the car windows open. The seats and rug were soaked. Since it had rained overnight.

   _____

   _____

   _____

3. After cutting fish at the restaurant all day. Jenny smelled like a cat food factory. She couldn't wait to take a hot, perfumed bath.

   _____

   _____

4. Franco raked out the soggy leaves. That were at the bottom of the cement fishpond. When two bullfrogs jumped out at him. He dropped the rake and ran.

   _____

   _____

5. Because he had eaten and drunk too much. He had to leave the party early. His stomach was like a volcano. That was ready to erupt.

   _____

   _____

   _____

2   *-ING* AND *TO* FRAGMENTS

When an *-ing* word appears at or near the start of a word group, a fragment may result. Such fragments often lack a subject and part of the verb. Underline the word groups in the examples below that contain *-ing* words. Each is a fragment.

Example 1

I spent all day in the employment office. Trying to find a job that suited me. The prospects looked bleak.

Example 2

Lola surprised Tony on the nature hike. Picking blobs of resin off pine trees. Then she chewed them like bubble gum.

Example 3

Mel took an aisle seat on the bus. His reason being that he had more legroom there.

People sometimes write *-ing* fragments because they think the subject in one sentence will work for the next word group as well. In the first example above, they might think the subject *I* in the opening sentence will also serve as the subject for "Trying to find a job that suited me." But the subject must actually be *in* the sentence.

How to Correct *-ing* Fragments

1   Attach the fragment to the sentence that comes before or the sentence that comes after it, whichever makes sense. Example 1 above could read, "I spent all day in the employment office, trying to find a job that suited me." (Note that here a comma is used to set off "trying to find a job that suited me," which is extra material placed at the end of the sentence.)

2   Add a subject and change the *-ing* verb part to the correct form of the verb. Example 2 could read, "She picked blobs of resin off pine trees."

3   Change *being* to the correct form of the verb *be* (*am, are, is, was, were*). Example 3 could read, "His reason was that he had more legroom there."

How to Correct *to* Fragments

When *to* appears at or near the start of a word group, a fragment sometimes results.

To remind people of their selfishness. Otis leaves handwritten notes on cars that take up two parking spaces.

The first word group in the selection above is a fragment. It can be corrected by adding it to the sentence that comes after it:

> To remind people of their selfishness, Otis leaves handwritten notes on cars that take up two parking spaces.

(Note that here a comma is used to set off "To remind people of their selfishness," which is introductory material in the sentence.)

Practice I

Underline the *-ing* fragment in each of the following selections. Then make the fragment a sentence by rewriting it, using the method described in parentheses.

Example   The dog eyed me with suspicion. <u>Not knowing whether its master was at home.</u> I hesitated to open the gate.
(Add the fragment to the sentence that comes before it.)

Not knowing whether its master was at home, I hesitated to open

the gate.

1. Eli lay in bed after the alarm rang. Wishing that he had $100,000. Then he would not have to go to work.
    (Add the fragment to the preceding sentence.)

    _____

    _____

2. Investigating the strange, mournful cries in his neighbor's yard. George found a puppy tangled in its leash.
    (Add the fragment to the sentence that comes after it.)

    _____

    _____

3. I had to drive to the most remote parking lot to get a space. As a result, being late for class.
    (Add the subject *I* and change *being* to the correct form of the verb *was*.)

    _____

    _____

Practice 2

Underline the *-ing* or *to* fragment in each selection. Then rewrite each selection correctly, using one of the methods of correction described on pages 98–99.

1. Glistening with dew. The gigantic web hung between the branches of the tree. The spider waited patiently for a visitor.

    _____

    _____

    _____

2. Martha is pleased with the carpet of Astroturf in her kitchen. Claiming that crumbs settle in the grass so she never sees them.

    _____

    _____

    _____

3. Ron picked through the box of chocolates. Removing the kinds he didn't like. He saved these for his wife and ate the rest.

    _____

    _____

    _____

4. The grass I was walking on suddenly became squishy. Having hiked into a marsh of some kind.

    _____

    _____

    _____

5. Steve drove quickly to the bank. To cash his paycheck. Otherwise, he would have no money for the weekend.

    _____

    _____

    _____

3   ADDED-DETAIL FRAGMENTS

Added-detail fragments lack a subject and a verb. They often begin with one of the following words.

also	except	including
especially	for example	such as

See if you can locate and underline the one added-detail fragment in each of the following examples:

Example 1

Tony has trouble accepting criticism. <u>Except from Lola.</u> She has a knack for tact.

Example 2

There is

My apartment has its drawbacks. For example, no hot water in the morning.

Example 3

I've worked at many jobs while in school. Among them, busboy, painter, and security guard.

Among the many jobs I've worked at while in school have been busboy, painter, and sec. guard.

People often write added-detail fragments for much the same reason they write *-ing* fragments. They think the subject and verb in one sentence will serve for the next word group as well. But the subject and verb must be in *each* word group.

How to Correct
Added-Detail Fragments

1   Attach the fragment to the complete thought that precedes it. Example 1 could read: "Tony has trouble accepting criticism, except from Lola." (Note that here a comma is used to set off "except from Lola," which is extra material placed at the end of the sentence.)

2   Add a subject and a verb to the fragment to make it a complete sentence. Example 2 could read: "My apartment has its drawbacks. For example, there is no hot water in the morning."

3   Change words as necessary to make the fragment part of the preceding sentence. Example 3 could read: "Among the many jobs I've worked at while in school have been busboy, painter, and security guard."

Practice I

Underline the fragment in each selection below. Then make it a sentence by rewriting it, using the method described in parentheses.

Example   My husband and I share the household chores. <u>Including meals.</u> I do the cooking and he does the eating.
(Add the fragment to the preceding sentence.)

My husband and I share the household chores, including meals.

1.   Bill is very accident-prone. For example, managing to cut his hand while crumbling a bar of shredded wheat.
(Correct the fragment by adding the subject *he* and changing *managing* to *managed.*)

2.   Tina's job in the customer service department depressed her. All day, people complained. About missing parts, rude salespeople, and errors on bills.
(Add the fragment to the preceding sentence.)

3.   My mother is always giving me household hints. For example, using club soda on stains. Unfortunately, I never remember them.
(Correct the fragment by adding the subject and verb *she suggests.*)

Practice 2

Underline the added-detail fragment in each selection. Then rewrite that part of the selection needed to correct the fragment. Use one of the three methods of correction described on page 101.

1.   My little boy is constantly into mischief. Such as tearing the labels off all the cans in the cupboard.

2. The old house was filled with expensive woodwork. For example, a hand-carved mantel and a mahogany banister.

_____

_____

3. Andy used to have many bad eating habits. For instance, chewing with his mouth open.

_____

_____

4. I put potatoes in the oven without first punching holes in them. A half hour later, there were several explosions. With potatoes splattering all over the walls of the oven.

_____

_____

5. Janet looked forward to seeing former classmates at the high school reunion. Including the football player she had had a wild crush on. She wondered if he had grown fat and bald.

_____

_____

4 MISSING-SUBJECT FRAGMENTS

Underline the word group in which the subject is missing in each example below.

Example 1

One illustration of my father's generosity is that he visits sick friends in the hospital. And takes along get-well cards with a few dollars folded in them.

Example 2

The weight lifter grunted as he heaved the barbells into the air. Then, with a loud groan, dropped them.

People write missing-subject fragments because they think the subject in one sentence will apply to the next word group as well. But the subject, as well as the verb, must be in each word group to make it a sentence.

How to Correct
Missing-Subject Fragments

1   Attach the fragment to the preceding sentence. Example 1 could read: "One illustration of my father's generosity is that he visits sick friends in the hospital and takes along get-well cards with a few dollars folded in them."

2   Add a subject (which can often be a pronoun standing for the subject in the preceding sentence). Example 2 could read: "Then, with a loud groan, he dropped them."

Practice

Underline the missing-subject fragment in each selection. Then rewrite that part of the selection needed to correct the fragment. Use one of the two methods of correction described above.

1.   Fred went to the refrigerator to get milk for his breakfast cereal. And discovered about one tablespoon of milk left in the carton.

_____

_____

2.   At the laundromat, I loaded the dryer with wet clothes. Then noticed the "Out of order" sign taped over the coin slot.

_____

_____

3.   Our neighborhood's most eligible bachelor got married this weekend. But did not invite us to the wedding. We all wondered what the bride was like.

_____

_____

4.   Larry's father could not accept his son's lifestyle. Also, was constantly criticizing Larry's choice of friends.

_____

_____

5.   Wanda stared at the blank page in desperation. And decided that the first sentence of a paper is always the hardest to write.

_____

_____

> **A REVIEW: HOW TO CHECK FOR SENTENCE FRAGMENTS**
>
> 1   Read your paper aloud from the *last* sentence to the *first*. You will be better able to see and hear whether each word group you read is a complete thought.
>
> 2   Ask yourself of any word group you think is a fragment: Does this contain a subject and a verb and express a complete thought?
>
> 3   More specifically, be on the lookout for the most common fragments:
>
> - Dependent-word fragments (starting with words like *after, because, since, when,* and *before*)
>
> - *-ing* and *to* fragments (*-ing* or *to* at or near the start of a word group)
>
> - Added-detail fragments (starting with words like *for example, such as, also,* and *especially*)
>
> - Missing-subject fragments (a verb is present but not the subject)

 Review Test 1

Turn each of the following word groups into a complete sentence. Use the space provided.

Examples   Feeling very confident

Feeling very confident, I began my speech.

Until the rain started

We played softball until the rain started.

1. Before you sit down

---

2. When the noise stopped

---

3. To get to the game on time

---

4. During my walk along the trail

---

5. Because I was short on cash

_____

6. Lucy, whom I know well

_____

7. Up in the attic

_____

8. Through hard work

_____

9. Which I agreed to do

_____

10. Was ready for a change

_____

 ## Review Test 2

Underline the fragment in each selection. Then correct the fragment in the space provided.

Example   Sam received all kinds of junk mail. <u>Then complained to the post office.</u> Eventually, some of the mail stopped coming.

Then he complained to the post office.

1. After seeing an offensive mouthwash ad on television. I resolved never to buy that brand again.

_____

_____

2. People worked together on the assembly line. Moving quickly and efficiently. They wanted to make as much money as possible.

_____

_____

3. Mark was offered several different jobs. And accepted one that featured a four-day workweek.

_____

_____

4. Our yard sale was an enormous success. We sold everything. Except the self-portrait of my grandfather.

   _____

   _____

5. While they were taking a midnight walk. Tony and Lola saw hundreds of lightning bugs flickering over the lake. They were also attacked by hundreds of man-of-war mosquitoes.

   _____

   _____

6. Andy always wins at hide-and-seek. Peeking through his fingers as he counts to one hundred. The other kids will soon catch on.

   _____

   _____

7. Tamika has worked on the crossword puzzle all day. All the while, mumbling each clue out loud. I hope she finishes soon.

   _____

   _____

8. Italian food is mouth-watering. Especially pizza. Spaghetti is delicious, too.

   _____

   _____

9. Lola looked at the enormous diamond on Holly's finger. And decided it was fake. The diamond was the size of a small headlight.

   _____

   _____

10. I often take pictures in my backyard. For instance, of a squirrel stealing sunflower seeds from a bird feeder.

    _____

    _____

Review Test 3

In the space provided, write *C* in front of the four word groups that are complete sentences; write *frag* in front of the six fragments. The first two items are done for you.

    frag   1. When Lola prepares for a day at the beach.

    C   2. She first selects a colorful bikini with a matching beach coat.

         3. Second, gathering together a pair of large, dark sunglasses, a beach bag and towel, suntan lotion, and a very comfortable lounge chair.

         4. Also, a large-brimmed hat in an unusual bright color.

         5. In addition, she takes along a radio to listen to her favorite music.

         6. Occasionally bringing along a good book to read as well.

         7. She also tucks into the beach bag some fattening snacks.

         8. Such as potato chips and oatmeal cookies.

         9. Before leaving, she checks to make sure her fingernail polish matches her toenail polish.

         10. Then on her way to a great afternoon at the lake.

Now correct the fragments you have found. Attach each fragment to the sentence that comes before or after it, or make whatever other change is needed to turn the fragment into a sentence. Use the space provided. The first one is corrected for you.

1. *When Lola prepares for a day at the beach, she first selects a colorful bikini with a matching beach coat.*

2. _____

_____

3. _____

_____

4. _____

_____

5. _____

_____

6. _____

_____

Review Test 4

Write quickly for five minutes about the high school you attended. Don't worry about spelling, punctuation, finding exact words, or organizing your thoughts. Just focus on writing as many words as you can without stopping.

After you have finished, go back and make whatever changes are needed to correct any fragments in your writing.

Run-Ons

A run-on occurs when two sentences are run together with no adequate sign given to mark the break between them. Shown below are four run-on sentences and four correctly marked sentences. See if you can complete the statement that explains how each run-on has been corrected.

1. A man coughed in the movie theater the result was a chain reaction of copy-cat coughing. *Run-on*

    A man coughed in the movie theater. The result was a chain reaction of copycat coughing. *Correct*

    The run-on has been corrected by using a _____ and a capital letter to separate the two complete thoughts.

2. I heard laughter inside the house, no one answered the bell. *Run-on*

    I heard laughter inside the house, but no one answered the bell. *Correct*

    The run-on has been corrected by using a joining word, _____, to connect the two complete thoughts.

3. A car sped around the corner, it sprayed slush all over the pedestrians. *Run-on*

    A car sped around the corner; it sprayed slush all over the pedestrians. *Correct*

    The run-on has been corrected by using a _____ to connect the two closely related thoughts.

4. I had a campus map, I still could not find my classroom building. *Run-on*

    Although I had a campus map, I still could not find my classroom building. *Correct*

    The run-on has been corrected by using the subordinating word _____ to connect the two closely related thoughts.

Answers are on page 518.

WHAT ARE RUN-ONS?

A *run-on* is two complete thoughts that are run together with no adequate sign given to mark the break between them.[*] As a result of the run-on, the reader is confused, unsure of where one thought ends and the next one begins. Some run-ons have no punctuation at all to mark the break between the thoughts. Such run-ons are known as *fused sentences:* they are fused or joined together as if they were only one thought.

Fused Sentences

Rita decided to stop smoking she didn't want to die of lung cancer.

The exam was postponed the class was canceled as well.

In other run-ons, known as *comma splices,* a comma is used to connect or "splice" together the two complete thoughts. However, a comma alone is *not enough* to connect two complete thoughts. Some connection stronger than a comma alone is needed.

Comma Splices

Rita decided to stop smoking, she didn't want to die of lung cancer.

The exam was postponed, the class was canceled as well.

Comma splices are the most common kind of run-on. Students sense that some kind of connection is needed between thoughts, and so they put a comma at the dividing point. But the comma alone is *not sufficient*—a stronger, clearer mark between the two thoughts is needed.

---

[*]Some instructors refer to each complete thought in a run-on sentence as an *independent clause.* A *clause* is simply a group of words having a subject and a verb. A clause may be *independent* (expressing a complete thought and able to stand alone) or *dependent* (not expressing a complete thought and not able to stand alone). A run-on sentence is two independent clauses that are run together with no adequate sign given to mark the break between them.

A Warning:
Words That Can Lead to Run-Ons

People often write run-ons when the second complete thought begins with one of the following words:

I	we	there	now
you	they	this	then
he, she, it		that	next

Remember to be on the alert for run-ons whenever you use one of these words in your writing.

CORRECTING RUN-ONS

Here are four common methods of correcting a run-on:

1 Use a period and a capital letter to separate the two complete thoughts. (In other words, make two separate sentences of the two complete thoughts.)

Rita decided to stop smoking. She didn't want to die of lung cancer.
The exam was postponed. The class was canceled as well.

2 Use a comma plus a joining word (*and, but, for, or, nor, so, yet*) to connect the two complete thoughts.

Rita decided to stop smoking, for she didn't want to die of lung cancer.
The exam was postponed, and the class was canceled as well.

3 Use a semicolon to connect the two complete thoughts.

Rita decided to stop smoking; she didn't want to die of lung cancer.
The exam was postponed; the class was canceled as well.

4 Use subordination.

Because Rita didn't want to die of lung cancer, she decided to stop smoking.
When the exam was postponed, the class was canceled as well.

The following pages will give you practice in all four methods of correcting run-ons. The use of subordination will be explained even further on page 469, in a section of the book that deals with sentence variety.

METHOD 1:
PERIOD AND A CAPITAL LETTER

One way of correcting a run-on is to use a period and a capital letter at the break between the two complete thoughts. Use this method especially if the thoughts are not closely related or if another method would make the sentence too long.

Practice 1

Locate the split in each of the following run-ons. Each is a *fused sentence*—that is, each consists of two sentences that are fused or joined together with no punctuation at all between them. Reading each sentence aloud will help you "hear" where a major break or split in the thought occurs. At such a point, your voice will probably drop and pause.

Correct the run-on by putting a period at the end of the first thought and a capital letter at the start of the second thought.

Example   Gary was not a success at his job, $\overset{H}{\text{h}}$is mouth moved faster than his hands.

1. Jerry's motorized wheelchair broke down he was unable to go to class.

2. The subway train hurtled through the station a blur of spray paint and graffiti flashed in front of my eyes.

3. Jenny panicked the car had stalled on a treacherous traffic circle.

4. Half the class flunked the exam the other half of the students were absent.

5. One reason for the high cost of new furniture is the cost of good wood one walnut tree sold recently for $40,000.

6. The wedding reception began to get out of hand guests started to throw cake at each other.

7. Larry's pitchfork turned over the rich earth earthworms poked their heads out of new furrows.

8. There were a lot of unusual people at the party a few of the women had shaved heads.

9. Carol talks all the time her tongue is getting calluses.

10. Hundreds of crushed cars were piled in neat stacks the rusted hulks resembled flattened tin cans.

Practice 2

Locate the split in each of the following run-ons. Some of the run-ons are fused sentences, and some of them are *comma splices*—run-ons spliced or joined together only with a comma. Correct each run-on by putting a period at the end of the first thought and a capital letter at the start of the next thought.

1. I wish Carl wouldn't fall asleep in class, his snoring drowns out the lecture.
2. The crime rate in this country is increasing, every eight seconds another home is burglarized.
3. Our car radio is not working properly we get whistling noises and static instead of music.
4. That shopping mall has the smell of death about it half the stores are empty.
5. Cats sleep in all sorts of unusual places, our new cat likes to curl up in the bathroom sink.
6. Every day, Americans use 450 billion gallons of water this amount would cover New York City to a depth of 96 feet.
7. The driver had an unusual excuse for speeding, he said he had just washed his car and was trying to dry it.
8. The telephone rang at least fifteen times nobody felt like getting up to answer it.
9. Some of our foods have misleading names, for example, English muffins were actually invented in America.
10. The gunslinger lay dead on the barroom floor his last words were, "You don't have the guts to pull that trigger."

Practice 3

Write a second sentence to go with each sentence below. Start the second sentence with the word given in the margin.

Example   *He*   My dog's ears snapped up. *He had heard a wolf howling on television.*

They   1. I could not find my car keys. _____

_____

Then   2. The first thing Marcus ate for dessert was a peach. _____

_____

She 3. My daughter began screaming. _____

_____

It 4. The toaster oven was acting strangely. _____

_____

There 5. Cars had to stop suddenly at the intersection. _____

_____

METHOD 2: COMMA AND A JOINING WORD

Another way of correcting a run-on is to use a comma plus a joining word to connect the two complete thoughts. Joining words (also called *coordinating conjunctions*) include *and, but, for, or, nor, so,* and *yet.* Here is what the four most common joining words mean:

and in addition, along with

Lola was watching Monday night football, and she was doing her homework as well.

(*And* means *in addition:* Lola was watching Monday night football; *in addition,* she was doing her homework as well.)

but however, except, on the other hand, just the opposite

I voted for the president two years ago, but I would not vote for him today.

(*But* means *however:* I voted for the president two years ago; *however,* I would not vote for him today.)

for because, the reason why, the cause for something

Saturday is the worst day to shop, for people jam the stores.

(*For* means *because:* Saturday is the worst day to shop *because* people jam the stores.) If you are not comfortable using *for,* you may want to use *because* instead of *for* in the activities that follow. If you do use *because,* omit the comma before it.

so   as a result, therefore

Our son misbehaved again, so he was sent upstairs without dessert.

(*So* means *as a result:* Our son misbehaved again; *as a result,* he was sent upstairs without dessert.)

Practice 1

Insert the comma and the joining word (*and, but, for, so*) that logically connect the two thoughts in each sentence. You will notice that some of the run-ons are *fused sentences* (there is no punctuation between the two complete thoughts) and some are *comma splices* (there is only a comma between the two complete thoughts).

for
Example   A trip to the zoo always depresses me, I hate to see animals in cages.

1. The telephone was ringing someone was at the front door as well.

2. Something was obviously wrong with the meat loaf it was glowing in the dark.

3. Nick and Fran enjoyed the movie, they wished the seats had been more comfortable.

4. Brett moved from Boston to Los Angeles he wanted to get as far away as possible from his ex-wife.

5. I decided to go back to school I felt my brain was turning to slush.

6. Lola loved the rose cashmere sweater, she had nothing to wear with it.

7. Art's son has joined the Army, his daughter is thinking of joining, too.

8. Lydia began working the second shift she is not able to eat supper with her family anymore.

9. Fred remembered to get the hamburger he forgot to buy the hamburger rolls.

10. My TV wasn't working I walked over to a friend's house to watch the game.

Practice 2

Add a complete and closely related thought to go with each of the following statements. Use a comma plus the joining word in the margin when you write the second thought.

Example   *but*   I was sick with the flu, <u>*but I still had to study for the test.*</u>

so   1. The night was hot and humid _____

_____

but   2. Fred wanted to get a pizza _____

_____

and   3. Lola went shopping in the morning _____

_____

for   4. I'm going to sell my car _____

_____

but   5. I expected the exam to be easy _____

_____

METHOD 3: SEMICOLON

A third method of correcting a run-on is to use a semicolon to mark the break between two thoughts. A *semicolon* (;) is made up of a period and a comma and is sometimes called a *strong comma*. The semicolon signals more of a pause than a comma alone but not quite the full pause of a period.

Semicolon Alone

Here are some earlier sentences that were connected with a comma plus a joining word. Notice that a semicolon, unlike a comma, can be used alone to connect the two complete thoughts in each sentence:

Lola was watching Monday night football; she was doing her homework as well.
I voted for the president two years ago; I would not vote for him today.
Saturday is the worst day to shop; people jam the stores.

The occasional use of the semicolon can add variety to sentences. For some people, however, the semicolon is a confusing mark of punctuation. Keep in mind that if you are not comfortable using it, you can and should use one of the other methods of correcting a run-on sentence.

Practice

Insert a semicolon where the break occurs between the two complete thoughts in each of the following sentences.

Example   She had a wig on; it looked more like a hat than a wig.

1.   Our *TV Guide* subscription just ran out nobody remembered to renew it.
2.   Suzie wanted to watch a *Star Trek* rerun the rest of the family insisted on turning to the network news.
3.   Bonnie put a freshly baked batch of chocolate-chip cookies on the counter to cool everyone gathered round for samples.
4.   About $25 million worth of pizza is eaten each year an average of 300 new pizza parlors open every week.
5.   Nate never heard the third-base coach screaming for him to stop he was out at home plate by ten feet.

Semicolon with a Transition

A semicolon is sometimes used with a transitional word and a comma to join two complete thoughts:

I figured the ball game would cost me about five dollars; however, I didn't consider the high price of food and drinks.

Fred and Martha have a low-interest mortgage on their house; otherwise, they would move to another neighborhood.

Sharon didn't understand the teacher's point; therefore, she asked him to repeat it.

Note: Sometimes transitional words do not join complete thoughts but are merely interrupters in a sentence (see pages 259–260):

My parents, moreover, plan to go on the trip.

I believe, however, that they'll change their minds.

Common Transitional Words

Here is a list of common transitional words (also known as *adverbial conjunctions*).

however	moreover	therefore
on the other hand	in addition	as a result
nevertheless	also	consequently
instead	furthermore	otherwise

Practice 1

Choose a logical transitional word from the box above and write it in the space provided. In addition, put a semicolon *before* the transition and a comma *after* it.

Example   It was raining harder than ever ____ ; *however,* ____ Bobby was determined to go to the amusement park.

1. The tree must be sprayed with insecticide _____ the spider mites will kill it.

2. I helped the magician set up his props _____ I agreed to let him saw me in half.

3. Fred never finished paneling his basement _____ he hired a carpenter to complete the job.

4. My house was robbed last week _____ I bought a watchdog.

5. Juanita is taking five courses this semester _____ she is working forty hours a week.

Practice 2

Punctuate each sentence by using a semicolon and a comma.

Example   A band rehearses in the garage next door ;as a result, I'm thinking of moving.

1. I arrived early to get a good seat however there were already a hundred people outside the door.

2. Foul language marred the live boxing match as a result next time the network will probably use a tape delay.
3. The fluorescent lights in the library gave Jan a headache furthermore they distracted her by making a loud humming sound.
4. The broken shells on the beach were like tiny razors consequently we walked along with extreme caution.
5. Ted carefully combed and recombed his hair nevertheless his bald spot still showed.

METHOD 4: SUBORDINATION

A fourth method of joining together related thoughts is to use subordination. *Subordination* is a way of showing that one thought in a sentence is not as important as another thought. Here are three earlier sentences that have been recast so that one idea is subordinated to (made less emphatic than) the other idea:

Because Rita didn't want to die of lung cancer, she decided to stop smoking.
The wedding reception began to get out of hand when the guests started to throw cake at each other.
Although Suzie wanted to watch a *Star Trek* rerun, the rest of the family insisted on turning to the network news.

Common Dependent Words

Notice that when we subordinate, we use dependent words like *because, when,* and *although.* Here is a brief list of common dependent words:

after	before	unless
although	even though	until
as	if	when
because	since	while

Subordination is explained in full on page 469.

Practice 1

Choose a logical dependent word from the box on the previous page and write it in the space provided.

Example _____Although_____ going up a ladder is easy, looking down can be difficult.

1. The instructor is lowering my grade in the course _____ I was late three times for class.

2. _____ the airplane dropped a few feet, my stomach rose a few feet.

3. _____ the football game was being played, we sent out for a pizza.

4. _____ the football game was over, we went out for another pizza.

5. You should talk to a counselor _____ you decide on your courses for next semester.

Practice 2

Rewrite the five sentences below, taken from this chapter, so that one idea is subordinate to the other. Use one of the dependent words in the box in each case.

Example My house was burglarized last week; I bought a watchdog.
        Because my house was burglarized last week, I bought a watchdog.

Note: As in the example above, use a comma if a dependent statement starts a sentence.

1. Sharon didn't understand the instructor's point; she asked him to repeat it.

   _____

   _____

2. Fred remembered to get the hamburger; he forgot to get the hamburger rolls.

   _____

   _____

3. Michael gulped two cups of strong coffee; his heart started to flutter.

   _____

   _____

4.   A car sped around the corner; it sprayed slush all over the pedestrians.

_____

_____

5.   Lola loved the rose cashmere sweater; she had nothing to wear with it.

_____

_____

A REVIEW: HOW TO CHECK FOR RUN-ONS

1   To see if a sentence is a run-on, read it aloud and listen for a break marking two complete thoughts. Your voice will probably drop and pause at the break.

2   To check an entire paper, read it aloud from the *last* sentence to the *first*. Doing so will help you hear and see each complete thought.

3   Be on the lookout for words that can lead to run-on sentences:

I	he, she, it	they	this	then
you	we	there	that	next

4   Correct run-on sentences by using one of the following methods:
- Period and a capital letter
- Comma and a joining word (*and, but, for,* or *so*)
- Semicolon
- Subordination (as explained above and on page 469)

 Review Test I

Some of the run-ons that follow are *fused sentences,* having no punctuation between the two complete thoughts; others are *comma splices,* having only a comma between the two complete thoughts.

Correct the run-ons by using one of the following three methods:

- Period and a capital letter
- Comma and a joining word (*and, but, for, so*)
- Semicolon

Use whichever method seems most appropriate in each case.

and

Example   Fred pulled the cellophane off the cake, the icing came along with it.

1. I found the cat sleeping on the stove the dog was eating the morning mail.

2. Yoko has a twenty-mile drive to school she sometimes arrives late for class.

3. I lifted the empty Coke bottle above me a few more drops fell out of it and into my thirsty mouth.

4. These pants are guaranteed to wear like iron they also feel like iron.

5. I saw a black-and-white blob on the highway soon the odor of skunk wafted through my car.

6. She gets A's in her math homework by using her pocket calculator she is not allowed to use the calculator at school.

7. Flies were getting into the house the window screen was torn.

8. Martha moans and groans upon getting up in the morning she sounds like a crazy woman.

9. Lola met Tony at McDonald's they shared a large order of fries.

10. The carpet in their house needs to be replaced the walls should be painted as well.

 Review Test 2

Correct the run-on in each sentence by using subordination. Choose from among the following dependent words:

after	before	unless
although	even though	until
as	if	when
because	since	while

Example   Tony hated going to a new barber, he was afraid of butchered hair.

Because Tony was afraid of butchered hair, he hated going to a

new barber.

1. The meal and conversation were enjoyable, I kept worrying about the check.

   _____

   _____

2. My wet fingers stuck to the frosty ice-cube tray, I had to pry them loose.

   _____

   _____

3. I take a late afternoon nap, my mind and body are refreshed and ready for my night course.

   _____

   _____

4. Our daughter jumped up screaming a black spider was on her leg.

   _____

   _____

5. I wanted badly to cry I remained cold and silent.

   _____

   _____

6. Jan does the food shopping every two weeks she first cashes her paycheck at the bank.

   _____

   _____

7. Follow the instructions carefully, you'll have the computer set up and working in no time.

   _____

   _____

8. Every child in the neighborhood was in the backyard, Frank stepped outside to investigate.

   _____

   _____

9. My first year in college was not a success, I spent most of my time in the game room.

   _____

   _____

10. A burglar was in our upstairs bedroom going through our drawers, we were in the den downstairs watching television.

_____

_____

 ## Review Test 3

On separate paper, write six sentences, each of which has two complete thoughts. Use a period and a capital letter between the thoughts in two of the sentences. Use a comma and a joining word (_and, but, or, nor, for, so, yet_) to join the thoughts in another two sentences. Use a semicolon to join the thoughts in the final two sentences.

In addition, select two of the six sentences and rewrite them so each uses a dependent word and contains a subordinated thought.

 ## Review Test 4

Write quickly for five minutes about a frightening experience you have had. Don't worry about spelling, punctuation, finding exact words, or organizing your thoughts. Just focus on writing as many words as you can without stopping.

After you have finished, go back and make whatever changes are needed to correct any run-on sentences in your writing.

Standard English Verbs

INTRODUCTORY PROJECT

Underline what you think is the correct form of the verb in each of the sentences below.

That radio station once (play, played) top-forty hits.
It now (play, plays) classical music.
When Jean was a little girl, she (hope, hoped) to become a movie star.
Now she (hope, hopes) to be accepted at law school.
At first, my father (juggle, juggled) with balls of yarn.
Now that he is an expert, he (juggle, juggles) with raw eggs.

On the basis of the above examples, see if you can complete the following statements.

1. The first sentence in each pair refers to an action in the (past time, present time), and the regular verb has an _____ ending.

2. The second sentence in each pair refers to an action in the (past time, present time), and the regular verb has an _____ ending.

Answers are on page 519.

Many people have grown up in communities where nonstandard verb forms are used in everyday life. Such forms include *they be, it done, we has, you was, she don't,* and *it ain't.* Community dialects have richness and power but are a drawback in college and the world at large, where standard English verb forms must be used. Standard English helps ensure clear communication among English-speaking people everywhere, and it is especially important in the world of work.

This chapter compares the community dialect and the standard English forms of a regular verb and three common irregular verbs.

REGULAR VERBS: DIALECT AND STANDARD FORMS

The chart below compares community dialect (nonstandard) and standard English forms of the regular verb *talk.*

TALK

Community Dialect (Do not use in your writing)		**Standard English** (Use for clear communication)	
Present Tense			
I talks	we talks	I talk	we talk
you talks	you talks	you talk	you talk
he, she, it talk	they talks	he, she, it talks	they talk
Past Tense			
I talk	we talk	I talked	we talked
you talk	you talk	you talked	you talked
he, she, it talk	they talk	he, she, it talked	they talked

One of the most common nonstandard forms results from dropping the endings of regular verbs. For example, people might say "Rose work until ten o'clock tonight" instead of "Rose work*s* until ten o'clock tonight." Or they'll say "I work overtime yesterday" instead of "I work*ed* overtime yesterday." To avoid such nonstandard usage, memorize the forms shown above for the regular verb *talk.* Then use the activities that follow to help make the inclusion of verb endings a writing habit.

Present Tense Endings

The verb ending -*s* or -*es* is needed with a regular verb in the present tense when the subject is *he, she, it,* or any one person or thing.

He	He lifts weights.
She	She runs.
It	It amazes me.
One person	Their son Ted swims.
One person	Their daughter Terry dances.
One thing	Their house jumps at night with all the exercise.

Practice 1

All but one of the ten sentences that follow need -*s* or -*es* endings. Cross out the nonstandard verb forms and write the standard forms in the spaces provided. Mark the one sentence that needs no change with a *C*.

ends   **Example**   The sale ~~end~~ tomorrow.

_____   1. Renée hate it when I criticize her singing.

_____   2. Whenever my sister tries to tell a joke, she always mess it up.

_____   3. Ice cream feel good going down a sore throat.

_____   4. Frank cover his ears every time his baby sister cries.

_____   5. "Dinner sure smell good," said Fran as she walked into the kitchen.

_____   6. My brother wants to be an astronaut so he can see stars.

_____   7. The picture on our television set blur whenever there is a storm.

_____   8. My mother think women should get equal pay for equal work.

_____   9. Sometimes Alonso pretend that he is living in a penthouse.

_____   10. It seem as if we are working more and more but getting paid less and less.

Practice 2

Rewrite the short selection below, adding present tense -*s* verb endings wherever needed.

> Charlotte react badly when she get caught in a traffic jam. She open the dashboard compartment and pull out an old pack of Marlboros that she keep for such occasions. She light up and drag heavily, sucking the smoke deep into her lungs. She get out of the car and look down the highway, trying to see where the delay is. Back in the car, she drum her fingers on the steering wheel. If the jam last long enough, she start talking to herself and angrily kick off her shoes.

_____

_____

_____

_____

_____

_____

_____

_____

_____

_____

_____

_____

Past Tense Endings

The verb ending -*d* or -*ed* is needed with a regular verb in the past tense.

Yesterday we finished painting the house.
I completed the paper an hour before class.
Fred's car stalled on his way to work this morning.

Practice 1

All but one of the ten sentences that follow need -*d* or -*ed* endings. Cross out the nonstandard verb forms and write the standard forms in the spaces provided. Mark the one sentence that needs no change with a *C*.

jumped   ***Example***   The cat ~~jump~~ on my lap when I sat down.

_____   1. As the burglar alarm went off, three men race out the door.

_____   2. Lola's new lipstick was so red that it glow in the dark.

_____   3. Stan smelled gas when he walk into the apartment.

_____   4. As soon as the pilot sight the runway, he turned on his landing lights.

_____   5. While the bear stare hungrily at him, the tourist reached for his camera.

_____   6. Susie studied for three hours and then decide to get some sleep.

_____   7. Just as Miss Muffet seated herself, a large spider joined her.

_____   8. Frank hurried to cash his paycheck because he need money for the weekend.

_____   9. The waiter dropped the tray with a loud crash; bits of broken glass scatter all over the floor.

_____   10. A customer who twisted his ankle in the diner's parking lot decide to sue.

Practice 2

Rewrite this selection, adding past tense -*d* or -*ed* verb endings where needed.

Bill's boss shout at Bill. Feeling bad, Bill went home and curse his wife. Then his wife scream at their son. Angry himself, the son went out and cruelly tease a little girl who live next door until she wail. Bad feelings were pass on as one person wound the next with ugly words. No one manage to break the vicious circle.

_____

_____

_____

_____

_____

_____

_____

THREE COMMON IRREGULAR VERBS: DIALECT AND STANDARD FORMS

The following charts compare the nonstandard and standard dialects of the common irregular verbs *be, have,* and *do.* (For more on irregular verbs, see the next chapter, beginning on page 135.)

BE

Community Dialect
(Do not use in your writing)

Standard English
(Use for clear communication)

Present Tense

I be (or is)	we be	I am	we are
you be	you be	you are	you are
he, she, it be	they be	he, she, it is	they are

Past Tense

I were	we was	I was	we were
you was	you was	you were	you were
he, she, it were	they was	he, she, it was	they were

HAVE

Community Dialect
(Do not use in your writing)

Standard English
(Use for clear communication)

Present Tense

I has	we has	I have	we have
you has	you has	you have	you have
he, she, it have	they has	he, she, it has	they have

Past Tense

I has	we has	I had	we had
you has	you has	you had	you had
he, she, it have	they has	he, she, it had	they had

DO

Community Dialect (Do not use in your writing)			**Standard English** (Use for clear communication)	

Present Tense

Community Dialect		Standard English	
~~I does~~	~~we does~~	I do	we do
you does	~~you does~~	you do	you do
~~he, she~~, it do	~~they does~~	he, she, it does	they do

Past Tense

Community Dialect		Standard English	
~~I done~~	~~we done~~	I did	we did
you done	~~you done~~	you did	you did
~~he, she~~, it done	~~they done~~	he, she, it did	they did

Note: Many people have trouble with one negative form of *do.* They will say, for example, "She don't listen" instead of "She doesn't listen," or they will say "This pen don't work" instead of "This pen doesn't work." Be careful to avoid the common mistake of using *don't* instead of *doesn't.*

Practice 1

Underline the standard form of the irregular verb *be, have,* or *do.*

1. This week, my Aunt Agatha (have, has) a dentist's appointment.
2. She (does, do) not enjoy going to the dentist.
3. She (is, are) always frightened by the shiny instruments.
4. The drills (is, are) the worst thing in the office.
5. When Aunt Agatha (was, were) a little girl, she (have, had) a bad experience at the dentist's.
6. The dentist told her he (was, were) going to pull out all her teeth.
7. Aunt Agatha (do, did) not realize that he (was, were) only joking.
8. Her parents (was, were) unprepared for her screams of terror.
9. From then on, she (has, had) a bad attitude toward dentists.
10. Even now, she refuses to keep an appointment unless I (am, are) with her in the waiting room.

Practice 2

Cross out the nonstandard verb form in each sentence. Then write the standard form of *be, have,* or *do* in the space provided.

_____   1. If it be not raining tomorrow, we're going camping.

_____   2. You is invited to join us.

_____   3. You has to bring your own sleeping bag and flashlight.

_____   4. It don't hurt to bring a raincoat also, in case of a sudden shower.

_____   5. The stars is beautiful on a warm summer night.

_____   6. Last year we have a great time on a family camping trip.

_____   7. We done all the cooking ourselves.

_____   8. The food tasted good even though it have some dead leaves in it.

_____   9. Then we discovered that we has no insect repellent.

_____   10. When we got home, we was covered with mosquito bites.

Practice 3

Fill in each blank with the standard form of *be, have,* or *do.*

My mother sings alto in our church choir. She _____ to go to choir practice every Friday night and _____ expected to know all the music. If she _____ not know her part, the other choir members _____ things like glare at her and _____ likely to make nasty comments, she says. Last weekend, my mother _____ house guests and _____ not have time to learn all the notes. The music _____ very difficult, and she thought the other people _____ going to make fun of her. But they _____ very understanding when she told them that she _____ laryngitis and couldn't make a sound.

Review Test 1

Underline the standard verb form.

1. Paul (pound, pounded) the mashed potatoes until they turned into glue.
2. The velvety banana (rest, rests) on the shiny counter.
3. My neighbor's daughter (have, has) a brand new Toyota.
4. It (is, be) fire-engine red with black leather upholstery.
5. The tree in the backyard (have, had) to be cut down.
6. When Rashid (talk, talks) about his ex-wife, his eyes grow hard and cold.
7. Every time my heart (skip, skips) a beat, I worry about my health.
8. My friend Pat (do, does) everything at the last minute.
9. The pattern on the wallpaper (look, looks) like fuzzy brown spiders marching in rows.
10. My hand (tremble, trembled) when I gave my speech in front of the class.

 Review Test 2

Cross out the nonstandard verb forms in the sentences that follow. Then write the standard English verb forms in the space above, as shown.

Example   She ~~watch~~ *watches* closely while the children ~~plays~~ *play* in the water.

1. The stores was all closed by the time the movie were over.
2. If you does your assignment on time, that instructor are going to like you.
3. The boxer pull his punches; the fight were fixed.
4. The tires is whitewalls; they be very good-looking.
5. He typically start to write a research paper the night before it be due.
6. It don't matter to him whether he have to stay up all night.
7. Jeannette anchor the relay team, since she be the fastest runner.
8. I done Bill a favor that I hope he don't forget.
9. Last night I sneak into the kitchen and remove some Hershey's Kisses from the candy jar.
10. I add the figures again and again, but I still weren't able to understand the bank statement.

Irregular Verbs

A BRIEF REVIEW
OF REGULAR VERBS

Every verb has four principal parts: present, past, past participle, and present participle. These parts can be used to build all the verb tenses (the times shown by a verb).

The past and past participle of a regular verb are formed by adding -*d* or -*ed* to the present. The *past participle* is the form of the verb used with the helping verb *have, has,* or *had* (or some form of be with passive verbs). The *present participle* is formed by adding -*ing* to the present. Here are the principal forms of some regular verbs:

Present	Past	Past Participle	Present Participle
laugh	laughed	laughed	laughing
ask	asked	asked	asking
touch	touched	touched	touching
decide	decided	decided	deciding
explode	exploded	exploded	exploding

Most verbs in English are regular.

LIST OF IRREGULAR VERBS

Irregular verbs have irregular forms in the past tense and past participle. For example, the past tense of the irregular verb *grow* is *grew;* the past participle is *grown.*

Almost everyone has some degree of trouble with irregular verbs. When you are unsure about the form of a verb, you can check the list of irregular verbs on the following pages. (The present participle is not shown on this list because it is formed simply by adding -*ing* to the base form of the verb.) Or you can check a dictionary, which gives the principal parts of irregular verbs.

Present	Past	Past Participle
arise	arose	arisen
awake	awoke *or* awaked	awoke *or* awaked
be (am, are, is)	was (were)	been
become	became	become
begin	began	begun
bend	bent	bent
bite	bit	bitten
blow	blew	blown
break	broke	broken
bring	brought	brought
build	built	built
burst	burst	burst
buy	bought	bought
catch	caught	caught
choose	chose	chosen
come	came	come
cost	cost	cost
cut	cut	cut
do (does)	did	done
draw	drew	drawn
drink	drank	drunk
drive	drove	driven
eat	ate	eaten
fall	fell	fallen
feed	fed	fed
feel	felt	felt
fight	fought	fought
find	found	found
fly	flew	flown
freeze	froze	frozen
get	got	got *or* gotten
give	gave	given
go (goes)	went	gone
grow	grew	grown
have (has)	had	had
hear	heard	heard
hide	hid	hidden
hold	held	held
hurt	hurt	hurt
keep	kept	kept
know	knew	known

Present	*Past*	*Past Participle*
lay	laid	laid
lead	led	led
leave	left	left
lend	lent	lent
let	let	let
lie	lay	lain
light	lit	lit
lose	lost	lost
make	made	made
meet	met	met
pay	paid	paid
ride	rode	ridden
ring	rang	rung
rise	rose	risen
run	ran	run
say	said	said
see	saw	seen
sell	sold	sold
send	sent	sent
shake	shook	shaken
shrink	shrank	shrunk
shut	shut	shut
sing	sang	sung
sit	sat	sat
sleep	slept	slept
speak	spoke	spoken
spend	spent	spent
stand	stood	stood
steal	stole	stolen
stick	stuck	stuck
sting	stung	stung
swear	swore	sworn
swim	swam	swum
take	took	taken
teach	taught	taught
tear	tore	torn
tell	told	told
think	thought	thought
wake	woke *or* waked	woken *or* waked
wear	wore	worn
win	won	won
write	wrote	written

Practice I

Cross out the incorrect verb form in the following sentences. Then write the correct form of the verb in the space provided.

began   ***Example***   When the mud slide started, the whole neighborhood ~~begun~~ going downhill.

_____ 1. The game-show contestant learned she had chose the box with a penny in it.

_____ 2. The mechanic done an expensive valve job on my engine without getting my permission.

_____ 3. Charlotte has wore that ring since the day Clyde bought it for her.

_____ 4. She has wrote a paper that will make you roar with laughter.

_____ 5. The gas station attendant gived him the wrong change.

_____ 6. My sister be at school when a stranger came asking for her at our home.

_____ 7. The basketball team has broke the school record for most losses in a year.

_____ 8. Because I had lended him the money, I had a natural concern about what he did with it.

_____ 9. I seen that stray dog nosing around the yard yesterday.

_____ 10. I knowed her face from somewhere, but I couldn't remember just where.

Practice 2

For each of the italicized verbs in the following sentences, fill in the three missing forms in the order shown in the box:

a. Present tense, which takes an -s ending when the subject is *he, she, it,* or any *one person or thing* (see page 128)

b. Past tense

c. Past participle—the form that goes with the helping verb *have, has,* or *had*

Example My little nephew loves to *break* things. Every Christmas he (a) _____*breaks*_____ his new toys the minute they're unwrapped. Last year he (b) _____*broke*_____ five toys in seven minutes and then went on to smash his family's new china platter. His mother says he won't be happy until he has (c) _____*broken*_____ their hearts.

1. Mary Beth wears contact lenses in order to *see* well. In fact, she (a) _____ so poorly without the lenses that the world is a multicolored blur. Once, when she lost one lens, she thought she (b) _____ a frog in the sink. She had really (c) _____ a lump of green soap.

2. When I was younger, I used to hate it when my gym class had to *choose* sides for a baseball game. Each captain, of course, (a) _____ the better players first. Since I was nearsighted and couldn't see a fly ball until it fell on my head, I would often have to wait half the period until one or the other captain (b) _____ me. If I had had my way, I would have (c) _____ to play chess.

3. My father loves to *take* pictures. Whenever we go on vacation, he (a) _____ at least ten rolls of film along. Last year, he (b) _____ over two hundred pictures of the same mountain scenery. Only after he had (c) _____ his last shot were we allowed to climb the mountain.

4. Instructors must love to *speak* to their classes. My English instructor (a) _____ so much that he has to get a drink of water midway through his lecture. Last Wednesday, he (b) _____ for the entire class period. I guess he never heard that old expression "Speak only when you're (c) _____ to."

5. Our next-door neighbor's pet poodle loves to *swim*. When there is no lake or pond handy, she (a) _____ in the family bathtub. Two summers ago, Fifi (b) _____ across the river in which the family was fishing. She won't be satisfied until she has (c) _____ the English Channel.

6. Convertibles may be old-fashioned, but they are fun to *drive*. My cousin has a sky-blue Chevrolet convertible which she (a) _____ to work. One day she (b) _____ with the top down and then forgot to put it back up again. That night it rained, and the seat was so wet the next day that she has (c) _____ with the top up ever since.

7. Annabelle loves buying new things to *wear*. She (a) _____ a different outfit every day of the year. Last year, she never (b) _____ the same clothing twice. She often complains that she gets tired of her clothes long before they're (c) _____ out.

8. My eight-year-old nephew likes to *blow* up balloons. Every year he (a) _____ up several dozen for his parents' New Year's Eve party. Last year, he (b) _____ up fifty balloons, including one in the shape of an American flag. When he tiptoed downstairs at midnight, he was thrilled to see all the guests saluting the balloon he had (c) _____ up.

9. Every year, I can't wait for summer vacation to *begin*. As soon as it (a) _____, I can get to work on all the things around the house that I had to ignore during school. This past May, the minute my exams were over, I (b) _____ cleaning out the garage, painting the windowsills, and building a bookcase. I must have (c) _____ half a dozen projects. Unfortunately, it's now Labor Day, and I haven't finished any of them.

10. We always have trouble getting our younger son, Teddy, to stop watching television and *go* to sleep. He never (a) _____ to his room until 10 or 11 P.M. In the past, when he finally (b) _____ upstairs, we did not check on him, since there was no TV set in his room. The night we finally did decide to look in on Teddy, we found him reading *TV Guide* with a flashlight under the covers and told him things had (c) _____ too far.

TROUBLESOME IRREGULAR VERBS

Three common irregular verbs that often give people trouble are *be, have,* and *do.* See pages 131–132 for a discussion of these verbs. Three sets of other irregular verbs that can lead to difficulties are *lie-lay, sit-set,* and *rise-raise.*

Lie–Lay

The principal parts of *lie* and *lay* are as follows:

Present	Past	Past Participle
lie	lay	lain
lay	laid	laid

To lie means *to rest* or *recline. To lay* means *to put something down.*

To Lie	To Lay
Tony *lies* on the couch.	I *lay* the mail on the table.
This morning he *lay* in the tub.	Yesterday I *laid* the mail on the counter.
He has *lain* in bed all week with the flu.	I have *laid* the mail where everyone will see it.

Practice

Underline the correct verb. Use a form of *lie* if you can substitute *recline.* Use a form of *lay* if you can substitute *place.*

1. Martha is the sort of person who (lies, lays) her cards on the table.
2. I am going to (lie, lay) another log on the fire.
3. (Lying, Laying) down for an hour after supper helps Fred regain his energy.
4. I have (lain, laid) all the visitors' coats in the master bedroom.
5. Frankenstein (lay, laid) on the table, waiting for lightning to recharge his batteries.

Sit–Set

The principal parts of *sit* and *set* are as follows:

Present	Past	Past Participle
sit	sat	sat
set	set	set

To sit means *to take a seat* or *to rest*. *To set* means *to put* or *to place*.

To Sit	To Set
I *sit* down during work breaks.	Tony *sets* out the knives, forks, and spoons.
I *sat* in the doctor's office for three hours.	His sister already *set* out the dishes.
I have always *sat* in the last desk.	They have just *set* out the dinnerware.

Practice

Underline the correct form of the verb. Use a form of *sit* if you can substitute *rest*. Use a form of *set* if you can substitute *place*.

1. During family arguments I try to (sit, set) on the fence instead of taking sides.
2. I walked three blocks before (sitting, setting) down the heavy suitcases.
3. Lorenzo (sat, set) the grapefruit on the teacher's desk.
4. That poor man has not (sat, set) down once today.
5. You can (sit, set) the laundry basket on top of the washer.

Rise-Raise

The principal parts of *rise* and *raise* are as follows:

Present	Past	Past Participle
rise	rose	risen
raise	raised	raised

To rise means *to get up* or *to move up*. *To raise* (which is a regular verb with simple *-ed* endings) means *to lift up* or *to increase in amount*.

To Rise	To Raise
The soldiers *rise* at dawn.	I'm going to *raise* the stakes in the card game.
The crowd *rose* to applaud the batter.	I *raised* the shades to let in the sun.
Dracula has *risen* from the grave.	I would have quit if the company had not *raised* my salary.

Practice

Underline the correct verb. Use a form of *rise* if you can substitute *get up* or *move up*. Use a form of *raise* if you can substitute *lift up* or *increase*.

1. Even though I can sleep late on Sunday if I want to, I usually (rise, raise) early.
2. Some dealers (rise, raise) rather than lower their prices before a sale.
3. After five days of steady rain, the water in the dam had (risen, raised) to a dangerous level.
4. The landlord (rose, raised) the rent in order to force the tenants out of the apartment.
5. The cost of living (rises, raises) steadily from year to year.

Review Test 1

Cross out the incorrect verb form. Then write the correct form of the verb in the space provided.

_____ 1. While I was kneading the meat loaf, someone rung the doorbell.

_____ 2. My first-grade teacher, Ms. Rickstein, teached me the meaning of fear.

_____ 3. Lola brang a sweatshirt, for she knew the mountains got cold at night.

_____ 4. We done the grocery shopping on Thursday evening.

_____ 5. She had went home early from the dance, for she didn't like any of the people she had seen there.

_____ 6. The police officer came with me when I drived home to get my owner's registration card.

_____ 7. The boy next door growed six inches in less than a year.

_____ 8. We had gave the landlord notice three times that our plumbing system needed repairs, and each time he failed to respond.

_____ 9. I had ate so much food at the buffet that I needed to loosen my belt.

_____ 10. Last summer I swum the width of that river and back again.

 ## Review Test 2

Write short sentences that use the form requested for the following irregular verbs.

Example Past of *ride:* ___The Lone Ranger rode into the sunset.___

1. Past of *break:*_____

2. Past participle of *bring:*_____

3. Past participle of *grow:* _____

4. Past of *choose:* _____

5. Present of *do:* _____

6. Past of *drink:* _____

7. Past participle of *write:* _____

8. Present of *give:* _____

9. Past participle of *begin:*_____

10. Present of *go:* _____

Subject–Verb Agreement

A verb must agree with its subject in number. A *singular subject* (one person or thing) takes a singular verb. A *plural subject* (more than one person or thing) takes a plural verb. Mistakes in subject-verb agreement are sometimes made in the following situations:

1   When words come between the subject and the verb.
2   When a verb comes before the subject.
3   With indefinite pronouns.
4   With compound subjects.
5   With *who, which,* and *that.*

Each situation is explained on the following pages.

WORDS BETWEEN THE SUBJECT AND THE VERB

Words that come between the subject and the verb do not change subject-verb agreement. In the following sentence,

The breakfast cereals in the pantry are made mostly of sugar.

the subject (*cereals*) is plural and so the verb (*are*) is plural. The words *in the pantry* that come between the subject and the verb do not affect subject–verb agreement. To help find the subject of certain sentences, you should cross out prepositional phrases (explained on page 87):

One ~~of the crooked politicians~~ was jailed for a month.
The posters ~~on my little brother's wall~~ included rock singers, monsters, and blond television stars.

Following is a list of common prepositions:

about	before	by	inside	over
above	behind	during	into	through
across	below	except	of	to
among	beneath	for	off	toward
around	beside	from	on	under
at	between	in	onto	with

Practice

Underline the subject and lightly cross out any words that come between the subject and the verb. Then double-underline the verb choice in parentheses that you believe is correct.

Example The price of the stereo speakers (is, are) too high for my wallet.

1. The blue stain on the sheets (comes, come) from the cheap dish towel that I put in the washer with them.
2. The sport coat, along with the two pairs of pants, (sells, sell) for just fifty dollars.
3. The roots of the apple tree (is, are) very shallow.
4. Nick's sisters, who wanted to be at his surprise party, (was, were) unable to come because of flooded roads.
5. The dust-covered photo albums in the attic (belongs, belong) to my grandmother.
6. The cost of personal calls made on office telephones (is, are) deducted from our pay.
7. Two cups of coffee in the morning (does, do) not make up a hearty breakfast.
8. The moon as well as some stars (is, are) shining brightly tonight.
9. The electrical wiring in the apartment (is, are) dangerous and needs replacing.
10. Chapter 4 of the psychology book, along with six weeks of class notes, (is, are) to be the basis of the test.

VERB BEFORE THE SUBJECT

A verb agrees with its subject even when the verb comes *before* the subject. Words that may precede the subject include *there, here,* and, in questions, *who, which, what,* and *where.*

Inside the storage shed are the garden tools.
At the street corner were two panhandlers.
There are times I'm ready to quit my job.
Where are the instructions for the microwave oven?

If you are unsure about the subject, ask *who* or *what* of the verb. With the first sentence above, you might ask, "What are inside the storage shed?" The answer, garden *tools,* is the subject.

Practice

Underline the subject in each sentence. Then double-underline the correct verb in parentheses.

1. There (is, are) long lines at the checkout counter.
2. Scampering to the door to greet Martha Grencher (was, were) her two little dogs.
3. Filling the forest floor (was, were) dozens of pine cones.
4. There (is, are) pretzels in the kitchen if you want something to go with the cheese.
5. At the end of the line, hoping to get seats for the movie, (was, were) Janet and Maureen.
6. There (is, are) rats nesting under the backyard woodpile.
7. Swaggering down the street (was, were) several tough-looking boys.
8. On the very top of that mountain (is, are) a house for sale.
9. At the soap opera convention, there (was, were) fans from all over the country.
10. Under a large plastic dome on the side of the counter (lies, lie) a single gooey pastry.

INDEFINITE PRONOUNS

The following words, known as *indefinite pronouns,* always take singular verbs:

(*-one* words)	(*-body* words)	(*-thing* words)	
one	nobody	nothing	each
anyone	anybody	anything	either
everyone	everybody	everything	neither
someone	somebody	something	

Note: *Both* always takes a plural verb.

Practice

Write the correct form of the verb in the space provided.

ignores, ignore

1. Everyone in the neighborhood _____ Charlie Brown.

dances, dance

2. Nobody _____ the way he does.

deserves, deserve

3. Either of our football team's guards _____ to be an all-state guard.

was, were

4. Both of the race drivers _____ injured.

appears, appear

5. Everyone who received an invitation _____ to be here.

offers, offer

6. No one ever _____ to work on that committee.

owns, own

7. One of my sisters _____ a VW convertible.

has, have

8. Somebody _____ been taking shopping carts from the super-market.

thinks, think

9. Everyone that I talked to _____ the curfew is a good idea.

has, have

10. Each of the candidates _____ talked about withdrawing from the race.

COMPOUND SUBJECTS

Subjects joined by *and* generally take a plural verb.

> <u>Yoga</u> and <u>biking</u> are Lola's ways of staying in shape.
> <u>Ambition</u> and <u>good luck</u> are the keys to his success.

When subjects are joined by *or, either . . . or, neither . . . nor, not only . . . but also,* the verb agrees with the subject closer to the verb.

> Either the restaurant <u>manager</u> or his <u>assistants</u> <u>deserve</u> to be fired for the spoiled meat used in the stew.

The nearer subject, *assistants,* is plural, and so the verb is plural.

Practice

Write the correct form of the verb in the space provided.

matches,
match

1. This tie and shirt _____ the suit, but the shoes look terrible.

has, have

2. The kitchen and the bathroom _____ to be cleaned.

is, are

3. A good starting salary and a bonus system _____ the most attractive features of my new job.

plan, plans

4. Neither Ellen nor her brothers _____ to work at a temporary job during their holiday break from college.

is, are

5. For better or worse, working on his van and playing video games _____ Pete's main interests in life.

WHO, WHICH, AND THAT

When *who, which,* and *that* are used as subjects, they take singular verbs if the word they stand for is singular and plural verbs if the word they stand for is plural. For example, in the sentence

Gary is one of those people <u>who</u> <u>are</u> very private.

the verb is plural because *who* stands for *people,* which is plural. On the other hand, in the sentence

Gary is a person <u>who</u> <u>is</u> very private.

the verb is singular because *who* stands for *person,* which is singular.

Practice

Write the correct form of the verb in the space provided.

was, were

1. I removed the sheets that _____ jamming my washer.

stumbles,
stumble

2. This job isn't for people who _____ over tough decisions.

blares, blare

3. The radio that _____ all night belongs to my insomniac neighbor.

gives, give   4. The Saturn is one of the small American cars that _____ high
gasoline mileage.

appears,   5. The strange smell that _____ in our neighborhood on rainy
appear   days is being investigated.

Review Test 1

In the following sentences, underline the subject. Then complete each sentence
using *is, are, was, were, have,* or *has.*

Example   The <u>hot dogs</u> in that luncheonette *are hazardous to your health.*

1. Neither of the songs ___are___ *is* _____

2. The new state tax on alcohol and cigarettes ___*is*___ _____
_____

3. The shadowy figure behind the cemetery walls ___*is*___ _____
_____

4. The movie actress and her agent ___*is* are___ _____

5. Larry is one of those people who ___*is* are___ _____

6. The football coach, along with ten of his assistants, ___*are* is___
_____

7. Coming up the back alley ___*is Thone*___ _____

8. Someone sitting in the left-field bleachers of the ballpark ___*is*___
_____

9. The first several weeks that I spent in college ___*are*___ _____

10. Tony's gentle voice and pleasant smile ___*are*___ _____

Review Test 2

Underline the correct word in the parentheses.

1. Excessive use of alcohol, caffeine, or cigarettes (damages, <u>damage</u>) a mother's
unborn child.

2. Neither of the newspaper articles (gives, <u>give</u>) all the facts of the murder case.

3. There (is, <u>are</u>) five formulas that we have to memorize for the test.

4. The rug and the wallpaper in that room (has, <u>have</u>) to be replaced.
5. The old man standing under the park trees (<u>does</u>, do) not look happy.
6. The scratch on the record (<u>was</u>, were) there when I bought it.
7. Heavy snows and months of subfreezing temperatures (is, <u>are</u>) two reasons why I moved to Florida.
8. I don't enjoy <u>people</u> who (likes, <u>like</u>) to play pranks.
9. The price of the set of dishes you like so much (<u>is</u>, are) $345.
10. What time in the morning (does, <u>do</u>) planes leave for Denver?

⬤ Review Test 3

There are eight mistakes in subject-verb agreement in the following passage. Cross out each incorrect verb and write the correct form above it. In addition, underline the subject of each of the verbs that must be changed.

There are several things that <u>makes</u> Tracy want to quit her job as a waitress. First *make* of all, she is never permitted to sit down. Even when there is no customers seated at *are* her tables, she must find something useful to do, such as folding napkins or refilling ketchup bottles. By the end of the night, her feet feel like two chunks of raw hamburger. Second, she finds it difficult to be cheerful all of the time, one of the qualities that is *are* expected of her. People who go out to eat in a restaurant wants to enjoy themselves, *want* and they don't like their spirits dampened by a grouchy waitress. This means that when Tracy feels sick or depressed, she can't let her feelings show. Instead, she has to pretend that the occasion is as pleasant for her as it is for her customers, night after night. Neither of these problems, however, bother her as much as people who are fussy. Both *bothers* the child who demands extra fudge sauce on her ice cream and the adult who asks for cleaner silverware has to be satisfied. In addition, each night at least one of the cus- *have* tomers at her tables insist on being a perfectionist. As Tracy learned her first day on *insists* the job, the customer is always right—even if he complains that the peas have too many wrinkles. Though she may feel like dumping the peas in the customer's lap, Tracy must pretend that each of her customers are royalty and hurry to find some less wrinkled *is* peas. Sometimes she wishes people would just stay home and eat.

Consistent
Verb Tense

KEEPING TENSES CONSISTENT

Do not shift tenses unnecessarily. If you begin writing a paper in the present tense, don't shift suddenly to the past. If you begin in the past, don't shift without reason to the present. Notice the inconsistent verb tenses in the following selection:

> Smoke spilled from the front of the overheated car. The driver opens up the hood, then jumped back as steam billows out.

The verbs must be consistently in the present tense:

> Smoke spills from the front of the overheated car. The driver opens up the hood, then jumps back as steam billows out.

Or the verbs must be consistently in the past tense:

> Smoke spilled from the front of the overheated car. The driver opened up the hood, then jumped back as steam billowed out.

Practice

In each selection one verb must be changed so that it agrees in tense with the other verbs. Cross out the incorrect verb and write the correct form in the space at the left.

looked **Example** I gave away my striped sweater after three people told me I ~~look~~ like a giant bee.

_____ 1. Mike peels and eats oranges at movies; the smell caused other people to move away from him.

_____ 2. The nursing program attracted Juanita, but she weighed the pluses and minuses and then decides to enroll in the x-ray technician course instead.

_____ 3. I grabbed for the last bag of pretzels on the supermarket shelf. But when I pick it up, I discovered there was a tear in the cellophane bag.

_____ 4. Ruby waits eagerly for the mail carrier each day. Part of her hoped to get a letter in which someone declares he is madly in love with her and will cherish her forever.

_____ 5. The first thing Jerry does every day is weigh himself. The scale informed him what he can eat that day.

_____ 6. My sister sprinkles detergent flakes on my head and then ran around telling everyone that I had dandruff.

_____ 7. When Norm peeled back the old shingles, he discovers the roof was rotted through.

_____ 8. My father knocked on the bedroom door. When he asks me if he could come in, I said, "Not right now."

_____ 9. Fred is so unaggressive that when a clerk overcharged him for an item, he pays the money and makes no comment.

_____ 10. When my doctor told me I needed an operation, I swallow hard and my stomach churned.

● Review Test I

Change verbs where needed in the following selection so that they are consistently in the past tense. Cross out each incorrect verb and write the correct form above it, as shown in the example. You will need to make nine corrections.

Last week, I began driving to work, as usual. I drove up the expressway ramp and

merged

~~merge~~ into three lanes of speeding cars. I turned on the radio and settle in for another

twenty-five minutes of tension and pressure. Then, about five miles on, I saw

something unusual. Up ahead, stranded on the narrow concrete island that separated

three lanes of eastbound traffic from three lanes of westbound traffic, was a small

brown dog. Streams of zooming cars pass the animal like two rushing rivers. Several

times, the dog attempt to cross the road. He moves gingerly onto the highway, only to

jump back at the approach of a car. I realize it was only a matter of time before the

panicky dog bolt into the traffic and kill itself. I didn't know what to do. I slow my car

down a little and wondered if I should pull onto the shoulder. Then, I heard a welcome

sound—a police siren. Someone must have called the state police about the dog. In my

rearview mirror, I saw the patrol car and a white van labeled "Animal Control." I drove

on, confident that the dog would be rescued and relieve that someone had cared enough

to save its small life.

Review Test 2

Change verbs where needed in the following selection so that they are consistently in the past tense. Cross out each incorrect verb and then write the correct form in the space provided. You will need to make ten corrections in all.

The first time I tried to parallel park on my own was a memorable experience. My first mistake was trying to move into the parking place hood first. I got the car's front end close to the curb, but the rear end remains out in the street. I then backed out and pull up beside the car in front of the parking place. This is where I make my second

5   mistake. Because I was worried that someone might steal my place, I fail to pull up enough alongside the car. So when I backed in, my rear wheels are against the curb while the car's hood was out in the street blocking traffic. I then had to pull out, and I attempt to park once more. As I backed in the second time, I remember my teacher's advice. She trained me not to turn the wheels in until the steering wheel of my car is

10 even with the rear bumper of the car in front of the parking place. I did this and the car slips neatly into the space, with only a few inches left between the tires and the curb. As I was congratulating myself on my success, the car behind me pulls out, leaving a parking space big enough for a Mack truck.

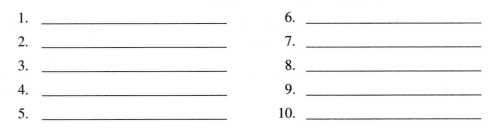

1. _____   6. _____

2. _____   7. _____

3. _____   8. _____

4. _____   9. _____

5. _____   10. _____

Additional Information about Verbs

The purpose of this special chapter is to provide additional information about verbs. Some people will find the grammar terms here a helpful reminder of earlier school learning about verbs. For them, the terms will increase their understanding of how verbs function in English. Other people may welcome more detailed information about terms used elsewhere in the text. In either case, remember that the most common mistakes that people make when writing verbs have been treated in earlier sections of the book.

VERB TENSE

Verbs tell us the time of an action. The time that a verb shows is usually called *tense.* The most common tenses are the simple present, past, and future. In addition, there are nine other tenses that enable us to express more specific ideas about time than we could with the simple tenses alone. Shown on the next page are the twelve verb tenses and examples of each tense. Read them over to increase your sense of the many different ways of expressing time in English.

Tenses	Examples
Present	I *work.* Tamika *works.*
Past	Howard *worked* on the lawn.
Future	You *will work* overtime this week.
Present perfect	Gail *has worked* hard on the puzzle. They *have worked* well together.
Past perfect	They *had finished* the work before their shift ended.
Future perfect	The volunteers *will have worked* many unpaid hours.
Present progressive	I *am* not *working* today. You *are working* the second shift. The clothes dryer *is* not *working* properly.
Past progressive	She *was working* outside. The plumbers *were working* here this morning.
Future progressive	The sound system *will be working* by tonight.
Present perfect progressive	Married life *has* not *been working* out for that couple.
Past perfect progressive	I *had been working* overtime until recently.
Future perfect progressive	My sister *will have been working* at that store for eleven straight months by the time she takes a vacation next week.

The perfect tenses are formed by adding *have, has,* or *had* to the past participle (the form of the verb that ends, usually, in *-ed*). The progressive tenses are formed by adding *am, is, are, was,* or *were* to the present participle (the form of the verb that ends in *-ing*). The perfect progressive tenses are formed by adding *have, has,* or *had* plus *been* to the present participle.

Certain tenses are explained in more detail on the following pages.

Present Perfect
(*have* or *has* + past participle)

The present perfect tense expresses an action that began in the past and has recently been completed or is continuing in the present.

The city has just agreed on a contract with the sanitation workers.
Tony's parents have lived in that house for twenty years.
Lola has watched *Star Trek* reruns since she was a little girl.

Past Perfect
(*had* + past participle)

The past perfect tense expresses a past action that was completed before another past action.

Lola had learned to dance by the time she was five.
The class had just started when the fire bell rang.
Bad weather had never been a problem on our vacations until last year.

Present Progressive
(*am, is,* or *are* + *-ing* form)

The present progressive tense expresses an action still in progress.

I am taking an early train into the city every day this week.
Karl is playing softball over at the field.
The vegetables are growing rapidly.

Past Progressive
(*was* or *were* + *-ing* form)

The past progressive expresses an action that was in progress in the past.

I was spending twenty dollars a week on cigarettes before I quit.
Last week, the store was selling many items at half price.
My friends were driving over to pick me up when the accident occurred.

Practice

For the sentences that follow, fill in the present or past perfect or the present or past progressive of the verb shown. Use the tense that seems to express the meaning of each sentence best.

Example *park* This summer, Mickey _____*is parking*_____ cars at a French restaurant.

walk 1. We _____ for five miles before we realized we were lost.

feel 2. The new mail carrier _____ good about his job until the first dog bit him.

place 3. After an hour, the waiter _____ only a basket of stale rolls on our table.

try 4. All last winter, my little brother _____ to get a job carrying groceries at the supermarket.

grow 5. This year, Aunt Agatha _____ tomatoes—she must have about five hundred already.

look 6. I _____ everywhere for the paper; finally, I found it under the cat.

study 7. Miriam _____ French for three years so she can talk to her poodle.

see 8. James loves karate; he _____ every Bruce Lee movie in existence.

watch 9. Rita _____ soap operas for four hours a day in the two months she was unemployed.

throw 10. The pitcher _____ to second; unfortunately, the runner was on third.

VERBALS

Verbals are words formed from verbs. Verbals, like verbs, often express action. They can add variety to your sentences and vigor to your writing style. The three kinds of verbals are *infinitives, participles,* and *gerunds.*

Infinitive

An infinitive is *to* plus the base form of the verb.

I started *to practice.*
Don't try *to lift* that table.
I asked Russ *to drive* me home.

Participle

A participle is a verb form used as an adjective (a descriptive word). The present participle ends in *-ing.* The past participle ends in *-ed* or has an irregular ending.

Favoring his *cramped* leg, the *screaming* boy waded out of the pool.
The *laughing* child held up her *locked* piggy bank.
Using a shovel and a bucket, I scooped water out of the *flooded* basement.

Gerund

A gerund is the *-ing* form of a verb used as a noun.

Studying wears me out.
Playing basketball is my main pleasure during the week.
Through *jogging,* you can get yourself in shape.

Practice

In the space beside each sentence, identify the italicized word as a participle (*P*), an infinitive (*I*), or a gerund (*G*).

_____   1. The *sobbing* child could not find his parents.

_____   2. *Gossiping* with neighbors is my favorite pastime.

_____   3. *Painting* the front porch is a chore Fred promises to get to every spring.

_____   4. All my brother ever wants *to do* is watch music videos.

_____   5. Lola always liked *to race* through a pile of dead leaves.

_____   6. My boss's *graying* hair gives him a look of authority.

_____   7. *Glowing* embers were all that remained of the fire.

_____   8. It doesn't matter if you win or lose—just try *to break* even.

_____   9. *Holding* her nose, my mother asked, "What's that awful smell?"

_____   10. *Smoking* a pipe makes that man look sophisticated.

ACTIVE AND PASSIVE VERBS

When the subject of a sentence performs the action of a verb, the verb is in the *active voice.* When the subject of a sentence receives the action of a verb, the verb is in the *passive voice.*

The passive form of a verb consists of a form of the verb *be* plus the past participle of the main verb. Look at the active and passive forms of the verbs below.

Active	*Passive*
Lola *ate* the vanilla pudding. (The subject, *Lola,* is the doer of the action.)	The vanilla pudding *was eaten by* Lola. (The subject, *pudding,* does not act. Instead, something happens to it.)
The plumber *replaced* the hot-water heater. (The subject, *plumber,* is the doer of the action.)	The hot-water heater *was replaced by* the plumber. (The subject, *heater,* does not act. Instead, something happens to it.)

In general, active verbs are more effective than passive ones. Active verbs give your writing a simpler and more vigorous style. The passive form of verbs is appropriate, however, when the performer of the action is unknown or is less important than the receiver of the action. For example:

My house was vandalized last night.
(The performer of the action is unknown.)
Mark was seriously injured as a result of your negligence.
(The receiver of the action, *Mark,* is being emphasized.)

Practice

Change the sentences on the next page from the passive to the active voice. Note that you may have to add a subject in some cases.

Examples   The moped bicycle was ridden by Tony.

Tony rode the moped bicycle. _____

The basketball team was given a standing ovation.

The crowd gave the basketball team a standing ovation. _____

(Here a subject had to be added.)

1. The surprise party was organized by Charlotte.

   _____

2. Many people were offended by the comedian.

   _____

3. The old woman's groceries are paid for by the neighbors.

   _____

4. The horse chestnuts were knocked off the trees by the boys.

   _____

5. The devil was driven out of Regan by the exorcist.

   _____

6. The huge moving van was loaded by four perspiring men.

   _____

7. A tray of glasses was dropped by the inexperienced waiter.

   _____

8. Umbrellas are always being lost by my forgetful Aunt Agatha.

   _____

9. Stan Musial's National League hitting record was finally broken by Pete Rose.

   _____

10. A bomb was found in the suitcase by the airport security staff.

    _____

 Review Test

On separate paper, write three sentences apiece that use:

1. Present perfect tense
2. Past perfect tense
3. Present progressive tense
4. Past progressive tense
5. Infinitive
6. Participle
7. Gerund
8. Passive voice (when the subject is unknown or is less important than the receiver of an action—see page 163)

Pronoun Reference, Agreement, and Point of View

INTRODUCTORY PROJECT

Read each pair of sentences below. Then see if you can choose the correct letter in each of the statements that follow.

1. a. None of the nominees for "best actress" showed <u>their</u> anxiety as the names were being read.
   b. None of the nominees for "best actress" showed <u>her</u> anxiety as the names were being read.
2. a. At the mall, <u>they</u> are already putting up Christmas decorations.
   b. At the mall, <u>shop owners</u> are already putting up Christmas decorations.
3. a. I go to the steak house often because <u>you</u> can get inexpensive meals there.
   b. I go to the steak house often because <u>I</u> can get inexpensive meals there.

In the first pair, (a, b) uses the underlined pronoun correctly because the pronoun refers to *None,* which is a singular word.

In the second pair, (a, b) is correct because otherwise the pronoun reference would be unclear.

In the third pair, (a, b) is correct because the pronoun point of view should not be shifted unnecessarily.

Answers are on page 521.

Pronouns are words that take the place of nouns (persons, places, or things). In fact, the word *pronoun* means *for a noun.* Pronouns are shortcuts that keep you from unnecessarily repeating words in writing. Here are some examples of pronouns:

> Martha shampooed *her* dog. (*Her* is a pronoun that takes the place of *Martha.*)
> As the door swung open, *it* creaked. (*It* replaces *door.*)
> When the motorcyclists arrived at McDonald's, *they* removed *their* helmets. (*They* and *their* replace *motorcyclists.*)

This section presents rules that will help you avoid three common mistakes people make with pronouns. The rules are as follows:

1 A pronoun must refer clearly to the word it replaces.
2 A pronoun must agree in number with the word or words it replaces.
3 Pronouns should not shift unnecessarily in point of view.

PRONOUN REFERENCE

A sentence may be confusing and unclear if a pronoun appears to refer to more than one word or if the pronoun does not refer to any specific word. Look at this sentence:

> We never buy fresh vegetables at that store because they charge too much.

Who charges too much? There is no specific word that *they* refers to. Be clear:

> We never buy fresh vegetables at that store because the owners charge too much.

Here are sentences with other kinds of faulty pronoun reference. Read the explanations of why they are faulty and look carefully at the ways they are corrected.

Faulty	*Clear*
Lola told Gina that she had gained weight.	Lola told Gina, "You've gained weight."
(*Who* had gained weight: Lola or Gina? Be clear.)	(Quotation marks, which can sometimes be used to correct an unclear reference, are explained on page 174.)

Faulty	*Clear*
My older brother is an electrician, but I'm not interested in it. (There is no specific word that *it* refers to. It would not make sense to say, "I'm not interested in electrician.")	My older brother is an electrician, but I'm not interested in becoming one.
Our instructor did not explain the assignment, which made me angry. (Does *which* mean that the instructor's failure to explain the assignment made you angry or that the assignment itself made you angry? Be clear.)	I was angry that the instructor did not explain the assignment.

Practice

Rewrite each of the following sentences to make clear the vague pronoun reference. Add, change, or omit words as necessary.

Example   Lana thanked Rita for the gift, which was very thoughtful of her.

Lana thanked Rita for the thoughtful gift.

1. Mario insisted to Harry that it was his turn to drive.

   _____

   _____

2. I failed two of my courses last semester because they graded unfairly.

   _____

   _____

3. Don was offered an accounting job, which pleased his parents very much.

   _____

   _____

4. When Tony questioned the mechanic, he became very upset.

   _____

   _____

5. I was very nervous about the biology exam, which was unexpected.

   _____

   _____

6. Paul told his younger brother that the dog had chewed his new running shoes.

_____

_____

7. My cousin is an astrologer, but I don't believe in it.

_____

_____

8. Liz told Elaine that she had been promoted.

_____

_____

9. Whenever I start enjoying a new television show, they take it off the air.

_____

_____

10. When the center fielder heard the crack of the bat, he raced toward the fence but was unable to catch it.

_____

_____

PRONOUN AGREEMENT

A pronoun must agree in number with the word or words it replaces. If the word a pronoun refers to is singular, the pronoun must be singular; if the word is plural, the pronoun must be plural. (Note that the word a pronoun refers to is known as the *antecedent.*)

Lola agreed to lend me her Billy Joel albums.

The gravediggers sipped coffee during their break.

In the first example, the pronoun *her* refers to the singular word *Lola;* in the second example, the pronoun *their* refers to the plural word *gravediggers.*

Practice

Write the appropriate pronoun (*they, their, them, it*) in the blank space in each of the following sentences.

Example   My credit cards got me into debt, so I burned _____*them*_____.

1. After the hikers arrived at the camp, _____ removed _____ heavy packs.
2. That breakfast cereal is delicious, but _____ has almost no nutrients.
3. I never miss my favorite television shows anymore, for I use a video-cassette recorder to tape _____.
4. The heat was so oppressive during the race that _____ caused several runners to pass out.
5. Fran's parents went to a marriage counselor, and _____ are getting along better now.

Indefinite Pronouns

The following words, known as *indefinite pronouns,* are always singular.

(-one words)	(-body words)	
one	nobody	each
anyone	anybody	either
everyone	everybody	neither
someone	somebody	

Either of the apartments has (its) drawbacks.

One of the girls lost (her) skateboard.

Everyone in the class must hand in (his) paper tomorrow.

In each example, the pronoun is singular because it refers to one of the indefinite pronouns. There are two important points to remember about indefinite pronouns.

Point 1: In the last example above, if the members of the class were all female, the pronoun would be *her.* If the students were a mixed group of men and women, the pronoun form would be *his or her:*

Everyone in the class must hand in *his or her* paper tomorrow.

Some writers follow the traditional practice of using *his* to refer to both men and women. Some use *his or her* to avoid an implied sexual bias. Perhaps the best practice, though, is to avoid using either *his* or the somewhat awkward *his or her.* This can be done by rewriting a sentence in the plural:

All students in the class must hand in their papers tomorrow.

Here are some examples of sentences that can be rewritten in the plural.

A young child is seldom willing to share her toys with others.
Young children are seldom willing to share their toys with others.

Anyone who does not wear his seatbelt will be fined.
People who do not wear their seatbelts will be fined.

A newly elected politician should not forget his or her campaign promises.
Newly elected politicians should not forget their campaign promises.

Point 2: In informal spoken English, *plural* pronouns are often used with the indefinite pronouns. Instead of saying

Everybody has *his or her* own idea of an ideal vacation.

we are likely to say

Everybody has *their* own idea of an ideal vacation.

Here are other examples:

Everyone in the class must pass in *their* papers.
Everybody in our club has *their* own idea about how to raise money.
No one in our family skips *their* chores.

In such cases, the indefinite pronouns are clearly plural in meaning. Also, the use of such plurals helps people to avoid the awkward *his or her.* In time, the plural pronoun may be accepted in formal speech or writing. Until that happens, however, you should use the grammatically correct singular form in your writing.

Practice

Underline the correct pronoun.

Example   Neither of those houses has (its, their) own garage.

1. Neither of the boys brought (his, their) homework in today.
2. Each waitress is responsible for (her, their) own section.
3. It seems as though no one in my fraternity wants to pay (his, their) dues these days.
4. None of the boys remembered to bring (his, their) radio.
5. Each of my sisters has (her, their) own room.
6. Any man who purchased one of those ill-made suits probably wasted (his, their) money.
7. Almost every woman on our street leaves for (her, their) job about the same time each morning.
8. Before a discussion in our women's club, each member must decide on one question that (she, they) wants to ask.
9. Either of the travel routes has (their, its) share of places to see.
10. Any player on the men's team who gains weight is in danger of losing (his, their) job.

PRONOUN POINT OF VIEW

Pronouns should not shift their point of view unnecessarily. When writing a paper, be consistent in your use of first-, second-, or third-person pronouns.

Type of Pronoun	*Singular*	*Plural*
First-person pronouns	I (my, mine, me)	we (our, us)
Second-person pronouns	you (your)	you (your)
Third-person pronouns	he (his, him)	they (their, them)
	she (her)	
	it (its)	

Note: Any person, place, or thing, as well as any indefinite pronoun like *one, anyone, someone,* and so on (page 169), is a third-person word.

For instance, if you start writing in the first person *I*, don't jump suddenly to the second person *you*. Or if you are writing in the third person *they*, don't shift unexpectedly to *you*. Look at the examples.

Inconsistent	**Consistent**
One reason that *I* like living in the city is that *you* always have a wide choice of sports events to attend. (The most common mistake people make is to let *you* slip into their writing after they start with another pronoun.)	One reason that *I* like living in the city is that *I* always have a wide choice of sports events to attend.
Someone who is dieting should have the help of friends; *you* should also have plenty of willpower.	*Someone* who is dieting should have the help of friends; *he or she* should also have plenty of willpower.
Students who work while *they* are going to school face special problems. For one thing, *you* seldom have enough study time.	Students who work while *they* are going to school face special problems. For one thing, *they* seldom have enough study time.

Practice

Cross out inconsistent pronouns in the following sentences and write the correction above the error.

Example   I work much better when the boss doesn't hover over ~~you~~ *me* with instructions on what to do.

1. What I don't like about eating Chinese food is that you always feel hungry an hour later.

2. Students may not leave the exam room unless you have finished the exam.

3. These days people never seem to get the recognition they deserve, no matter how hard you work.

4. If our pets could talk, we would find it easier to take care of them. As it is, you can never be sure what a pet means by a bark or a meow.

5. Whenever a woman feels she is being discriminated against, you should register a complaint.

6. If a person plans to make a complaint, you should check all the facts first.

7. I work at a shop where you do not get paid for all the holidays you should.

8. If you think you're coming down with cold symptoms, one should take action right away.

9. Once we were at the campsite, you had only a radio as contact with the outside world.

10. In our office, we can have a long coffee break anytime you want it.

 ## Review Test 1

Underline the correct word in the parentheses.

1. When the moon and stars come out, (it, the night) is beautiful.
2. If a person drives defensively, (he or she, they) will be constantly aware of other drivers' actions on the road.
3. Hitting the wall with her skateboard, she chipped (it, the skateboard).
4. Persons wanting old furniture should check the newspaper classified section; also, (they, you) might stop at yard sales.
5. We drove for hours and (we, you) got scared by the heavy fog.
6. Lonnie is the kind of player that always gives (his, their) best for the team.
7. Although we had a delightful vacation, (you, we) are always glad to get home.
8. I've always loved butterfly exhibits, so I decided to start collecting (them, butterflies).
9. When Sally asked why she was being given a ticket, (he, the officer) said she had run a stop sign.
10. I buy my clothes at the outlet store because (it has, they have) the best prices.

Review Test 2

Cross out the pronoun error in each sentence and write the correction in the space provided at the left. Then circle the letter that correctly describes the type of error that was made.

Examples ___Students___ ~~Anyone~~ turning in their papers late will be penalized.
Mistake in: a. pronoun reference (b.) pronoun agreement

___Paul___ When Clyde takes his son Paul to the park, ~~he~~ enjoys himself.
Mistake in: (a.) pronoun reference b. pronoun point of view

___we___ From where we stood, ~~you~~ could see three states.
Mistake in: a. pronoun agreement (b.) pronoun point of view

_____ 1. After throwing the dog a stick, I took it home.
Mistake in: a. pronoun reference b. pronoun agreement

_____ 2. Everyone on the women's team was in the locker room packing their travel bag.
Mistake in: a. pronoun agreement b. pronoun point of view

_____ 3. Ralph walks the dog so he won't get fat.
Mistake in: a. pronoun reference b. pronoun point of view

_____ 4. One of the children forgot to put on their rubbers.
Mistake in: a. pronoun agreement b. pronoun point of view

_____ 5. I've been taking allergy pills, and now it doesn't bother me as much.
Mistake in: a. pronoun reference b. pronoun agreement

_____ 6. When people face a common problem, your personal relationship often becomes stronger.
Mistake in: a. pronoun agreement b. pronoun point of view

_____   7. Everyone who was at the dance has their own memories of the sudden fire.
            Mistake in: a. pronoun reference   b. pronoun agreement

Hint: You may want to rewrite item 7 in the plural, using the lines below.

_____

_____

_____   8. Sometimes our instructor has Ted write on the board because chalk dust makes
       him sneeze.
            Mistake in: a. pronoun reference   b. pronoun point of view

_____   9. Even though I closed the bedroom door, you could still hear the television
       downstairs.
            Mistake in: a. pronoun agreement   b. pronoun point of view

_____   10. If a person walks through those woods, you will see at least ten kinds of nesting
       birds.
            Mistake in: a. pronoun agreement   b. pronoun point of view

Hint: You may want to rewrite item 10 in the plural, using the lines below.

_____

_____

Pronoun
Types

Answers are on page 522.

INTRODUCTORY PROJECT

In each pair, put a check beside the sentence that you think uses pronouns correctly.

Ali and *I* enrolled in a computer course. _____

Ali and *me* enrolled in a computer course. _____

The police officer pointed to my sister and *me*. _____

The police officer pointed to my sister and *I*. _____

Lola prefers men *whom* take pride in their bodies. _____

Lola prefers men *who* take pride in their bodies. _____

The players are confident that the league championship is *theirs'*. _____

The players are confident that the league championship is *theirs*. _____

Them concert tickets are too expensive. _____

Those concert tickets are too expensive. _____

Our parents should spend some money on *themself* for a change. _____

Our parents should spend some money on *themselves* for a change. _____

Answers are on page 522.

This section describes some common types of pronouns: subject and object pronouns, relative pronouns, possessive pronouns, demonstrative pronouns, and reflexive pronouns.

SUBJECT AND OBJECT PRONOUNS

Pronouns change their form depending upon the place that they occupy in a sentence. Here is a list of subject and object pronouns:

Subject Pronouns	Object Pronouns
I	me
you	you (no change)
he	him
she	her
it	it (no change)
we	us
they	them

Subject Pronouns

Subject pronouns are subjects of verbs.

They are getting tired. (*They* is the subject of the verb *are getting.*)
She will decide tomorrow. (*She* is the subject of the verb *will decide.*)
We women organized the game. (*We* is the subject of the verb *organized.*)

Several rules for using subject pronouns, and mistakes people sometimes make, are explained starting below.

Rule 1: Use a subject pronoun in a sentence with a compound (more than one) subject.

Incorrect	Correct
Nate and *me* went shopping yesterday.	Nate and *I* went shopping yesterday.
Him and *me* spent lots of money.	*He* and *I* spent lots of money.

If you are not sure what pronoun to use, try each pronoun by itself in the sentence. The correct pronoun will be the one that sounds right. For example, "*Me* went shopping yesterday" does not sound right; "*I* went shopping yesterday" does.

Rule 2:   Use a subject pronoun after forms of the verb *be*. Forms of *be* include *am, are, is, was, were, has been, have been,* and others.

It was *I* who telephoned.
It may be *they* at the door.
It is *she.*

The sentences above may sound strange and stilted to you, since they are seldom used in conversation. When we speak with one another, forms such as "It was me," "It may be them," and "It is her" are widely accepted. In formal writing, however, the grammatically correct forms are still preferred. You can avoid having to use the pronoun form after *be* simply by rewording a sentence. Here is how the preceding examples could be reworded:

I was the one who telephoned.
They may be at the door.
She is here.

Rule 3:   Use subject pronouns after *than* or *as* when a verb is understood after the pronoun.

You read faster than I (read). (The verb *read* is understood after *I*.)
Tom is as stubborn as I (am). (The verb *am* is understood after *I*.)
We don't go out as much as they (do). (The verb *do* is understood after *they*.)

Notes

a   Avoid mistakes by simply adding the "missing" verb at the end of the sentence.
b   Use object pronouns after *than* or *as* when a verb is not understood after the pronoun.

The law applies to you as well as me.
Our boss paid Monica more than me.

Object Pronouns

Object pronouns (*me, him, her, us, them*) are the objects of verbs or prepositions. (Prepositions are connecting words like *for, at, about, to, before, by, with,* and *of.* See also page 87.)

> Rita chose *me.* (*Me* is the object of the verb *chose.*)
> We met *them* at the ball park. (*Them* is the object of the verb *met.*)
> Don't mention UFOs to *us.* (*Us* is the object of the preposition *to.*)
> I live near *her.* (*Her* is the object of the preposition *near.*)

People are sometimes uncertain about what pronoun to use when two objects follow the verb.

Incorrect	**Correct**
I spoke to George and *he.*	I spoke to George and *him.*
She pointed at Jamila and *I.*	She pointed at Jamila and *me.*

Hint: If you are not sure what pronoun to use, try each pronoun by itself in the sentence. The correct pronoun will be the one that sounds right. For example, "I spoke to he" doesn't sound right; "I spoke to him" does.

Practice 1

Underline the correct subject or object pronoun in each of the following sentences. Then show whether your answer is a subject or an object pronoun by circling the *S* or *O* in the margin. The first one is done for you as an example.

S (O) 1. I left the decision to (her, she).

S O 2. My sister and (I, me) decided to combine funds to buy our parents' Christmas present.

S O 3. He arrived sooner than (they, them).

S O 4. Give more spaghetti to Hal and (her, she). *object P*

S O 5. Marge and (she, her) gave the car an oil change.

S O 6. The two people failed for cheating on the test were Mary and (he, him).

S O 7. (She, Her) and Barbara are jealous of my success.

S O 8. (We, Us) fellows decided to get up a football game.

S O 9. I don't feel he is a better volleyball player than (me, I). *Comparison.*

S O 10. (Her, She) and (I, me) are not talking to each other.

Practice 2

Write in a subject or an object pronoun that fits in the space provided. Try to use as many different pronouns as possible. The first one is done for you as an example.

1. Lola ran after Sue and _____ *me* _____ to return the suntan lotion she had borrowed.

   Direct Object

2. Mr. Spud, our football coach, asked Gary and _____ me _____ to play on both offense and defense.

3. Pull the map out of the glove compartment and give it to _____ him (us)

4. The bowling team presented _____ they us _____ with a bronze trophy.

5. The instructor caught Ted and _____ me _____ whispering together during the exam.

   I compar

6. No one was dressed up as much as _____ I _____ was.

7. My sister and _____ I _____ decided to care for the stray puppy.

8. I'm tired of _____ them _____ and their polite artificial smiles.

   objet

9. The block party was organized by _____ us or them _____ and our neighbors.

   Preposition

10. My uncle entertained _____ us _____ kids with his John Wayne imitation.

RELATIVE PRONOUNS

Relative pronouns do two things at once. First, they refer to someone or something already mentioned in the sentence. Second, they start a short word group that gives additional information about this someone or something. Here is a list of relative pronouns, followed by some example sentences:

who	which
whose	that
whom	

The only friend *who* really understands me is moving away.
The child *whom* Ben and Arlen adopted is from Korea.
Chocolate, *which* is my favorite food, upsets my stomach.
I guessed at half the questions *that* were on the test.

In the example sentences, *who* refers to *friend, whom* refers to *child, which* refers to *chocolate,* and *that* refers to *questions.* In addition, each of these relative pronouns begins a group of words that describes the person or thing being referred to. For example, the words *whom Ben and Arlene adopted* tell which child the sentence is about, and the words *which is my favorite food* give added information about chocolate.

Points to Remember about Relative Pronouns

Point 1:   *Whose* means *belonging to whom.* Be careful not to confuse *whose* with *who's,* which means *who is.*

Point 2:   *Who, whose,* and *whom* all refer to people. *Which* refers to things. *That* can refer to either people or things.

I don't know *whose* book this is.
Don't sit on the chair *which* is broken.
Let's elect a captain *that* cares about winning.

Point 3:   *Who, whose, whom,* and *which* can also be used to ask questions. When they are used in this way, they are called *interrogative* pronouns:

Who murdered the secret agent?
Whose fingerprints were on the bloodstained knife?
To *whom* have the detectives been talking?
Which suspect is going to confess?

Note: In informal usage, *who* is generally used instead of *whom* as an interrogative pronoun. Informally, we can say or write, "*Who* are you rooting for in the game?" or "*Who* did the instructor fail?" More formal usage would use *whom:* "*Whom* are you rooting for in the game?" and "*Whom* did the instructor fail?"

Point 4:   *Who* and *whom* are used differently. *Who* is a subject pronoun. Use *who* as the subject of a verb:

Let's see *who* will be teaching the course.

Whom is an object pronoun. Use *whom* as the object of a verb or a preposition:

Dr. Kelsey is the instructor *whom* I like best.
I haven't decided for *whom* I will vote.

You may want to review the material on subject and object pronouns on pages 177–179.

Here is an easy way to decide whether to use *who* or *whom*. Find the first verb after the place where the *who* or *whom* will go. See if it already has a subject. If it does have a subject, use the object pronoun *whom*. If there is no subject, give it one by using the subject pronoun *who*. Notice how *who* and *whom* are used in the sentences that follow:

> I don't know *who* sideswiped my car.
> The suspect *whom* the police arrested finally confessed.

In the first sentence, *who* is used to give the verb *sideswiped* a subject. In the second sentence, the verb *arrested* already has a subject, *police*. Therefore, *whom* is the correct pronoun.

Practice 1

Underline the correct pronoun in each of the following sentences.

1. My grandfather, (who, which) is seventy-nine, goes bowling every Friday.
2. The plant (who, that) Nita got for her birthday finally died.
3. I wish I had a relative (who, whom) would give me a million dollars.
4. I don't know to (who, whom) I should send my complaint letter.
5. Nobody knew (who, whom) was responsible for the mistake.

Practice 2

Write five sentences using *who*, *whose*, *whom*, *which*, and *that*.

POSSESSIVE PRONOUNS

Here is a list of possessive pronouns:

my, mine	her, hers	your, yours
your, yours	its	their, theirs
his	our, ours	

Possessive pronouns show ownership or possession.

> Clyde revved up *his* motorcycle and blasted off.
> The keys are *mine.*

Points to Remember about Possessive Pronouns

Point 1:   A possessive pronoun *never* uses an apostrophe. (See also page 241.)

Incorrect	**Correct**
That coat is *hers'*.	That coat is *hers.*
The card table is *theirs'*.	The card table is *theirs.*

Point 2:   Do not use any of the following nonstandard forms to show possession.

Incorrect	**Correct**
I met a friend of *him.*	I met a friend of *his.*
Can I use *you* car?	Can I use *your* car?
Me sister is in the hospital.	*My* sister is in the hospital.
That magazine is *mines.*	That magazine is *mine.*

Practice

Cross out the incorrect pronoun form in each of the sentences that follow. Write the correct form in the space at the left.

_____My_____   **Example**   ~~Me~~ car has broken down again.

_____   1.   That car won't be safe until you get its' brakes fixed.

_____   2.   If you are a friend of him, you're welcome to stay with us.

_____   3.   The seat you are sitting on is mines.

_____   4.   The neighbors called they dogs to chase the cat off the lawn.

_____   5.   The coffeepot is ours'.

DEMONSTRATIVE PRONOUNS

Demonstrative pronouns point to or single out a person or thing. There are four demonstrative pronouns:

this	these
that	those

Generally speaking, *this* and *these* refer to things close at hand; *that* and *those* refer to things farther away.

Is anyone using *this* spoon?

I am going to throw away *these* magazines.

I just bought *that* white Volvo at the curb.

Pick up *those* toys in the corner.

Note: Do not use *them, this here, that there, these here,* or *those there* to point out. Use only *this, that, these,* or *those.*

Incorrect	**Correct**
Them tires are badly worn.	*Those* tires are badly worn.
This here book looks hard to read.	*This* book looks hard to read.
That there candy is delicious.	*That* candy is delicious.
Those there squirrels are pests.	*Those* squirrels are pests.

Practice 1

Cross out the incorrect form of the demonstrative pronoun and write the correct form in the space provided.

Those **Example** ~~Them~~ clothes need washing.

_____ 1. That there dog will bite you if it gets a chance.

_____ 2. This here fingernail is not growing straight.

_____ 3. Them girls cannot be trusted.

_____ 4. Carry in those there shopping bags if you want to help.

_____ 5. The place where I'd like to live is that there corner house.

Practice 2

Write four sentences using *this, that, these,* and *those.*

_____

_____

_____

_____

REFLEXIVE PRONOUNS

Reflexive pronouns are ones that refer to the subject of a sentence. Here is a list of reflexive pronouns:

singular	plural
myself	ourselves
yourself	yourselves
himself	themselves
herself	
itself	

Sometimes the reflexive pronoun is used for emphasis:

You will have to wash the dishes *yourself.*
We *ourselves* are willing to forget the matter.
The president *himself* turns down his living room thermostat.

Points to Remember about Reflexive Pronouns

Point 1: In the plural *-self* becomes *-selves.*

Lola washes *herself* in Calgon bath oil.
They treated *themselves* to a Bermuda vacation.

Point 2: Be careful not to use any of the following incorrect forms as reflexive pronouns.

Incorrect	**Correct**
He believes in *hisself.*	He believes in *himself.*
We drove the children *ourself.*	We drove the children *ourselves.*
They saw *themself* in the fun house mirror.	They saw *themselves* in the fun house mirror.
I'll do it *meself.*	I'll do it *myself.*

Practice

Cross out the incorrect form of the reflexive pronoun and write the correct form in the space at the left.

themselves   ***Example***   She believes that God helps those who help ~~themself~~.

_____ 1. Tony considers hisself the strongest wrestler in the class.

_____ 2. The striking players are only making theirselves look greedy.

_____ 3. You must carry your luggage yourselfs.

_____ 4. Many firefighters themself do not have smoke detectors in their homes.

_____ 5. We decided to finish the basement by ourself.

 ## Review Test I

Underline the correct word in the parentheses.

1. I'm going to leave if (that, that there) waiter doesn't come over here soon.
2. Though secured by a chain, the snarling German shepherd still terrified Lee and (I, me).
3. That FM radio is (mine, mines).
4. Watching Alan and (I, me) dancing made him grit his teeth.
5. My aunts promised (us, we) girls a trip to Canada for graduation.
6. The service manager did not remember (who, whom) worked on my car.
7. I think (those, those there) people should be kicked out of the theater for talking.

8. The giggling boys only made (themself, themselves) look foolish.

9. If the decision were up to (they, them), my position in the company would be that of full-time pencil sharpener.

10. If (she, her) and Sandy had reported the leak, the cellar would not have flooded.

 ## Review Test 2

Cross out the pronoun error in each sentence and write the correct form above it.

Example   Terry and ~~me~~ *I* have already seen the movie.

1. Our friends have gotten theirselves into debt by overusing credit cards.

2. This here heat pump will save on your energy bill.

3. Watching the football game, us fans soon realized that our team would lose.

4. If you and her get confused about directions, stop and check at a service station.

5. Dmitri felt both sorry for and angry at the drug addict whom tried to steal his car.

6. Before he took a foul shot, the basketball player crossed hisself for good luck.

7. Jane and me refused to join the union.

8. The parents theirselfs must share the blame for their child's failure in school.

9. Our class painted more colorful posters than them.

10. You and me have got to have a talk.

Review Test 3

On separate paper, write sentences that use correctly each of the following words or word groups.

Example   Peter and him   *The coach suspended Peter and him.*

1. those
2. Sue and she
3. faster than I
4. ours
5. Lola and me

6. whom
7. yourselves
8. with Linda and him
9. you and I
10. the neighbors and us

Adjectives
and
Adverbs

INTRODUCTORY PROJECT

Write in an appropriate word to complete each of the sentences below.

1. The teenage years were a _____beautiful_____ time for me.
2. The mechanic listened _____good_____ while I described my car problem.
3. Basketball is a _____better_____ game than football.
4. My brother is the _____youngest_____ person in our family.

Now see if you can complete the following sentences.

The word inserted in the first sentence is an (adjective, adverb); it describes the word *time.*

The word inserted in the second sentence is an (adjective, adverb); it ends

in the two letters _____ and describes the word *listened.*

The word inserted in the third sentence is a comparative adjective; it is

preceded by *more* or ends in the two letters _____.

The word inserted in the fourth sentence is a superlative adjective; it is

preceded by *most* or ends in the three letters _____.

Answers are on page 523.

Adjectives and adverbs are descriptive words. Their purpose is to make the meanings of the words they describe more specific.

ADJECTIVES

What Are Adjectives?

Adjectives describe nouns (names of persons, places, or things) or pronouns.

> Dena is a *kind* woman. (The adjective *kind* describes the noun *woman.*)
> He is *tired.* (The adjective *tired* describes the pronoun *he.*)

Adjectives usually come before the word they describe (as in *kind woman*). But they also come after forms of the verb *be* (*is, are, was, were,* and so on). Less often, they follow verbs such as *feel, look, smell, sound, taste, appear, become,* and *seem.*

> That bureau is *heavy.* (The adjective *heavy* describes the bureau.)
> The children are *restless.* (The adjective *restless* describes the children.)
> These pants are *itchy.* (The adjective *itchy* describes the pants.)

Using Adjectives to Compare

For most *short* adjectives, add *-er* when comparing two things and *-est* when comparing three or more things.

> I am *taller* than my brother, but my father is the *tallest* person in the house.
> The farm market sells *fresher* vegetables than the corner store, but the *freshest* vegetables are the ones grown in my own garden.

For most *longer* adjectives (two or more syllables), add *more* when comparing two things and *most* when comparing three or more things.

> Backgammon is *more enjoyable* to me than checkers, but chess is the *most enjoyable* game of all.
> My mother is *more talkative* than my father, but my grandfather is the *most talkative* person in the house.

Points to Remember about Adjectives

Point 1: Be careful not to use both an *-er* ending and *more,* or both an *-est* ending and *most.*

Incorrect

Football is a *more livelier* game than baseball.

Tod Traynor was voted the *most likeliest* to succeed in our high school class.

Correct

Football is a *livelier* game than baseball.

Tod Traynor was voted the *most likely* to succeed in our high school class.

Point 2: Pay special attention to the following four words, each of which has irregular forms.

	Comparative (Two)	**Superlative (Three or More)**
bad	worse	worst
good, well	better	best
little	less	least
much, many	more	most

Practice 1

Fill in the comparative or superlative forms for the following words. Two are done for you as examples.

	Comparative (Two)	**Superlative (Three or More)**
fast	faster	fastest
timid	more timid	most timid
kind	_____	_____
ambitious	_____	_____
generous	_____	_____
fine	_____	_____
likable	_____	_____

Practice 2

Add to each sentence the correct form of the word in the margin.

Example   **bad**   The _____worst_____ day of my life was the one when my house caught fire.

comfortable   1. My jeans are the _____most_____ pants I own.

difficult   2. My biology exam was the _____ of my five exams.

easy   3. The _____easiest_____ way to get a good grade in the class is to take effective notes.

little   4. I made _____more_____ money in my job as a delivery boy than I did as a golf caddy.

good   5. The _____most_____ pay I ever made was as a drill press operator in a machine shop.

long   6. The ticket lines for the rock concert were the _____longest_____ I had ever seen.

memorable   7. The _____ days of my childhood were the ones I spent on trips with my grandfather.

experienced   8. I am a _____ driver than my sister, but my brother is the _____ driver in the family.

bad   9. This year's drought is _____ than last year's; forecasters are saying that next year's drought may be the _____ of this century.

good   10. The diner's cheesecake is _____ than its custard pie.

ADVERBS

What Are Adverbs?

Adverbs describe verbs, adjectives, or other adverbs. They usually end in *-ly*.

Dena spoke *kindly* to the confused man. (The adverb *kindly* describes the verb *spoke.*)

The man said he was *completely* alone in the world. (The adverb *completely* describes the adjective *alone.*)

Dena listened *very* sympathetically to his story. (The adverb *very* describes the adverb *sympathetically.*)

A Common Mistake
with Adjectives and Adverbs

Perhaps the most common mistake that people make with adjectives and adverbs is to use an adjective instead of an adverb after a verb.

Incorrect	*Correct*
Tony breathed *heavy*.	Tony breathed *heavily*.
I rest *comfortable* in that chair.	I rest *comfortably* in that chair.
She learned *quick*.	She learned *quickly*.

Practice

Underline the adjective or adverb needed.

1. Her pink top clashed (violent, violently) with her orange skirt.
2. If I had not run (quick, quickly), the dog would have caught me.
3. The crowd pushed (angry, angrily) toward the box office window.
4. Sam peered with (considerable, considerably) effort through the grimy cellar window.
5. The trees swayed (gentle, gently) in the wind.
6. I was (real, really) tired.
7. I exercise (regular, regularly), and my eating habits are also (regular, regularly).
8. Sarah sat very (quiet, quietly) on the stairs, listening to her parents quarrel (angry, angrily) in the kitchen.
9. I listened (careful, carefully) to the doctor's (exact, exactly) instructions.
10. (Slow, Slowly) but (sure, surely), I improved my grades in school.

Well and *Good*

Two words often confused are *well* and *good*. *Good* is an adjective; it describes nouns. *Well* is usually an adverb; it describes verbs. *Well* (rather than *good*) is also used when referring to a person's health.

I became a *good* swimmer. (*Good* is an adjective describing the noun *swimmer.*)

For a change, two-year-old Tommy was *good* during the church service. (*Good* is an adjective describing Tommy and comes after *was,* a form of the verb *be.*)

Tanya did *well* on that exam. (*Well* is an adverb describing the verb *did.*)

I explained that I wasn't feeling *well*. (*Well* is used in reference to health.)

Practice

Write *well* or *good* in the sentences that follow.

1. He writes ___*Well*___ enough to pass the course.
2. We always have a ___*good*___ time at the county fair.
3. The mayor and district attorney know each other very ___*well*___.
4. Jim has not been feeling ___*Well*___ lately.
5. I did not do _____ when I took the typing test.

● Review Test 1

Cross out the adjective or adverb error in each sentence and write the correction in the space at the left.

frequently   **Examples**   My boss ~~frequent~~ tells me to slow down.

harder   For me, the country is a ~~more harder~~ place to live than the city.

_____   1. Make sure the job is done safe.

_____   2. He was found guilty of the charges, and the judge lectured him harsh.

_____   3. I am the taller of the five children in my family.

_____   4. Hal swam effortless through the water, not making a single awkward movement.

_____   5. At this time it is importanter to be in school than to have a full-time job.

_____   6. His eyes are his most attractivest feature.

_____   7. I slept light, for the stereo blared noisily upstairs.

_____   8. Mr. Scott is the helpfulest of my instructors.

_____   9. Despite reforms, conditions at the prison are more worse than before.

_____   10. Tony didn't feel good after eating diced eggplant in clam sauce.

Review Test 2

Write a sentence that uses each of the following adjectives and adverbs correctly.

1. nervous _____

2. nervously _____

3. good _____

4. well _____

5. carefully _____

6. most honest _____

7. easier _____

8. best _____

9. more useful _____

10. loudest _____

Misplaced
Modifiers

INTRODUCTORY PROJECT

Because of misplaced words, each of the sentences below has more than one possible meaning. In each case, see if you can explain both the intended meaning and the unintended meaning. Also, circle the words that you think create the confusion because they are misplaced.

1. The farmers sprayed the apple trees wearing masks.

    Intended meaning: _____

    Unintended meaning: _____

2. The woman reached out for the faith healer who had a terminal disease.

    Intended meaning: _____

    Unintended meaning: _____

Answers are on page 523.

WHAT MISPLACED MODIFIERS ARE AND HOW TO CORRECT THEM

Misplaced modifiers are words that, because of awkward placement, do not describe the words the writer intended them to describe. Misplaced modifiers often confuse the meaning of a sentence. To avoid them, place words as close as possible to what they describe.

Misplaced Words	*Correctly Placed Words*
They could see the Goodyear blimp *sitting on the front lawn.* (The Goodyear blimp was sitting on the front lawn?)	Sitting on the front lawn, they could see the Goodyear blimp. (The intended meaning—that the Goodyear blimp was visible from the front lawn—is now clear.)
We had a hamburger after the movie, *which was too greasy for my taste.* (The movie was too greasy for your taste?)	After the movie, we had a hamburger, which was too greasy for my taste. (The intended meaning—that the hamburger was greasy—is now clear.)
Our phone *almost* rang fifteen times last night. (The phone almost rang fifteen times, but in fact did not ring at all?)	Our phone rang almost fifteen times last night. (The intended meaning—that the phone rang a little under fifteen times—is now clear.)

Other single-word modifiers to watch out for include *only, even, hardly, nearly,* and *often.* Such words should be placed immediately before the word they modify.

Practice 1

Underline the misplaced word or words in each sentence. Then rewrite the sentence, placing related words together and thereby making the meaning clear.

Example   Anita returned the hamburger to the supermarket <u>that was spoiled</u>.

Anita returned the hamburger that was spoiled to the

supermarket.

1. They finally found a Laundromat driving around in their car.

_____

_____

2. I read that Chuck Yeager was a pilot who broke the sound barrier in the library.

_____

_____

3. Evelyn was thinking about her lost chemistry book taking the elevator.

_____

_____

4. Lola selected a doughnut from the bakery filled with banana cream.

_____

_____

5. Howard almost worked twenty hours overtime to pay some overdue bills.

_____

_____

6. Tickets have gone on sale for next week's championship game in the college bookstore.

_____

_____

7. I returned the orange socks to the department store that my uncle gave me.

_____

_____

8. The camper saw the black bear looking through the binoculars.

_____

_____

9. I nearly earned two hundred dollars last week.

_____

_____

10. Mushrooms should be stored in the refrigerator enclosed in a paper bag.

_____

_____

Practice 2

Rewrite each sentence, adding the *italicized* words. Make sure that the intended meaning is clear and that two different interpretations are not possible.

Example   I borrowed a pen for the essay test. (Insert *that ran out of ink.*)

For the essay test, I borrowed a pen that ran out of ink.

1.   We agreed to go out to dinner tonight. (Insert *in our science class.*)

_____

_____

2.   Bob and I decided to get married. (Insert *on a rainy day in June* to show when the decision was made.)

_____

_____

3.   Suki decided to hail a taxi. (Insert *weighed down with heavy packages.*)

_____

_____

4.   I've looked everywhere for an instruction book on how to play the guitar. (Insert *without success.*)

_____

_____

5.   Mother told me to wash the car. (Insert *over the phone.*)

_____

_____

 Review Test 1

Write *M* for *misplaced* or *C* for *correct* in front of each sentence.

_____   1. Larry spotted the missing dog on his way to the bank.

_____   2. Larry, while on his way to the bank, spotted the missing dog.

_____   3. Marie brought a casserole right out of the oven to the new neighbors.

_____   4. Marie brought a casserole to the new neighbors right out of the oven.

_____   5. My sister smiled at the usher in the theater with long sideburns.

_____   6. My sister smiled at the usher with long sideburns in the theater.

_____   7. A cheerful man with one leg hopped onto the bus.

_____   8. A cheerful man hopped onto the bus with one leg.

_____   9. The weary hunter shot at the ducks sitting in his car.

_____   10. Sitting in his car, the weary hunter shot at the ducks.

_____   11. Bill saw a kangaroo at the window under the influence of whiskey.

_____   12. Bill saw a kangaroo under the influence of whiskey at the window.

_____   13. Under the influence of whiskey, Bill saw a kangaroo at the window.

_____   14. I was attacked by a stray dog working in the yard.

_____   15. While working in the yard, I was attacked by a stray dog.

_____   16. He remembered with dismay that he had to wash the windows.

_____   17. He remembered that he had to wash the windows with dismay.

_____   18. With dismay, he remembered that he had to wash the windows.

_____   19. Ana received a sports car for her birthday that has a sun roof.

_____   20. Ana received a sports car that has a sun roof for her birthday.

 ## Review Test 2

Underline the five misplaced modifiers in the following passage. Then correct them in the spaces provided on the next page.

Before heading to work in the morning, joggers almost fill all the streets. They quietly pound the sidewalks wearing brightly colored sweatsuits and sneakers. Groups of early feeding pigeons and squirrels scatter as the joggers move easily down the streets. The joggers are gazed at by people who are waiting at bus stops wearing expressions of wonder

5   and envy. Occasionally, a jogger stops to tie a shoelace kneeling on the cement. The joggers pass supermarkets and vegetable trucks parked at loading ramps. On rainy days, the runners watch for slick spots on the sidewalk, but they don't worry about the rain or cold. Pushing on at a steady pace, they count the number of miles traveled. Finally, the joggers take quick showers and think about the workday ahead back at their homes. They will return

10   to their special world of running the next morning.

1. _____
   _____

2. _____
   _____

3. _____
   _____

4. _____
   _____

5. _____
   _____

Dangling Modifiers

Because of dangling words, each of the sentences below has more than one possible meaning. In each case, see if you can explain both the intended meaning and the unintended meaning.

1. Munching leaves from a tall tree, the children were fascinated by the eighteen-foot-tall giraffe.

   Intended meaning: _____

   Unintended meaning: _____

2. Arriving home after ten months in the service, the neighbors threw a block party for Michael.

   Intended meaning: _____

   _____

   Unintended meaning: _____

   _____

Answers are on page 524.

WHAT DANGLING MODIFIERS ARE AND HOW TO CORRECT THEM

A modifier that opens a sentence must be followed immediately by the word it is meant to describe. Otherwise, the modifier is said to be *dangling,* and the sentence takes on an unintended meaning. For example, in the sentence

> While sleeping in his backyard, a Frisbee hit Bill on the head.

the unintended meaning is that the *Frisbee* was sleeping in his backyard. What the writer meant, of course, was that *Bill* was sleeping in his backyard. The writer should have placed *Bill* right after the modifier:

> While sleeping in his backyard, *Bill* was hit on the head by a Frisbee.

The sentence could also be corrected by placing the subject within the opening word group:

> While *Bill* was sleeping in his backyard, a Frisbee hit him on the head.

Other sentences with dangling modifiers follow. Read the explanations of why they are dangling and look carefully at the ways they are corrected.

Dangling	**Correct**
Having almost no money, my survival depended on my parents. (*Who* has almost no money? The answer is not *survival* but *I.* The subject *I* must be added.)	Having almost no money, *I* depended on my parents for survival. *Or:* Since *I* had almost no money, I depended on my parents for survival.
Riding his bike, a German shepherd bit Tony's ankle. (*Who* is riding the bike? The answer is not *German shepherd,* as it unintentionally seems to be, but *Tony.* The subject *Tony* must be added.)	Riding his bike, *Tony* was bitten on the ankle by a German shepherd. *Or:* While *Tony* was riding his bike, a German shepherd bit him on the ankle.
When trying to lose weight, all snacks are best avoided. (*Who* is trying to lose weight? The answer is not *snacks* but *you.* The subject *you* must be added.)	When trying to lose weight, *you* should avoid all snacks. *Or:* When *you* are trying to lose weight, avoid all snacks.

These examples make clear two ways of correcting a dangling modifier. Decide on a logical subject and do one of the following:

1 Place the subject *within* the opening word group:

Since *I* had almost no money, I depended on my parents for survival.

Note: In some cases an appropriate subordinating word, such as *since,* must be added, and the verb may have to be changed slightly as well.

2 Place the subject right *after* the opening word group:

Having almost no money, *I* depended on my parents for survival.

Sometimes even more rewriting is necessary to correct a dangling modifier. What is important to remember is that a modifier must be placed as close as possible to the word that it modifies.

Practice I

Rewrite each sentence to correct the dangling modifier. Mark the one sentence that is correct with a *C.*

1. Folded into a tiny square, I could not read the message.

   _____

   _____

2. Wading into the lake, tadpoles swirled around my ankles.

   _____

   _____

3. Soaked to the skin, Chris was miserable waiting in the unsheltered doorway.

   _____

   _____

4. Hanging on the wall, I saw a photograph of my mother.

   _____

   _____

5. Settling comfortably into the chair, the television captured my attention for the next hour.

   _____

   _____

6. Driving home after a tiring day at work, the white line became blurry.

   _____

   _____

7. Soaring high over the left-field fence, the batter hit his first home run.

   _____

   _____

8. Threadbare and dirty, Martha knew the time had come to replace the rug.

   _____

   _____

9. After spending most of the night outdoors in a tent, the sun rose and we went into the house.

   _____

   _____

10. Hot and sizzling, we bit into the apple tarts.

   _____

   _____

Practice 2

Complete the following sentences. In each case, a logical subject should follow the opening words.

Example   Checking the oil stick, *I saw that my car was a quart low.* _____

1. Since failing the first test, _____

2. Before learning how to dance, _____

3. While flying the kite, _____

4. After taking my coffee break, _____

5. Though very tired, _____

Review Test 1

Write *D* for *dangling* or *C* for *correct* in front of each sentence. Remember that the opening words are a dangling modifier if they are not followed immediately by a logical subject.

1. Hanging in the closet for a year, Lola forgot she owned an aqua dress.

2. Lola forgot she owned an aqua dress that had been hanging in the closet for a year.

3. Having eaten several spicy tacos, my stomach began an Indian war dance.

4. Having eaten several spicy tacos, I began to feel my stomach doing an Indian war dance.

5. Hitching a ride, I was picked up by a Mack truck.

6. Hitching a ride, a Mack truck picked me up.

7. While waiting for the bus, rain began to fall.

8. While waiting for the bus, it began to rain.

9. While I was waiting for the bus, rain began to fall.

10. Being tired, my chores were not finished.

11. Because I was tired, I did not finish my chores.

12. While I was practicing yoga exercises, a mail carrier rang the doorbell.

13. While practicing yoga exercises, a mail carrier rang the doorbell.

14. Containing dangerous chemicals, people are not swimming in the lake.

15. Containing dangerous chemicals, the lake is not open for swimming.

16. Because the lake contains dangerous chemicals, it is not open for swimming.

17. Falling heavily, Toshio broke his arm.

18. Falling heavily, Toshio's arm was broken.

19. Just before finishing the book, the power failed.

20. Just before I finished the book, the power failed.

Review Test 2

Underline the five dangling modifiers in the following passage. Then correct them in the spaces provided below.

When my brother Rick gets hold of a best-seller, he forgets that the rest of the world exists. Absorbed in his book, dinner is forgotten. He must be reminded to eat even when we have meat loaf, his favorite meal. Rick not only ignores the other people in the family but also forgets his chores. Reading after breakfast, lunch, and dinner, a lot of dishes pile

5   up and wastebaskets are not emptied. We try to understand; in fact, we think he's lucky. Sitting in the middle of a room, his book seems to drown out the television, radio, and screaming children. Never wanting any sleep, his book still has his attention at 1 A.M. We bought a new rocking chair once when Rick was in the middle of a best-seller. Rocking away, his eyes never left the pages long enough to notice it. Only after finishing the book

10 did he ask, "When did we get the new chair?"

1. _____

_____

2. _____

_____

3. _____

_____

4. _____

_____

5. _____

_____

Parallelism

INTRODUCTORY PROJECT

Read aloud each pair of sentences below. Put a check mark beside the sentence that reads more smoothly and clearly and sounds more natural.

Pair 1

I use my TV remote control to change channels, to adjust the volume, and for turning the set on and off.

✓ I use my TV remote control to change channels, to adjust the volume, and to turn the set on and off.

Pair 2

✓ One option the employees had was to take a cut in pay; the other was longer hours of work.

One option the employees had was to take a cut in pay; the other was to work longer hours.

Pair 3

The refrigerator has a cracked vegetable drawer, one of the shelves is missing, and a strange freezer smell.

✓ The refrigerator has a cracked vegetable drawer, a missing shelf, and a strange freezer smell.

Answers are on page 524.

PARALLELISM EXPLAINED

Words in a pair or a series should have a parallel structure. By balancing the items in a pair or a series so that they have the same structure, you will make your sentences clearer and easier to read. Notice how the parallel sentences that follow read more smoothly than the nonparallel ones.

Nonparallel (Not Balanced)	*Parallel (Balanced)*
I attended three classes in the morning, studied most of the afternoon, and my sales job was in the evening.	I attended three classes in the morning, studied most of the afternoon, and worked at my sales job in the evening. (A balanced series of past tense verbs: *attended, studied, worked.*)
Mel spends his free time reading, listening to music, and he watches TV sports.	Mel spends his free time reading, listening to music, and watching TV sports. (A balanced series of *-ing* words: *reading, listening, watching.*)
After the camping trip I was exhausted, irritable, and wanted to eat.	After the camping trip I was exhausted, irritable, and hungry. (A balanced series of descriptive words: *exhausted, irritable, hungry.*)
My hope for retirement is to be healthy, to live in a comfortable house, and having plenty of money.	My hope for retirement is to be healthy, to live in a comfortable house, and to have plenty of money. (A balanced series of *to* verbs: *to be, to live, to have.*)
Nightly, Fred puts out the trash, checks the locks on the doors, and the burglar alarm is turned on.	Nightly, Fred puts out the trash, checks the locks on the doors, and turns on the burglar alarm. (Balanced verbs and word order: *puts out the trash, checks the locks, turns on the burglar alarm.*)

Balancing sentences is not a skill you need worry about when writing first drafts. But when you rewrite, you should try to put matching words and ideas into matching structures. Such parallelism will improve your writing style.

Practice I

The unbalanced part of each sentence is italicized. Rewrite this part so that it matches the rest of the sentence.

Example   In the afternoon, I changed two diapers, ironed several shirts, and *was watching* soap operas. _watched_

1. After the exercise class, I woke up with stiff knees, throbbing legs, and *arms that ached.* _aching arms_

2. Our favorite restaurant specializes in delicious omelets, *soups that are freshly made,* and inexpensive desserts. _freshly made soups_

3. The man running the checkout counter was tall, thin, and *having a bad temper.* _had a bad temper_

4. Caulking the windows, *to replace weather stripping,* and painting the garage are my chores for the weekend. _replacing weather strippings_

5. With her pale skin and *her eyes that were green,* she appeared ghostly in the moonlight. _green eyes_

6. As a Barbra Streisand fan, I love to see her movies and *hearing her sing.* _heard her sing_

7. After calling the police, checking the area hospitals, and *we prayed,* we could only wait. _praying_

8. The stars appeared on talk shows, signed autographs, and *were attending* opening nights in order to promote their latest movie. _attended_

9. Our teenage daughter ties up the phone for hours, giggling with her girlfriends, deciding what to wear, and *complaints about her strict parents.* _complaining about her strict parents_

10. In Allan's nightmare, he was audited by the IRS, investigated by *Sixty Minutes,* and *bill collectors were chasing him.* _and chased by chased bill collectors._

Practice 2

Complete the following statements. The first two parts of each statement are parallel in form; the part that you add should be parallel in form as well.

Example   Three things I like about myself are my sense of humor, my thoughtfulness, and <u>my self-discipline.</u>

1. Among the drawbacks of apartment living are noisy neighbors, yearly rent
    increases, and _____

2. Three bad habits I have resolved to change are losing my temper, showing up
    late for appointments, and _____

3. The best features of my part-time job are good pay, flexible hours, and

    _____

4. Cigarette smoking is expensive, disgusting, and _____

5. Lessons I had to learn after moving from my parents' home included how to
    budget my money, how to take care of my own laundry, and _____

    _____

 ## Review Test I

Cross out the unbalanced part of each sentence. Then rewrite the unbalanced part so that it matches the other item or items in the sentence.

Example   I enjoy watering the grass and ~~to work~~ in the garden.
             <u>working</u>

1. Our production supervisor warned Jed to punch in on time, dress appropriately
   for the job, and he should stop taking extra breaks.

   _____

2. On his ninetieth birthday, the old man mused that his long life was due to hard
   work, a loving wife, and because he had a sense of humor.

   _____

3. The philosopher's advice is to live for the present, find some joy in each day, and by helping others.

_____

4. Freshly prepared food, an attractive decor, and having prompt service are signs of a good restaurant.

_____

5. Martha has tickets for reckless driving, speeding, and she parked illegally.

_____

6. Washing clothes, cooking meals, and to take care of children used to be called "women's work."

_____

7. Our compact car provides better mileage; more comfort is provided by our station wagon.

_____

8. As the first bartender to arrive each day, Elena must slice lemons, get ice, and she has to check the inventory.

_____

9. Last week I finished my term paper, took all my final exams, and an interview for a summer job.

_____

10. On our ideal vacation, I enjoy lazing in the sun, eating delicious food, and to be with special friends.

_____

 ## Review Test 2

On separate paper, write five sentences of your own that use parallel structure. Each sentence should contain three items in a series. Use the same formats provided for the five sentences on page 208: past tense verbs; *-ing* words; descriptive words; *to* verbs; and present tense verbs and word order.

Review Test 3

There are six nonparallel parts in the following passage. The first is corrected for you as an example. Underline and correct the other five.

My sister used to drive an old VW "Bug." With its dented body, torn upholstery, and <u>fenders that were rusted</u>, the car was a real eyesore. Worse, though, the car was in terrible shape mechanically. The engine coughed, the tailpipe rattled, and there were squealing brakes. My father spent many hours searching for cures for the car's many ailments. He often spoke about pushing the car off a cliff or to explode it and put it out of its misery. He **5** wasn't serious, of course, but one day the little car saved my father the trouble. As Kathy was driving one afternoon, smoke began pouring through the backseat of the car. My sister parked on the side of the road and began to check the engine. Quickly, another motorist pulled over, jumped out of his car, and pushing my sister away from the VW. The car smoldered a few minutes and then bursting into flames. Firefighters arrived in about ten **10** minutes but were too late. The car's tires had melted, its body was black, the glass popping out of the windows, and the steering wheel was twisted. When Kathy told the family what had happened, everyone was sympathetic. I suspect, however, that my father shed no tears that the Bug was gone from our lives.

1. _____rusty fenders_____

2. _____

3. _____

4. _____

5. _____

6. _____

Section 2: Mechanics

Paper Format

INTRODUCTORY PROJECT

Which of the paper openings below seems clearer and easier to read?

A

	Finding Faces
	It takes just a little imagination to find faces in the
	objects around you. For instance, clouds are sometimes
	shaped like faces. If you lie on the ground on a partly

B

	"finding faces"
	It takes just a little imagination to find faces in the objects
	around you. For instance, clouds are sometimes shaped like
	faces. If you lie on the ground on a partly cloudy day, chan-
	ces are you will be able to spot many well-known faces

What are three reasons for your choice?

_____

_____

_____

_____

Answers are on page 524.

GUIDELINES FOR PREPARING PAPERS

Here are guidelines to follow in preparing a paper for an instructor.

1 Use full-sized theme or typewriter paper, 8½ by 11 inches.

2 Keep wide margins (1 to 1½ inches) all around the paper. In particular, do not crowd the right-hand and bottom margins. The white space makes your paper more readable; also, the instructor has room for comments.

3 If you write by hand:

Use a blue or black pen (*not* a pencil).

Be careful not to overlap letters or to make decorative loops on letters.

On narrow-ruled paper, write on every other line.

Make all your letters distinct. Pay special attention to *a, e, i, o,* and *u*—five letters that people sometimes write illegibly.

Keep your capital letters clearly distinct from your small letters. You may even want to print all capital letters.

4 Center the title of your paper on the first line of page one. Do *not* put quotation marks around the title or underline the title or put a period after the title. Capitalize all the major words in a title, including the first word. Small connecting words within a title, such as *of, for, the, in,* and *to,* are not capitalized.

5 Skip a line between the title and the first line of your text. Indent the first line of each paragraph about five spaces (half an inch) from the left-hand margin.

6 Make commas, periods, and other punctuation marks firm and clear. Leave a slight space after each period. When you type, leave a double space after a period.

7 Whenever possible, avoid breaking a word at the end of a line. If you must break a word, break only between syllables (see page 205). Do not break words of one syllable.

8 Put your name, the date, and the course number where your instructor asks for them.

Also keep in mind these important points about the *title* and the *first sentence* of your paper:

9 The title should be several words that tell what the paper is about. It should usually *not* be a complete sentence. For example, if you are writing a paper about your jealous sister, the title could simply be "My Jealous Sister."

10 Do not rely on the title to help explain the first sentence of your paper. The first sentence must be independent of the title. For instance, if the title of your paper is "My Jealous Sister," the first sentence should *not* be, "She has been this way as long as I can remember." Rather, the first sentence might be, "My sister has always been a jealous person."

Practice 1

Identify the mistakes in format in the following lines from a student theme. Explain the mistakes in the spaces provided. One mistake is described for you as an example.

	"The generation gap in our house"
	When I was a girl, I never argued with my parents about
	differences between their attitude and mine. My father
	would deliver his judgment on an issue and that was alw-
	ays the end of the matter. There was no discussion permit-
	ted, so I gradually began to express my disagreement in other

1. *Hyphenate only between syllables (al-ways).*
2. _____
3. _____
4. _____
5. _____
6. _____

Practice 2

As already stated, a title should tell in several words what a paper is about. Often a title can be based on the sentence that expresses the main idea of a paper.

Following are five main-idea sentences from student papers. Write a suitable and specific title for each paper, basing the title on the main idea.

Example Title: *Aging Americans as Outcasts*

Our society treats aging Americans as outcasts in many ways.

1. Title: _____

Selfishness is a common trait in young children.

2. Title: _____

Exercising every morning offers a number of benefits.

3. Title: _____

My teenage son is a stubborn person.

4. Title: _____

To survive in college, a person must learn certain essential study skills.

5. Title: _____

Only after I was married did I fully realize the drawbacks and values of single life.

Practice 3

In four of the five following sentences, the writer has mistakenly used the title to help explain the first sentence. But as has already been stated, you must *not* rely on the title to help explain your first sentence.

Rewrite the sentences so that they stand independent of the title. Write *Correct* under the one sentence that is independent of the title.

Example   Title: Flunking an Exam
First sentence: I managed to do this because of several bad habits.

Rewritten: *I managed to flunk an exam because of several*

bad habits.

1.   Title: The Worst Day of My Life
First sentence: It began when my supervisor at work gave me a message to call home.

Rewritten: _____

_____

2.   Title: Catholic Church Services
First sentence: They have undergone many changes in the last few years.

Rewritten: _____

_____

3.   Title: An Embarrassing Incident
First sentence: This happened to me when I was working as a waitress at the Stanton Hotel.

Rewritten: _____

_____

4. Title: The Inability to Share
    First sentence: The inability to share can cause great strains in a relationship.

    Rewritten: _____

    _____

5. Title: Offensive Television Commercials
    First sentence: Many that I watch are degrading to human dignity.

    Rewritten: _____

    _____

  Review Test

Use the space provided below to rewrite the following sentences from a student paper, correcting the mistakes in format.

	"my husband's Grandfather"
	He was seventy-four when I first met him, and yet in many
	ways he was the youngest person I ever knew. I couldn't help
	being impressed with the strength of his handshake, the
	tightness of his jaw, and the firm muscles of his body. When
	he learned that I was a jogger, he invited me to go running.

Capital Letters

You probably know a good deal about the uses of capital letters. Answering the questions below will help you check your knowledge.

1. Write the full name of a person you know: _____

2. In what city and state were you born? _____

3. What is your present street address? _____

4. Name a country where you want to travel: _____

5. Name a school that you attended: _____

6. Give the name of a store where you buy food: _____

7. Name a company where you or anyone you know works: _____

8. What day of the week gives you the best chance to relax? _____

9. What holiday is your favorite?_____

10. What brand of toothpaste do you use?_____

11. Give the brand name of a candy or chewing gum you like: _____

12. Name a song or a television show you enjoy: _____

13. Write the title of a magazine or newspaper you read: _____

Items 14-16: Three capital letters are needed in the lines below. Underline the words you think should be capitalized. Then write them, capitalized, in the spaces provided.

on Super Bowl Sunday, my roommate said, "let's buy some snacks and invite a few friends over to watch the game." i knew my plans to write a term paper would have to be changed.

14. _____ 15. _____ 16. _____

Answers are on page 525.

MAIN USES OF CAPITAL LETTERS

Capital letters are used with

1 First word in a sentence or direct quotation.
2 Names of persons and the word *I*.
3 Names of particular places.
4 Names of days of the week, months, and holidays.
5 Names of commercial products.
6 Titles of books, magazines, articles, films, television shows, songs, poems, stories, papers that you write, and the like.
7 Names of companies, associations, unions, clubs, religious and political groups, and other organizations.

Each use is illustrated on the pages that follow.

First Word in a Sentence or Direct Quotation

Our company has begun laying people off.
The doctor said, "This may hurt a bit."
"My husband," said Martha, "is a light eater. When it's light, he starts to eat."

Note: In the third example, *My* and *When* are capitalized because they start new sentences. But *is* is not capitalized, because it is part of the first sentence.

Names of Persons and the Word *I*

At the picnic, I met Tony Curry and Lola Morrison.

Names of Particular Places

After graduating from Gibbs High School in Houston, I worked for a summer at a nearby Holiday Inn on Clairmont Boulevard.

But: Use small letters if the specific name of a place is not given.

After graduating from high school in my hometown, I worked for a summer at a nearby hotel on one of the main shopping streets.

Names of Days of the Week, Months, and Holidays

This year Memorial Day falls on the last Thursday in May.

But: Use small letters for the seasons—summer, fall, winter, spring.

In the early summer and fall, my hay fever bothers me.

Names of Commercial Products

The consumer magazine rates highly Cheerios breakfast cereal, Howard Johnson's ice cream, and Jif peanut butter.

But: Use small letters for the *type* of product (breakfast cereal, ice cream, peanut butter, or whatever).

Titles of Books, Magazines, Articles, Films, Television Shows, Songs, Poems, Stories, Papers That You Write, and the Like

My oral report was on *The Diary of a Young Girl* by Anne Frank.

While watching *The Young and the Restless* on television, I thumbed through *Cosmopolitan* magazine and *The New York Times*.

Names of Companies, Associations, Unions, Clubs, Religious and Political Groups, and Other Organizations

A new bill before Congress is opposed by the National Rifle Association.

My wife is Jewish; I am Roman Catholic. We are both members of the Democratic Party.

My parents have life insurance with Prudential, auto insurance with Allstate, and medical insurance with Blue Cross and Blue Shield.

Practice

Cross out the words that need capitals in the sentences that follow. Then write the capitalized forms of the words in the space provided. The number of spaces tells you how many corrections to make in each case.

Example   Rhoda said, "~~why~~ should I bother to *eat* this ~~hershey's~~ bar? I should just apply it directly to my hips."   <u> Why </u>   <u> Hershey's </u>

1. Vince wanted to go to the halloween party dressed as a thanksgiving turkey, but he was afraid someone might try to carve him.

    _____   _____

2. Laurie called upstairs, "if you're not ready in five minutes, i'm leaving without you."

    _____   _____

3. The old ford rattled its way from connecticut to florida on four balding goodyear tires.

    _____   _____   _____   _____

4. Among the dusty boxes in the attic lay a stack of old *life* magazines dating back to world war II.

    _____   _____   _____   _____

5. Juanita King, a member of the northside improvement association, urged the city to clean up the third Street neighborhood.

    _____   _____   _____   _____

6. At soundworks, a discount store on washington boulevard, she purchased a panasonic stereo amplifier.

    _____   _____   _____   _____

7. Tom finished basic training at fort gordon and was transferred to a base near Stuttgart, germany.

    _____   _____   _____

8. On thursday nights Martha goes to the weight watchers' meeting at a nearby high school.

    _____   _____   _____

9. The two films they enjoyed most during the horror film festival held in february were *return of dracula* and *alien*.

    _____   _____   _____   _____

10. My sister bought a pair of gloria vanderbilt jeans at the burlington mall.

    _____   _____   _____   _____

OTHER USES OF CAPITAL LETTERS

Capital letters are also used with

1 Names that show family relationships.
2 Titles of persons when used with their names.
3 Specific school courses.
4 Languages.
5 Geographic locations.
6 Historical periods and events.
7 Races, nations, and nationalities.
8 Opening and closing of a letter.

Each use is illustrated on the pages that follow.

Names That Show Family Relationships

Aunt Fern and Uncle Jack are selling their house.
I asked Grandfather to start the fire.
Is Mother feeling better?

But: Do not capitalize words like *mother, father, grandmother, grandfather, uncle, aunt,* and so on when they are preceded by *my* or another possessive word.

My aunt and uncle are selling their house.
I asked my grandfather to start the fire.
Is my mother feeling better?

Titles of Persons When Used with Their Names

I wrote an angry letter to Senator Blutt.
Can you drive to Dr. Stein's office?
We asked Professor Bushkin about his attendance policy.

But: Use small letters when titles appear by themselves, without specific names.

I wrote an angry letter to my senator.
Can you drive to the doctor's office?
We asked our professor about his attendance policy.

Specific School Courses

My courses this semester include Accounting I, Introduction to Data Processing, Business Law, General Psychology, and Basic Math.

But: Use small letters for general subject areas.

This semester I'm taking mostly business courses, but I have a psychology course and a math course as well.

Languages

Lydia speaks English and Spanish equally well.

Geographic Locations

I lived in the South for many years and then moved to the West Coast.

But: Use small letters in giving directions.

Go south for about five miles and then bear west.

Historical Periods and Events

One essay question dealt with the Battle of the Bulge in World War II.

Races, Nations, Nationalities

The census form asked whether I was Caucasian, African American, Native American, Hispanic, or Asian.
Last summer I hitchhiked through Italy, France, and Germany.
The city is a melting pot for Koreans, Vietnamese, and Mexican Americans.

But: Use small letters when referring to *whites* or *blacks.*

Both whites and blacks supported our mayor in the election.

Opening and Closing of a Letter

Dear Sir:	Sincerely yours,
Dear Madam:	Truly yours,

Note: Capitalize only the first word in a closing.

Practice

Cross out the words that need capitals in the following sentences. Then write the capitalized forms of the words in the spaces provided. The number of spaces tells you how many corrections to make in each case.

1. When aunt esther died, she left all her money to her seven cats and nothing to my uncle.

    _____   _____

2. This fall I'm taking night courses in spanish and aerobic exercise I.

    _____   _____   _____

3. Tony was referred to dr. purdy's office because his regular dentist was on vacation.

    _____   _____

4. The hispanic family in the apartment upstairs has just moved here from the southwest.

    _____   _____

5. My accounting courses are giving me less trouble than intermediate math 201.

    _____   _____

UNNECESSARY USE OF CAPITALS

Practice

Many errors in capitalization are caused by adding capitals where they are not needed. Cross out the incorrectly capitalized letters in the following sentences and write the correct forms in the spaces provided. The number of spaces tells you how many corrections to make in each sentence.

1. During the Summer I like to sit in my backyard, Sunbathe, and read Magazines like *Glamour* and *People*.

    _____ _____ _____

2. Every Week I seem to be humming another Tune. Lately I have been humming the Melody for the latest Pepsi commercial on television.

    _____ _____ _____

3. After High School I traveled to twenty States, including Alaska, and then I decided to enroll in a local College.

    _____ _____ _____ _____

4. The Title of my Paper was "The End of the Civil War." My Instructor did not give me a good Grade for it.

    _____ _____ _____ _____

5. My Friend Jesse said, "People no longer have to go to College and get a Degree in order to find a good job and succeed in Life."

    _____ _____ _____ _____

Review Test 1

Cross out the words that need capitals in the following sentences. Then write the capitalized forms of the words in the spaces provided. The number of spaces tells you how many corrections to make in each sentence.

Example   During halftime of the ~~saturday~~ afternoon football game, my sister said, "~~let's~~ get some hamburgers from ~~wendy's~~ or put a pizza in the oven."

   Saturday   _Let's_   _Wendy's_

1. Stanley was disgusted when he was told he couldn't order lipton tea at the chinese restaurant.

   _____   _____

2. When my grandfather came to america from the ukraine, which was then a part of russia, he spoke no english.

   _____   _____   _____   _____

3. Nikki said, "i've been working as a waitress at the red lobster since last march."

   _____   _____   _____   _____

4. My math 101 course meets on tuesdays in wister hall.

   _____   _____   _____   _____

5. Every election Day, my mother takes a day off from her job as a nurse at memorial hospital to serve as a poll watcher for the democrats.

   _____   _____   _____   _____

6. Lola said, "my favorite episode of *star trek* is the one in which Mr. Spock falls in love."

   _____   _____   _____

7. At the corner of thirteenth and market streets is a newsstand where people can buy magazines from as far away as france.

   _____   _____   _____   _____   _____

8. When aunt esther's pontiac finally broke down, she decided to get a toyota.

   _____   _____   _____   _____

9. The college is showing the movie *stagecoach* on friday night as part of its john wayne film festival.

   _____   _____   _____   _____

10. On our trip to washington, we visited the lincoln memorial, sat through a session of the United States senate, and then fell asleep at a concert at the kennedy center.

    _____   _____   _____

    _____   _____   _____

 ## Review Test 2

On separate paper, write:

- Seven sentences demonstrating the seven main uses of capital letters.
- Eight sentences demonstrating the eight other uses of capital letters.

Numbers
and
Abbreviations

INTRODUCTORY PROJECT

Put a check beside the item in each pair that you think uses numbers correctly.

I finished the exam by 8:55, but my grade was only 65 percent. _____

I finished the exam by eight-fifty-five, but my grade was only sixty-five percent. _____

9 people are in my biology lab, but there are 45 in my lecture group. _____

Nine people are in my biology lab, but there are forty-five in my lecture group. _____

Put a check beside the item in each pair that you think uses abbreviations correctly.

Both of my bros. were treated by Dr. Lewis after the mt. climbing accident. _____

Both of my brothers were treated by Dr. Lewis after the mountain climbing accident. _____

I spent two hrs. finishing my Eng. paper and handed it to my instructor, Ms. Peters, right at the deadline. _____

I spent two hours finishing my English paper and handed it to my instructor, Ms. Peters, right at the deadline. _____

Answers are on page 525.

NUMBERS

Rule 1: Spell out numbers that take no more than two words. Otherwise, use numerals—the numbers themselves.

> Last year Tina bought nine new records.
> Ray struck out fifteen batters in Sunday's softball game.

But

> Tina now has 114 records in her collection.
> Already this season Ray has recorded 168 strikeouts.

You should also spell out a number that begins a sentence:

> One hundred fifty first-graders throughout the city showed flu symptoms today.

Rule 2: Be consistent when you use a series of numbers. If some numbers in a sentence or paragraph require more than two words, then use numerals throughout the selection.

> This past spring, we planted 5 rhodos, 15 azaleas, 50 summersweet, and 120 myrtle around our house.

Rule 3: Use numbers to show dates, times, addresses, percentages, exact sums of money, and parts of a book.

> John Kennedy was killed on November 22, 1963.
> My job interview was set for 10:15. (*But:* Spell out numbers before *o'clock.* For example: The time was then changed to eleven o'clock.)
> Janet's new address is 118 North 35th Street.
> Almost 40 percent of my meals are eaten at fast-food restaurants.
> The cashier rang up a total of $18.35. (*But:* Round amounts may be expressed as words. For example: The movie has a five-dollar admission charge.)
> Read Chapter 6 in your math textbook and answer questions 1 to 5 on page 250.

Practice

Use the three rules to make the corrections needed in these sentences.

1. Why do I always wind up with 5 exams in 3 days?
2. 2 teenage girls were responsible for the shoplifting.
3. My appointment was for eight-thirty in the evening.
4. However, the doctor didn't arrive until 9 o'clock.
5. I worked overtime last week and received a paycheck for two hundred and eighty-two dollars.
6. Steve lives at twenty-three West Pine Street.
7. Fred and Martha were married on May thirty-first, nineteen-fifty-six.
8. Our son has decorated his room with two wall posters, five record-album covers, and over 215 baseball cards.
9. Sears' fifty percent off sale on certain items ends on Friday.
10. Our team was penalized 5 yards for having 12 players on the field.

ABBREVIATIONS

While abbreviations are a helpful time-saver in note-taking, you should avoid most abbreviations in formal writing. Listed below are some of the few abbreviations that can acceptably be used in compositions. Note that a period is used after most abbreviations.

1   Mr., Mrs., Ms., Jr., Sr., and Dr. when used with proper names:

    Mr. Rollin   Ms. Peters   Dr. Coleman

2   Time references:

    A.M. or a.m.   P.M. or p.m.   B.C.; A.D.

3   First or middle initial in a signature:

    T. Alan Parker   Linda M. Evans

4 Organizations, technical words, and trade names known primarily by their initials:

ABC   CIA   UNESCO   GM   STP   LTD

Practice

Cross out the words that should not be abbreviated and correct them in the spaces provided.

1. My cous. moved into her own apt. after she had a fight with her parents.

   _____   _____

2. Next Wed. I finish my last class of the semester.

   _____

3. Linda gets depressed when all her charge acct. bills arrive before the first of the mo.

   _____   _____

4. After the mov. men broke my recliner, I wrote an angry letter to the pres. of the co.

   _____   _____   _____

5. Inez has lost fifteen lbs. on the diet she started three wks. ago.

   _____   _____

6. My favor. actor is George C. Scott, esp. in old movies like *Dr. Strangelove.*

   _____   _____

7. That sec. from the temp. agency can type seventy-eight words a min.

   _____   _____   _____

8. My younger bro. is a drum major with his h. s. marching band.

   _____   _____   _____

9. Our new Honda gets twenty-eight miles a gal. on city sts.

   _____   _____

10. At 11:15 A.M., Dr. Liu came out of the hosp. operating rm. and told me that my wife was fine.

   _____   _____

Review Test

Cross out the mistake or mistakes in numbers and abbreviations and correct them in the spaces provided.

1. Nothing was left in the refrigerator except 2 overripe pears.

   _____

2. As usual, the train pulled into the sta. forty min. late.

   _____   _____

3. On Saturdays, the hardware store on Central Avenue doesn't open until ten-fifteen.

   _____

4. Even though I had paid all my premiums on time, my insur. co. refused to reimburse me for my loss.

   _____   _____

5. Dr. Engler's driver's lic. was revoked after he got into a traffic accident on Wayne Ave.

   _____   _____

6. I can still remember when it cost only 8 cents to mail a first-class letter and three cents for a postcard.

   _____

7. Last Wed. I fell asleep at 9 P.M. watching the pres. address a joint session of Congress on television.

   _____   _____

8. My little brother has had bronchitis six times this year and has missed 32 days of school.

   _____

9. The nice thing about double feat. is that you can see two mov. for the price of one.

   _____   _____

10. Can you believe that the thrift shop on Seventeenth Street is selling two-hundred-and-fifty-dollar down coats for $49.95?

    _____

Section 3: Punctuation

End Marks

INTRODUCTORY PROJECT

Add the end mark needed in each of the following sentences.

1. All week I have been feeling depressed
2. What is the deadline for handing in the paper
3. The man at the door wants to know whose car is double-parked
4. That truck ahead of us is out of control

Answers are on page 526.

A sentence always begins with a capital letter. It always ends with a period, a question mark, or an exclamation point.

PERIOD (.)

Use a period after a sentence that makes a statement.

> More single parents are adopting children.
> It has rained for most of the week.

Use a period after most abbreviations.

Mr. Brady	B.A.	Dr. Ballard
Ms. Peters	A.M.	Tom Ricci, Jr.

QUESTION MARK (?)

Use a question mark after a *direct* question.

> When is your paper due?
> How is your cold?
> Tom asked, "When are you leaving?"
> "Why doesn't everyone take a break?" Rosa suggested.

Do not use a question mark after an *indirect* question (a question not in the speaker's exact words).

> She asked when the paper was due.
> He asked how my cold was.
> Tom asked when I was leaving.
> Rosa suggested that everyone take a break.

EXCLAMATION POINT (!)

Use an exclamation point after a word or sentence that expresses strong feeling.

> Come here!
> Ouch! This pizza is hot!
> That truck just missed us!

Note: Be careful not to overuse exclamation points.

Practice

Add a period, a question mark, or an exclamation point, as needed, to each of the following sentences.

1. How long will the store sale continue
2. Watch out for that bump in the road
3. The copper bracelet on her arm helps her arthritis
4. Does Barbara's room always look as if a hurricane came for a visit
5. Dr. Kirby specializes in acupuncture of the wallet
6. Manny, Moe, and Jack are always working on their cars
7. Watch out or you'll step on my sunglasses
8. He asked if I had read Tolkien's *The Lord of the Rings*
9. "It will take hours to clean up this mess " Ellen cried.
10. Little Alan asked his uncle, "Is your mustache a wig "

Apostrophe

INTRODUCTORY PROJECT

1. You're the kind of person who believes he's going to be a big success without doing any hard work, but the world doesn't work that way.

   What is the purpose of the apostrophe in *You're, he's,* and *doesn't?*

   _____

2. the eagle's nest
   Fred's feet
   my mother's briefcase
   the children's drawings
   Babe Ruth's bat

   What is the purpose of the *'s* in all the examples above?

   _____

3. The piles of old books in the attic were starting to decay. One book's spine had been gnawed away by mice.
   Two cars were stolen yesterday from the mall parking lot. Another car's antenna was ripped off.

   In the sentence pairs above, why is the *'s* used in each second sentence but not in the first?

   _____

   _____

Answers are on page 526.

The two main uses of the apostrophe are

1   To show the omission of one or more letters in a contraction.
2   To show ownership or possession.

Each use is explained on the pages that follow.

APOSTROPHE IN CONTRACTIONS

A contraction is formed when two words are combined to make one word. An apostrophe is used to show where letters are omitted in forming the contraction. Here are two contractions:

have + not   = haven't (the *o* in *not* has been omitted)
I + will   = I'll (the *wi* in *will* has been omitted)

The following are some other common contractions:

I + am	= I'm		it + is	= it's
I + have	= I've		it + has	= it's
I + had	= I'd		it + not	= isn't
who + is	= who's		could + not	= couldn't
do + not	= don't		I + would	= I'd
did + not	= didn't		they + are	= they're
let + us	= let's		there + is	= there's

Note: *will* + *not* has an unusual contraction: *won't.*

Practice I

Combine the following words into contractions. One is done for you.

he + is	= ___*he's*___		we + are	= _____
are + not	= _____		has + not	= _____
you + are	= _____		who + is	= _____
they + have	= _____		does + not	= _____
would + not	= _____		where + is	= _____

Practice 2

Write the contraction for the words in parentheses.

Example   He (could not) _____*couldn't*_____ come.

1. (I will) _____ be with you shortly if (you will) _____
    just wait a minute.

2. (It is) _____ such a long drive to the ballpark that Clyde (would
    not) _____ go there if you paid him.

3. You (should not) _____ drink any more if (you are)
    _____ hoping to get home safely.

4. Alice's husband (is not) _____ the aggressive type, and her
    former husbands (were not) _____ either.

5. (I would) _____ like to know (who is) _____ in
    charge of the cash register and why (it is) _____ taking so long
    for this line to move.

Note: Even though contractions are common in everyday speech and in written
dialogue, usually it is best to avoid them in formal writing.

Practice 3

Write five sentences using the apostrophe in different contractions.

1. _____

2. _____

3. _____

4. _____

5. _____

Four Contractions to Note Carefully

Four contractions that deserve special attention are *they're, it's, you're,* and *who's.*
Sometimes these contractions are confused with the possessive words *their, its,
your,* and *whose.* The chart on the following page shows the difference in meaning
between the contractions and the possessive words.

Contractions	*Possessive Words*
they're (means *they are*)	their (means *belonging to them*)
it's (means *it is* or *it has*)	its (means *belonging to it*)
you're (means *you are*)	your (means *belonging to you*)
who's (means *who is*)	whose (means *belonging to whom*)

Note: Possessive words are explained further on page 241.

Practice

Underline the correct form (the contraction or the possessive word) in each of the following sentences. Use the contraction whenever the two words of the contraction (*they are, it is, you are, who is*) would also fit.

1. (They're, Their) going to hold the party in (they're, their) family room.
2. (You're, Your) not going to be invited if you insist on bringing (you're, your) accordion.
3. (Who's, Whose) going with us, and (who's, whose) car are we taking?
4. (It's, Its) too early to go to bed and (it's, its) too late in the day to take a nap.
5. If (your, you're) not going to drive by (they're, their) house, (it's, its) going to be impossible for them to get home tonight.

APOSTROPHE TO SHOW OWNERSHIP OR POSSESSION

To show ownership or possession, we can use such words as *belongs to, owned by,* or (most commonly) *of.*

> the knapsack *that belongs to* Lola
> the house *owned by* my mother
> the sore arm *of* the pitcher

But the apostrophe plus *s* (if the word does not end in *-s*) is often the quickest and easiest way to show possession. Thus we can say:

> Lola's knapsack
> my mother's house
> the pitcher's sore arm

Points to Remember

I   The *'s* goes with the owner or possessor (in the examples given, *Lola, mother,* and *pitcher*). What follows is the person or thing possessed (in the examples given, *knapsack, house,* and *sore arm*). An easy way to determine the owner or possessor is to ask the question "To whom does it belong?" In the first example, the answer to the question "To whom does the knapsack belong?" is *Lola.* Therefore, the *'s* goes with *Lola.*

2   There should always be a break between the word and the *'s.*

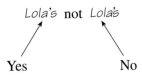

Lola's not Lola's

Yes   No

Practice I

Rewrite the italicized part of each of the sentences below, using the *'s* to show possession. Remember that the *'s* goes with the owner or possessor.

Examples   *The motorcycle owned by Clyde* is a frightening machine.

Clyde's motorcycle

The roommate of my brother is a sweet and friendly person.

My brother's roommate

1. The *sneakers owned by Lola* were stolen.

_____

2. As a joke, he put on *the lipstick that belongs to Veronica.*

_____

3. *The house of his brother* was burglarized.

_____

4. *The tires belonging to the car* are badly worn.

_____

5. *The bicycle owned by Jan* was stolen from the bike rack outside school.

_____

6. I discovered the *nest of the blue jay* while pruning the tree.

_____

7. I don't like *the title of my paper.*

_____

8. *The arthritis of my mother* gets progressively worse.

_____

9. *The boyfriend belonging to my sister* is a gorgeous-looking man.

_____

10. It is a *game belonging to anybody* at this point.

_____

Practice 2

Underline the word in each sentence that needs an 's. Then write the word correctly in the space at the left. One is done for you as an example.

children's   1. The <u>children</u> voices carried downstairs.

_____   2. Georgia husband is not a take-charge guy.

_____   3. My friend computer is also a typewriter.

_____   4. When the teacher anger became apparent, the class quickly grew quiet.

_____   5. His girlfriend apple pie made his stomach rebel.

_____   6. Albert dog looks like a porcupine without its quills.

_____   7. Under the couch were several of our daughter toys.

_____   8. My boss car was stolen.

_____   9. That wine tastes like last night rain.

_____   10. The dentist charged $50 to fix our son tooth.

Practice 3

Add an *'s* to each of the following words to make it the possessor or owner of something. Then write sentences using the words. Your sentences can be serious or playful. One is done for you as an example.

1. Cary _____*Cary's*_____

   _*Cary's hair is bright red.*_____

2. neighbor _____

   _____

3. car _____

   _____

4. sister _____

   _____

5. doctor _____

   _____

Apostrophe versus Possessive Pronouns

Do not use an apostrophe with possessive pronouns. They already show ownership. Possessive pronouns include *his, hers, its, yours, ours,* and *theirs.*

Incorrect	*Correct*
The bookstore lost its' lease.	The bookstore lost its lease.
The racing bikes were theirs'.	The racing bikes were theirs.
The change is yours'.	The change is yours.
His' problems are ours', too.	His problems are ours, too.
His' skin is more tanned than hers'.	His skin is more tanned than hers.

Apostrophe versus Simple Plurals

When you want to make a word plural, just add an *s* at the end of the word. Do *not* add an apostrophe. For example, the plural of the word *movie* is *movies,* not *movie's* or *movies'*. Look at this sentence:

When Sally's cat began catching birds, the neighbors called the police.

The words *birds* and *neighbors* are simple plurals, meaning more than one bird, more than one neighbor. The plural is shown by adding *-s* only. (More information about plurals starts on page 288.) On the other hand, the *'s* after *Sally* shows possession—that Sally owns the cat.

Practice

In the space provided under each sentence, add the one apostrophe needed and explain why the other words ending in *s* are simple plurals.

Example Sarahs yard is full of gophers.

Sarahs: *Sarah's, meaning "yard of Sarah"*

gophers: *simple plural meaning more than one gopher*

1. The sharp odor of the cheese and onions made Rons eyes water.

   onions: _____

   Rons: _____

   eyes: _____

2. My mothers recipe for chicken pot pie is famous among our relatives and friends.

   mothers: _____

   relatives: _____

   friends: _____

3. Sailors ran to their battle stations; the ships alarm had sounded.

   Sailors: _____

   stations: _____

   ships: _____

4. The kites string broke when it got caught in the branches of a tree.

   kites: _____

   branches: _____

5. We met two guys after our colleges football game and went with them to the movies that night.

   guys: _____

   colleges: _____

   movies: _____

6. Originally, the cuffs of mens pants were meant for cigar ashes.

   cuffs: _____

   mens: _____

   pants: _____

   ashes: _____

7. We almost drowned when our inner tubes turned over in the rivers rushing currents.

   tubes: _____

   rivers: _____

   currents: _____

8. That movie directors specialty is films about vampires.

   directors: _____

   films: _____

   vampires: _____

9. The secretary made copies of the companys tax returns for the previous three years.

   copies: _____

   companys: _____

   returns: _____

   years: _____

10. Scientists are exploring Africas Congo region for living relatives of the dinosaurs.

    Scientists: _____

    Africas: _____

    relatives: _____

    dinosaurs: _____

Apostrophe with Plural Words Ending in -s

Plurals that end in -s show possession simply by adding the apostrophe, rather than an apostrophe plus *s*.

Both of my *neighbors'* homes have been burglarized recently.
The many *workers'* complaints were ignored by the company.
All the *campers'* tents were damaged by the hailstorm.

Practice

In each sentence, cross out the one plural word that needs an apostrophe. Then write the word correctly, with the apostrophe, in the space provided.

Example   ___*bosses'*___   My two ~~bosses~~ tempers are much the same: explosive.

_____   1. Icy water from the hose froze on many of the firefighters coats.

_____   2. Other drivers mistakes have led to my three car accidents.

_____   3. Two of my friends cars have been stolen recently.

_____   4. My grandparents television has a 50-inch screen.

_____   5. All of the soldiers uniforms will be replaced.

 ## Review Test I

In each sentence cross out the two words that need apostrophes. Then write the words correctly in the spaces provided.

1. Youre right and Im wrong, though I hate to admit it.

   _____   _____

2. The divers stomach began to cramp as he struggled to the waters surface.

   _____   _____

3. A baby birds throat muscles wont work when its stomach is full.

   _____   _____

4. In the rabbits frenzy to escape the traps hold, it chewed off its hind leg.

   _____   _____

5. If youre rich and caught speeding in Finland, youll pay a stiffer fine than someone who is poorer.

   _____   _____

6. Marlons motorcycle gang roared down Main Street and terrorized the small towns inhabitants.

   _____   _____

7. Im amazed by my sisters perfect recall of how much she has weighed for every important social event.

   _____   _____

8. A golfers chance of making a hole in one is nearly ten times better than a bowlers chance of bowling a perfect game.

   _____   _____

9. If youre thinking of entering the contest, youll need to pay an admission fee of $10.

   _____   _____

10. I flinched as someones hands covered my eyes and a voice said, "Dont turn around."

    _____   _____

 Review Test 2

Rewrite the following sentences, changing the underlined words into either (1) a contraction or (2) a possessive.

1. I do not think the diet of Sarita has helped her lose weight.

   _____

2. I have been warned by friends about the false charms of Michael.

   _____

3. The house of the Murphys uses the rays of the sun as a heating source.

   _____

4. The bill of the plumber was very high, but his work was not very good.

   _____

5. The menu of the restaurant is not very extensive.

   _____

   _____

Quotation Marks

INTRODUCTORY PROJECT

Read the following scene and underline all the words enclosed within quotation marks. Your instructor may also have you dramatize the scene, with one person reading the narration and two persons acting the two speaking parts of Clyde and Sam. The two speakers should imagine the scene as part of a stage play and try to make their words seem as real and true-to-life as possible.

At a party that Clyde and Charlotte recently had, Clyde got angry at a guy named Sam who kept bothering Clyde's wife. "Listen, man," Clyde said, "what's this thing you have for my wife? There are lots of other chicks at this party."

"Be cool," Sam said. "Charlotte is a very sweet person. I enjoy talking with her."

"I'm saying it just one more time," Clyde said. "Lay off my wife or get the blazes out of my party."

Sam, a mean hunk of a man, just looked at Clyde and grinned. "You've got good booze here. Why should I leave? Come on, Charlotte," he said, taking her arm. "Let's sit by the window."

Clyde went to his basement and was back a minute later holding a two-by-four. "I'm giving you a choice," Clyde said. "Leave by the door or I'll slam you out the window."

Sam left by the door.

1. On the basis of the above selection, what is the purpose of quotation marks?

    _____

2. Do commas and periods that come after a quotation go inside or outside the quotation marks?

    _____

Answers are on page 527.

246

The two main uses of quotation marks are:

I   To set off the exact words of a speaker or writer
2   To set off the titles of short works

Each use is explained on the pages that follow.

QUOTATION MARKS TO SET OFF
THE WORDS OF A SPEAKER OR WRITER

Use quotation marks when you want to show the exact words of a speaker or writer:

"Who left the cap off the toothpaste?" Lola demanded.
(Quotation marks set off the exact words that Lola spoke.)

Ben Franklin wrote, "Keep your eyes wide open before marriage, half shut afterward."
(Quotation marks set off the exact words that Ben Franklin wrote.)

"You're never too young," my Aunt Fern often tells me, "to have a heart attack."
(Two pairs of quotation marks are used to enclose the aunt's exact words.)

Maria complained, "I look so old some days. Even makeup doesn't help. I feel as though I'm painting a corpse!"
(Note that the end quotes do not come until the end of Maria's speech. Place quotation marks before the first quoted word of a speech and after the last quoted word. As long as no interruption occurs in the speech, do not use quotation marks for each new sentence.)

Punctuation Hint: In the four examples above, notice that a comma sets off the quoted part from the rest of the sentence. Also observe that commas and periods at the end of a quotation always go *inside* quotation marks.

Complete the following statements that explain how capital letters, commas, and periods are used in quotations. Refer to the four examples as guides.

- Every quotation begins with a ___*Capital*___ letter.
- When a quotation is split (as in the sentence about Aunt Fern), the second part does not begin with a capital letter unless it is a ___*new*___ sentence.
- ___*Commas*___ are used to separate the quoted part of a sentence from the rest of the sentence.
- Commas and periods that come at the end of a quote go _____ quotation marks.

The answers are *capital, new, Commas,* and *inside.*

Practice I

Insert quotation marks where needed in the sentences that follow.

1. "Have more trust in me," Lola said to her mother."
2. The instructor asked Sharon, "Why are your eyes closed?"
3. Christ said, "I come that you may have life, and have it more abundantly."
4. "I refuse to wear those itchy wool pants!" Ralph shouted at his parents.
5. His father replied, "We should give all the clothes you never wear to the Salvation Army."
6. The nervous boy whispered hoarsely over the telephone, "Is Linda home?"
7. "When I was ten," Lola said, "I spent my entire summer playing Monopoly."
8. Tony said, "When I was ten, I spent my whole summer playing basketball."
9. The critic wrote about the play, It runs the gamut of emotions from A to B.
10. "The best way to tell if a mushroom is poisonous," the doctor solemnly explained, "is if you find it in the stomach of a dead person."

Practice 2

Rewrite the following sentences, adding quotation marks where needed. Use a capital letter to begin a quotation, and use a comma to set off a quoted part from the rest of the sentence.

Example I'm getting tired Sally said.

"I'm getting tired," Sally said.

1. Fred said I'm going with you.

   Fred said "I'm going with you."

2. "Everyone passed the test" the instructor informed them.

   _____

3. My parents asked "where were you?"

   _____

4. "I hate that commercial" he muttered."

   _____

5." If you don't leave soon," he warned, "you'll be late for work."

   _____

Practice 3

1. Write three quotations that appear in the first part of a sentence.

Example *"Let's go shopping," I suggested.*

a. _____

b. _____

c. _____

2. Write three quotations that appear at the end of a sentence.

Example *Bob asked, "Have you had lunch yet?"*

a. _____

b. _____

c. _____

3. Write three quotations that appear at the beginning and end of a sentence.

Example *"If the bus doesn't come soon," Mary said, "we'll freeze."*

a. _____

b. _____

c. _____

Indirect Quotations

An indirect quotation is a rewording of someone else's comments rather than a word-for-word direct quotation. The word *that* often signals an indirect quotation.

Direct Quotation	*Indirect Quotation*
George said, "My son is a dare-devil."	George said that his son is a dare-devil.
(George's exact spoken words are given, so quotation marks are used.)	(We learn George's words *in*directly, so no quotation marks are used.)
Carol's note to Arnie read, "I'm at the neighbors'. Give me a call."	Carol left a note for Arnie that said she would be at the neighbors' and he should give her a call.
(The exact words that Carol wrote in the note are given, so quotation marks are used.)	(We learn Carol's words *in*directly, so no quotation marks are used.)

Practice I

Rewrite the following sentences, changing words as necessary to convert the sentences into direct quotations. The first one is done for you as an example.

1. Nick asked Fran if she had mailed the party invitations.

    Nick asked Fran, "Have you mailed the party invitations?"

2. Fran replied that she thought Nick was going to write them this year.

    _____

    _____

3. Nick said that writing invitations was a woman's job.

    _____

    _____

4. Fran exclaimed that Nick was crazy.

    _____

    _____

5. Nick replied that she had much better handwriting than he did.

    _____

    _____

Practice 2

Rewrite the following sentences, converting each direct quotation into an indirect statement. In each case you will have to add the word *that* or *if* and change other words as well.

Example   The barber asked Fred, "Have you noticed how your hair is thinning?"

   The barber asked Fred if he had noticed how his hair was

   thinning.

1.   He said, "As the plane went higher, my heart sank lower."

   _____

2.   The designer said, "Shag rugs are back in style."

   _____ That _____

3.   The foreman asked Jake, "Have you ever operated a lift truck?"

   _____ if he _____

4.   My nosy neighbor asked, "Were Ed and Ellen fighting?"

   _____

5.   Martha complained, "I married a man who eats Tweeties cereal for breakfast."

   _____

   _____

QUOTATION MARKS TO SET OFF
THE TITLES OF SHORT WORKS

Titles of short works are usually set off by quotation marks, while titles of long works are underlined. Use quotation marks to set off the titles of such short works as articles in books, newspapers, or magazines; chapters in a book; short stories; poems; and songs. On the other hand, you should underline the titles of books, newspapers, magazines, plays, movies, record albums, and television shows. See the examples on the next page.

Note: In printed form the titles of long works are set off by italics—slanted type that looks *like this.*

Quotation Marks	*Underlines*
the article "The Toxic Tragedy"	in the book Who's Poisoning America
the article "New Cures for Headaches"	in the newspaper The New York Times
the article "When the Patient Plays Doctor"	in the magazine Family Health
the chapter "Connecting with Kids"	in the book Straight Talk
the story "The Dead"	in the book Dubliners
the poem "Birches"	in the book The Complete Poems of Robert Frost
the song "Some Enchanted Evening"	in the album South Pacific
	the television show Jeopardy
	the movie Rear Window

Practice

Use quotation marks or underlines as needed.

1. The young couple opened their brand-new copy of Cooking Made Easy to the chapter titled Meat Loaf Magic.

2. Annabelle borrowed Hawthorne's novel The Scarlet Letter from the library because she thought it was about a varsity athlete.

3. Did you know that the musical West Side Story is actually a modern version of Shakespeare's tragedy Romeo and Juliet?

4. I used to think that Richard Connell's short story The Most Dangerous Game was the scariest piece of suspense fiction in existence—until I began reading Bram Stoker's classic novel Dracula.

5. Every year at Easter, we watch a movie like The Robe on television.

6. During the past year, Time featured an article about DNA titled Building Blocks of the Future.

7. My father still remembers the way that Julie Andrews sang I Could Have Danced All Night in the original Broadway production of My Fair Lady.

8. As I stand in the supermarket checkout line, I always look at a feature titled Life in These United States in the <u>Reader's Digest</u>.

9. My favorite Simon and Garfunkel song is Mrs. Robinson, which can be found in their album <u>Bookends</u>.

10. Absentmindedly munching a Dorito, Hana opened the latest issue of <u>News-week</u> to its cover story, The Junk Food Explosion.

OTHER USES OF QUOTATION MARKS

I To set off special words or phrases from the rest of a sentence:

Many people spell the words "all right" as one word, "alright," instead of correctly spelling them as two words.
I have trouble telling the difference between "principal" and "principle."

2 To mark off a quote within a quote. For this purpose, single quotes (' ') are used:

Ben Franklin said, "The noblest question in the world is, 'What good may I do in it?'"
"If you want to have a scary experience," Nick told Fran, "read Stephen King's story 'The Mangler' in his book *Night Shift*."

 Review Test I

Place quotation marks around the exact words of a speaker or writer in the sentences that follow.

1. Is something wrong with your car again? the mechanic asked Fred.

2. Murphy's law states, Whatever can go wrong, will.

3. John Kennedy once said, Ask not what your country can do for you; ask what you can do for your country.

4. The sign read, Be careful how you drive. You may meet a fool.

5. Martha said, Turn on the burglar alarm when you leave the house, Fred.

6. Tony asked the struggling old lady if he could help with her heavy bag. Go to blazes, you masher, she said.

7. Listen, I confided to my sister, Neil told me he is going to ask you to go out with him.

8. The sign in the tough Western saloon read, Carry out your own dead.

9. When the ball hit Willie Wilson in the head and bounced into the outfield, Eric remarked, That was a heads-up play.

10. A woman who was one of Winston Churchill's political enemies once remarked to him, If you were my husband, I would put poison in your coffee. Churchill's reply was, Madam, if I were your husband, I would drink it.

 ## Review Test 2

1. Write a sentence in which you quote a favorite expression of someone you know. Identify the relationship of the person to you.

   Example *My brother Sam often says after a meal, "That wasn't bad*
   _____
                at all."
   _____

   _____

   _____

2. Write a quotation that contains the words *Tony asked Lola*. Write a second quotation that includes the words *Lola replied*.

   _____

   _____

   _____

3. Write a sentence that interests or amuses you from a book. Identify the title and author of the book.

   Example *In her book At Wit's End, Erma Bombeck advises, "Never go to a*
   _____
                doctor whose office plants have died."
   _____

   _____

   _____

   _____

4. Write a sentence that interests you from a newspaper. Identify the title and the author (if given) of the article.
5. Write a sentence that interests you from a magazine. Identify the title and the author of the article.

_____

_____

_____

Review Test 3

Go through the comics section of a newspaper to find a comic strip that amuses you. Be sure to choose a strip where two or more characters are speaking to each other. Write a full description that will enable people who have not read the comic strip to visualize it clearly and appreciate its humor. Describe the setting and action in each panel and enclose the words of the speakers in quotation marks.

Comma

INTRODUCTORY PROJECT

A comma often (though not always) signals a minor break or pause in a sentence. Each of the six pairs of sentences below illustrates one of six main uses of the comma. Read each pair of sentences aloud and place a comma wherever you feel a slight pause occurs.

1. a. Joel watched the eleven o'clock news a movie a *Honeymooners* rerun and the station sign-off.
    b. Please endorse your check write your account number on the back and fill out a deposit slip.

2. a. Even though I was safe indoors I shivered at the thought of the bitter cold outside.
    b. To start the car depress the accelerator and then turn the ignition key.

3. a. The opossum an animal much like the kangaroo carries its young in a pouch.
    b. George Derek who was recently arrested was a high school classmate of mine.

4. a. I had enrolled in the course during preregistration but my name did not appear on the class list.
    b. A police cruiser blocked the busy intersection and an ambulance pulled up on the sidewalk near the motionless victims.

5. a. Emily said "Why is it so hard to remember your dreams the next day?"
    b. "After I left the interview" said David "I couldn't remember a word I had said."

6. a. Hollis has driven over 1500000 accident-free miles in his job as a long-distance trucker.
    b. The Gates Trucking Company of 1800 Industrial Highway Jersey City New Jersey gave Hollis an award on October 23 1992 for his superior safety record.

Answers are on page 528.

SIX MAIN USES OF THE COMMA

Commas are used mainly as follows:

1 To separate items in a series.
2 To set off introductory material.
3 On both sides of words that interrupt the flow of thought in a sentence.
4 Between two complete thoughts connected by *and, but, for, or, nor, so, yet.*
5 To set off a direct quotation from the rest of a sentence.
6 For certain everyday material.

You may find it helpful to remember that the comma often marks a slight pause, or break, in a sentence. These pauses or breaks occur at the points where the six main comma rules apply. Read aloud the sentence examples given on the following pages for each of the comma rules and listen for the minor pauses or breaks that are signaled by commas.

At the same time, you should keep in mind that commas are far more often overused than underused. As a general rule, you should *not* use a comma unless a given comma rule applies or unless a comma is otherwise needed to help a sentence read clearly. A good rule of thumb is that "when in doubt" about whether to use a comma, it is often best to "leave it out."

After reviewing each of the comma rules that follow, you will practice adding commas that are needed and omitting commas that are not needed.

1 Comma between Items in a Series

Use a comma to separate items in a series.

Magazines, paperback novels, and textbooks crowded the shelves.
Hard-luck Sam needs a loan, a good-paying job, and a close friend.
Pat sat in the doctor's office, checked her watch, and chewed gum nervously.
Lola bit into the ripe, juicy apple.
More and more people entered the crowded, noisy stadium.

Note

A comma is used between two descriptive words in a series only if *and* inserted between the words sounds natural. You could say:

Lola bit into the ripe *and* juicy apple.
More and more people entered the crowded *and* noisy stadium.

But notice in the following sentences that the descriptive words do not sound natural when *and* is inserted between them. In such cases, no comma is used.

The model wore a light sleeveless blouse. ("A light *and* sleeveless blouse" doesn't sound right, so no comma is used.)

Dr. Van Helsing noticed two tiny puncture marks on his patient's neck. ("Two *and* tiny puncture marks" doesn't sound right, so no comma is used.)

Practice 1

Place commas between items in a series.

1. Becky brought a cake iced with red white and blue frosting to the Fourth of July picnic.
2. My brother did the laundry helped clean the apartment waxed the car and watched ABC's *Wide World of Sports*.
3. You can make a Big Mac by putting two all-beef patties special sauce lettuce cheese pickles and onions on a sesame-seed bun.

Practice 2

Cross out the one comma that is not needed. Add the one comma that is needed between items in a series.

1. Cold eggs burnt bacon, and watery orange juice are the reasons, I've never returned to that diner for breakfast.
2. Bill relaxes, by reading Donald Duck Archie, and Bugs Bunny comic books.
3. Tonight I've got to work at the restaurant for three hours finish writing a paper, and study, for an exam.

2 Comma after Introductory Material

Use a comma to set off introductory material.

Fearlessly, Lola picked up the slimy slug.

Just to annoy Tony, she let it crawl along her arm.

Although I have a black belt in karate, I decided to go easy on the demented bully who had kicked sand in my face.

Mumbling under her breath, the woman picked over the tomatoes.

Note:

a   If the introductory material is brief, the comma is sometimes omitted. In the activities here, you should include the comma.

b   A comma is also used to set off extra material placed at the end of a sentence. Here are two earlier sentences in the book where this comma rule applied:

I spent all day at the employment office, trying to find a job that suited me.
Tony has trouble accepting criticism, except from Lola.

Practice 1

Place commas after introductory material.

1.   When I didn't get my paycheck at work I called up the business office. According to the office computer I was dead.
2.   After seeing the accident Susan wanted to stop driving forever. Even so she went driving to work next morning over the ice-covered roads.
3.   To get her hair done Faye goes to a beauty salon all the way across town. Once there she enjoys listening to the gossip in the beauty shop. Also she likes looking through *Cosmopolitan* and other magazines in the shop.

Practice 2

Cross out the one comma that is not needed. Add the one comma that is needed after introductory material.

1.   Even though Tina had an upset stomach she went bowling with her husband.
2.   Looking back over the last ten years I can see several decisions I made that really changed my life.
3.   Instead of going with my family to the mall I decided to relax at home and to call up some friends.

3   Commas around Words Interrupting the Flow of Thought

Use a comma on both sides of words that interrupt the flow of thought in a sentence.

The car, cleaned and repaired, is ready to be sold.
Martha, our new neighbor, used to work as a bouncer at Rexy's Tavern.
Taking long walks, especially after dark, helps me sort out my thoughts.

Usually you can "hear" words that interrupt the flow of thought in a sentence. However, if you are not sure if certain words are interrupters, remove them from the sentence. If it still makes sense without the words, you know the words are interrupters and that the information they give is nonessential. Such nonessential information is set off with commas. In the following sentence,

> Susie Hall, who is my best friend, won a new car in the *Reader's Digest* sweepstakes.

the words *who is my best friend* are extra information, not needed to identify the subject of the sentence, *Susie Hall.* Put commas around such nonessential information. On the other hand, in the sentence

> The woman who is my best friend won a new car in the *Reader's Digest* sweepstakes.

the words *who is my best friend* supply essential information needed for us to identify the woman. If the words were removed from the sentence, we would no longer know which woman won the sweepstakes. Commas are not used around such essential information.

Here is another example:

> *The Shining,* a novel by Stephen King, is the scariest book I've ever read.

Here the words *a novel by Stephen King* are extra information, not needed to identify the subject of the sentence, *The Shining.* Commas go around such nonessential information. On the other hand, in the sentence

> Stephen King's novel *The Shining* is the scariest book I've ever read.

the words *The Shining* are needed to identify the novel. Commas are not used around such essential information.

Most of the time you will be able to "hear" words that interrupt the flow of thoughts in a sentence and will not have to think about whether the words are essential or nonessential.[*]

---

[*] Some instructors refer to nonessential or extra information that is set off by commas as a *nonrestrictive* clause or phrase. Essential information that interrupts the flow of thought is called a *restrictive* clause or phrase. No commas are used to set off a restrictive clause.

Practice 1

Add commas to set off interrupting words.

1. Friday is the deadline, the absolute final deadline, for your papers to be turned in.
2. The nursery rhyme told how the cow, a weird creature, jumped over the moon. The rhyme also related how the dish, who must also have been strange, ran away with the spoon.
3. Tod, voted the most likely to succeed in our high school graduating class, has just made the front page of our newspaper. He was arrested with other members of the King Kongs, a local motorcycle gang, for creating a disturbance in the park.

Practice 2

Cross out the one comma that is not needed. Add the two commas that are needed to set off interrupting words.

1. My sister's cat, which she got from the animal shelter, woke her, when her apartment caught on fire.
2. A bulging biology textbook, its pages stuffed with notes, and handouts, lay on the path to the college parking lot.
3. A baked potato, with its crispy skin and soft inside, rates as one of my all-time favorite, foods.

4   Comma between Complete Thoughts Connected by a Joining Word

Use a comma between two complete thoughts connected by *and, but, for, or, nor, so, yet.*

My parents threatened to throw me out of the house, so I had to stop playing the drums.

The polyester bed sheets had a gorgeous design on them, but they didn't feel as comfortable as plain cotton sheets.

The teenage girls walked the hot summer streets, and the teenage boys drove by in their shined-up cars.

Notes

a The comma is optional when the complete thoughts are short:

Hal relaxed but Bob kept working.
The soda was flat so I poured it away.
We left school early for the furnace broke down.

b Be careful not to use a comma in sentences having *one* subject and a *double* verb. The comma is used only in sentences made up of two complete thoughts (two subjects and two verbs). In the sentence

Mary lay awake that stormy night and listened to the thunder crashing.

there is only one subject (*Mary*) and a double verb (*lay* and *listened*). No comma is needed. Likewise, the sentence

The quarterback kept the ball and plunged across the goal line for a touchdown.

has only one subject (*quarterback*) and a double verb (*kept* and *plunged*); therefore, no comma is needed.

Practice

Place a comma before a joining word that connects two complete thoughts (two subjects and two verbs). The four sentences that have only one subject and a double verb do not need commas.

1. The outfielder raced to the warning track and caught the fly ball over his shoulder.
2. The sun set in a golden glow behind the mountain and a single star sparkled in the night sky.
3. Arturo often tries to cut back on his eating but he always gives up after a few days.
4. Her voice became very dry during the long speech and beads of perspiration began to appear on her forehead.
5. Cheryl learned two computer languages in high school and then began writing her own programs.

6. I spent all of Saturday morning trying to fix my car, but I still wound up taking it to a garage in the afternoon.
7. She felt like shouting but didn't dare open her mouth.
8. He's making a good living selling cosmetics to beauty shops, but he still has regrets about not having gone to college.
9. Crazy Bill often goes into bars and asks people to buy him a drink.
10. He decided not to take the course in advanced math, for he wanted to have time for a social life during the semester.

5   Comma with Direct Quotations

Use a comma to set off a direct quotation from the rest of a sentence.

> "Please take a number," said the deli clerk.
> Fred told Martha, "I've just signed up for a Dale Carnegie course."
> "Those who sling mud," a famous politician once said, "usually lose ground."
> "Reading this book," complained Stan, "is about as interesting as watching paint dry."

Note: A comma or a period at the end of a quotation goes inside quotation marks. See also page 247.

Practice 1

Add commas to set off quotations from the rest of the sentence.

1. "I can't wait to have a fish filet and some fries," said Lola to Tony as she pulled into the order lane at the fast-food restaurant. She asked, "What can I get you, Tony?"
2. "Two quarter-pounders with cheese, two large fries, and a large Coke," responded Tony.
3. "Good grief," said Lola. "It's hard to believe you don't weigh three hundred pounds. In fact," she continued, "how much do you weigh?".

Practice 2

Cross out the one comma that is not needed. Add the commas that are needed to set off a quotation from the rest of a sentence.

1. "You better hurry," Thelma's mother warned, "or you're going to miss the last bus, of the morning."
2. "It really worries me," said Marty, "that you haven't seen a doctor, about that strange swelling under your arm."
3. The student sighed in frustration, and then raised his hand. "My computer has crashed again," he called out to the instructor.

6   Comma with Everyday Material

Use a comma with certain everyday material as shown in the following sections.

Persons Spoken To

Sally, I think that you should go to bed.
Please turn down the stereo, Mark.
Please, sir, can you spare a dollar?

Dates

Our house was burglarized on October 28, 1997, and two weeks later on November 11, 1997.

Addresses

Lola's sister lives at Greenway Village, 342 Red Oak Drive, Los Angeles, California 90057.

Note: No comma is used before the zip code.

Openings and Closings of Letters

Dear Vanessa,   Sincerely,
Dear John,   Truly yours,

Note: In formal letters, a colon is used after the opening:

Dear Sir:
Dear Madam:

Numbers

Government officials estimate that Americans spend about 785,000,000 hours a year filling out federal forms.

Practice

Place commas where needed.

1. I am sorry sir but you cannot sit at this table.
2. On May 6 1954 Roger Bannister became the first person to run a mile in under four minutes.
3. Redeeming the savings certificate before June 30 2000 will result in a substantial penalty.
4. A cash refund of one dollar can be obtained by sending proof of purchase to Seven Seas P.O. Box 760 El Paso Texas 79972.
5. Leo turn off that TV set this minute!

UNNECESSARY USE OF COMMAS

Remember that if no clear comma rule applies for using a comma, it is usually better not to use a comma. As stated earlier, "when in doubt, leave it out." Following are some typical examples of unnecessary commas.

Sharon told me, that my socks were different colors.
(A comma is not used before *that* unless the flow of thought is interrupted.)

The union negotiations, dragged on for three days.
(Do not use a comma between a simple subject and verb.)

I waxed all the furniture, and cleaned the windows.
(Use a comma before *and* only with more than two items in a series or when *and* joins two complete thoughts.)

Jasmin carried, the baby into the house.
(Do not use a comma between a verb and its object.)

I had a clear view, of the entire robbery.
(Do not use a comma before a prepositional phrase.)

Practice

Cross out the one comma that does not belong in each sentence. Do not add any commas.

1. When I arrived to help with the moving, Jerome said to me, that the work was already done.
2. After the flour and milk have been mixed, eggs must be added, to the recipe.
3. Because my sister is allergic to cat fur, and dust, our family does not own a cat or have any dust-catching drapes or rugs.
4. The guys on the corner, asked, "Have you ever taken karate lessons?"
5. As the heavy Caterpillar tractor, rumbled up the street, our house windows rattled.
6. Las Vegas, Miami Beach, San Diego, and Atlantic City, are the four places she has worked as a bartender.
7. Thomas Farley, the handsome young man, who just took off his trousers, is an escaped mental patient.
8. Hal wanted to go to medical school, but he does not have the money, and was not offered a scholarship.
9. Joyce reads, a lot of fiction, but I prefer stories that really happened.
10. Because Mary is single, her married friends do not invite her, to their parties.

Review Test I

Insert commas where needed. In the space provided under each sentence, summarize briefly the rule that explains the use of the comma or commas.

1. After I fell and fractured my wrist I decided to sell my skateboard.

   _____

2. She asked her son "Are you going to church with me tomorrow?"

   _____

3. The weather bureau predicts that sleet fire or brimstone will fall on Washington today.

   _____

4. The ignition system in his car as well as the generator was not working properly.

   _____

5. Tony asked Lola "Have you ever had nightmares in which some kind of monster was ready to swallow you?"

   _____

6. They attacked their bathroom with Lysol Comet and Fantastik.

   _____

7. The pan of bacon fat heating on the stove burst into flame and he quickly set a lid on the pan to put out the fire.

   _____

8. Clyde's bad cough which he had had for almost a week began to subside.

   _____

9. I wear thick socks while hiking but I still return from a trip with blistered feet.

   _____

10. When they found pencil shavings in the soup the guests decided they were not hungry.

   _____

Review Test 2

1. Write a sentence telling of three items you want to get the next time you go to the store. _____

   _____

2. Write a sentence that describes three things you would like to get done this week. _____

   _____

3. Write two sentences, starting the first one with *If a prowler came into my bedroom* and the second one with *Also.* _____

   _____

   _____

   _____

4. Write two sentences describing how you relax after getting home from school or work. Start the first sentence with *After* or *When.* Start the second sentence with *Next.* _____

   _____

   _____

   _____

   _____

5. Write a sentence about a selfish or generous person you know. Use the words *a selfish person* or *a generous person* right after his or her name.

   _____

   _____

6. Write a sentence that tells something about your favorite magazine or television show. Use the words *which is my favorite magazine* or *which is my favorite television show* after the name of the magazine or show.

   _____

   _____

7. Write two complete thoughts about foods you enjoy. Use *and* to join the two complete thoughts. _____

   _____

8. Write two complete thoughts about a person you know. The first thought should tell of something you like about the person. The second thought should tell of something you don't like. Join the thoughts with *but*.

   _____

   _____

   _____

9. Invent a line that Lola might say to Tony. Use the words *Lola said* in the

   sentence. _____

   _____

10. Write a remark that you made to someone today. Use the words *I said*

    somewhere in the middle of the sentence. _____

    _____

 ## Review Test 3

On separate paper, write six sentences, with each sentence demonstrating one of the six main comma rules.

Other Punctuation Marks

COLON (:)

The colon is a mark of introduction. Use the colon at the end of a complete statement to do the following:

1 Introduce a list.

My little brother has three hobbies: playing video games, racing his Hot Wheels cars all over the floor, and driving me crazy.

2 Introduce a long quotation.

Janet's paper was based on a passage from George Eliot's novel *Middlemarch:* "If we had a keen vision and feeling of all ordinary human life, it would be like hearing the grass grow and the squirrel's heart beat, and we should die of that roar which lies on the other side of silence. As it is, the quickest of us walk about well wadded with stupidity."

3 Introduce an explanation.

There are two ways to do this job: the easy way and the right way.

Two minor uses of the colon are after the opening in a formal letter (*Dear Sir or Madam:*) and between the hour and the minute when writing the time (*The bus will leave for the game at 11:45*).

Practice

Place colons where needed.

1. Lin had an excellent excuse for being late for work an early-morning power failure that stopped her alarm clock.
2. I ordered the following items from Sears two pairs of jeans, four plaid flannel shirts, and a wide leather belt.
3. In her speech, Mrs. Wagner quoted William Hazlitt "Man is the only animal that laughs and weeps, for he is the only animal that is struck with the difference between what things are and what they ought to be."

SEMICOLON (;)

The semicolon signals more of a pause than the comma alone but not quite the full pause of a period. Use a semicolon to do the following:

1   Join two complete thoughts that are not already connected by a joining word such as *and, but, for,* or *so.*

The chemistry lab blew up; Professor Thomas was fired.
I once stabbed myself with a pencil; a black mark has been under my skin ever since.

2   Join two complete thoughts that include a transitional word such as *however, otherwise, moreover, furthermore, therefore,* or *consequently.*

I cut and raked the grass; moreover, I weeded the lawn.
Sally finished typing the paper; however, she forgot to bring it to class.

Note: The first two uses of the semicolon are treated in more detail on pages 117–118.

3   Mark off items in a series when the items themselves contain commas.

This fall I won't have to work on Labor Day, September 7; Veterans' Day, November 11; or Thanksgiving Day, November 26.
At the final Weight Watchers' meeting, prizes were awarded to Sally Johnson, for losing 20 pounds; Irving Ross, for losing 26 pounds; and Betty Mills, the champion loser, who lost 102 pounds.

Practice

Place semicolons where needed.

1.   There's an old saying about law school: in the first year, they scare you to death in the second year, they work you to death and in the third year, they bore you to death.
2.   I find some television commercials for soap ads ridiculous for example, people are always grinning as the shower spray pelts their teeth.
3.   The following persons have been elected to the National Board of Bank Executives: Ellen Green, First National Bank Jay Hunt, Fidelity State Bank and M. O. Granby, Farmers' Regional Bank.

DASH (—)

A dash signals a degree of pause longer than a comma but not as complete as a period. Use the dash to set off words for dramatic effect.

I suggest—no, I insist—that you stay for dinner.

The prisoner walked toward the electric chair—grinning.

A meaningful job, a loving wife, and a car that wouldn't break down all the time—these are the things he wanted in life.

Practice

Place dashes where needed.

1. The car is in excellent condition except that the brakes don't always work.
2. I can be ready in ten minutes in fact, I'm ready now.
3. Hunting, fishing, and doing odd jobs around the house rather than going to work these are the activities I enjoy.

HYPHEN (-)

Use a hyphen in the following ways:

I With two or more words that act as a single unit describing a noun.

The society ladies nibbled at the deep-fried grasshoppers.

A white-gloved waiter then put some snails on their table.

Note: Your dictionary will often help when you are unsure about whether to use a hyphen between words.

2 To divide a word at the end of a line of writing or typing.

Although it had begun to drizzle, the teams decided to play the champion-ship game that day.

Notes

a Always divide a word between syllables. Use your dictionary (see page 278) to be sure of correct syllable divisions.

b Do not divide words of one syllable.

c Do not divide a word if you can avoid dividing it.

Practice

Place hyphens where needed.

1. I went food shopping with about sixty five dollars in my pocket and came back with about sixty five cents.
2. The ten year old girl was remarkably self confident when she was giving her speech.
3. My wife's aunt and uncle, who live in a split level house, have been unable to prevent mildew from forming on the walls of the lower level.

PARENTHESES ( )

Use parentheses to do the following:

1 Set off extra or incidental information from the rest of a sentence.

The chapter on drugs in our textbook (pages 142–178) contains some frightening statistics.
The normal body temperature of a cat (101 to 102°) is 3° higher than the temperature of its owner.

2 Enclose letters or numbers that signal items in a series.

Three steps to follow in previewing a textbook are to (1) study the title, (2) read the first and last paragraphs, and (3) study the headings and subheadings.

Note: Do not use parentheses too often in your writing.

Practice

Add parentheses where needed.

1. For tomorrow we must study the charts pages 16–20 in the first chapter of our biology text.
2. To make better use of your time, you should prepare 1 a daily list of things to do and 2 a weekly study schedule.
3. A recent study revealed that people who are heavy coffee drinkers five or more cups a day suffer many more ill effects than those whose coffee intake is less.

Review Test 1

At the appropriate spot or spots, place the punctuation mark shown in the margin.

Example   The singles dance was a success I met several people I wanted to see again.

:
1. Before you go anywhere, finish your chores the laundry, the dishes, and the vacuuming.

—
2. The Easter Bunny, Santa Claus, and the Tooth Fairy these were the idols of my youth.

-
3. Tom's self important manner makes him boring to be with.

( )
4. The two most important steps in writing an effective paper are 1 to make a point of some kind and 2 to provide specific evidence to support that point.

:
5. Albert Einstein once said "It is in fact nothing short of a miracle that the modern methods of instruction have not yet entirely strangled the holy curiosity of inquiry; for this delicate little plant, aside from stimulation, stands mainly in need of freedom; without this it goes to wrack and ruin without fail."

;
6. Sally bought a second remote-control unit for the television set as a result, she can change the channels as often as her husband does.

—
7. I asked the waiter to return the steak which seemed to consist of more fat than meat to the kitchen.

-
8. Fred always brings a pair of wide angle binoculars to the football games.

( )
9. The television set is relatively new having been bought only a year ago but has been to the repair shop three times.

;
10. Angelo had a lot of studying to do: for sociology, he had to read two articles for his math course, he had to interpret an entire page of graphs and for English, he had to catch up on his journal.

Review Test 2

On separate paper, write two sentences for each of the following punctuation marks: colon, semicolon, dash, hyphen, parentheses.

Section 4: Word Use

Dictionary Use

INTRODUCTORY PROJECT

The dictionary is an indispensable tool, as will be apparent if you try to answer the following questions *without* using the dictionary.

1. Which one of the following words is spelled incorrectly?

   fortutious   macrobiotics   stratagem

2. If you wanted to hyphenate the following word correctly, at which points would you place the syllable divisions?

   h i e r o g l y p h i c s

3. What common word has the sound of the first *e* in the word *chameleon?*
4. Where is the primary accent in the following word?

   o c/t o/g e/n a r/i/a n

5. What are two separate meanings of the word *earmark?*

Your dictionary is a quick and sure authority on all these matters: spelling, syllabication, pronunciation, and word meanings. And as the chapter ahead will show, it is a source for many other kinds of information as well.

Answers are on page 529.

The dictionary is a valuable tool. To take advantage of it, you need to understand the main kinds of information that a dictionary gives about a word. Look at the information provided for the word *dictate* in the following entry from the *American Heritage Dictionary,* paperback edition.*

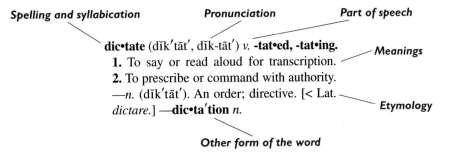

Spelling and syllabication   Pronunciation   Part of speech

dic•tate (dĭk′tāt′, dĭk-tāt′) *v.* **-tat•ed, -tat•ing.**
1. To say or read aloud for transcription.
2. To prescribe or command with authority.
—*n.* (dĭk′tāt′). An order; directive. [< Lat. *dictare.*] —**dic•ta′tion** *n.*

Meanings

Etymology

Other form of the word

SPELLING

The first bit of information, in the boldface (heavy type) entry itself, is the spelling of *dictate.* You probably already know the spelling of *dictate,* but if you didn't, you could find it by pronouncing the syllables in the word carefully and then looking it up in the dictionary.

Use your dictionary to correct the spelling of the following words:

alright _____   elavater _____

assosiation _____   plesure _____

awkwerd _____   balence _____

diferent _____   beleiving _____

omited_____   libary _____

opinyon_____   apetite _____

critikal_____   happyness _____

embarasment_____   usualy _____

probaly _____   suprise _____

* © 1983 Houghton Mifflin Company. Reprinted by permission from *American Heritage Dictionary of the English Language,* Paperback Edition.

SYLLABICATION

The second bit of information that the dictionary gives, also in the boldface entry, is the syllabication of *dic•tate*. Note that a dot separates each syllable (or part) of the word.

Use your dictionary to mark the syllable divisions in the following words. Also indicate how many syllables are in each word.

b e l i e v e	(_____ syllables)
t r e a c h e r o u s	(_____ syllables)
d i s s a t i s f i e d	(_____ syllables)
u n p r e c e d e n t e d	(_____ syllables)

Noting syllable divisions will enable you to *hyphenate* a word: divide it at the end of one line of writing and complete it at the beginning of the next line. You can correctly hyphenate a word only at a syllable division, and you may have to check your dictionary to make sure of a particular word's syllable divisions.

PRONUNCIATION

The third bit of information in the dictionary entry is the pronunciation of *dictate:* (dĭk'tāt') or (dĭk-tāt'). You already know how to pronounce *dictate,* but if you did not, the information within the parentheses would serve as your guide. Use your dictionary to complete the following exercises that relate to pronunciation.

Vowel Sounds

You will probably use the pronunciation key in your dictionary mainly as a guide to pronouncing different vowel sounds (vowels are the letters *a, e, i, o,* and *u*). Here is the pronunciation key that appears on every other page of the paperback *American Heritage Dictionary:*

ă pat ā pay â care ä father ĕ pet ē be ĭ pit ī tie î pier ŏ pot ō toe ô paw, for oi noise oŏ took o͞o boot ou out th thin *th* this ŭ cut û urge yo͞o abuse zh vision ə about, item, edible, gallop, circus

The key tells you, for example, that the sound of the short *a* is pronounced like the *a* in *pat,* the sound of the long *a* is like the *a* in *pay,* and the sound of the short *i* is like the *i* in *pit.*

Now look at the pronunciation key in your dictionary. The key is probably located in the front of the dictionary or at the bottom of every page. What common word in the key tells you how to pronounce each of the following sounds?

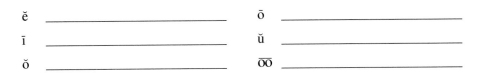

ĕ _____   ō _____

ī _____   ŭ _____

ŏ _____   o͞o _____

(Note that the long vowel always has the sound of its own name.)

The Schwa (ə)

The symbol ə looks like an upside-down *e.* It is called a *schwa,* and it stands for the unaccented sound in such words as *about, item, edible, gallop,* and *circus.* More approximately, it stands for the sound *uh*—like the *uh* that speakers sometimes make when they hesitate. Perhaps it would help to remember that *uh,* as well as ə, could be used to represent the schwa sound.

Here are some of the many words in which the sound appears: *socialize* (sō′shə līz or sō′shuh līz); *legitimate* (lə jĭt′ə mĭt or luh jĭt′uh mĭt); *oblivious* (ə blĭv′ē əs or uh blĭv′ē uhs). Open your dictionary to any page, and you will almost surely be able to find three words that make use of the schwa in the pronunciation in parentheses after the main entry. Write three such words and their pronunciations in the following spaces:

1. _____

2. _____

3. _____

Accent Marks

Some words contain both a primary accent, shown by a heavy stroke (′), and a secondary accent, shown by a lighter stroke (′). For example, in the word *vicissitude* (vĭ sĭs′ĭ to͞od′), the stress, or accent, goes chiefly on the second syllable (sĭs′), and, to a lesser extent, on the last syllable (to͞od′).

Use your dictionary to add stress marks to the following words:

soliloquy (sə lĭl ə kwē)
diatribe (dī ə trīb)
rheumatism (ro͞o mə tīz əm)
representation (rĕp rĭ zĕn tā shən)

Full Pronunciation

Use your dictionary to write out the full pronunciation (the information given in parentheses) for each of the following words:

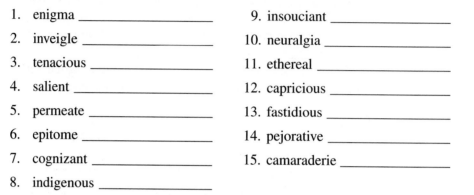

1. enigma _____
2. inveigle _____
3. tenacious _____
4. salient _____
5. permeate _____
6. epitome _____
7. cognizant _____
8. indigenous _____

9. insouciant _____
10. neuralgia _____
11. ethereal _____
12. capricious _____
13. fastidious _____
14. pejorative _____
15. camaraderie _____

Now practice pronouncing each word. Use the pronunciation key in your dictionary as an aid to sounding out each syllable. Do *not* try to pronounce a word all at once; instead, work on mastering *one syllable at a time*. When you can pronounce each of the syllables in a word successfully, then say them in sequence, add the accent, and pronounce the entire word.

OTHER INFORMATION ABOUT WORDS

Parts of Speech

The dictionary entry for *dictate* includes the abbreviation *v.* This means that the meanings of *dictate* as a verb will follow. The abbreviation *n.* is then followed by the meaning of *dictate* as a noun.

At the front of your dictionary, you will probably find a key that will explain the meanings of abbreviations used in the dictionary. Use the key to fill in the meanings of the following abbreviations:

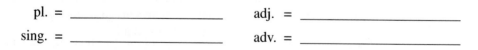

pl. = _____   adj. = _____

sing. = _____   adv. = _____

Principal Parts of Irregular Verbs

Dictate is a regular verb and forms its principal parts by adding *-d, -d,* and *-ing* to the stem of the verb. When a verb is irregular, the dictionary lists its principal parts. For example, with *begin* the present tense comes first (the entry itself, *begin*). Next comes the past tense (*began*), and then the past participle (*begun*)—the form of the verb used with such helping words as *have, had,* and *was.* Then comes the present participle (*beginning*)—the *-ing* form of the word.

Look up the principal parts of the following irregular verbs and write them in the spaces provided. The first one has been done for you.

Present	Past	Past Participle	Present Participle
see	saw	seen	seeing
go			
ride			
speak			

Plural Forms of Irregular Nouns

The dictionary supplies the plural forms of all irregular nouns (regular nouns form the plural by adding *-s* or *-es*). Give the plurals of the following nouns:

cemetery   _____

knife   _____

veto   _____

neurosis   _____

Note: See page 295 for more information about plurals.

Meanings

When a word has more than one meaning, the meanings are numbered in the dictionary, as with the verb *dictate.* In many dictionaries, the most common meanings are presented first. The introductory pages of your dictionary will explain the order in which meanings are presented.

Use the sentence context to try to explain the meaning of the underlined word in each of the following sentences. Write your definition in the space provided. Then look up and record the dictionary meaning of the word. Be sure you pick out the meaning that fits the word as it is used in the sentence.

1. The surgeons first <u>flushed</u> the patient's chest cavity with sterile fluid.

   Your definition: _____

   Dictionary definition: _____

2. Several well-known actors make <u>cameo</u> appearances in the director's first movie.

   Your definition: _____

   Dictionary definition: _____

   _____

3. The spy story was so <u>riveting</u> I stayed awake till 2 A.M. reading it.

   Your definition: _____

   Dictionary definition: _____

Etymology

Etymology refers to the history of a word. Many words have origins in foreign languages, such as Greek (Gk) or Latin (L). Such information is usually enclosed in brackets and is more likely to be present in a hardbound desk dictionary than in a paperback one. Good desk dictionaries include the following:

The American Heritage Dictionary
The Random House College Dictionary
Webster's New Collegiate Dictionary
Webster's New World Dictionary

A good desk dictionary will tell you, for example, that the word *cannibal* derives from the name of the man-eating tribe, the Caribs, that Christopher Columbus discovered on Cuba and Haiti.

See if your dictionary says anything about the origins of the following words.

bikini _____

_____

sandwich _____

_____

tantalize _____

_____

breakfast _____

_____

Usage Labels

As a general rule, use only standard English words in your writing. If a word is not standard English, your dictionary will probably give it a usage label like one of the following: *informal, nonstandard, slang, vulgar, obsolete, archaic, rare.*

Look up the following words and record how your dictionary labels them. Remember that a recent hardbound desk dictionary will always be the best source of information about usage.

break (meaning *a stroke of luck*) _____

ain't _____

uptight _____

well-heeled _____

cop-out _____

Synonyms

A *synonym* is a word that is close in meaning to another word. Using synonyms helps you avoid unnecessary repetition of the same word in a paper. A paperback dictionary is not likely to give you synonyms for words, but a good desk dictionary will. (You might also want to own a *thesaurus,* a book that lists synonyms and antonyms. An *antonym* is a word approximately opposite in meaning to another word.)

Consult a desk dictionary that gives synonyms for the following words, and write the synonyms in the spaces provided.

fear _____

answer _____

love _____

Review Test

Items 1–5: Use your dictionary to answer the following questions.

1. How many syllables are in the word *cinematography?* _____

2. Where is the primary accent in the word *domesticity?* _____

3. In the word *oppressive,* the *o* is pronounced like
   a. schwa.
   b. short *o.*
   c. long *u.*
   d. long *o.*

4. In the word *culpable,* the *a* is pronounced like
   a. short *a.*
   b. long *a.*
   c. short *i.*
   d. schwa.

5. In the word *negotiate,* the first *e* is pronounced like
   a. short *e.*
   b. long *e.*
   c. schwa.
   d. short *i.*

Items 6–10: There are five misspelled words in the following sentence. Cross out each misspelled word and write the correct spelling in the spaces provided.

The college I plan to transferr to will accept my psikology credits, the counseler told me, but I will not recieve credit for my courses in introductory mathamatics and basic English.

6. _____

7. _____

8. _____

9. _____

10. _____

Spelling
Improvement

INTRODUCTORY PROJECT

See if you can circle the word that is misspelled in each of the following pairs:

akward	*or*	awkward
exercise	*or*	exercize
business	*or*	buisness
worried	*or*	worryed
shamful	*or*	shameful
begining	*or*	beginning
partys	*or*	parties
sandwichs	*or*	sandwiches
heroes	*or*	heros

Answers are on page 529.

Poor spelling often results from bad habits developed in early school years. With work, such habits can be corrected. If you can write your name without misspelling it, there is no reason why you can't do the same with almost any word in the English language. Following are seven steps you can take to improve your spelling.

STEP 1: USING THE DICTIONARY

Get into the habit of using the dictionary. When you write a paper, allow yourself time to look up the spelling of all those words you are unsure about. Do not overlook the value of this step just because it is such a simple one. Just by using the dictionary, you can probably make yourself a 95 percent better speller.

STEP 2: KEEPING A PERSONAL SPELLING LIST

Keep a list of words you misspell and study the words regularly. Use the space on the inside front cover of this book as a starter. When you accumulate additional words, you may want to use a back page of your English notebook.

Hint: When you have trouble spelling long words, try to break each word down into syllables and see whether you can spell the syllables. For example, *misdemeanor* can be spelled easily if you can hear and spell in turn its four syllables: *mis-de-mean-or.* The word *formidable* can be spelled easily if you hear and spell in turn its four syllables: *for-mi-da-ble.* Remember, then: try to see, hear, and spell long words in terms of their syllable parts.

STEP 3: MASTERING COMMONLY CONFUSED WORDS

Master the meanings and spellings of the commonly confused words on pages 298–314. Your instructor may assign twenty words for you to study at a time and give you a series of quizzes until you have mastered all the words.

STEP 4: USING ELECTRONIC AIDS

There are three electronic aids that may help your spelling. First, many *electronic typewriters* on the market today will beep automatically when you misspell or mistype a word. They include built-in dictionaries that will then give you the correct spelling. Smith-Corona, for example, has a series of portable typewriters with an "Auto-Spell" feature that start at around $100 at discount stores.

Second, a *computer with a spell-checker* will identify incorrect words and suggest correct spellings. If you know how to write on a computer, you will have no trouble learning how to use the spell-check feature.

Third, *electronic spell-checkers* are pocket-size devices that look much like the pocket calculators you may carry to your math class. They are the latest example of how technology can help the learning process. Electronic spellers can be found in the typewriter or computer section of any discount store, at prices in the $100 range. The checker includes a tiny keyboard. You type out the word the way you think it is spelled, and the checker quickly provides you with the correct spelling of related words. Some of these checkers even *pronounce* the word aloud for you.

STEP 5: UNDERSTANDING BASIC SPELLING RULES

Explained briefly here are three rules that may improve your spelling. While exceptions sometimes occur, the rules hold true most of the time.

1   ***Change y to i.***   When a word ends in a consonant plus *y*, change *y* to *i* when you add an ending.

try	+	ed	=	tried	marry	+	es	= marries
worry	+	es	=	worries	lazy	+	ness	= laziness
lucky	+	ly	=	luckily	silly	+	est	= silliest

2   ***Final silent e.***   Drop a final *e* before an ending that starts with a vowel (the vowels are *a, e, i, o,* and *u*).

hope	+	ing	=	hoping	sense	+	ible	= sensible
fine	+	est	=	finest	hide	+	ing	= hiding

Keep the final *e* before an ending that starts with a consonant.

use	+	ful	=	useful	care	+	less	= careless
life	+	like	=	lifelike	settle	+	ment	= settlement

3 *Doubling a final consonant.* Double the final consonant of a word when all the following are true:

a The word is one syllable or is accented on the last syllable.
b The word ends in a single consonant preceded by a single vowel.
c The ending you are adding starts with a vowel.

sob	+	ing	=	sobbing	big	+	est	= biggest
drop	+	ed	=	dropped	omit	+	ed	= omitted
admit	+	ing	=	admitting	begin	+	ing	= beginning

Practice

Combine the following words and endings by applying the three rules above.

1. study + ed   = _____
2. advise + ing   = _____
3. carry + es   = _____
4. stop + ing   = _____
5. terrify + ed   = _____

6. compel + ed   = _____
7. retire + ing   = _____
8. hungry + ly   = _____
9. expel + ing   = _____
10. judge + es   = _____

STEP 6: UNDERSTANDING PLURALS

Most words form their plurals by adding *-s* to the singular.

Singular	*Plural*
blanket	blankets
pencil	pencils
street	streets

Some words, however, form their plurals in special ways, as shown in the rules that follow.

l Words ending in *-s, -ss, -z, -x, -sh,* or *-ch* usually form the plural by adding *-es.*

kiss	kisses		inch	inches
box	boxes		dish	dishes

2   Words ending in a consonant plus *y* form the plural by changing *y* to *i* and adding *-es.*

party	parties	county	counties
baby	babies	city	cities

3   Some words ending in *f* change the *f* to *v* and add *-es* in the plural.

leaf	leaves	life	lives
wife	wives	yourself	yourselves

4   Some words ending in *o* form their plurals by adding *-es.*

potato	potatoes	mosquito	mosquitoes
hero	heroes	tomato	tomatoes

5   Some words of foreign origin have irregular plurals. When in doubt, check your dictionary.

antenna	antennae	crisis	crises
criterion	criteria	medium	media

6   Some words form their plurals by changing letters within the word.

man	men	foot	feet
tooth	teeth	goose	geese

7   Combined words (words made up of two or more words) form their plurals by adding *-s* to the main word.

brother-in-law	brothers-in-law
passer-by	passers-by

Practice

Complete these sentences by filling in the plural of the word at the left.

grocery   1. I carried six bags of _____ into the house.

town   2. How many _____ did you visit during the tour?

supply   3. While the Lone Ranger waited at the campsite, Tonto rode into town to get

    some _____.

body   4. Because the gravediggers were on strike, _____ piled up in the
    morgue.

lottery   5. She plays two state _____ in hopes of winning a fortune.

pass   6. Hank caught six _____ in a losing cause.

tragedy   7. That woman has had to endure many _____ in her life.

watch   8. I have found that cheap _____ work better for me than expensive
    ones.

suit   9. To help himself feel better, he went out and bought two _____ .

boss   10. I have not one but two _____ to worry about every day.

STEP 7: MASTERING A BASIC WORD LIST

Make sure you can spell all the words in the following list. They are some of the
words used most often in English. Again, your instructor may assign twenty words
for you to study at a time and give you a series of quizzes until you have mastered
the words.

ability	among	bargain	cereal
absent	angry	beautiful	certain
accident	animal	because	change
across	another	become	cheap
address	20 answer	before	chief
advertise	anxious	begin	children
advice	apply	being	church
after	approve	believe	cigarette
again	argue	between	clothing
against	around	40 bottom	collect
all right	attempt	breathe	color
almost	attention	building	comfortable
a lot	awful	business	company
always	awkward	careful	condition
although	balance	careless	60 conversation

daily
danger
daughter
decide
death
deposit
describe
different
direction
distance
doubt
dozen
during
each
early 120
earth
education
either
English
80 enough
entrance
everything
examine
exercise
expect
family
flower
foreign
friend
garden
general
grocery
guess
happy
heard 140
heavy
height
himself
holiday
100 house
however
hundred
hungry
important
instead

intelligence
interest
interfere
kitchen
knowledge
labor
language
laugh
leave
length
lesson
letter
listen
loneliness
making
marry
match
matter
measure
medicine
middle
might
million
minute
mistake
money
month
morning
mountain
much 180
needle
neglect
newspaper
noise
none
nothing
number
ocean
offer
often
omit
only
operate
opportunity
original

ought
pain
paper
pencil
people 200
perfect
period
personal
picture
place
pocket
possible
potato
president
pretty
problem
promise
property
psychology
public
question
quick
raise
ready
really 220
reason
receive
recognize
remember
repeat
restaurant
ridiculous
said
same
sandwich
send
sentence
several
shoes
should
since
sleep
smoke
something
soul 240

started
state
straight
street
strong
student
studying
success
suffer
surprise
teach
telephone
theory
thought
thousand
through
ticket
tired
today
together
tomorrow
tongue
tonight
touch
travel
truly
understand
unity
until
upon
usual
value
vegetable
view
visitor
voice
warning
watch
welcome
window
would
writing
written
year
yesterday

Review Test

Use the three spelling rules to spell the following words.

1. cry   +   es   = _____ cries

2. believe +   able = _____ believable

3. bury   +   ed   = _____ buried

4. date   +   ing   = _____ dating

5. lonely   +   est   = _____ loneliest

6. large   +   er   = _____ larger

7. skim   +   ed   = _____ skimmed

8. rare   +   ly   = _____ rarely

Circle the correctly spelled plural in each pair.

9. beliefs	believs
10. churchs	churches
11. bullys	bullies
12. countries	countrys
13. womans	women
14. potatos	potatoes

Circle the correctly spelled word (from the basic word list) in each pair.

15. foreign	foriegn
16. condicion	condition
17. restarant	restaurant
18. opportunity	oportunity
19. entrance	enterance
20. surprise	surprize

Omitted Words and Letters

INTRODUCTORY PROJECT

Some people drop small connecting words such as *of, and,* or *in* when they write. They may also drop the *-s* endings of plural nouns. See if you can find and circle the six places with dropped letters or words in the passage below.

Two glass bottle of apple juice lie broken the supermarket aisle. Suddenly, a toddler who has gotten away from his parents appears at the head of the aisle. He spots the broken bottles and begins to run toward them. His chubby body lurches along like wind-up toy, and his arm move excitedly up and down. Luckily, alert shopper quickly reacts to the impending disaster and blocks the toddler's path. Then the shopper waits with crying, frustrated little boy until his parents show up.

Answers are on page 530.

Be careful not to leave out words or letters when you write. The omission of words like *a, an, of, to,* or *the* or the *-s* ending needed on nouns or verbs may confuse and irritate your readers. They may not want to read what they regard as careless work.

FINDING OMITTED WORDS AND LETTERS

Finding omitted words and letters, like finding many other sentence-skills mistakes, is a matter of careful proofreading. You must develop your ability to look carefully at a page to find places where mistakes may exist.

The exercises here will give you practice in finding omitted words and omitted *-s* endings on nouns. Another section of this book (pages 128–129) gives you practice in finding omitted *-s* endings on verbs.

Practice

Add the missing word (*a, an, the, of,* or *to*) as needed.

Example Some people regard television as *a* tranquilizer that provides
temporary relief from *the* pain and anxiety *of* modern life.

1. When I began eating box of chicken I bought at the fast-food restaurant, I found several pieces that consisted of lot crust covering nothing but chicken bones.

2. Sally had instructor who tried light a piece of chalk, thinking it was cigarette.

3. In his dream, Harry committed perfect crime: he killed his enemy with icicle, so murder weapon was never found.

4. Dr. Yutzer told me not worry about sore on my foot, but I decided to get second opinion.

5. As little girl ate vanilla sugar cone, ice cream dripped out hole at the bottom onto her pants.

6. When thick black clouds began form and we felt several drops rain, we knew picnic would be canceled.

7. After spending most her salary on new clothes, Susan looks like something out of fashion magazine.

8. As wasps buzzed around room, I ran for can of Raid.

9. Sam put pair wet socks in oven, for he wanted dry them out quickly.

10. Because weather got hot and stayed hot for weeks, my flower garden started look like dried flower arrangement.

The Omitted -s Ending

The plural form of regular nouns usually ends in -s. One common mistake that some people make with plurals is to omit this -s ending. People who drop the ending from plurals when speaking also tend to do it when writing. This tendency is especially noticeable when the meaning of the sentence shows that a word is plural.

> Ed and Mary pay two hundred dollar a month for an apartment that has only two room.

The -s ending has been omitted from *dollars* and *rooms*.

The activities that follow will help you correct the habit of omitting the -s endings from plurals.

Practice I

Add -s endings where needed.

Example   Bill beat me at several game of darts.

1. When Rita's two boyfriend met each other last night, they almost came to blow.

2. My brother let out a choice selection of curse when he dropped his watch in the sand.

3. We were expected to write an essay of several paragraph on key event leading up to the Civil War.

4. Sunlight reflected off the windshield of the many car in the parking lot.

5. A number of house along the elevated subway route have been torn down to make room for two new highway that are being built.

6. Rainy day depress me, especially during those time when I am depressed already.

7. Our drive along the shoreline was marred by the billboard that seem to have popped up everywhere.

8. There were no folding chair in the room; instead, people were asked to sit on pillow spread around the floor.

9. From the top of either of those watchtower, you can see four different state.

10. Motorist waited restlessly as several tow truck worked to remove the tractor trailer spread-eagled across the highway.

Practice 2

Write sentences that use plural forms of the following pairs of words.

Example   girl, bike   *The little girls raced their bikes down the street.*

1. paper, grade _____

   _____

2. pillow, bed _____

   _____

3. sock, shoe _____

   _____

4. day, night _____

   _____

5. game, loss _____

   _____

Note: People who drop the -*s* ending on nouns also tend to omit endings on verbs. Pages 128–130 will help you correct the habit of dropping endings on verbs.

Review Test I

In each of the following sentences, two small connecting words are needed. Write them in the spaces provided, and write a caret (∧) at each place in the sentence where a connecting word should appear.

_____   1.   Like ostriches, the two men hunched over car's hood buried their heads in
_____   the engine.

_____   2.   Each time I put my bare foot down on hot asphalt road, I think I left layer of
_____   skin behind.

_____   3.   Lisa sneaked out of diner when the waitress wasn't looking; she didn't have
_____   enough money leave a tip.

_____   4.   Vince held lighted match to his car door, trying unfreeze the lock.
_____

_____   5.   I can't remember the name the book we were assigned read for Friday's class.
_____

Review Test 2

Add the two -s endings needed in each sentence.

_____   1.   Fred keeps two giant jar of multicolored vitamin on the counter.
_____

_____   2.   The grimy fingerprint of the workers had smudged the electric switchplate in
_____   the living and dining rooms.

_____   3.   If I could just get together a thousand dollar, I think all my money problem
_____   could be solved.

_____   4.   Lola had big plan for the weekend, but all Tony wanted to do was watch a series
_____   of football game on television.

_____   5.   When Eddie opened the package of shirt from the laundry, he discovered that
_____   many button were missing.

Commonly Confused Words

HOMONYMS

The commonly confused words shown below (also known as *homonyms*) have the same sounds but different meanings and spellings. Complete the activities for each set of words, and check off and study the words that give you trouble.

all ready	pair	threw
already	pear	through
brake	passed	to
break	past	too
		two
coarse	peace	
course	piece	wear
		where
hear	plain	
here	plane	weather
		whether
hole	principal	
whole	principle	whose
		who's
its	right	
it's	write	your
		you're
knew	than	
new	then	
know	their	
no	there	
	they're	

all ready   completely prepared
already   previously; before

We were *all ready* to go, for we had eaten and packed *already* that morning.

Fill in the blanks: I was _____ to start ordering breakfast when I found out that the restaurant had _____ shifted to its luncheon menu.

Write sentences using *all ready* and *already.*

_____

_____

brake   stop
break   come apart

Dot slams the *brake* pedal so hard that I'm afraid I'll *break* my neck in her car.

Fill in the blanks: Al tried to put the _____ on his appetite, but the luscious rum cake made him _____ all his resolutions.

Write sentences using *brake* and *break*.

_____

_____

coarse   rough
course   part of a meal; a school subject; direction; certainly (with *of*)

During the *course* of my career as a waitress, I've dealt with some very *coarse* customers.

Fill in the blanks: Weaving a coarse wall hanging with _____ yarns is part of the arts and crafts _____.

Write sentences using *coarse* and *course*.

_____

_____

hear   perceive with the ear
here   in this place

If I *hear* another insulting ethnic joke *here*, I'll leave.

Fill in the blanks: My mother always says, "Come _____ if you can't _____ what I'm saying."

Write sentences using *hear* and *here*.

_____

_____

hole   an empty spot
whole   entire

> If there is a *hole* in the tailpipe, I'm afraid we will have to replace the *whole* exhaust assembly.

Fill in the blanks: The _____ in the wallboard gives the _____ living room a neglected look.

Write sentences using *hole* and *whole.*

_____

_____

its   belonging to it
it's   shortened form for *it is* or *it has*

> The kitchen floor has lost *its* shine because *it's* been used as a roller skating rink by the children.

Fill in the blanks: _____ the chemistry course with _____ lab requirement that worries me.

Write sentences using *its* and *it's.*

_____

_____

knew   past tense of *know*
new   not old

> We *knew* that the *new* television comedy would be canceled quickly.

Fill in the blanks: If you _____ in advance all the _____ turns your life would take, you might give up.

Write sentences using *knew* and *new.*

_____

_____

know   to understand
no   a negative

I never *know* who might drop in even though *no* one is expected.

Fill in the blanks: When that spoiled boy's parents say _____ to him, we all _____ a temper tantrum is likely to result.

Write sentences using *know* and *no.*

_____

_____

pair   a set of two
pear   a fruit

The dessert consisted of a *pair* of thin biscuits topped with vanilla ice cream and poached *pear* halves.

Fill in the blanks: The grove of _____ trees is one of the places where the _____ of escaped convicts was spotted last week.

Write sentences using *pair* and *pear.*

_____

_____

passed   went by; succeeded in; handed to
past   by, as in "I drove past the house"; a time before the present

After Edna *passed* the driver's test, she drove *past* all her friends' houses and honked the horn.

Fill in the blanks: In her _____ jobs, Nadia had _____ up several opportunities for promotion because she did not want to seem aggressive.

Write sentences using *passed* and *past.*

_____

_____

peace   calm
piece   a part

> The *peace* of the little town was shattered when a *piece* of a human body was found in the town dump.

Fill in the blanks: The judge promised to give the troublemaker more than just

a _____ of his mind if the boy ever disturbed the

_____ again.

Write sentences using *peace* and *piece*.

_____

_____

plain   simple
plane   aircraft

> The *plain* box contained a very expensive model *plane* kit.

Fill in the blanks: That _____ -looking man boarding the

_____ is actually a famous movie director.

Write sentences using *plain* and *plane.*

_____

_____

principal main; a person in charge of a school; amount of money borrowed
principle a law or standard

> My *principal* goal in child rearing is to give my daughter strong *principles* to live by.

Fill in the blanks: The school _____ defended the school's

_____ regarding a dress code for students.

Write sentences using *principal* and *principle.*

_____

_____

Note: It might help to remember that the *e* in *principle* is also in *rule*—the meaning of *principle*.

right   correct; opposite of *left;* privilege
write   what you do in English

It is my *right* to refuse to *write* my name on your petition.

Fill in the blanks: Ellen wanted to _____ and thank Steve for his flowers, but she didn't think it _____ to keep leading him on.

Write sentences using *right* and *write.*

_____

_____

than   used in comparisons
then   at that time

I glared angrily at my boss, and *then* I told him our problems were more serious *than* he suspected.

Fill in the blanks: I went to the front porch to get my newspaper, and _____ I made my breakfast. The news on the front page was no more cheerful _____ it had been the day before.

Write sentences using *than* and *then.*

_____

_____

Note: It might help to remember that *then* is also a time signal.

their   belonging to them
there   at that place; a neutral word used with verbs like *is, are, was, were, have,* and *had*
they're   shortened form of *they are*

The tenants *there* are complaining because *they're* being cheated by *their* landlords.

Fill in the blanks: Indians once lived _____, building a unique culture within _____ cliff cities; now _____ gone.

Write sentences using *their, there,* and *they're.*

_____

_____

_____

threw   past tense of *throw*
through from one side to the other; finished

> When a character in a movie *threw* a cat *through* the window, I had to close my eyes.

Fill in the blanks: My favorite sweat socks went _____ hundreds of washings before they started to disintegrate; then my mother _____ them away.

Write sentences using *threw* and *through.*

_____

_____

to   a verb part, as in *to smile;* toward, as in "I'm going to heaven."
too overly, as in "The pizza was too hot"; also, as in "The coffee was hot, too."
two the number 2

> Lola drove *to* the store *to* get some ginger ale. (The first *to* means *toward;* the second *to* is a verb part that goes with *get.*)
> The sport jacket is *too* tight; the slacks are tight, *too.* (The first *too* means *overly;* the second *too* means *also.*)
> The *two* basketball players leaped for the jump ball. (2)

Fill in the blanks: _____ Arlene, the _____ holidays just meant _____ much company and _____ little rest.

Write sentences using *to, too,* and *two.*

_____

_____

_____

wear   to have on
where   in what place

I work at a nuclear reactor, *where* one must *wear* a radiation-detection badge at all times.

Fill in the blanks: If you _____ your jacket buttoned up, no one will see _____ the stain is.

Write sentences using *wear* and *where.*

_____

_____

weather   atmospheric conditions
whether   if it happens that; in case; if

Because of the threatening *weather,* it's not certain *whether* or not the game will be played.

Fill in the blanks: The _____ is glorious, but I don't know _____ the water is warm enough for swimming.

Write sentences using *weather* and *whether.*

_____

_____

whose   belonging to whom
who's   shortened form for *who is* and *who has*

The man *who's* the author of the latest diet book is a man *whose* ability to cash in on the latest craze is well known.

Fill in the blanks: Rashad is determined to find out _____ van is in the street and _____ been watching him from it with binoculars.

Write sentences using *whose* and *who's.*

_____

_____

your   belonging to you
you're   shortened form of *you are*

Since *your* family has a history of heart disease, *you're* the kind of person who should take extra health precautions.

Fill in the blanks: When _____ always the last person chosen for a team, _____ self-confidence dwindles away.

Write sentences using *your* and *you're.*

_____

_____

OTHER WORDS FREQUENTLY CONFUSED

Following is a list of other words that people frequently confuse. Complete the activities for each set of words, and check off and study the ones that give you trouble.

a	beside	fewer
an	besides	less
accept	can	former
except	may	latter
advice	clothes	loose
advise	cloths	lose
affect	desert	quiet
effect	dessert	quite
among	does	though
between	dose	thought

a   Both *a* and *an* are used before other words to mean, approximately, *one.*
an

Generally you should use *an* before words starting with a vowel (*a, e, i, o, u*):

   an absence   an exhibit   an idol   an offer   an upgrade

Generally you should use *a* before words starting with a consonant (all other letters):

   a pen   a ride   a digital clock   a movie   a neighbor

Fill in the blanks: Lola bought her mother _____ orchid and _____ slinky nightgown for her birthday.

Write sentences using *a* and *an.*

_____

_____

accept   receive; agree to
except   exclude; but

   If I *accept* your advice, I'll lose all my friends *except* you.

Fill in the blanks: _____ for one detail, my client is willing to _____ this offer.

Write sentences using *accept* and *except.*

_____

_____

advice   noun meaning *an opinion*
advise   verb meaning *to counsel, to give advice*

   Jake never listened to his parents' *advice,* and he ended up listening to a cop *advise* him of his rights.

Fill in the blanks: Martha Grencher's doctor said, "I _____ you to follow my diet rather than take the _____ of the minister who promised you could lose weight through prayer."

Write sentences using *advice* and *advise.*

_____

_____

affect   verb meaning *to influence*
effect   verb meaning *to bring about something;* noun meaning *result*

My sister Sally cries for *effect,* but my parents caught on and her act no longer *affects* them.

Fill in the blanks: The loud music began to _____ my hearing, creating a high-pitched ringing _____ in my ears.

Write sentences using *affect* and *effect.*

_____

_____

among   implies three or more
between implies only two

We selfishly divided the box of candy *between* the two of us rather than *among* all the members of the family.

Fill in the blanks: _____ the twenty-five girls on the camping trip, arguments developed only _____ the two counselors.

Write sentences using *among* and *between.*

_____

_____

beside   along the side of
besides in addition to

Fred sat *beside* Martha. *Besides* them, there were ten other people at the Tupperware party.

Fill in the blanks: I love this class; _____ the fact that the course has thought-provoking content, I sit _____ a Tom Cruise look-alike.

Write sentences using *beside* and *besides.*

_____

_____

can   refers to the ability to do something
may   refers to permission or possibility

If you *can* work overtime on Saturday, you *may* take Monday off.

Fill in the blanks: When she _____ speak English fluently, she _____ be eligible for that job.

Write sentences using *can* and *may.*

_____

_____

clothes   articles of dress
cloths   pieces of fabric

I tore up some old *clothes* to use as polishing *cloths.*

Fill in the blanks: I keep some _____ next to me to wipe up any food spills before they reach the baby's _____.

Write sentences using *clothes* and *cloths.*

_____

_____

desert   noun meaning *a stretch of dry land;* verb meaning *to abandon one's post or duty*
dessert   noun meaning *last part of a meal*

Don't *desert* us now; order a sinful *dessert* along with us.

Fill in the blanks: When it's time to order _____, that man's appetite will never _____ him.

Write sentences using *desert* and *dessert.*

_____

_____

does   form of the verb *do*
dose   an amount of medicine

Martha *does* not realize that a *dose* of brandy is not the best medicine for the flu.

Fill in the blanks: _____ she understand the importance of taking only the prescribed _____?

Write sentences using *does* and *dose.*

_____

_____

fewer   used with things that can be counted
less   refers to amount, value, or degree

I missed *fewer* classes than Rafael, but I wrote *less* effectively than he did.

Fill in the blanks: I've had _____ attacks of nerves since I began drinking _____ coffee.

Write sentences using *fewer* and *less.*

_____

_____

former   refers to the first of two items named
latter   refers to the second of two items named

I turned down both the service station job and the shipping clerk job; the *former* involved irregular hours and the *latter* offered very low pay.

Fill in the blanks: Howard doesn't like babies or dogs: the _____ cry when they see him and the _____ try to bite him.

Write sentences using *former* and *latter.*

_____

_____

Note: Be sure to distinguish *latter* from *later* (meaning *after some time*). Very often people will use the word *latter* when in fact they mean *later.*

loose   not fastened; not tight-fitting
lose   misplace; fail to win

I am afraid I'll *lose* my ring: it's too *loose* on my finger.

Fill in the blanks: Lola told Tony, "You look dumpy when you wear a

_____ -fitting shirt. You _____ all the wonderful

lines of your chest."

Write sentences using *loose* and *lose.*

_____

_____

quiet   peaceful
quite   entirely; really; rather

After a busy day, the children were still not *quiet,* and their parents were
quite tired.

Fill in the blanks: My friends regarded Bob as _____ a catch, but

he was just too _____ for me.

Write sentences using *quiet* and *quite.*

_____

_____

though   despite the fact that
thought   past tense of *think*

Though I enjoyed the dance, I *thought* the cover charge of $5 was too high.

Fill in the blanks: _____ Pam is now content, she once

_____ her unhappiness would never end.

Write sentences using *though* and *thought.*

_____

_____

INCORRECT WORD FORMS

Following is a list of incorrect word forms that people sometimes use in their writing. Complete the activities for each word, and check off and study the words that give you trouble.

being that	could of	would of
can't hardly	must of	irregardless
couldn't hardly	should of	

being that   Incorrect! Use *because* or *since*.

I'm going to bed now ~~being that~~ *because* I must get up early tomorrow.

Correct the following sentences.

1. Being that she's a year older than I am, Mary thinks she can run my life.

2. I think school will be canceled, being that the bus drivers are on strike.

3. Being that I didn't finish the paper, I didn't go to class.

can't hardly   Incorrect! Use *can hardly* or *could hardly*.
couldn't hardly

Small store owners ~~can't~~ *can* hardly afford to offer large discounts.

Correct the following sentences.

1. I can't hardly understand why Nelson would cut class when he's madly in love with the instructor.

2. You can't hardly imagine how I felt when I knocked over my aunt's favorite plant.

3. You couldn't hardly see last night because of the heavy fog.

could of Incorrect! Use *could have, must have, should have, would have.*
must of
should of
would of

I should ~~of~~ *have* applied for a loan when my credit was good.

Correct the following sentences.

1. Anita must of gone home from work early.

2. I should of started reading the textbook early in the semester.

3. If the game had been canceled, they would of been very disappointed.

4. If Shirelle had wanted to, she could of come with us.

irregardless   Incorrect! Use *regardless.*

~~Irregardless~~ *Regardless* of what anyone says, he will not change his mind.

Correct the following sentences.

1. They decided to buy the house irregardless of the price.

2. That company insures people irregardless of their age or state of health.

3. Irregardless of the risk, I started mountain climbing as a hobby.

 Review Test 1

These sentences check your understanding of *its, it's; there, their, they're; to, too, two;* and *your, you're.* Underline the correct word in the parentheses. Rather than guess, look back at the explanations of the words when necessary.

1. Some stores will accept (your, you're) credit card but not (your, you're) money.

2. I know (its, it's) late, but (its, it's) important to get this job done properly.

3. (There, Their, They're) is a good baseball game down at the playground, but (there, their, they're) (to, too, two) busy to walk down (there, their, they're).

4. (Its, It's) been an hour since I put the TV dinner in the oven, but (its, it's) still not ready.

5. (There, Their, They're) going to be away for (to, too, two) weeks and want me to go over to (there, their, they're) yard to water (there, their, they're) rosebushes.

6. (Your, You're) going to have to do a better job on (your, you're) final exam if you expect to pass the course.

7. That issue is (to, too, two) hot for any politician (to, too, two) handle.

8. If (your, you're) hoping to get good grades on (your, you're) essay tests, you need to improve (your, you're) handwriting.

9. (There, Their, They're) planning to trade in (there, their, they're) old car for a new one before taking (there, their, they're) vacation.

10. (Your, You're) going to have to put aside individual differences and play together for the benefit of (your, you're) team.

Review Test 2

The sentences that follow check your understanding of a variety of commonly confused words. Underline the correct word in the parentheses. Rather than guess, look back at the explanations of the words when necessary.

1. I try to get (through, threw) each day without a cigarette. Once I (through, threw) away my latest magazines because their tempting cigarette ads were (affecting, effecting) my resolve.

2. We weren't sure (whether, weather) or not a storm was brewing until several hours had passed. (Then, Than) the air became (quiet, quite), clouds formed, and we (knew, new) enough to run indoors.

3. (Being that, Since) "Stormy (Weather, Whether)" is her favorite song, I (should of, should have) gotten her an album with that song on it.

4. Take my (advice, advise) and hurry down (to, too, two) the radio station. You'll get a (pair, pear) of free tickets to the rock concert.

5. For Lola the (principal, principle) (course, coarse) of the meal—a (desert, dessert) of French vanilla ice cream and blueberry pie—was yet (to, too, two) come.

6. (Its, It's) obvious why people are not eating the cheese; (there, their, they're) frightened by (its, it's) unusual smell.

7. The first (course, coarse) of the meal was soup. Its (principal, principle) ingredient was onion, to which I'm allergic. Trying to be polite, I ate one mouthful, but (than, then) I began to sneeze uncontrollably.

8. As he (passed, past) by the church, he (though, thought) of the Sunday mornings he had spent (there, their, they're) in the (passed, past).

9. The night after I watched the chiller movie, I dreamed that (a, an) gigantic (hole, whole) opened up in the earth, swallowed a whole city, and (than, then) tried to swallow me, (to, too, two).

10. "I'm going to let you be my (knew, new) woman," the man declared. "(Your, You're) my (peace, piece) of property from now on."

"(Whose, Who's) messed up (your, you're) head?" the woman replied. "I can't believe I (hear, here) you (right, write). (Where, Wear) are you at? I think you have been (affected, effected) by the sun."

 Review Test 3

On separate paper, write short sentences using the ten words shown below.

there	then	you're	affect	who's
past	advise	too (meaning *also*)	its	break

Effective Word Choice

INTRODUCTORY PROJECT

Put a check beside the sentence in each pair that you feel makes more effective use of words.

1. After the softball game, we wolfed down a few burgers and drank a couple of brews. _____

   After the softball game, we ate hamburgers and drank beer. _____

2. A little birdie told me you're getting married next month. _____

   Someone told me you're getting married next month. _____

3. The personality adjustment inventories will be administered on Wednesday.

   _____

   Psychological tests will be given on Wednesday. _____

4. I must say I think that the referee in the game, in my personal opinion, made the right decision in the situation. _____

   I think the referee made the right decision. _____

Now see if you can circle the correct number in each case:

Pair (1, 2, 3, 4) contains a sentence with slang; pair (1, 2, 3, 4) contains a sentence with a cliché; pair (1, 2, 3, 4) contains a sentence with pretentious words; and pair (1, 2, 3, 4) contains a wordy sentence.

Answers are on page 531.

Choose your words carefully when you write. Always take the time to think about your word choices rather than simply using the first word that comes to mind. You want to develop the habit of selecting words that are appropriate and exact for your purposes. One way you can show your sensitivity to language is by avoiding slang, clichés, pretentious words, and wordiness.

SLANG

We often use slang expressions when we talk because they are so vivid and colorful. However, slang is usually out of place in formal writing. Here are some examples of slang expressions:

> The party was a *real horror show.*
> I don't want to *lay a guilt trip* on you.
> Our boss is not *playing with a full deck.*
> Dad *flipped out* when he learned that Jan had *totaled* the car.

Slang expressions have a number of drawbacks. They go out of date quickly, they become tiresome if used excessively in writing, and they may communicate clearly to some readers but not to others. Also, the use of slang can be an evasion of the specific details that are often needed to make one's meaning clear in writing. For example, in "The party was a real horror show," the writer has not provided the specific details about the party necessary for us to understand the statement clearly. Was it the setting, the food and drink (or lack of same), the guests, the music, the hosts, the writer, or what that made the party such a dreadful experience? In general, then, you should avoid the use of slang in your writing. If you are in doubt about whether an expression is slang, it may help to check a recently published hardbound dictionary.

Practice

Rewrite the following sentences, replacing the italicized slang words with more formal ones.

Example   My friend had *wheels,* so we decided to *cut out* of the *crummy* dance.

We decided to use my friend's car to leave the boring dance.

1. If you don't *get your act together* in this course, you're going to be *blown away* by the midterm exam.

   _____

   _____

2. Living with a roommate is a *drag,* but the *extra bread* helps when the rent is due.

   _____

   _____

3. The football game was a *real wipeout;* we *got our butts kicked.*

   _____

   _____

4. If people keep *bad-mouthing* Gene, soon no one will *hang out* with him.

   _____

   _____

5. I *pushed the panic button* when the instructor called on me. My brain went *out to lunch.*

   _____

   _____

CLICHÉS

Clichés are expressions that have been worn out through constant use. Some typical clichés are:

all work and no play	saw the light
at a loss for words	short but sweet
better late than never	sigh of relief
drop in the bucket	singing the blues
easier said than done	taking a big chance
had a hard time of it	time and time again
in the nick of time	too close for comfort
in this day and age	too little, too late
it dawned on me	took a turn for the worse
it goes without saying	under the weather
last but not least	where he/she is coming
make ends meet	from
on top of the world	word to the wise
sad but true	work like a dog

Clichés are common in speech but make your writing seem tired and stale. Also, they are often an evasion of the specific details that you must work to provide in your writing. You should, then, avoid clichés and try to express your meaning in fresh, original ways.

Practice 1

Underline the cliché in each of the following sentences. Then substitute specific, fresh words for the trite expression.

Example   My parents supported me through some trying times.

rough years

1. The physical exam didn't shed any light on why I was getting headaches.

_____

2. I heaved a sigh of relief when I learned my final grade for the course was a B.

   _____

3. The record began selling like hotcakes as soon as it was released.

   _____

4. Helen could not have cared less whom Pete was dating.

   _____

5. Since my mother was feeling under the weather, she didn't go to work.

   _____

Practice 2

Write a short paragraph describing the kind of day you had. Try to put as many clichés as possible into your writing. For example, "I had a long hard day. I had a lot to get done, and I kept my nose to the grindstone." By making yourself aware of clichés in this way, you should lessen the chance that they will appear in your writing.

PRETENTIOUS WORDS

Some people feel they can improve their writing by using fancy and elevated words rather than more simple and natural words. They use artificial and stilted language that more often obscures their meaning than communicates it clearly. Here are some unnatural-sounding sentences:

   The football combatants left the gridiron.
   His instructional technique is a very positive one.
   At the counter, we inquired about the arrival time of the aircraft.
   I observed the perpetrator of the robbery depart from the retail establishment.

The same thoughts can be expressed more clearly and effectively by using plain, natural language, as below:

   The football players left the field.
   He is a good instructor.
   At the counter, we asked when the plane would arrive.
   I saw the robber leave the store.

Here is a list of some other inflated words and the simple words that could replace them.

Inflated Words	Simpler Words
component	part
delineate	describe
facilitate	help
finalize	finish
initiate	begin
manifested	shown
subsequent to	after
to endeavor	to try
transmit	send

Practice

Cross out the artificial words in each sentence. Then substitute clear, simple language for the artificial words.

Example   Sally was ~~terminated~~ from her ~~employment~~.

Sally was fired from her job.

1. My television receiver is not operative.

   _____

2. We made an expedition to the mall to see the new fall apparel.

   _____

3. José indicated an aversion to fish.

   _____

4. The fans expressed their displeasure when the pitcher threw the ball erratically.

   _____

5. How long have you resided in that municipality?

   _____

WORDINESS

Wordiness—using more words than necessary to express a meaning—is often a sign of lazy or careless writing. Your readers may resent the extra time and energy they must spend when you have not done the work needed to make your writing direct and concise. Here are examples of wordy sentences:

> At this point in time in our country, the amount of violence seems to be increasing every day.
> I called to the children repeatedly to get their attention, but my shouts did not get any response from them.

Omitting needless words improves the sentences:

> Violence is increasing in our country.
> I called to the children repeatedly, but they didn't respond.

Here is a list of some wordy expressions that could be reduced to single words.

Wordy Form	*Short Form*
a large number of	many
a period of a week	a week
arrive at an agreement	agree
at an earlier point in time	before
at the present time	now
big in size	big
due to the fact that	because
during the time that	while
five in number	five
for the reason that	because
good benefit	benefit
in every instance	always
in my own opinion	I think
in the event that	if
in the near future	soon
in this day and age	today
is able to	can
large in size	large
plan ahead for the future	plan
postponed until later	postponed
red in color	red
return back	return

Practice

Rewrite the following sentences, omitting needless words.

Example   Starting as of the month of June, I will be working at the store on a full-time basis.

As of June, I will be working at the store full time.

1.   Because of the fact that it was raining, I didn't go shopping.

2.   As far as I am concerned, in my opinion I do not feel that prostitution should be legalized.

3.   Please do not hesitate to telephone me if you would like me to come into your office for an interview.

4.   During the time that I was sick and out of school, I missed a total of three math tests.

5.   Well-paying jobs are all too few and far between unless a person has a high degree of training.

 ## Review Test I

Certain words are italicized in the following sentences. In the space provided, identify whether the words are slang (*S*), clichés (*C*), or pretentious words (*PW*). Then replace them with more effective words.

_____   1. If the boss starts *putting heat* on me again, I'm going to quit.

_____   2. Because of the rain, I wore a jacket that *has seen better days.*

_____   3. Ted won't help us unless we offer *a monetary reward.*

_____   4. When my younger brother did not get home from the party until 2 A.M., my mother decided *to put her foot down.*

_____   5. My upset stomach was *alleviated* by the antacid.

_____ 6. The vacation spot was a *total ripoff;* the weather and the food were both *the pits.*

_____

_____ 7. Phan *saw the error of his ways* and began to work harder.

_____

_____ 8. I needed *a respite from my exertions* after I finished typing the long report.

_____

_____ 9. I *jumped for joy* when I heard about the promotion.

_____

_____ 10. *You could have wiped me off the floor* when I learned my old girlfriend was on drugs.

_____

 ## Review Test 2

Rewrite the following sentences, omitting needless words.

1. At this point in time, I cannot say with any degree of certainty that I am planning to participate in the blood drive.

_____

_____

2. Due to the fact that there was no consensus of opinion, the committee agreed that it should meet again.

_____

_____

3. As far as Jay is concerned, he thinks that a working day of eight hours of work is too demanding for the average American worker.

_____

_____

4. For the price of $600, you can purchase outright this car of mine.

_____

_____

5. Without a doubt, the importance of the question of abortion as an issue cannot be denied.

_____

_____

Reinforcement of the Skills

INTRODUCTION

To reinforce the sentence skills presented in Part Two, this part of the book consists of mastery tests, combined mastery tests, proofreading tests, and editing tests. Four *mastery tests* appear for each of the skills where errors occur most frequently; two *mastery tests* are provided for each of the remaining skills. A series of *combined mastery tests* measure your understanding of important related skills. *Editing* and *proofreading tests* offer practice in finding and correcting one kind of error in a brief passage. *Combined editing tests* then offer similar practice—except that the passages contain a variety of mistakes. Both the editing and the proofreading tests will help you become a skillful editor and proofreader. All too often, students can correct mistakes in practice sentences but are unable to do so in their own writing. They must learn to look carefully for errors and to make a habit of checking closely for each skill. Appendix C provides progress charts that will help you keep track of your performance on these tests.

Mastery Tests

SUBJECTS AND VERBS

● Mastery Test 1

Draw one line under the subjects and two lines under the verbs. To help find subjects, cross out prepositional phrases as necessary. (Be sure to underline all the parts of a verb. Also, remember that you may find more than one subject and one verb in a sentence.)

1. My son pours chocolate milk on his cereal.
2. A solution to the problem popped suddenly into my head.
3. The salad and potatoes fed only half the guests.
4. That man on the corner may ask you for a quarter.
5. The fallen power line jumped and sparked on the street.
6. Lola likes to walk barefoot across the campus.
7. Nick and Fran sang together and banged on the piano.
8. The flashing lights of the police car appeared unexpectedly in my rearview mirror.
9. Juan often plays the stereo but almost never watches television.
10. We sat by a large rock, munched peanuts, and talked for hours.

Score: Number correct _____ × 10 = _____ %

SUBJECTS AND VERBS

🔵 Mastery Test 2

Draw one line under the subjects and two lines under the verbs. To help find subjects, cross out prepositional phrases as necessary. (Be sure to underline all the parts of a verb. Also, remember that you may find more than one subject and one verb in a sentence.)

1. I may hitchhike to the Mardi Gras this year.

2. Those tulips make my eyes itch.

3. Carol will be studying all day for the test.

4. Strange behavior in our house is the norm rather than the exception.

5. The prices of jewelry items in that specialty store have been reduced.

6. Fred and Martha refuse to drive their car at night.

7. I walked out to the garage last night and ran into a rug on the clothesline.

8. The rising tide will start to wash away that sand castle.

9. Harriet buys clothing impulsively, sends off for lots of mail-order items, and in general quickly spends her money.

10. The girls paddled their canoe across the lake and visited some boys at the camp on the other side.

Score: Number correct _____ × 10 = _____ %

SUBJECTS AND VERBS

 ## Mastery Test 3

Draw one line under the subjects and two lines under the verbs. To help find subjects, cross out prepositional phrases as necessary. (Be sure to underline all the parts of a verb. Also, remember that you may find more than one subject and one verb in a sentence.)

1. Lola believes in extrasensory perception.

2. The drawer of the bureau sticks on rainy days.

3. The little boy squirmed impatiently in his father's arms.

4. The window fan made a clanking sound and kept them awake at night.

5. The shrubs are starting to grow too close to the side of the house.

6. Three members of the basketball team have been suspended from school.

7. Jerry began to study seriously before final exams.

8. The newspaper boy shouted out the headlines and soon sold all his papers.

9. They won a lifetime supply of dish detergent on the game show but do not have any room for it in their house.

10. The shattered glass, cracked foundations, and fallen signs throughout the city resulted from earthquake tremors.

Score: Number correct _____ × 10 = _____%

SUBJECTS AND VERBS

 Mastery Test 4

Draw one line under the subjects and two lines under the verbs. To help find subjects, cross out prepositional phrases as necessary. (Be sure to underline all the parts of a verb. Also, remember that you may find more than one subject and one verb in a sentence.)

1. The nail under the rug barely missed my toe.

2. I have studied over eight hours for my biology test.

3. Tony and Lola just bought matching sweatshirts.

4. The game has been postponed because of bad weather.

5. Our families played badminton and volleyball at the picnic.

6. Behind all that mud you will see my daughter's face.

7. The beginning of that movie should not be missed.

8. Fred began to exercise seriously after his heart attack.

9. Hakim has been thinking about the job offer but has not made a decision yet.

10. The people on the tour bus dozed, read magazines, talked to each other, or snapped pictures.

Score: Number correct _____ × 10 = _____%

FRAGMENTS

 ## Mastery Test I

Each word group in the student paragraph below is numbered. In the space provided, write *C* if a word group is a complete sentence; write *frag* if it is a fragment. You will find ten fragments in the paragraph.

1. _____
2. _____
3. _____
4. _____
5. _____
6. _____
7. _____
8. _____
9. _____
10. _____
11. _____
12. _____
13. _____
14. _____
15. _____
16. _____
17. _____
18. _____
19. _____
20. _____

[1]I was seventeen on the night I died. [2]In the spring of 1982. [3]I had a severe case of the flu. [4]And had spent the first three days of my illness in bed. [5]Running a temperature between 102° and 106°. [6]Getting up only to take care of the necessities of life. [7]On Friday, the sixth day of my illness, rain from early morning on. [8]The wind howled outside, the house was damp and chilly, and my fever seemed higher than ever. [9]In late afternoon, I took my pillow and blanket into the living room. [10]Because I was sick of bed and had decided to lie on the sofa and watch television. [11]I watched Oprah Winfrey and read a magazine for a while. [12]Then I must have fallen asleep. [13]When I was suddenly conscious again. [14]I was in the middle of total darkness. [15]And total silence. [16]I was absolutely terrified. [17]Because I was sure that I had died. [18]Then, somewhere in the blackness ahead of me, I saw and recognized a small, dissolving spot of light. [19]I slowly realized that it was coming from the television set. [20]And that there had been a power failure.

Score: Number correct _____ × 5 = _____%

FRAGMENTS

 Mastery Test 2

Underline the fragment in each item. Then make whatever changes are needed to turn the fragment into a sentence.

Example   In grade school, I didn't want to wear glasses, ̶A̶nd avoided having to
get them by memorizing the Snellen eye chart.

1. I rang their doorbell for ten minutes. Finally deciding no one was home. I stalked away in disgust.

2. According to the latest weather report. Heavy rains will fall for the next twenty-four hours. Flash floods are expected.

3. A ceiling should be painted a very light color. Such as white or pale beige. Then, the room will seem larger.

4. My classes all being in the afternoon this semester. I can sleep until noon every day. My roommate hates me for it.

5. The plumber told us he could fix the leak in our shower. But would not be able to come until next month.

6. I spent an hour in the mall parking lot yesterday. Looking for my gray compact car. There were hundreds of other cars just like it in the lot.

7. Tony filled in the three-page application. Then he waited to see the personnel manager. Who would interview him for the position.

8. Suddenly the pitcher turned around. And threw to first base. But the runner was already standing on second.

9. Staggering under the weight of the heavy laundry basket. Nick stumbled down the basement steps. Then he discovered the washer was not working.

10. My brother spends a lot of time at the mall. There is an arcade there called Space Port. Where he meets his friends and plays video games.

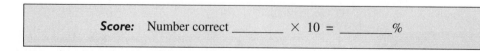

Score: Number correct _____ × 10 = _____ %

FRAGMENTS

 ## Mastery Test 3

Underline the fragment in each item. Then make whatever changes are needed to turn the fragment into a sentence.

1. Susie turned in her exam book. Then she walked out of the room. Wondering if she had passed.

2. The manager was fined $1,000. He had knocked the umpire's cap off his head. And kicked it across the infield.

3. Lola's typewriter was giving her trouble. All the *y*'s were losing their tails. And looked like *v*'s.

4. My little brother enjoys playing practical jokes. On anyone who visits our house. He even tells people that our house is haunted.

5. Because she had not studied for the exam. Susie was very nervous. If she got a passing grade, it would be a miracle.

6. Customers were lined up ten-deep at every entrance. Waiting for the store to open. Everything was on sale at 50 percent off.

7. Fran often gets up very early. Sometimes as early as 6 A.M. She says she thinks most clearly in the mornings.

8. We loaded the car with camping gear. Including a four-burner Coleman stove and a portable television.

9. Frank has a terrible problem. Unless he can scrape together a hundred dollars for his monthly installment. He will lose his new Honda.

10. The unusual meeting began at 3 P.M. But adjourned at 3:05 P.M. Nobody could think of anything to talk about.

Score: Number correct _____ × 10 = _____%

FRAGMENTS

● Mastery Test 4

Underline and then correct the ten fragments in the following passage.

When my mother was a young girl. She spent several summers on her aunt and uncle's farm. To this day she has vivid memories of the chores she did on the farm. Such as shucking corn for dinners and for canning. As she pulled off the moist brown cornsilk. Yellow worms would wiggle on the ear or drop off into her lap. Another task was preparing string beans. Which had to be picked over before the beans would be cooked. My mother and her aunt spent hours snapping the ends off the beans. And tossing each one into a large basin. But the chore my mother remembers most clearly is preparing a chicken for Sunday dinner. Her aunt would head for the chicken yard. Somehow, the chickens seemed to know her purpose. They ran wildly in all directions. Fluttering and squawking, or fleeing into the henhouse. When Aunt Helen found the right chicken. She picked it up and gave its neck a quick twist. Killing it instantly. Back in the kitchen, she and my mother would gut the chicken. And pluck its feathers out, down to the last tiny pinfeather. One special treat came out of this bloody chore. My mother always got the chicken feet to play with. Their long white tendons still attached. As my mother pulled on the tendons, the claws opened and closed like mechanical toys. My mother loved to terrorize her friends with these moving claws.

Score: Number correct _____ × 10 = _____%

RUN-ONS

 ## Mastery Test I

In the space provided, write *R-O* beside run-on sentences. Write *C* beside sentences that are punctuated correctly. Some of the run-ons have no punctuation between the two complete thoughts; others have only a comma.

Correct each run-on by using (1) a period and a capital letter, (2) a comma and a joining word, or (3) a semicolon. Do not use the same method of correction in each case.

Examples

R-O   I applied for the job, _{but} I never got called in for an interview.

R-O   Carla's toothache is getting worse, _s she should go to a dentist soon.

_____ 1. I had a very bad headache I felt light-headed and feverish as well.

_____ 2. Our children have the newest electronic games the house sounds like a pinball arcade.

_____ 3. Two men held up the ski shop, they were wearing bank tellers' masks.

_____ 4. Swirls of dust flew across the field good topsoil vanished into the distance.

_____ 5. I cannot get a definite commitment from Beth I decided not to count on her.

_____ 6. The soup was too hot to eat, so I dropped in two ice cubes and cooled it off quickly.

_____ 7. The course on the history of UFOs sounded interesting it turned out to be very dull.

_____ 8. That clothing store is a strange place to visit, you keep walking up to dummies that look like real people.

_____ 9. Martha throws out old pieces of soap, for she can't stand the sharp edges of the worn-down bars.

_____ 10. The oil warning light came on Gerry foolishly continued to drive the car.

Score: Number correct _____ × 10 = _____ %

RUN-ONS

Mastery Test 2

Correct the run-on in each item by using subordination. Choose from among the following dependent words:

after	before	unless
although	even though	until
as	if	when
because	since	while

Example The bus drivers are on strike, I had to walk to work today.

Because the bus drivers are on strike, I had to walk to work today.

1. Nick pulled the cellophane off the cake, the icing came along with it.

   _____

   _____

2. Sherrie was late for the job interview she still got the job.

   _____

   _____

3. I threw some potatoes into the oven I then prepared the salmon loaf.

   _____

   _____

4. Winters in New England are very cold Cindy decided to move to the Sun Belt.

   _____

   _____

5. I've been using a calculator for a year, I've almost forgotten the multiplication tables.

   _____

   _____

Score: Number correct _____ × 20 = _____%

RUN-ONS

 ## Mastery Test 3

In the space provided, write *R-O* beside run-ons. Write *C* beside sentences that are punctuated correctly. Some of the run-ons have no punctuation between the two complete thoughts; others have only a comma.

    Correct each run-on by using (1) a period and capital letter, (2) a comma and a joining word, or (3) a semicolon. Do not use the same method of correction in each case.

_____   1. Lola does yoga exercises every morning she strongly believes in a healthy body.

_____   2. Fast cars and fast people can be lots of fun, but they can also be very dangerous.

_____   3. I wondered why the time was passing so slowly then I realized my watch had stopped.

_____   4. Bill can crush walnuts with his teeth he is also good at biting the caps off of beer bottles.

_____   5. At one time Bill used to bend nails with his teeth this practice ended when a wise guy slipped him a hardened nail.

_____   6. My dentist teaches part-time in a neighborhood clinic he refers to himself as a drill instructor.

_____   7. An improperly placed goldfish bowl can start a house fire, sunlight reflects and magnifies through the bowl glass.

_____   8. At the crack of dawn, our neighbors start up their lawn mowers, and the Saturday-morning symphony begins.

_____   9. Fred had a bad headache yesterday, moreover, his arthritis was bothering him.

_____   10. As a little girl, she pretended she was a hairdresser her closet was full of bald dolls.

Score: Number correct _____ × 10 = _____ %

RUN-ONS

 ### Mastery Test 4

Correct the run-on in each sentence by using subordination. Choose from among the following dependent words:

after	before	unless
although	even though	until
as	if	when
because	since	while

1. My boss needs me to work overtime, I can't study for the test.

   _____

   _____

2. A storm was predicted for later in the day we still decided to go for a hike.

   _____

   _____

3. Fred's shirt sleeve caught on fire, his wife quickly dumped a pitcher of iced tea on it.

   _____

   _____

4. I was very tired at the end of the day, I still managed to complete a paper for my English class.

   _____

   _____

5. Marilyn took a year of accounting courses in school she decided to switch to another major.

   _____

   _____

Score: Number correct _____ × 20 = _____%

STANDARD ENGLISH VERBS

 ## Mastery Test 1

Underline the correct words in the parentheses.

1. The radio announcer said that traffic (is, are) tied up for six miles because of an accident that just (happen, happened) on the expressway.

2. My new pen (scratch, scratches) when I write with it; it (make, makes) little cuts in the paper.

3. Before I (mail, mailed) the letter, the postal rate went up, so I (need, needed) an extra stamp.

4. Rodrigo (have, has) a new tuxedo that (make, makes) him look just like a movie star.

5. They (do, does) not plan to give a New Year's Eve party this year, for they (have, has) painful memories of last year's.

6. Tim (is, be) terrific at home repairs; for example, he (fix, fixes) broken appliances just like a professional.

7. Just as Stanley (walk, walked) around the corner, he saw someone trying to steal his bicycle, so he (yell, yelled) for the police.

8. Little Danny (pile, piled) the blocks into a tower, but it (collapse, collapsed) with a loud crash, scattering all over the floor.

9. We (suspect, suspected) from the start that it (was, were) the neighbor's boy who took our lawn furniture.

10. My two sisters (was, were) thrilled when I (turn, turned) up with three tickets to the rock concert.

Score: Number correct _____ × 5 = _____%

STANDARD ENGLISH VERBS

 ## Mastery Test 2

Cross out the nonstandard verb form and write the correct form in the space provided.

_____seems_____   ***Example***   The job offer ~~seem~~ too good to be true.

_____   1. When I was learning how to drive, I strip the gears on my father's car.

_____   2. My parents is going to throw me a big party when I graduate.

_____   3. Bill prefer riding his motorcycle to just about any other activity.

_____   4. Vince do well on every exam he takes.

_____   5. Lucille change into comfortable clothes right after she gets home from a day of work.

_____   6. I remember how my mittens used to steam when I place them on the living room radiator.

_____   7. It was so cold that my breath turn into sharp white puffs of smoke when I exhaled.

_____   8. When Ida have her work breaks during the day, she often reads a magazine.

_____   9. Tea contain so much caffeine that it stimulates some people more than coffee.

_____   10. When I were little, my father would punish me just for expressing my opinion.

Score: Number correct _____ × 10 = _____%

STANDARD ENGLISH VERBS

 ### Mastery Test 3

Part 1: Fill in each blank with the appropriate standard verb form of *be, have,* or *do* in present or past tense.

People _____ really funny at amusement parks. They
_____ to prove that they _____ absolutely
     2
fearless, so they _____ crazy things such as stand up while the
           4
roller coaster _____ on its way downhill at ninety miles per
      5
hour. A normally careful driver _____ accidents on purpose; he
        6
_____ this to see how many cars he can hit in the Demolition
    7
Derby. I wonder if our parents _____ equally crazy things
        8
when they _____ young kids and needed to prove to the world
     9
that they _____ courage.
     10

Part 2: Fill in each blank with the appropriate form of the regular verb shown in parentheses. Use present or past tense as needed.

When Joanne (*rush*) _____ she often gets into trouble. Last
      11
Monday, while in a hurry to catch her train, she (*park*) _____
      12
her car too close to a shiny green Camaro that was in the next space
on the lot. When she (*arrive*) _____ at the station in the
      13
afternoon and (*open*) _____ her car door, Joanne (*realize*)
      14
_____ she could not back out of the parking space without
   15
hitting the other car. In addition, its driver was waiting impatiently and (*scowl*)
_____ as she (*watch*) _____ Joanne
    16   17
struggling with the wheel. Joanne finally got out of the space, but she (*scrape*)
_____ a two-inch strip off the Camaro's fender. The angry
    18
driver of the other car (*calm*) _____ down only when Joanne
      19
(*agree*) _____ to pay.
      20

Score: Number correct _____ × 5 = _____%

STANDARD ENGLISH VERBS

Mastery Test 4

Part I: Fill in each blank with the appropriate standard verb form of *be, have,* or *do* in the present or past tense.

My cousin Rita _____ determined to lose ten pounds, so
1
she _____ put herself on a rigid diet that _____
2   3
not allow her to eat anything that she enjoys. Last weekend while the
family _____ at Aunt Agatha's house for dinner, all Rita
4
_____ to eat _____ a can of Diet Delight
5   6
peaches. We _____ convinced that Rita meant business when
7
she joined an exercise club whose members _____ to work out
8
on enormous machines and _____ fifty sit-ups just to get
9
started. If Rita succeeds, we _____ going to be proud.
10

Part 2: Fill in each blank with the appropriate form of the regular verb shown in parentheses. Use present or past tense as needed.

Have you ever (*notice*) _____ what (*happen*)
11
_____ at a children's playground? Very often one child
12
(*struggle*) _____ with another to be first on the sliding
13
board, while a third child (*compete*) _____ with a fourth
14
for the sandbox. Meanwhile, each parent (*wait*) _____
15
patiently on a nearby park bench and (*ignore*) _____
16
his or her offspring. Just yesterday, I saw a young father whose
daughter had (*drag*) _____ him to the playground.
17
He (*stare*) _____ at his watch while she (*scream*)
18
_____ happily from the top of the jungle gym. He must have
19
been counting the minutes until they (*return*) _____ home.
20

Score: Number correct _____ × 5 = _____%

IRREGULAR VERBS

Mastery Test 1

Underline the correct word in the parentheses.

1. Juan had (wrote, written) me five times before the letters stopped.
2. Did you see the damage that maniac (did, done) to the laundromat?
3. The fever made me hallucinate, and I (saw, seen) monkeys at the foot of my bed.
4. After dicing the vegetables, Sarah (freezed, froze) them.
5. I (drank, drunk) at least six cups of coffee while working on the paper.
6. That last commercial (came, come) close to making me scream.
7. The foreman asked why I had (went, gone) home early from work the day before.
8. I should have (wore, worn) heavier clothes to the picnic.
9. If I hadn't (threw, thrown) away the receipt, I could have gotten my money back.
10. Willy (brang, brought) his volleyball to the picnic.
11. I would have (become, became) very angry if you had not intervened.
12. I was exhausted because I had (swam, swum) two lengths of the pool.
13. Albert (eat, ate) four slices of almond fudge cake before he got sick.
14. How long has your watch been (broke, broken)?
15. If we had (knew, known) how the weather would be, we would not have gone on the trip.
16. The children had (did, done) the dishes as a surprise for their mother.
17. Teresa has (rode, ridden) all over the city looking for an apartment.
18. The burglar (ran, run) like a scared rabbit when he heard the alarm.
19. Someone had (took, taken) the wrong coat from the restaurant rack.
20. The trucker (drived, drove) all night; his eyes looked like poached eggs.

Score: Number correct _____ × 5 = _____ %

IRREGULAR VERBS

 ## Mastery Test 2

Cross out the incorrect verb form. Write the correct form in the space provided.

_____ 1. The mop that I left by the door has froze stiff.

_____ 2. My car was stole, and I had no way of getting to school.

_____ 3. Someone leaved a book in the classroom.

_____ 4. Our gym teacher speaked on physical fitness, but we slept through the lecture.

_____ 5. That sweater was tore yesterday.

_____ 6. After I had loosed weight, the pants fit perfectly.

_____ 7. Ellen awaked from a sound sleep with the feeling there was someone in the house.

_____ 8. Life has dealed Lonnell a number of hard moments.

_____ 9. Father begun to yell at me as I walked in the door.

_____ 10. The sick puppy laid quietly on the veterinarian's table.

_____ 11. The instructor didn't remember that I had spoke to him.

_____ 12. While Alvin sung in the church choir, his mother beamed with pride and pleasure.

_____ 13. I would have went on vacation this week, but my boss asked me to wait a month.

_____ 14. When the boys throwed stones at us, we decided to throw some back.

_____ 15. I blowed up the balloon until it exploded in my face.

_____ 16. The body that the men taked out of the water was a terrible thing to see.

_____ 17. Rich breaked the video game that I lent him.

_____ 18. If the phone had rang once more, my mother would have tossed a pot at it.

_____ 19. A sudden banging on the door shaked me out of sleep.

_____ 20. Granny has wore the same dress to every wedding and funeral for twenty years.

Score: Number correct _____ × 5 = _____%

IRREGULAR VERBS

 Mastery Test 3

Write in the space provided the correct form of the verb shown in the margin.

sink   1. The fishing rod slipped out of his hand and _____ to the bottom
            of the pond.

choose   2. I _____ the blueberry pie for dessert because the pudding
            looked watery.

write   3. Pat had _____ the essay three times, but it still needed revision.

lie   4. As soon as I _____ down to take a nap, the phone rang.

catch   5. Fred _____ a cold while defrosting the refrigerator.

sell   6. The brothers worked on their old station wagon for a month and then
            _____ _____ it for twice as much as they paid for it.

ride   7. Eric _____ the bucking bronco for a full thirty seconds before
            he was tossed into the sawdust.

hide   8. How did my little brother ever guess where his Christmas present was
            _____?

speak   9. If I _____ only when I was spoken to, I'd never get a word in
            edgewise.

shake   10. Susie's hands _____ as she handed in her paper.

Score: Number correct _____ × 10 = _____%

IRREGULAR VERBS

🖤 Mastery Test 4

Write in the space provided the correct form of the verb shown in the margin.

ring
1. Sometimes the doorbell has _____ for several minutes before my grandfather notices the sounds.

shrink
2. My new designer jeans _____ three sizes in the wash.

lend
3. Stella _____ someone her notebook and then forgot who had borrowed it.

rise
4. If taxes had not _____ so much this year, I could have afforded a vacation.

sleep
5. I turned in my term paper and then _____ for ten hours.

sting
6. Kim didn't see the bee in her sleeve and was _____ the moment she put her jacket on.

wear
7. Nick jogs five miles a day and has _____ out three pairs of running shoes this year.

burst
8. Lola blew the biggest bubble I have ever seen. Then it _____, leaving shreds of pink bubble gum all over her face.

keep
9. I should have _____ my old coat instead of contributing it to the church rummage sale.

drive
10. We _____ for fifteen miles without seeing a single McDonald's.

Score: Number correct _____ × 10 = _____%

SUBJECT-VERB AGREEMENT

Mastery Test I

Underline the correct verb in the parentheses. Note that you will first have to determine the subject in each sentence. To help find subjects in certain sentences, you may find it helpful to cross out prepositional phrases.

1. The four flights of stairs up to my apartment (is, are) as steep as Mount Everest sometimes.
2. The sweater and the books on the table (belongs, belong) to Keiko.
3. One of their sons (has, have) been expelled from school.
4. My brother and I (has, have) season tickets to the games.
5. Nick and Fran (enjoys, enjoy) watching old movies on television.
6. Either of the television sets (gives, give) excellent picture quality.
7. There (is, are) about ten things I must get done today.
8. Hurrying down the street after their father (was, were) two small children.
9. Here (is, are) the screwdriver you were looking for all weekend.
10. No one in this world (is, are) going to get out alive.
11. The plywood under your carpets (is, are) rotting.
12. Sex and violence (is, are) the mainstays of many drive-in movies.
13. Jill is one of those people who (loses, lose) their temper quickly.
14. Not only the manager but also the owners of the ball club (is, are) responsible for the poor performance of the team.
15. There (is, are) a great deal of work yet to be done.
16. One of the women on the bowling team (has, have) won a million dollars in the state lottery.
17. The study of statistics (is, are) important for a psychology major.
18. My father is a person who (cares, care) more about time with his family than about success in his job.
19. The carpenter and the electrician (is, are) working at the house today.
20. I tug and pull, but the line of supermarket carts (seems, seem) welded together.

Score: Number correct _____ × 5 = _____ %

SUBJECT-VERB AGREEMENT

Mastery Test 2

In the space provided, write the correct form of the verb shown in the margin.

is, are

1. The chain-link fence surrounding the school grounds _____ ready to collapse.

plays, play

2. I envy people who _____ a musical instrument well.

is, are

3. Inside the bakery shop carton _____ your favorite pastries.

has, have

4. Someone on the team _____ forgotten her warm-up jacket.

wants, want

5. Because I spilled a beaker of sulfuric acid, nobody in my chemistry lab _____ to work with me.

is, are

6. At the end of the long movie line _____ about twenty people who will not get into the next show.

looks, look

7. Neither of the coats _____ good on you.

is, are

8. A little time for rest and relaxation _____ what I need right now.

was, were

9. The shirts that she thought _____ too expensive are now on sale.

shops, shop

10. Raquel and her mother _____ together on Thursday nights.

Score: Number correct _____ × 10 = _____%

SUBJECT-VERB AGREEMENT

 ## Mastery Test 3

Cross out the incorrect form of the verb. In addition, underline the subject that goes with the verb. Then write the correct form of the verb in the space provided. Mark the one sentence that is correct with a *C*.

_____ 1. The price of the computer games have been reduced.

_____ 2. The marigolds that was planted yesterday were accidentally mowed over today.

_____ 3. Many tables at the auction was covered with very old books.

_____ 4. Brenda checked with the employment agencies that was helping her look for a job.

_____ 5. Trucks and cars uses our street heavily since road construction began.

_____ 6. The old woman rooting through those trash baskets have refused to enter a nursing home.

_____ 7. The vicious gossip about our new neighbor have begun to anger me.

_____ 8. Sam is one of those people who rips pages out of library books rather than copy them on a duplicator.

_____ 9. The plastic slipcovers on their furniture has started to turn yellow.

_____ 10. Either my willpower or my lust for chocolate has to win out.

Score: Number correct _____ × 10 = _____%

SUBJECT-VERB AGREEMENT

● Mastery Test 4

Cross out the incorrect form of the verb. In addition, underline the subject that goes with the verb. Then write the correct form of the verb in the space provided. Mark the one sentence that is correct with a *C*.

_____ 1. Why has Cindy and Karen quit their jobs as telephone repair persons?

_____ 2. One actress at the rehearsals have become ill from the heat.

_____ 3. The buildings across the street is all going to be demolished.

_____ 4. Those old coats in your closet has dust lying on their shoulders.

_____ 5. Archery and soccer is the new sports at our school.

_____ 6. If only there was more hours in the day, I could get all my work done.

_____ 7. Two pieces of dry toast and a soft-boiled egg is all Rita is allowed to eat for breakfast.

_____ 8. One of the waitresses at the diner have just won a free trip to Las Vegas.

_____ 9. Lola's long red silk scarf and her lipstick match perfectly.

_____ 10. Anything that parents tell their children usually get ignored.

Score: Number correct _____ × 10 = _____ %

CONSISTENT VERB TENSE

 ## Mastery Test 1

In each item, one verb must be changed so that it agrees in tense with the other verbs. Cross out the inconsistent verb and write the correct form in the space provided.

_____ 1. After he bought a stereo and collects a lot of records, my brother wound up listening mostly to his FM radio.

_____ 2. The little boy raced his Lionel train too fast, so that it topples off the track when it rounded a curve.

_____ 3. She let her mother cut her hair until her friends began saying that her hairstyle looks very strange.

_____ 4. The air pollution is so bad that the weather bureau urges people not to exercise outside until it cleared.

_____ 5. Sandy greeted the mailman and flips quickly through the letters he handed her to see if there was a letter from her boyfriend.

_____ 6. After the truck overturned, passing motorists parked their cars on the side of the road and walk back to look at the damage.

_____ 7. The lights went out and we all jump because we were watching a horror movie at the time.

_____ 8. The wind came up quickly, knocks down a lot of dead tree branches, and blew in the front window of the bank across the street.

_____ 9. After the wolf unsuccessfully huffed and puffed at the little pigs' brick house, he realizes he would have to hire a demolition contractor.

_____ 10. While in the hospital, she read lots of magazines, watched daytime television, shuffles up and down the corridor, and generally felt very bored.

Score: Number correct _____ × 10 = _____%

CONSISTENT VERB TENSE

● Mastery Test 2

In each item one verb must be changed so that it agrees in tense with the other verbs. Cross out the inconsistent verb and write the correct form in the space provided.

_____ 1. Lola likes to use lip gloss but hates the way it stains her fingers and never seemed to come off.

_____ 2. Tony reached way down into the bread bag. He skipped the first couple of pieces and grabs one of the fresher, bigger pieces from the middle.

_____ 3. Eric believes he is smarter than we are; he tried to show this all the time.

_____ 4. When I noticed the way my mother cocked her head, I realize that she had an earache.

_____ 5. When we asked for a fresh tablecloth, the waiter looks as though we were speaking Russian.

_____ 6. As the tourists walked through the forest, they check the trail markers that were posted along the way.

_____ 7. My eyes always close and my fingers get numb when I listened to an afternoon lecture in Professor Snorrel's class.

_____ 8. Billy graduated from Camden High School, works as a plumber's assistant for two years, and then returned to school.

_____ 9. At holiday dinners, many people continue to stuff themselves even when it seemed obvious that they are already full.

_____ 10. I wiped my hands on my trousers before I walk in for the job interview. I did not want the personnel officer to know my palms were sweating.

Score: Number correct _____ × 10 = _____%

PRONOUN REFERENCE, AGREEMENT, AND POINT OF VIEW

 ## Mastery Test I

Underline the correct word in the parentheses.

1. I realized that each of the coaches had done (her, their) best to motivate me.
2. Either of the television sets has (its, their) good and bad features.
3. I hated my job as an office mailboy because (I, you) got taken advantage of by everyone.
4. A player on the ice hockey team broke (his, their) arm last week.
5. I quit my pottery classes because (it, the ceramic dust) made me sneeze.
6. If (a person goes, people go) barefoot through the store, he or she can expect to meet a security guard.
7. We went to Disney World on a Sunday, and (you, we) had to wait an hour for every ride.
8. My cat got hold of a lollipop, and (it, the cat) got very sticky.
9. When Jack argues with Ted, (he, Ted) always gets in the last word.
10. One of my sisters has decided to separate from (her, their) husband.
11. I've been taking cold medicine, and now (it, the cold) is better.
12. The ten girls in our cabin developed a closeness that (you, we) could feel grow as the summer at camp progressed.
13. Sarah was nervous about her speech, but (it, the nervousness) didn't show.
14. Each of the men was asked to put (his, their) name on the petition.
15. When we reached the station, (you, we) realized that the train had left.
16. Has everybody in the sorority finished (her, their) work for the committee?
17. I went fishing yesterday and caught three (of them, fish).
18. No one in the men's dorm felt (he, they) had taken very good notes at the lecture.
19. When the Dolphins met the Cowboys in the playoff game, (they, the Dolphins) won.
20. If students work with irresponsible lab partners, (you, they) will find it difficult to get a good grade.

Score: Number correct _____ × 5 = _____ %

PRONOUN REFERENCE, AGREEMENT, AND POINT OF VIEW

 Mastery Test 2

In the space provided, write *PE* beside sentences that contain pronoun errors. Write *C* beside the two sentences that use pronouns correctly. Then cross out each pronoun error and write the correction above it.

_____PE_____ **Example** Each of the boys explained ~~their~~ *his* project.

_____ 1. Lola loves to run, but Tony's not interested in it.

_____ 2. My deepest thoughts and feelings are ones that you can hide easily.

_____ 3. If I don't have my activities for the day planned in advance, I waste too much time deciding what to do next.

_____ 4. My cousin is a religious man and has devoted much of his life to it.

_____ 5. They take too many taxes out of my weekly paycheck.

_____ 6. I have a carton full of pencils and pens here; where do you want me to put them?

_____ 7. One of the best swimmers on the team has badly sprained her back.

_____ 8. As we watched the lightning storm, you were in awe.

_____ 9. Elaine told Sue that she was being selfish.

_____ 10. Each of the women had pinned a gardenia in their hair.

Score: Number correct _____ × 10 = _____%

PRONOUN REFERENCE, AGREEMENT, AND POINT OF VIEW

● Mastery Test 3

In the space provided, write *PE* beside sentences that contain pronoun errors. Write *C* beside the two sentences that use pronouns correctly. Then cross out each pronoun error and write the correction above it.

_____   1. A person should always be extremely careful when using their chainsaw.

_____   2. Many people flick on the television as soon as they get in the house; this is a bad habit for you to get into.

_____   3. After I joined the shopping club, they began sending me stacks of junk mail.

_____   4. Many toys on the market today can both entertain children and educate them as well.

_____   5. The custard pie was so good that you kept going back for more.

_____   6. Lola told her mother that she was too impatient.

_____   7. A student in a late-afternoon class often has difficulty attending to their instructor.

_____   8. No one except a police officer is allowed to turn their car around on a toll road.

_____   9. When my broken wrist was set, I could feel the bones grinding against each other.

_____   10. At the bookstore in the mall, they have all the best-sellers in racks at the front.

Score: Number correct _____ × 10 = _____ %

PRONOUN REFERENCE, AGREEMENT, AND POINT OF VIEW

Mastery Test 4

In the space provided, write *PE* beside sentences that contain pronoun errors. Write *C* beside the two sentences that use pronouns correctly. Then cross out each pronoun error and write the correction above it.

_____	1. When the picture tube on the television burned out, I had to get a new one.
_____	2. People will enjoy the movie if they don't mind a sentimental ending.
_____	3. Everyone who donates their time for the project will receive free admission to the union picnic.
_____	4. People should never go for a job interview if you don't prepare in advance.
_____	5. If a person intends to pass a chemistry course, you have to be good at math.
_____	6. Tisha told her mother she needed a new pair of shoes.
_____	7. We wanted to see the exhibit, but you couldn't push through the crowds.
_____	8. Everyone in the class should be ready to deliver her report by next Monday.
_____	9. I enjoyed the volleyball match even though I'm not very good at it.
_____	10. I wanted a free pencil sharpener, but you first had to buy five dozen pencils.

Score: Number correct _____ × 10 = _____ %

PRONOUN TYPES

Mastery Test I

Underline the correct word in the parentheses.

1. Harold pretended to be at ease, but he didn't fool Susan or (me, I).   *D.O*
2. (This, This here) tree is full of sparrows at night.
3. I believe that coat is (hers', hers).
4. Talking intimately, Ellen and (I, me) didn't see Fred walking up to our front porch.
5. The two of you must give (yourself, yourselves) another chance.
6. Al and (I, me) are equally poor in math.
7. My car's front tires, (who, which) vibrate at high speeds, need to be realigned.
8. (Those, Them) newspapers have to be carried down to the incinerator.
9. That last hamburger on the grill is (yours', yours) if you want it.
10. Though the furry black tarantula was in a cage, it still scared Bill and (I, me).   *DO*
11. Whenever our neighbor sees me on the porch, he invites (hisself, himself) over.
12. You are getting more of your work done than (I, me).   *comparison*
13. Ted (hisself, himself) takes full responsibility for the accident.
14. The instructor glared at Sarah and (I, me) and then dismissed the class.   *ob of prep*
15. Though younger than (I, me), Andrea acts like my superior.
16. When I miss class, I get together later with a student (who, whom) takes good notes.
17. Of all the children in the class, Dora and (he, him) are the least reliable.
18. The professor asked Chico and (I, me) to volunteer.   *D.Ob*
19. I recently met a friend of (her, hers).
20. (Those, Them) boots weren't made for walking.

Score: Number correct _____ × 5 = _____%

PRONOUN TYPES

🟣 Mastery Test 2

Cross out the incorrect pronoun in each sentence and write the correct form in the space provided.

_____ 1. The coach's decision didn't suit Charlie or I.

_____ 2. Our instructor gave us homework in all of those there books.

_____ 3 That rabbit of yours' just became a mother again.

_____ 4. Joel won because he has played chess much longer than her.

_____ 5. Our brothers were very proud of themself when they caught the vandal in our neighborhood.

_____ 6. The women whom filed the class action suit were initially fired by the company.

_____ 7. The mail carrier says that Tyrell and me get more mail than all the other people on the block combined.

_____ 8. Lee never gets tired of talking about hisself.

_____ 9. Even the United States mail gets things done faster than her.

_____ 10. This here toothbrush looks as if someone used it to scrub potatoes.

_____ 11. Angela and me go hiking together each fall.

_____ 12. The firefighters theirselfs were puzzled by the source of the smoke in my basement.

_____ 13. Our garden is better cared for than theirs'.

_____ 14. The stone barely missed we and the children.

_____ 15. Them mosquitoes will bite you faster than you can blink your eyes.

_____ 16. If you want that old garden shovel, it's yours'.

_____ 17. I heard that her and her sister were expelled from school.

_____ 18. Julio is looking for someone to who he can sell his car.

_____ 19. Pete jogs on a more regular basis than me.

_____ 20. The pages are torn in many of them books.

Score: Number correct _____ × 5 = _____ %

ADJECTIVES AND ADVERBS

 Mastery Test 1

Part 1: Cross out the incorrect adjectival or adverbial form in each sentence. Then write the correct form in the space provided.

_____ 1. My mother spoke bluntly to the salesperson, and he responded aggressive. *ly*

_____ 2. The spade cut sharp and severed the tree root. *ly*

_____ (their) 3. Because the children were quietly during the movie, their parents were happy to buy them some ice cream. *quiet*

_____ 4. Our powerful singing rang out noisy in the packed theater. *noisily*

_____ *good* 5. Your cupcakes taste so well that they are rapidly disappearing. *good*

Part 2: Cross out the error in comparison in each sentence. Then write the correct form in the space provided.

_____ 6. Andy considers himself importanter than other people. *more*

_____ 7. Lola's hair is the most shortest that she has ever worn it. *shorter than*

_____ 8. Despite the reviews, I think *The Killer Frogs* was the entertainingest movie released this year.

_____ 9. Earthworms are less likelier to make me squeamish than are spiders.

_____ 10. I always do a more good job in preparing a meal than my brother does.

Score: Number correct _____ × 10 = _____ %

ADJECTIVES AND ADVERBS

 Mastery Test 2

Part I: Cross out the incorrect adjectival or adverbial form in each sentence. Then write the correct form in the space provided.

_____   1. For a week after his accident, Carlos could not walk steady.

_____   2. I didn't think the instructor had graded my paper fair.

_____   3. The sharp blade slipped easy between the chicken's bumpy skin and satiny flesh.

_____   4. My father was thoughtfully as he looked at the pictures in the old family album.

_____   5. Waitressing was easy for Marge, but since my coordination was not as well as hers, I was fired.

Part 2:   Add to each sentence the correct form of the word in the margin.

strong   6. Jerry, whose nickname is Goliath, is probably the _____ player on the football team.

graceful   7. The _____ sport at the Olympics is the figure-skating competition.

hard   8. My science exam was the _____ of my two tests.

little   9. That is the _____ of my many worries.

bad   10. I can't decide what to do; the _____ thing, though, would be to do nothing.

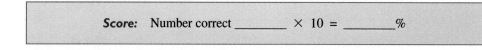

Score: Number correct _____ × 10 = _____%

MISPLACED MODIFIERS

Mastery Test I

Underline the misplaced word or words in each sentence. Then rewrite the sentence, placing related words together and making the meaning clear.

1. Every six hours the doctor told me to take a pill.

   _____

   _____

2. I bought a watch at the flea market that I wear every day.

   _____

   _____

3. Lola dozed by the pool growing redder by the minute.

   _____

   _____

4. We need another player on the team who can catch badly.

   _____

   _____

5. Elena almost got an A in every subject.

   _____

   _____

6. Mike signed a letter of intent to play football at Penn State in the family kitchen.

   _____

   _____

7. I threw the potatoes in the pot and tore open a box of peas in a bad mood.

   _____

   _____

8. My uncle bought a house from an elderly real estate agent with a large bay window.

   _____

   _____

Score: Number correct _____ × 12.5 = _____%

MISPLACED MODIFIERS

 ### Mastery Test 2

Underline the misplaced word or words in each sentence. Then rewrite the sentence, placing related words together and making the meaning clear.

1. Fran was attacked by a stray dog working in the yard.

   _____

   _____

2. I will never ride another horse wearing shorts.

   _____

   _____

3. Everyone we invited almost came to the party.

   _____

   _____

4. The boy struggled to reel in the large fish with shaking hands.

   _____

   _____

5. I bought a tire from an auto shop that flattened overnight.

   _____

   _____

6. Judy bought sheepskin seat covers for her Toyota that cost only thirty dollars.

   _____

   _____

7. Breakfast is served at the school cafeteria from 8 A.M. until the end of the school year.

   _____

   _____

8. Finding their house burglarized, the Murphys called the police when they came back from vacation.

   _____

   _____

Score: Number correct _____ × 12.5 = _____ %

DANGLING MODIFIERS

Mastery Test I

Underline the dangling modifier in each sentence. Then rewrite the sentence, correcting the dangling modifier.

1. Feeling extra lucky, the black cat didn't scare Diana.

_____

_____

2. After waiting all day, the moving truck finally arrived at our apartment.

_____

_____

3. Hot and sizzling, Lola bit into the apple tart.

_____

_____

4. Having faulty plumbing, we decided not to rent the apartment.

_____

_____

5. Waiting in line to be seated, the hostess finally called our names.

_____

_____

6. Out late the night before, Rita's eyes were red and strained.

_____

_____

7. Having won the championship game, the locker room was filled with cheering players.

_____

_____

8. While walking through the shopping mall, my head suddenly began to pound.

_____

_____

Score: Number correct _____ × 12.5 = _____%

DANGLING MODIFIERS

 ## Mastery Test 2

Underline the dangling modifier in each sentence. Then rewrite the sentence, correcting the dangling modifier.

1. While cutting the lawn, five mosquitoes bit me.

   _____

   _____

2. Smoking in the rest room, my math teacher caught Fred and me.

   _____

   _____

3. Shortly before giving birth, the doctor gave his wife a sedative.

   _____

   _____

4. Quickly taking the sheets off the clothesline, rain pelted our faces.

   _____

   _____

5. Dripping with perspiration, the air-conditioned store offered us relief.

   _____

   _____

6. While shopping at the store, my bike was stolen.

   _____

   _____

7. Hurrying to class, my English paper fell out of my notebook into a puddle.

   _____

   _____

8. After watching two movies at the drive-in, my stomach began rumbling for pizza.

   _____

   _____

Score: Number correct _____ × 12.5 = _____ %

PARALLELISM

Mastery Test I

The unbalanced part of each sentence is italicized. Rewrite this part so that it matches the rest of the sentence.

1. Long box office lines, *T-shirts that are overpriced,* and overcrowded parking lots—these are what I dislike about going to a rock concert.

   _____

2. My sister can do her math homework, cut my hair, and *be planning a party* while she watches television.
   plan a party

   _____

3. The sky got dark, a wind sprang up, and *there was a drop in the temperature.*

   _____

4. My magazines sometimes arrive torn, dirty, and *being late.*

   _____

5. Between work and dinner, she picked up her son at school, *was stopping at the drugstore,* and dropped the dog off at the vet's office.

   _____

6. The flowers that Robin entered in the show were healthy-looking, brilliantly colored, and *smelled sweet.*

   _____

7. I'd play golf day and night if it weren't for eating and *to have to sleep.*

   _____

8. The crowd showed excitement, happiness, and *there was patriotic spirit.*

   _____

9. If it weren't for Marie's indecision and *being insecure,* she could accomplish great things in the business world.

   _____

10. My nephew's career plans center on becoming a state trooper, training as a police officer, or *to join the FBI.*

    _____

Score: Number correct _____ × 10 = _____%

PARALLELISM

 ## Mastery Test 2

Draw a line under the unbalanced part of each sentence. Then rewrite the unbalanced part so that it matches the other items in the sentence.

1. My bedridden little brother asked for a bowl of cereal, a glass of orange juice, and to have a comic book to read.

   _____

2. Science fiction, popular music, and sports that are on television are the things my father enjoys most.

   _____

3. My sister's peculiar habits included yelling in her sleep and to do her homework in the bathtub.

   _____

4. That new blond-haired boy is both handsome as he is personable.

   _____

5. Lola enjoys novels, shopping for new clothes, and meeting new men.

   _____

6. Shoppers stop in pet stores to buy a pet, to pick up pet supplies, or just looking at the animals.

   _____

7. Our children can watch television, talk on the phone, and their homework all at the same time.

   _____

8. Frustrated, annoyed, and feeling depression, Steve returned to work after the strike.

   _____

9. Thelma likes people who have thoughtfulness and are unselfish.

   _____

10. His headache was so bad that Andy was ready to give all his money or the confessing of all his secrets to anyone who would stop the pain.

   _____

> *Score:*   Number correct _____ × 10 = _____ %

CAPITAL LETTERS

Mastery Test 1

Cross out the two capitalization errors in each of the following sentences. Then write the corrections in the spaces provided.

_____

_____

_____

_____

_____

_____

_____

_____

_____

_____

_____

_____

_____

_____

_____

_____

_____

_____

_____

_____

1. Our local nightspot, studio 84, will admit only people dressed in designer Jeans.

2. Lisa complained, "this pearl bracelet I bought at woolworth's has started to turn green."

3. Though howard no longer lives on third Street, he likes to return there on weekends to visit old friends.

4. Joe and Leslie love arizona, but we prefer colorado.

5. The statue in Boyle's Square is supposed to represent all the soldiers killed during the revolutionary war.

6. I hired a lawyer after my VW Rabbit was sideswiped by a united parcel delivery truck.

7. Yuri often works overtime on saturdays and sundays to help keep up with his bills.

8. Our neighbor, mr. charles Reynolds, accidentally backed into our maple tree today.

9. "last week I bought Adidas sneakers and a jogging sweatshirt," Janey said. "But my asthma is so bad that my Doctor won't let me start running."

10. I don't like instant coffee, but that's all that's served at the weight watchers' meetings on Wednesday nights.

Score: Number correct _____ × 5 = _____%

CAPITAL LETTERS

🔵 Mastery Test 2

Cross out the two capitalization errors in each of the following sentences. Then write the corrections in the spaces provided.

_____

_____   1. I asked the clerk, "do you have any italian olives?"

_____

_____   2. the third-grade children sang "Jingle Bells" during the school christmas ceremony.

_____   3. I drove lance to the auto shop to get the estimate on repairs to his 1970 thunderbird.

_____   4. "because of the bad weather conditions," said the manager, "our Store will be closing at four o'clock."

_____   5. I can't decide whether to buy the boots I saw at butler's or to see if I can find a better pair at Florsheim's on hudson Street.

_____   6. I am so brainwashed by Advertising that I always want to buy both skippy and Peter Pan peanut butter.

_____   7. Linda works at the farmers' National Bank in williamstown on Mondays, Wednesdays, and Fridays.

_____   8. He got low grades in his Math courses but straight A's in English and spanish.

_____   9. When the company transferred Rick's mother to the West coast, he wound up as a student at Beverly Hills High school.

_____   10. The epitaph on W. C. Fields' tombstone reads, "on the whole, I'd rather be in philadelphia."

_____

Score: Number correct _____ × 5 = _____%

CAPITAL LETTERS

 ## Mastery Test 3

Cross out the two capitalization errors in each of the following sentences. Then write the corrections in the spaces provided.

_____
_____ 1. My Uncle, a ranger at Olympia National Park, wrote a pamphlet titled "a Guide to Olympia's Wildflowers."

_____
_____ 2. Last summer I visited my aunt in israel and had a chance to learn some Hebrew and French, since she spoke both Languages.

_____
_____ 3. During the college's festival of marx brothers movies, Jean saw _Duck Soup_ for the first time.

_____
_____ 4. The book titled _A Study in Human Dignity_ tells the story of john merrick, a terribly deformed young man.

_____
_____ 5. Dave studied at the Culinary Institute of America before joining the staff at the greenbrier inn.

_____
_____ 6. As soon as his father came in the door, Frankie cried, "Who won, Dad? i'll bet the dodgers did."

_____
_____ 7. After visiting the smithsonian institution in Washington, we headed for a Chinese restaurant recommended by friends.

_____
_____ 8. Although he is a christian scientist, Harold Phipps decided to let the doctors treat his son with antibiotics.

_____
_____ 9. After the game we stopped off to get an early supper at a nearby burger king.

_____
_____ 10. Billy Joel's "The Piano Man" is tony's all-time favorite Song.

**Score:** Number correct _____ × 5 = _____%

CAPITAL LETTERS

 ## Mastery Test 4

Cross out the two capitalization errors in each of the following sentences. Then write the corrections in the spaces provided.

_____

_____ 1. "Why subscribe to *TV guide*," said Nick to Fran, "when there's a perfectly good TV listing in the sunday paper?"

_____

_____ 2. Someone smashed into Claude's toyota when it was parked on Pine street and stole all his tape cassettes.

_____

_____ 3. Sherry came home from work hungry and devoured three hershey bars and a bag of fritos; then she asked what was for supper.

_____

_____ 4. "You ought to quit smoking those camels," said Martha to her husband. "Even tiparillos would be less harmful."

_____

_____ 5. Corey was watching a soap opera, *General hospital,* on TV when a woman from bell Telephone called.

_____

_____ 6. I had no sooner sat down in dr. Stein's office last tuesday evening than his beeper began to sound.

_____

_____ 7. My Mother's first job was as a real estate salesperson for century 21.

_____

_____ 8. To Sam, labor day means staying up all night to watch the Jerry Lewis Telethon.

_____

_____ 9. Until the remodeling work is completed, our psychology classes will be held in wister hall.

_____

_____ 10. The dirty Sign on the back of the speeding truck read, "this driver is a professional."

Score: Number correct _____ × 5 = _____ %

NUMBERS AND ABBREVIATIONS

 ## Mastery Test I

Cross out the mistake in numbers or abbreviations in each sentence and correct it in the space provided.

_____ 1. In a panic, William grabbed the phone book and looked in the inside cover for the emergency number of the fire dept.

_____ 2. Did you know that an eight-ounce glass of tomato juice has only 50 calories?

_____ 3. Rod finally entered the ladies' room to investigate after he had waited a half hr. for his girlfriend.

_____ 4. By the time I graduated from high school, I had written 3 term papers, thirty-two book reports, and 120 spelling tests.

_____ 5. The federal govt. agreed to reimburse the citizens whose land was being incorporated into a protected wilderness area.

_____ 6. The basketball ref. called a technical foul on the screaming coach who had run out onto the court.

_____ 7. It took Sam all evening to do the twenty problems on page eighty-seven.

_____ 8. In Floyd's backyard were 125 old tires, 263 yards of rusty barbed wire, and three cast-iron bathtubs.

_____ 9. To discourage burglars, our automatic timer turns on a light and radio at 8 o'clock every night.

_____ 10. The overjoyed couple had won a thousand dollars a wk. for life in the state lottery drawing.

Score: Number correct _____ × 10 = _____%

NUMBERS AND ABBREVIATIONS

 ## Mastery Test 2

Cross out the mistake in numbers or abbreviations in each sentence and correct it in the space provided. Mark the one sentence that is correct with a *C*.

_____ 1. A delivery van was carelessly blocking the entrance to the hosp. emergency room.

_____ 2. From five potted tomato plants on the patio, Ruth harvested over ninety-five tomatoes.

_____ 3. Whenever I catch a cold, I take 2 aspirins every four hours.

_____ 4. Mrs. Ramirez stood patiently in line at the P.O. waiting to mail a package and several letters.

_____ 5. As she did, she studied the faces of the "Ten Most Wanted" crim. on the FBI poster.

_____ 6. After joining Weight Watchers, Martha lost thirty-two pounds in only 17 weeks.

_____ 7. I hurried to answer the phone, but it was only someone from the Rescue Squad requesting a contrib.

_____ 8. One of the actual questions on the test was when the War of Eighteen-Twelve was fought.

_____ 9. By mid-nineteen-ninety-nine, employment in service industries is expected to increase by 30 percent.

_____ 10. The trouble with Ms. Ryder, my history prof., is that she never gives any examples when she lectures.

Score: Number correct _____ × 10 = _____%

END MARKS

 ## Mastery Test 1

Add a period, a question mark, or an exclamation point, as needed, to each of the following sentences.

Note: End marks always go *inside* the quotation marks that appear in some sentences.

1. Even today women earn, on the average, only 59 percent of men's salaries
2. Are you going to watch the Miss America pageant this year
3. After interrupting the program, the radio announcer hurried to assure us, "This was only a test"
4. The strange meal consisted of sausage, potato chips, and watermelon
5. When will daylight saving time end this year
6. Karen screamed, "I don't ever want to see you again "
7. That tree has been attacked by some kind of insect
8. Watch out for an incoming Frisbee
9. Sometimes I get depressed and wonder if I will ever get my degree
10. Do you know how many cups of coffee it took me to finish this paper
11. The man threw open the window and yelled, "I'm mad at the world and I'm not going to take it anymore "
12. My little brother is always working on ways to be more obnoxious
13. In bold red letters, the ad proclaimed, "You too can be a star "
14. My Uncle Jack is so budget-conscious that the only book he ever reads is his bankbook
15. How much time do we have left to finish the test
16. Stanley yelled at the top of his voice, "Turn that stereo down before I smash it"
17. Fran asked, "Nick, will you type my sociology paper "
18. Get inside quickly or that dog will bite you—hurry
19. "One of the strangest phobias people have," said the professor, "is the fear of peanut butter sticking to the roof of the mouth"
20. Have you heard the one about the fellow at the shopping mall who wanted to buy the escalator because it was marked down

Score: Number correct _____ × 5 = _____%

END MARKS

Mastery Test 2

Add a period, a question mark, or an exclamation point, as needed, to each of the following sentences.

Note: End marks always go *inside* the quotation marks that appear in some sentences.

1. Uncle Arthur's mustache makes him look like a walrus
2. Do coleslaw and French fries come with every order
3. From the airplane window, the clouds looked like mashed potatoes
4. A voice from the stands screamed, "Strike the bum out "
5. How can you hold down two jobs and still go to college
6. With a loud crack, the rotted branch broke and fell from the tree
7. "On your way over," asked Fran, "could you pick up a case of Cokes "
8. Every time I take a shower, the kitchen ceiling begins to drip
9. The instructor asked me whether I had studied for the exam
10. "Somebody's been squeezing the bottom of the chocolates without eating them " Martha cried.
11. Annie wanted to know if I had finished bathing the dog
12. Why do I always get thirsty in the middle of the night
13. You're going to knock the vase off the table—watch out
14. I often wonder why more people don't buy live Christmas trees and plant them in their yards afterward
15. Must all our house guests bring screaming kids with them
16. The minute Aunt Agatha thought she had won, she jumped out of her seat and yelled "Bingo "
17. I'd think twice before I took one of his courses again
18. The water company wants to know if it can replace the meter in our basement
19. Have you tried that new Indian fast-food restaurant, Cash and Curry
20. It is better to keep one's mouth closed and be thought a fool than to open it and remove all doubt

Score: Number correct _____ × 5 = _____%

APOSTROPHE

 ## Mastery Test I

Cross out the word in each sentence that needs an apostrophe. Then write the word correctly in the space provided.

_____ 1. I walked casually around the parking lot, trying to conceal the fact that Id no idea where I left my car.

_____ 2. Martha ignored the police motorcycle officers siren and ended up in jail last night.

_____ 3. The man insisted that his name was Elmer Fudd, but I didnt believe him.

_____ 4. The blue whales tongue weighs about as much as forty men.

_____ 5. Lolas mother put on designer jeans and went along with Lola to the rock concert.

_____ 6. Tony had to remove wood ticks from his hair after a walk through the field behind his uncles house.

_____ 7. The womens room in that service station is always clean.

_____ 8. Youre going to cause trouble for yourself if your temper gets out of hand.

_____ 9. Some of the most violent crime years in our nations history occurred during the Great Depression.

_____ 10. Since Africas population increases by twenty million each month, its people face starvation.

Score:	Number correct _____	× 10 = _____%	

APOSTROPHE

🖋 Mastery Test 2

In the space provided under each sentence, add the one apostrophe needed and explain why the other word ending in *s* is a simple plural.

Example   Joans hair began to fall out two days after she dyed it.

Joans: _____ *Joan's, meaning "hair belonging to Joan"* _____

days: _____ *simple plural meaning more than one day* _____

1. The students gradually got used to the professors Japanese accent.

    students: _____

    professors: _____

2. Our tough sheriffs campaign promise is that he'll replace the electric chair with electric bleachers.

    sheriffs: _____

    bleachers: _____

3. My little sisters habit of sucking in noodles makes her an unpleasant dining companion.

    sisters: _____

    noodles: _____

4. When the students complained about the instructors assignment, he said, "You're not in high school anymore."

    students: _____

    instructors: _____

5. A football-sized nest of yellow jackets hung menacingly under the roofs rain gutter.

    jackets: _____

    roofs: _____

Score: Number correct _____ × 10 = _____ %

APOSTROPHE

 ## Mastery Test 3

In each sentence two apostrophes are missing or are used incorrectly. Cross out the two errors and write the corrections in the spaces provided.

_____
_____
1. Freds day started going sour when he noticed that everyone in the doughnut shop had gotten fatter doughnuts' than he did.

_____
_____
2. While the team was in the showers, someone tied all the players sneakers' together.

_____
_____
3. If youll check the noise in the attic, Ill stand by the phone in case you scream.

_____
_____
4. Despite the drivers warning that smoking was not allowed, several people lit cigarettes' in the back of the bus.

_____
_____
5. When I sat on the fender of Hassans car, he stared darts' at me until I slid off.

_____
_____
6. My brothers car phone was stolen by vandals' who broke his car window.

_____
_____
7. Sallys typing might improve if shed cut an inch off her nails.

_____
_____
8. Martha has been on Freds blacklist since she revealed that he sleeps with his' socks on.

_____
_____
9. The troopers face was stern as he told me that my drivers license had expired.

_____
_____
10. I never ride anymore in my uncles station wagon; its like being on a roller coaster.

Score: Number correct _____ × 5 = _____%

APOSTROPHE

● Mastery Test 4

In each sentence two apostrophes are missing or are used incorrectly. Cross out the two errors and write the corrections in the spaces provided.

_____

_____

1. I was shocked when the movie stars toupee blew off; I hadnt realized he was completely bald.

_____

_____

2. The skirts cheap lining puckered and scorched even though Eileens iron was set at the lowest possible heat level.

_____

3. The two boys boat capsized in the rivers rushing current.

_____

_____

4. Teds work always ends up on someone elses desk.

_____

_____

5. People in the dentists waiting room squirmed uneasily as a childs cries echoed down the hall.

_____

_____

6. When Jeans voice cracked during her solo, I thought shed faint with embarrassment.

_____

_____

7. Didnt you know that school will be closed next week because of a teachers conference?

_____

_____

8. My youngest sisters goldfish has jumped out of its' bowl many times.

_____

_____

9. "Its the muffler," the mechanic explained, crawling out from under Freds car.

_____

_____

10. Kevin knew he was headed for trouble when his dates father said that hed like to come along.

Score: Number correct _____ × 5 = _____ %

QUOTATION MARKS

 Mastery Test I

Place quotation marks where needed.

1. A friend of mine used to say, There's nothing wrong with you that a few birthdays won't cure.

2. The food critic wrote, The best test of a fast-food hamburger is to eat it after all the trimmings have been taken off.

3. After I finished James Thurber's story The Secret Life of Walter Mitty, I started to write a paper on it.

4. When I'm done exercising in the morning, said Lola, there's a smoky fragrance to my skin.

5. Well, this is just fine, he mumbled. The recipe calls for four eggs and I have only two.

6. Eating Lola's chili, Tony whispered, is a breathtaking experience.

7. After Bill pulled the flip-top cap off the can, he noticed that the label said, Shake well before drinking.

8. How would you feel, the instructor asked the class, if I gave you a surprise quiz today?

9. In a tired voice, Clyde asked, Did you ever wonder why kids have more energy at the end of a long day than they had when they got up?

10. When Dick Cavett first met Groucho Marx on a street corner, he said, Hello, Groucho, I'm a big fan of yours. Groucho's response was, If it gets any hotter, I could use a big fan.

Score: Number correct _____ × 10 = _____%

QUOTATION MARKS

 Mastery Test 2

Place quotation marks or underlines where needed.

1. The tag on the pillow read, Do not remove under penalty of law.

2. You two kids had better stop fighting this minute! ordered Aunt Esther in her most severe tone of voice.

3. If we don't hurry, we'll miss the beginning of the movie, Nick reminded Fran.

4. Honest men, said the cranky old man, are scarcer than the feathers on a frog.

5. The most famous line from George Orwell's novel 1984 is, Big Brother is watching you.

6. It never fails, complained Martha. Just as I lie down to take a nap, the telephone rings.

7. I know I'm getting old, Grandfather said. When I walked past the cemetery today, two guys ran after me with shovels.

8. There is a sign in the grocery store that reads, In God we trust. All others pay cash.

9. When Clyde got home from work, he said, At times I feel I'm in a rat race and the rats are winning. Charlotte consoled him by saying that everyone feels that way from time to time.

10. In a Consumer Reports article titled What's Inside Frozen Pot Pies? the editors write, The filth we discovered is not a health hazard. But it's unpleasant to discover that these pies contain big and little parts of aphids, flies, moths, weevils, cereal beetles, and rodent hairs.

Score: Number correct _____ × 10 = _____%

QUOTATION MARKS

Mastery Test 3

Place quotation marks or underlines where needed.

1. Abraham Lincoln once wrote, My father taught me to work. He did not teach me to love it.

2. Diana Ross's song It's My Turn is one of my all-time favorites.

3. Are you positive you locked the front door? asked Vince for the third time.

4. You know, Bill said to the bartender, there are times in my life when I kind of panic. I want to go to bed and never get up again.

5. When I know I have a long day ahead, Judy said, I always have trouble sleeping well the night before.

6. Cracking his knuckles, Harry complained, I wish people didn't have so many annoying habits.

7. Look out, you idiot! screamed the frightened pedestrian. Are you trying to kill somebody?

8. Immanuel Kant once wrote: Two things fill me with constantly increasing admiration and awe the longer and more earnestly I reflect on them—the starry heavens without and the moral law within.

9. The saying we learned in school was, Do unto others as you would have them do unto you. The saying that I now have on the wall of my study reads, Remember the golden rule: he who has the gold makes the rules.

10. One of the questions in Sharon's American literature test was to identify the book in which the following line appears: You don't know about me without you have read a book by the name of The Adventures of Tom Sawyer, but that ain't no matter.

Score: Number correct _____ × 10 = _____%

QUOTATION MARKS

Mastery Test 4

Place quotation marks or underlines where needed.

1. Tony's uncle likes to say to him, You're never too young to have a heart attack.

2. The preacher began his sermon with the words, Nobody will ever get out of this world alive.

3. I won't get nervous. I won't get nervous, Terry kept repeating to herself as she walked into the exam room.

4. The honest politician proclaimed to the crowd, I haven't the slightest idea of what I'm talking about.

5. Tony said to Lola, Guess how many jellybeans I can hold in my mouth at one time?

6. Ved complained, No one wants to go with me to Maniac for Hire, the new movie at the drive-in.

7. If an infielder makes a mistake during a softball game, Darryl yells from the bench, You're a disgrace to your base!

8. As a child I was ugly, said the comedian. Once my old man took me to the zoo. The guy at the gate thanked him for returning me.

9. Don't let your paintbrushes dry up, advises the book Saving Money Around the House. Instead, store them in motor oil.

10. I agree that the public has a right to know what is in a hot dog, said the president of the meat company. But does the public really want to know what's in a hot dog?

Score: Number correct _____ × 10 = _____%

COMMA

🗨 Mastery Test 1

Add commas where needed. Then refer to the box below to write, in the space provided, the letter of the one comma rule that applies in each sentence.

---

a. Between items in a series	d. Between complete thoughts
b. After introductory material	e. With direct quotations
c. Around interrupters	

_____ 1. The hot dogs that we bought tasted delicious but they reacted later like delayed time bombs.

_____ 2. Because it was the thing to do whenever he talked with the guys Tony pretended he had dated a lot of women.

_____ 3. Clyde had no idea what his weight was but Charlotte always knew hers.

_____ 4. Lola a good athlete surprised Tony by making forty-six of fifty foul shots.

_____ 5. The child's eyes glowed at the sight of the glittering tree colorful packages and stuffed stockings.

_____ 6. "Before you crack open another walnut" Tony's father warned him "remember that we're going to be eating shortly."

_____ 7. When she got back from the supermarket, she realized she had forgotten to get cereal grape jelly and Drano.

_____ 8. The old graveyard was filled with vampires werewolves crooked politicians and other monsters.

_____ 9. The problem with you David is that you take criticism personally.

_____ 10. Fred chose the shortest line at the post office but the woman in front of him suddenly began pulling a number of tiny packages out of her pockets.

Score: Number correct _____ × 10 = _____ %

COMMA

Mastery Test 2

Add commas where needed. Then refer to the box below to write, in the space provided, the letter of the one comma rule that applies in each sentence.

a. Between items in a series
b. After introductory material
c. Around interrupters
d. Between complete thoughts
e. With direct quotations

_____ 1. As soon as Sam finished the difficult problem he let out a satisfied grunt.

_____ 2. On Saturday if it doesn't rain we plan to take the kids to the ball game.

_____ 3. I don't care if I never see you your family or your vacation pictures again.

_____ 4. Tony quit his part-time job at a local gas station for he was being paid only $4.25 an hour.

_____ 5. "Aunt Agatha is so forgetful" my mother observed "that whenever she ties a string around her finger as a reminder, she forgets to look at the string."

_____ 6. The Washington, D.C., zoo purchases 50,000 pounds of meat 6,500 loaves of bread 114,000 live crickets and other foods for its animals each year.

_____ 7. My Aunt Esther loves watching the silly childish antics of the contestants on some game shows.

_____ 8. Although my classes don't begin until ten o'clock I still have trouble getting to the lecture hall on time.

_____ 9. A flock of snow geese their shiny wings flashing in the sun flew above the marshlands.

_____ 10. Mike brought a cassette tape recorder to class for he had broken two fingers and couldn't take notes.

Score: Number correct _____ × 10 = _____ %

COMMA

🗩 Mastery Test 3

Add commas where needed. Then refer to the box below to write, in the space provided, the letter of the one comma rule that applies in each sentence.

---

a.	Between items in a series	d.	Between complete thoughts
b.	After introductory material	e.	With direct quotations
c.	Around interrupters		

_____ 1. Clyde and Charlotte took Paul their son to see Walt Disney's *Bambi.*

_____ 2. The film covers the birth of Bambi the loss of his mother his escape from a forest fire and his growth to young fatherhood.

_____ 3. Just before the film started Clyde decided to get a giant box of Jujyfruits.

_____ 4. While he was at the refreshment counter, the houselights dimmed the stage curtains opened and the movie started.

_____ 5. Clyde hurried back down the dark aisle almost stumbling and slipped into the empty aisle seat that he thought was his.

_____ 6. While Clyde popped Jujyfruits into his mouth the woman next to him rested her head on his shoulder.

_____ 7. Clyde's eyes grew accustomed to the dark and he became aware suddenly of an elderly man standing near him in the aisle.

_____ 8. "Excuse me, Sir" the man said. "You're in my seat."

_____ 9. Hearing the man's voice, the woman looked up saw Clyde next to her and screamed.

_____ 10. "I'm really sorry, Madam," Clyde said. He got up quickly and then saw in front of him waving and laughing his wife and son.

Score: Number correct _____ × 10 = _____%

COMMA

🌑 Mastery Test 4

Do three things: (1) cross out the one comma that is not needed; (2) add the one comma that is needed; and (3) in the space provided, write the letter of the one rule that applies for each comma you added.

---

a. Between items in a series	d. Between complete thoughts
b. After introductory material	e. With direct quotations
c. Around interrupters	

_____ 1. On Friday, my day off I went, to get a haircut.

_____ 2. "When I have a headache" my aunt explained, "I simply close my eyes, and take several deep breaths."

_____ 3. The aliens in the science-fiction film visited our planet in peace but we greeted them, with violence.

_____ 4. A neat appearance warm smile, and positive attitude, will make an employer respond to you.

_____ 5. "Even, the greatest creations," the sign said "start from small seeds."

_____ 6. Frank does not like, cooked carrots and he cares even less for lima beans.

_____ 7. According to rumors our school janitor has made himself a millionaire, through real estate investments.

_____ 8. Hilda was not happy, about having to drop the math course but there were too many other demands being made on her time.

_____ 9. A jar of split-pea soup, which was all Bill had in the refrigerator did not make, for a very satisfactory meal.

_____ 10. Although Martha is normally, a careful and defensive driver she drives recklessly if she is in a bad mood.

Score: Number correct _____ × 10 = _____%

OTHER PUNCTUATION MARKS

Mastery Test I

At the appropriate spot (or spots), place the punctuation mark shown in the margin.

—   1. Martha screamed when she saw a water bug the kind that can travel sixty miles an hour race across her bathroom floor.

;   2. A canary's claws must be carefully clipped it is important not to nick the little veins in each one.

—   3. The town is so far north that it has only two seasons winter and August.

:   4. A search of Danny's pockets revealed these items an inch-long piece of wire, a crumpled baseball card, three small stones, and a dead grasshopper.

( )   5. The incoming line section should be a rigid dead-front type, completely encased with metal and self-supporting see diagram A.

-    6. "Seventy Six Trombones" is a toe tapping, finger snapping march from the Broadway classic *The Music Man.*

( )   7. Our country's national parks especially famous ones like Yosemite and Yellowstone must now deal with major crimes committed by summer visitors.

;   8. American Indians used poetic names for the months of the year for instance, December was "Moon When the Deer Shed Their Horns."

-    9. The slightly built burglar was well known as the most talented "second story" man in town.

:   10. *Consumer Reports* concludes its article on wood stoves by stating "You should first ask yourself if you *need* a wood stove to help lower your home-heating costs. Are you sure you've done as much as you can to save energy in other ways? Are you prepared for the inconveniences, major and minor, that a stove entails?"

Score: Number correct _____ × 10 = _____%

OTHER PUNCTUATION MARKS

 ## Mastery Test 2

Add colons, semicolons, dashes, hyphens, or parentheses as needed. Each sentence requires only one of the five kinds of punctuation marks.

1. Bargain hunters swarmed around the entrance to the store the manager quickly opened the doors.

2. The diagram of the reproductive cycle pages 24–25 must also be studied for the test.

3. Self centered people are often very insecure individuals.

4. There is one sure way to get in trouble with that instructor ask too many questions.

5. Tarzan, Superman, the Lone Ranger these were the heroes of his boyhood.

6. George Orwell has written "On the whole, human beings want to be good, but not too good, and not quite all the time. . . . Society has always to demand a little more from human beings than it will get in practice."

7. Two squirrels there they are on top of the fence are building a nest in the storage shed.

8. The three required books on our psychology reading list are *Towards a Psychology of Being,* by Abraham Maslow *On Becoming a Person,* by Carl Rogers and *Love and Will,* by Rollo May.

9. I don't know why the door to the gas station rest room is locked perhaps the owner is afraid someone will get inside to clean it.

10. This do it yourself repair book will save homeowners a lot of money.

Score: Number correct _____ × 10 = _____ %

DICTIONARY USE

Mastery Test I

Items 1–5:   Use your dictionary to answer the following questions.

1. How many syllables are in the word *decontaminate?* _____

2. Where is the primary accent in the word *interpretation?* _____

3. In the word *posterity,* the *i* is pronounced like
    a.   short *e.*
    b.   short *i.*
    c.   long *i.*
    d.   schwa.

4. In the word *secularize,* the *u* is pronounced like
    a.   schwa.
    b.   short *a.*
    c.   short *u.*
    d.   long *u.*

5. In the word *erratic,* the *e* is pronounced like
    a.   short *e.*
    b.   long *e.*
    c.   short *i.*
    d.   schwa.

Items 6–10:   There are five misspelled words in the following sentence. Cross out each misspelled word and write in the correct spelling in the spaces provided.

The canidate for mayor promised to reduce subway fares by a nickle, to crack down on criminels, and to bring new businesses to the city by ofering tax breaks.

6. _____   8. _____   10. _____

7. _____   9. _____

Score: Number correct _____ × 10 = _____%

DICTIONARY USE

Mastery Test 2

Items 1–5: Use your dictionary to answer the following questions.

1. How many syllables are in the word *rationalize?* _____

2. Where is the primary accent in the word *dilapidated?* _____

3. In the word *vicarious,* the second *i* is pronounced like
   a. long *e.*
   b. short *i.*
   c. long *i.*
   d. schwa.

4. In the word *cumbersome,* the *o* is pronounced like
   a. schwa.
   b. short *a.*
   c. short *o.*
   d. long *o.*

5. In the word *esoteric,* the second *e* is pronounced like
   a. short *e.*
   b. long *e.*
   c. short *i.*
   d. schwa.

Items 6–10: There are five misspelled words in the following sentence. Cross out each misspelled word and write the correct spelling in the space provided.

My mother's most precious possesion is her collection of crystel animals; she keeps them in a specal cabinet in the dineing room and won't allow anyone to handel them.

6. _____ 8. _____ 10. _____

7. _____ 9. _____

Score: Number correct _____ × 10 = _____%

SPELLING IMPROVEMENT

● Mastery Test I

Items 1–8:   Use the three spelling rules on pages 287–288 to spell the following words.

1. debate + able = _____

2. run   + ing   = _____

3. thorny + est   = _____

4. woe   + ful   = _____

5. swim   + er   = _____

6. happy + ly   = _____

7. hate   + ful   = _____

8. infer   + ed   = _____

Items 9–14:   Circle the correctly spelled plural in each pair.

9. knifes	knives	12. stories	storys
10. wishes	wishs	13. heros	heroes
11. decoys	decoies	14. ourselfs	ourselves

Items 15–20:   Circle the correctly spelled word (from the basic word list on pages 290-291) in each pair.

15. possible	possable	18. success	sucess
16. exercize	exercise	19. rediculous	ridiculous
17. receive	recieve	20. acident	accident

Score: Number correct _____ × 5 = _____%

SPELLING IMPROVEMENT

Mastery Test 2

Items 1–8:   Use the three spelling rules on pages 287-288 to spell the following words.

1. equip   + ed   = _____
2. excite   + ment = _____
3. heavy   + ly   = _____
4. flat   + est   = _____
5. carry   + ed   = _____
6. begin   + er   = _____
7. surprise   + ing   = _____
8. crazy   + ness   = _____

Items 9–14:   Circle the correctly spelled plural in each pair.

9. issues	issus	12. loaves	loafs
10. partys	parties	13. halfs	halves
11. worries	worrys	14. father-in-laws	fathers-in-law

Items 15–20:   Circle the correctly spelled word (from the basic word list on pages 290-291) in each pair.

15. measure	meazure	18. psycology	psychology
16. knowlege	knowledge	19. awkward	akward
17. alright	all right	20. recognize	recognise

Score: Number correct _____ × 5 = _____%

OMITTED WORDS AND LETTERS

Mastery Test 1

Part 1:   In the spaces provided, write in the two small connecting words needed in each sentence. Use carets (^) within the sentences to show where these words belong.

_____

_____

1. With only inning left play, the score was three to two.

_____

_____

2. In middle of the night, I heard a loud crash jumped out of bed, trembling.

_____

_____

3. Whenever Fran puts Frank Sinatra record on stereo, Nick goes to sleep.

_____

_____

4. If Martha thinks she is coming down with cold, she drinks a cup tea with honey.

_____

_____

5. The beautiful starlet slowly got out of her limousine, clutching small white poodle that resembled animated mop.

Part 2:   In the spaces provided, write in the two words that need -*s* endings in each sentence. Be sure to add the *s* to each word.

_____

_____

6. Our expense were getting out of control, so my husband and I began keeping a record of all our purchase.

_____

_____

7. All the section of two course Tony wanted were closed.

_____

_____

8. We had forgotten to make extra ice cube, so Melba volunteered to pick up two bag at the corner store.

_____

_____

9. A young couple in the laundromat started to roll their sock into ball and lob them at each other.

_____

_____

10. After several attempt, Vince was finally able to bench-press 250 pound.

Score: Number correct _____ × 5 = _____%

OMITTED WORDS AND LETTERS

● Mastery Test 2

Part 1: In the spaces provided, write in the two small connecting words needed in each sentence. Use carets (^) within the sentences to show where these words belong.

_____

_____
1. Tara called cable company when picture on her set resembled a crazy quilt.

_____

_____
2. When twenty inches rain fell in one day, our backyard resembled swimming pool.

_____
3. I have lost track how many parties our neighbor has given in past year.

_____

_____
4. Even though Bill had eaten three sandwiches lunch, he began eat a bag of doughnuts at three o'clock.

_____
5. The quarterback would have had better completion record if backs had not dropped so many passes this year.

_____

Part 2: In the spaces provided, write in the two words that need *-s* endings in each sentence. Be sure to add the *s* to each word.

_____

_____
6. The music store in the mall has two trade-in day a month when used CD are purchased for cash.

_____

_____
7. The pattern had worn off the linoleum floor in many place, and the wall were water-stained.

_____
8. Like small black freight train, long lines of ant moved across the sidewalk.

_____

_____
9. The director's chair on Larry's porch are imprinted with the name of the family members.

_____

_____
10. Everything from a group of stuffed parrot to several antique bicycle hung from the ceiling of the restaurant.

Score: Number correct _____ × 5 = _____%

COMMONLY CONFUSED WORDS

 ## Mastery Test 1

Choose the correct words in each sentence and write them in the spaces provided.

_____

_____

1. Last year the (hole, whole) publishing industry seemed to concentrate on turning out (knew, new) romantic novels.

_____

_____

2. We drove out into the (dessert, desert) (to, too, two) test our dune buggies.

_____

_____

3. The mechanic did not (know, no) what caused the (break, brake) in the fuel line of Fred's car.

_____

_____

4. My dog lost (its, it's) tail after being run over by a truck that had lost its (brakes, breaks).

_____

_____

5. (Irregardless, Regardless) of what her coworkers think, Susan always wears plain (clothes, cloths) to work.

_____

_____

6. Pete (could of, could have) used the money, but he refused to (accept, except) the check his parents offered him.

_____

_____

7. Morris can't stand to (hear, here) advice. He lives by the (principal, principle), "If I make my own decisions, I have only myself to praise or blame."

_____

_____

8. Kevin and Judy have to make (there, their, they're) handwriting neater and more legible if (there, their, they're) after good grades.

_____

_____

9. Just (among, between) us, I'd advise you not to take Dear Abby's (advice, advise) as gospel.

_____

_____

10. That lion over (there, their, they're) clawed at the attendant cleaning (it's, its) cage.

Score: Number correct _____ × 5 = _____%

COMMONLY CONFUSED WORDS

 ## Mastery Test 2

Choose the correct words in each sentence and write them in the spaces provided.

_____

_____

_____

_____

_____

_____

_____

_____

_____

_____

_____

_____

_____

_____

_____

_____

_____

_____

_____

_____

1. Laurie is going to (lose, loose) her job even though she was (among, between) the ten best salespeople in the company last year.

2. The (affect, effect) of the medication is that all my symptoms (accept, except) for a slight cough have disappeared.

3. (Its, It's) hard to deny the fact that (there, their, they're) are many fools in the world.

4. I (would of, would have) tried out for that role, but the director told me that she had (already, all ready) filled the part.

5. (Being that, Because) you never studied for the course, you (can hardly, can't hardly) blame the instructor for your F.

6. (There, Their, They're) are only (to, too, two) days left to take advantage of the store's January white sale.

7. Tony pushed the mower (through, threw) the heavy underbrush on the back lawn and (than, then) maneuvered it past a huge pile of rocks.

8. (It's, Its) very peaceful and (quite, quiet) along the stretch of the river that passes near our town.

9. The (weather, whether) was so bad that it caused a one-hour (brake, break) in the game.

10. Marilyn changed her seat to get away from the (to, too, two) (coarse, course) people on the bus.

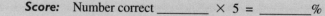

Score: Number correct _____ × 5 = _____%

COMMONLY CONFUSED WORDS

 ## Mastery Test 3

Cross out the two mistakes in usage in each sentence. Then write the correct words in the spaces provided.

_____ _____
1. A stranger in an black suit knocked on my neighbor's door and handed him a plane manila envelope.

_____ _____
2. Its not easy to find food in that refrigerator because it's shelves are crowded and poorly lit.

_____ _____
3. If this cough syrup dose its job, your going to be feeling better very soon.

_____ _____
4. Our psychology instructor should of canceled the last class before the holiday, for less than six students showed up.

_____ _____
5. Do you know that the cactus plant over their is the basis for a delicious desert?

_____ _____
6. When he tries to learn her how to drive, she sets up a mental block and refuses to except his instructions.

_____ _____
7. One affect of the strong wind is that some lose roof shingles have blown off the house.

_____ _____
8. Too get to the Washington Monument, you must ride two buses and take a subway, to.

_____ _____
9. I can't hardly recommend you buy that house, for there are termite wholes in the basement studs.

_____ _____
10. If the principle ingredient in that stew is octopus, I don't know whether I'll accept you're invitation to try it.

_____ _____

_____ _____

> ***Score:*** Number correct _____ × 5 = _____%

COMMONLY CONFUSED WORDS

 Mastery Test 4

Cross out the two mistakes in usage in each sentence. Then write the correct words in the spaces provided.

_____
_____

1. Beside the twins, the Fosters have three other children—more then anyone else on the block.

_____
_____

2. Larry should of realized by now that he could have past the course by studying harder.

_____
_____

3. Its to bad that the pair of you didn't apply for the job there.

_____
_____

4. Nothing was less appealing to Joel then the possibility of excepting the advice I had given him.

_____
_____

5. Regardless of what you say, I believe we could of learned our collie how to be a good watchdog.

_____
_____

6. I pursue both rug making and gardening: the latter allows me to be creative and the former allows me to enjoy the peace of nature.

_____
_____

7. I'll be quiet surprised if the promise of a delicious desert doesn't make my little sister agree to be quiet.

_____
_____

8. Being that it's sinking into the water, their must be too many people in the boat.

_____
_____

9. You're new car has been inspected and registered, so it's already to drive.

_____
_____

10. Whether or not I take that course depends on whose teaching it and how much righting is required.

> *Score:* Number correct _____ × 5 = _____ %

EFFECTIVE WORD CHOICE

 ## Mastery Test I

Certain words are italicized in the following sentences. In the space at the left, identify whether these words are slang (*S*), clichés (*C*), or pretentious words (*PW*). Then replace the words with more effective diction.

_____ 1. The man in the house on the corner *kicked the bucket* last night.

_____ 2. That book is by a millionaire who *didn't have a dime to his name* as a boy.

_____ 3. Marty has always *endeavored* to excel in his college courses.

_____ 4. The boss told Bob to *get his act together* or to resign.

_____ 5. I have a large *quantity* of chores to do this weekend.

_____ 6. Our team's chances of winning the league championship are *as dead as a doornail.*

_____ 7. The players were nervous; they didn't want to *blow* the championship game.

_____ 8. Donna *came out of her shell* after she joined the theater group at school.

_____ 9. When Julie's marriage *hit the rocks,* she decided to see a therapist.

_____ 10. Many people today *entertain anxieties* about our country's economy.

Score: Number correct _____ × 10 = _____%

EFFECTIVE WORD CHOICE

 ## Mastery Test 2

Certain words are italicized in the following sentences. In the space at the left, identify whether these words are slang (*S*), clichés (*C*), or pretentious words (*PW*). Then replace the words with more effective diction.

_____ 1. Kwan thought it was *too good to be true* when the boss told her to go home early.

_____

_____ 2. I won't be coming; square dancing just *isn't my thing*.

_____

_____ 3. Passing the course *is contingent* upon my grade in the final exam.

_____

_____ 4. I am *sick and tired of* her dog's digging up my backyard.

_____

_____ 5. If the boss starts *putting heat on me* again, I'm going to ask for a transfer.

_____

_____ 6. Long political speeches *bore me to tears*.

_____

_____ 7. I got so tired at Neil's party that I had to *sack out* on his living room couch.

_____

_____ 8. Nick scrubbed the countertop with Ajax until it was *clean as a whistle*.

_____

_____ 9. Margery is embarrassed about the fact that, after high school, she did not go on to *an institution of higher learning*.

_____

_____ 10. My husband and I have both lost weight as a result of our *reducing regimens*.

_____

Score: Number correct _____ × 10 = _____%

EFFECTIVE WORD CHOICE

 ## Mastery Test 3

The following sentences include examples of wordiness. Rewrite the sentences in the space provided, omitting needless words.

1. The fact of the matter is that I did not remember that I had an appointment to meet with you.

    _____

    _____

2. To make a long story short, my brother and his wife are going to go about getting a divorce.

    _____

    _____

3. At our company there are at present two coffee breaks, with each of them fifteen minutes long.

    _____

    _____

4. At this point in time, Lou would be wise to start working on the paper he has to write for English.

    _____

    _____

5. Permit us to take this opportunity to inform you that your line of credit has been increased.

    _____

    _____

Score: Number correct _____ × 20 = _____%

EFFECTIVE WORD CHOICE

 ## Mastery Test 4

The following sentences include examples of wordiness. Rewrite the sentences in the space provided, omitting needless words.

1. In my opinion, I think that all people, men and women both, should be treated exactly alike.

   _____

   _____

2. The exercises that Susan does every day of the week give her more energy with which to deal with everyday life.

   _____

   _____

3. I hereby wish to inform you in this letter that I will not be renewing my lease for the apartment.

   _____

   _____

4. All American citizens should consider it their duty to go out and vote on the day that has been scheduled to be Election Day every year.

   _____

   _____

5. In view of the fact that miracle drugs exist in our science today, our lifetimes will be extended longer than our grandparents'.

   _____

   _____

Score: Number correct _____ × 20 = _____%

Combined Mastery Tests

FRAGMENTS AND RUN-ONS

 ## Combined Mastery Test 1

Each of the word groups below is numbered. In the space provided, write *C* if a word group is a complete sentence, write *F* if it is a fragment, and write *R-O* if it is a run-on. Then correct the errors.

1. _____

2. _____

3. _____

4. _____

5. _____

6. _____

7. _____

8. _____

9. _____

10. _____

11. _____

12. _____

13. _____

14. _____

15. _____

16. _____

17. _____

18. _____

19. _____

20. _____

[1]The cheap motel room smelled musty. [2]As if the window had never been opened. [3]I snapped on the light, a roach sauntered across the floor. [4]Although the bed looked lumpy. [5]I flopped on it gratefully, totally exhausted. [6]I needed about ten hours' sleep. [7]Then I would get something to eat. [8]And start to plan how to get my life going in the right direction again.

[9]As the rest of the class scribbled furiously during the lecture. [10]Gene doodled in his notebook. [11]Weird stick figures marched across the page odd flowers blossomed on its borders. [12]Because he was so involved in his fantasy world. [13]Gene continued to draw. [14]After the lecture had ended.

[15]Gripping the scissors in one hand and her son's shoulder in the other. [16]Margaret attempted to give the squirming toddler a haircut. [17]Waving his fist angrily. [18]The boy knocked the shears out of his mother's hand. [19]The shears skidded across the floor they headed for the family's unsuspecting dog. [20]Who jumped backward suddenly and began to bark loudly.

Score: Number correct _____ × 5 = _____%

FRAGMENTS AND RUN-ONS

 ## Combined Mastery Test 2

In the space provided, indicate whether each item below contains a fragment (*F*) or a run-on (*R-O*). Then correct the error.

_____ 1. Since the game ended in a tie. The teams had to go into sudden-death, overtime. Not a single fan left the stadium.

_____ 2. Nick and Fran buy only name brands at the store, they feel economy brands are lower not just in price but in quality. I disagree with them.

_____ 3. The fire drills in school gave a welcome break to the daily routine. Students moved quickly and obediently. Clearing the building in a hurry.

_____ 4. Because the miracle soles on Fred's shoes have never worn down. He has used the same pair for the last four years. Martha is sick of looking at them.

_____ 5. An astrologer read my chart I didn't believe her. My friend was born on the same day, but we have completely different personalities.

_____ 6. My sister parked her cart in the checkout line at the market. Then dashed off to get final items on her list. I hate people who do that.

_____ 7. When Laurie left for college, her mother was devastated, she was not used to a lonely house. Her solution was to return to school herself.

_____ 8. Nick and Fran didn't have time to cook dinner. They stopped at McDonald's. To pick up Big Macs.

_____ 9. Because Harvey is only five feet three inches, he has trouble getting dates. He often fantasizes about being a seven-foot-tall basketball player then all the women in the world would look up to him.

_____ 10. Until I was twelve, I believed there really was a tooth fairy. She would leave a dollar under my pillow. Whenever I lost a tooth.

Score: Number correct _____ × 10 = _____%

VERBS

● Combined Mastery Test I

Each sentence contains a mistake involving (1) standard English or irregular verb forms, (2) subject-verb agreement, or (3) consistent verb tense. Cross out the incorrect verb and write the correct form in the space provided.

_____ 1. The quarterback had broke most of the school's passing records by his senior year.

_____ 2. The cost of the transmission and brake repairs are more than the car's worth.

_____ 3. The more my instructor tried to explain the material and the more he writes on the board, the more confused I got.

_____ 4. Nobody on the police force know the identity of the informer.

_____ 5. Lola likes to use lip gloss but hated the way it stains her fingers and never seems to come off.

_____ 6. Each of Ramona's boyfriends think he is the only man in her life.

_____ 7. The socks I bought at that store have wore thin after only three months.

_____ 8. Out of my little brother's mouth comes some of the most amazing words I have ever heard.

_____ 9. As soon as the store opened, customers race through the doors and hurried to the bargain racks.

_____ 10. We have not ate out at a restaurant since my wife lost her job.

Score: Number correct _____ × 10 = _____%

VERBS

● Combined Mastery Test 2

Each sentence contains a mistake involving (1) standard English or irregular verb forms, (2) subject-verb agreement, or (3) consistent verb tense. Cross out the incorrect verb and write the correct form in the space provided.

_____ 1. Lola was stang by some kind of bug during her hike in the woods.

_____ 2. My sister and I often gets into an argument at the dinner table.

_____ 3. The mechanic told me my car was going to be ready by noon, but he finishes working on it at five o'clock.

_____ 4. I had not did my math homework, so I was sure my instructor would give a surprise quiz.

_____ 5. Roaring down a quiet street at fifty miles an hour were Daisy on her new Honda.

_____ 6. You should have knowed better than to trust your little brother to deliver the message.

_____ 7. Carl watched suspiciously as a strange car drives back and forth in front of his house.

_____ 8. I should have brung an extra pen to the exam.

_____ 9. When Lola saw the children skipping home from school clutching their drawings, she remembered when she use to do the same thing.

_____ 10. Rob Revolting, lead singer of the Deadly Poisons, wears a black satin jump suit with a silver skull and crossbones on the front when he perform.

Score: Number correct _____ × 10 = _____ %

PRONOUNS

 ## Combined Mastery Test I

Choose the sentence in each pair that uses pronouns correctly. Then write the letter of that sentence in the space provided.

_____   1. a.   When I took my son to his first basketball game, he was amazed at how tall they were.
           b.   When I took my son to his first basketball game, he was amazed at how tall the players were.

_____   2. a.   You can't play the new software on the Macintosh because it's defective.
           b.   You can't play the new software on the Macintosh because the software is defective.

_____   3. a.   None of the players on the women's softball team felt proud about her performance in the championship game.
           b.   None of the players on the women's softball team felt proud about their performance in the championship game.

_____   4. a.   I've learned a lot about biking from Eddie, who is a much better biker than me.
           b.   I've learned a lot about biking from Eddie, who is a much better biker than I.

_____   5. a.   I wanted to browse through the store, but in every department a salesperson came up and asked to help you.
           b.   I wanted to browse through the store, but in every department a salesperson came up and asked to help me.

Score: Number correct _____ × 20 = _____%

PRONOUNS

 ## Combined Mastery Test 2

In the space provided, write *PE* beside each of the nine sentences that contain pronoun errors. Write *C* beside the sentence that uses pronouns correctly. Then cross out each pronoun error and write the correction above it.

_____   1. Diane received in the mail an ad that said you could make $600 a month addressing envelopes.

_____   2. We refereed the game ourselfs, for no officials were available.

_____   3. Before any more time is wasted, you and me must have a serious talk.

_____   4. One of the Boy Scouts left some live embers burning in his campfire.

_____   5. Everyone who works in the company must have their chest x-rayed every two years.

_____   6. The instructor gave George and I a warning look.

_____   7. Gina wanted to run in for some bread and milk, but it was so crowded that she decided not to bother.

_____   8. If them eggs have a bad smell, throw them away.

_____   9. When I visited a friend at the hospital, you had to pay two dollars just to use the parking lot.

_____   10. Alex called Franco at work to say that his father had had an accident.

Score: Number correct _____ × 10 = _____ %

FAULTY MODIFIERS AND PARALLELISM

 ## Combined Mastery Test I

In the space provided, indicate whether each sentence contains a misplaced modifier (*MM*), a dangling modifier (*DM*), or faulty parallelism (*FP*). Then correct the error in the space under the sentence.

_____ 1. My parents like to visit auctions, eat Mexican food, and watching horror movies.

_____

_____ 2. An old wreck of wars past, Admiral Hawkeye inspected the ship.

_____

_____ 3. I notified the police that my house had been burglarized by phone.

_____

_____ 4. Dulled by Novocaine, the dentist pulled my tooth.

_____

_____ 5. With sweaty hands and a voice that trembled, Alice read her paper aloud.

_____

_____ 6. At the age of six, my mother bought me a chemistry set.

_____

_____ 7. Cut and infected, Reggie took his dog to the vet.

_____

_____ 8. My neighbor mowed the lawn perspiring heavily.

_____

_____ 9. Midori decided to start a garden while preparing dinner.

_____

_____ 10. To earn extra money, Terry types term papers and is working at the Point Diner.

_____

Score: Number correct _____   × 10 = _____%

FAULTY MODIFIERS AND PARALLELISM

● Combined Mastery Test 2

In the space provided, indicate whether each sentence contains a misplaced modifier (*MM*), a dangling modifier (*DM*), or faulty parallelism (*FP*). Then correct the error in the space under the sentence.

_____   1. By studying harder, Barry's grades improved.

_____   2. We put the food back in the knapsack that we had not eaten.

_____   3. My doctor advised extra sleep, nourishing food, and that I should exercise regularly.

_____   4. Smelling up the room, I quickly put the trout in the freezer.

_____   5. Buying a foreign car will cause more family arguments for me than to buy an American car.

_____   6. Marty is the guy carrying packages with curly brown hair.

_____   7. My hopes for retirement are good health, having plenty of money, and beautiful companions.

_____   8. Filled with cigarette butts and used tea bags, I washed the disgusting cups.

_____   9. I asked Bonny to see a movie with me nervously.

_____   10. Frightened by the rising crime rate, an alarm system was installed in the house.

Score: Number correct _____ × 10 = _____%

CAPITAL LETTERS
AND PUNCTUATION

 ## Combined Mastery Test I

Each of the following sentences contains an error in capitalization or punctuation. Refer to the box below to write, in the space provided, the letter identifying the error. Then correct the error.

a. missing capital	c. missing quotation marks
b. missing apostrophe	d. missing comma

_____ 1. I wanted desperately to scratch the scab on my hand but I didn't want to take the risk of infecting it.

_____ 2. "Don't drive too close to the edge of the prairie, the old prospector warned the tourists, "or you're liable to fall off."

_____ 3. Did you know they're going to tear down the old school on second Street and put a McDonald's there?

_____ 4. The hamsters eyes glowed when some fresh lettuce was put into its cage.

_____ 5. Because the electric can opener was broken Fred was unable to make himself some chicken noodle soup.

_____ 6. Its not going to be easy to find a job that both pays well and involves interesting work.

_____ 7. The woman was asked why she wanted to be a mortician. "I enjoy working with people, she replied.

_____ 8. For my lonely uncle Russ, holidays are the worst time of the year.

_____ 9. Some people believe that voting should be mandatory not merely encouraged, in the United States.

_____ 10. Martha said to the woman behind her in the theater, "will you shut your mouth, please?"

Score: Number correct _____ × 10 = _____%

CAPITAL LETTERS AND PUNCTUATION

● Combined Mastery Test 2

Each of the following sentences contains an error in capitalization or punctuation. Refer to the box below to write, in the space provided, the letter identifying the error. Then correct the error.

a. missing capital	c. missing quotation marks
b. missing apostrophe	d. missing comma

_____ 1. There is nothing on the menu of that restaurant," Nick said, "that would not cause nausea in laboratory mice."

_____ 2. If you'll hold this package shut for me I'll be able to do a better job of taping it closed.

_____ 3. Lolas yoga class has been canceled this week, so she's decided to go running instead.

_____ 4. Fran said, "the directions called for a pinch of sugar in the stew, but I accidentally added a teaspoonful."

_____ 5. Roger just got a good job offer today so he won't have to stand in the unemployment line anymore.

_____ 6. Unless I start studying soon, I'm going to have to repeat sociology 101.

_____ 7. "Did you hear the news? Martha asked Fred. "A man who was attempting to walk around the world drowned today."

_____ 8. If youre going to stay up late, be sure to turn down the heat before going to bed.

_____ 9. I was able to return the hair dryer, even though I hadn't saved the receipt to the Sears catalog store.

_____ 10. The company has to pay double time when it calls employees in to work an extra shift on sunday.

Score: Number correct _____ × 10 = _____%	

WORD USE

 ## Combined Mastery Test I

Each of the following sentences contains a mistake identified in the left-hand margin. Underline the mistake and then correct it in the space provided.

Slang

1. Ralph was canned from his job yesterday for sleeping at his desk.

_____

Wordiness

2. I'm in college for the purpose of getting a degree in data processing.

_____

Cliché

3. Nick and Fran were able to depend upon their parents in their hour of need.

_____

Pretentious language

4. Eric improved his math skills by utilizing the tutoring center at school.

_____

Adverb error

5. Wilma has not done bad in her math course, even though she missed a week of classes because of illness.

_____

Error in comparison

6. This year my garden has been producing the abundantest crop of weeds in human history.

_____

Confused word

7. It's the second time our dog has broken it's chain and run away.

_____

Confused word

8. The doctor was concerned that the new allergy drug would effect my sense of balance.

_____

Confused word

9. There not too friendly in that store, but their merchandise is sold at bargain prices.

_____

Confused word

10. Whitney plans to move to an efficiency apartment hear in the city.

_____

Score: Number correct _____ × 10 = _____%

WORD USE

● Combined Mastery Test 2

Each of the following sentences contains a mistake identified in the left-hand margin. Underline the mistake and then correct it in the space provided.

Slang

1. That company has spent millions to hype its new shampoo.

_____

Wordiness

2. I plan to quit my job because of the fact that my boss treats me unfairly.

_____

Cliché

3. The catcher and pitcher had a sneaking suspicion that their signs were being stolen.

_____

Pretentious language

4. Bonnie wants to procure a VCR as soon as she has the money.

_____

Adverb error

5. Phil and Nancy are taking their relationship too serious, considering that they're still teenagers.

_____

Error in comparison

6. The book report for my psychology class is the most bad paper I've ever written.

_____

Confused word

7. Football has always been the principle sport at our school.

_____

Confused word

8. You're children are the ones who broke my front gate, so you're going to pay for the damage.

_____

Confused word

9. Whose the professor whose courses involve a lot of field trips?

_____

Confused word

10. Classes in college are far less regimented then the ones in high school.

_____

> *Score:*   Number correct _____ × 10 = _____%

Editing and Proofreading Tests

The passages in this section can be used in either of two ways:

1 As Editing Tests: Each passage contains a number of mistakes involving a single sentence skill. For example, the first passage on page 419 contains five fragments. Your instructor may ask you to proofread the passage to locate the five fragment errors. Spaces are provided at the bottom of the page for you to indicate which word groups are fragments. Your instructor may also have you correct the errors, either in the text itself or on separate paper. Depending on how well you do, you may also be asked to edit the second and third passages for fragments.

There are three passages for each skill area, and there are twelve skills covered in all. Here is a list of the skill areas:

2 As Guided Composition Activities: To give you practice in proofreading as well, your instructor may ask you to do more than correct the mistakes in each passage. You may be asked to rewrite the passage, correcting it for mistakes *and also* copying the rest of the passage perfectly. Should you miss one mistake involving a skill or make even one mistake in copying (for example, omitting a word, dropping a verb ending, misspelling a word, or misplacing an apostrophe), you may be asked to rewrite a different passage that deals with the same skill.

Here is how you would proceed. You would start with sentence fragments, rewriting the first passage, proofreading your paper carefully, and then showing it to your instructor. He or she will check it quickly to see that all the fragments have been corrected and that no mistakes have been made in copying. If the passage is error-free, the instructor will mark and initial the appropriate box in the progress chart on pages 534–535 and you can proceed to run-ons.

If even a single mistake is made, the instructor may question you briefly to see if you recognize and understand it. (Perhaps he or she will put a check beside the line in which the mistake appears and then ask if you can correct it.) You may then be asked to write the second passage under a particular skill. If necessary, you will keep working on that skill and rewrite the third passage (and even perhaps go on to repeat the first and second passages) as well. You will complete the program in guided composition when you successfully work through all twelve skills. Completing the twelve skills will strengthen your understanding of the skills, increase your chances of transferring the skills to actual writing situations, and markedly improve your proofreading ability.

In doing the passages, note the following points:

a For each skill you will be told the number of mistakes that appear in the passages. If you have trouble finding the mistakes, turn back and review the pages in this book that explain the skill in question.

b Here is an effective way to go about correcting a passage. First, read it over quickly. Look for and mark off mistakes in the skill area involved. For example, in your first reading of a passage that has five fragments, you may locate and mark only three fragments. If so, reread the passage carefully to find the remaining errors in the skill in question. Finally, make notes in the margin about how to correct each mistake. Only at this point should you begin to rewrite the passage.

c Be sure to proofread with care after you finish a passage. Go over your writing word for word, looking for careless errors. Remember that you may be asked to do another passage involving the same skill if you make even one mistake.

Test I: Fragments

Mistakes in each passage: 5

Passage A

[1]I am only thirty, but a trip to the movies recently made me realize that my youth is definitely past. [2]The science-fiction movie had attracted a large audience of younger kids and teenagers. [3]Before the movie began. [4]Groups of kids ran up and down the aisles, laughing, giggling, and spilling popcorn. [5]I was annoyed with them. [6]But thought, "At one time, I was doing the same thing. [7]Now I'm acting like one of the adults." [8]The thought was a little depressing, for I remembered how much fun it was not to care what the adults thought. [9]Soon after the movie began, a group of teenagers walked in and sat in the first row. [10]During the movie, they vied with each other. [11]To see who could make the loudest comment. [12]Or the most embarrassing noise. [13]Some of the adults in the theater complained to the usher, but I had a guilty memory about doing the same thing myself a few times. [14]In addition, a teenage couple was sitting in front of me. [15]Occasionally, these two held hands or the boy put his arm around the girl. [16]A few times, they sneaked a kiss. [17]Realizing that my wife and I were long past this kind of behavior in the movies. [18]I again felt like an old man.

Word groups with fragments: _____ _____ _____ _____ _____

Passage B

[1]For her biology class, Ann lay stretched out on the grass in the park. [2]Taking notes on the insect life she observed around her. [3]First, a clear-winged bug sat down from the heat. [4]And swayed on a blade of grass nearby. [5]Next, landing suddenly on her hand, a ladybug. [6]Ann could count the number of dots on its tiny, speckled body as it crawled around and under her fingers. [7]When the ladybug left, Ann picked up a low, flat rock. [8]Three black crickets slithered quickly away. [9]Seeking shelter under other rocks or leaves. [10]She watched one camouflage itself under a leaf. [11]Carefully, she removed the leaf and watched the cricket dig deeper into the underbrush. [12]It kept crawling away from the light. [13]Ann moved her eyes away for a second as a car went by. [14]When she looked back. [15]The cricket had disappeared.

Word groups with fragments: _____ _____ _____ _____ _____

Passage C

[1]One factor that causes you to forget is lack of motivation. [2]If you have no reason for remembering certain information. [3]You will probably forget it. [4]Dr. Joyce Brothers, a prominent psychologist, relates how she memorized facts on boxing. [5]To win $64,000 on a television quiz show. [6]She and her husband were college students at the time. [7]And, like most students, could use some extra money. [8]She was not as interested in boxing as she was in winning the money. [9]After she had won the money and used her memorized information for its purpose. [10]She promptly forgot the facts. [11]Another factor in forgetting is interference. [12]Previous learning can interfere with new learning. [13]Especially if there are similarities between the two. [14]If you have previously studied traditional math, you may experience difficulty learning the new math.

Word groups with fragments: _____   _____   _____   _____   _____

Test 2: Run-Ons (Fused Sentences)

Mistakes in each passage: 5

Passage A

¹Someday soon you may not have to get up in the morning and go to work you will, instead, work at home in front of your very own computer. ²Already many thousands of American workers are "telecommuters" they do at home what they used to do in the office. ³For instance, one secretary takes dictation from her boss over the telephone. ⁴Then she types the letters on her computer terminal. ⁵Stockbrokers or sales personnel can place orders and keep records right in their living rooms all they need is a computer hookup. ⁶A few banks and consulting firms give their employees a choice of working in the office or at home many other businesses as well plan to try this idea. ⁷Telecommuting has many advantages some of them are no commuting time, no expensive lunch hours, and an extra income tax deduction for a home office. ⁸You also have a chance to do your work without worrying about the boss looking over your shoulder.

Word groups with run-ons: _____ _____ _____ _____ _____

Passage B

¹Have you ever wondered what the hotels of the future might look like? ²You need not wonder any longer a hotel in Japan will give you a preview. ³The name of this hotel is the Capsule Inn its rooms rent for eleven dollars a night. ⁴Each room comes with a radio, a television set, and an alarm clock in addition, all the rooms are air-conditioned, but here any resemblance to a twentieth-century hotel ends. ⁵The rooms are small plastic capsules each capsule is about five feet high by five feet wide by seven feet deep. ⁶The capsules are stacked in a double layer guests have to crawl into bed through a large porthole entrance. ⁷Bathrooms and washing facilities, and sofas, chairs, and vending machines are located in common areas in other parts of the hotel. ⁸Believe it or not, this hotel is almost always full, perhaps because the price of the rooms is as small as the rooms themselves.

Word groups with run-ons: _____ _____ _____ _____ _____

Passage C

[1]The paperback book that we take for granted is a fairly new invention. [2]At one time, the only books available were hardcover ones that cost a few dollars—an expensive purchase for the average working person. [3]Then, in the 1930s, one publisher decided that there was a large market for a light, portable, inexpensive book the book would be cheaper to manufacture because it would have paper covers and a glued spine. [4]The publisher was right it took several years for the books to catch on. [5]World War II gave paperbacks the push they needed. [6]The government gave armed forces editions of paperbacks to men and women serving overseas the books were light enough to carry in a pack. [7]Many soldiers survived dull or frightening times by turning to the tattered books in their kits after the war, they brought the paperback habit home with them. [8]In the 1950s, however, paperbacks suffered a loss of respectability they were linked with trashy detective stories or soft-core sex. [9]Now, paperbacks are bought by almost everyone, and readers can find everything from best-selling novels to works of philosophy enclosed in soft covers.

Word groups with run-ons: _____   _____   _____   _____   _____

Test 3: Run-Ons (Comma Splices)

Mistakes in each passage: 5

Passage A

[1]"Typhoid Mary" is the name that was given to a woman who unknowingly spread death throughout New York City at the turn of the century. [2]Typhoid is caused by bacteria and is highly infectious, it causes fever, diarrhea, and often death. [3]Mary was a carrier of the disease, but she herself was unaffected by it. [4]Unfortunately, Mary worked as a cook, so she passed the disease to others through the food she touched. [5]Mary would take a job as cook to a household. [6]A few weeks later, several members of the family would become ill, sometimes typhoid would break out over a whole neighborhood. [7]After this happened several times, Mary became frightened, death appeared wherever she went, but she did not understand why or how. [8]Eventually, Mary was tracked down and arrested by public health authorities. [9]When she promised not to work as a cook again, she was released, she then vanished into the city. [10]But there were rumors that she continued to work as a cook, whenever typhoid broke out in the city for years afterward, "Typhoid Mary" was blamed.

Word groups with run-ons: _____ _____ _____ _____ _____

Passage B

[1]The worst job I ever had was as packager in the Thompson Laundry. [2]First of all, I hated the hours, I had to get up at five in the morning and work from six until two-thirty in the afternoon. [3]Second, the work was boring. [4]All day long, I folded clothes, wrapped them in brown paper, and sealed them with tape that never stuck to the paper. [5]Also, the heat in the "hole," which is what the workers called the place, was unbearable. [6]There were two little fans in the front of the store, they didn't help, however, because I was in the middle of twelve hot dryers. [7]It was always ten degrees hotter inside than it was out, on many summer days the temperature inside was at least a hundred degrees! [8]But I think the main reason I hated the job was Harry, my boss, Harry's favorite lines were, "My, you look tired today" and "All right, let's keep moving because there's a lot to do today." [9]I badly wanted to slug Harry or curse him, I did not control my temper easily. [10]Because he was always around watching me, I was never able to take little breaks along the way. [11]If I had had a chance to rest now and then, the job might have been more bearable.

Word groups with run-ons: _____ _____ _____ _____ _____

Passage C

[1]People are fond of pointing out how much there is wrong with television programming, and many shows do leave much to be desired. [2]But there is also much that is good about television, to begin with, television offers us an escape from our daily problems. [3]No matter what is bothering us, we can put our brains on hold for a while and enjoy some mindless fun, this only becomes a problem if we put our brains on hold for hours on end. [4]Another positive aspect of television is the wide choice of programs we have to choose from, it wasn't long ago that there were only three channels. [5]If you didn't find something you liked on one of those three, it was just your tough luck. [6]Since the development of cable television, it is not uncommon for a viewer to have over thirty different channels to choose from, this means more interests and tastes are being served. [7]The best thing about television, though, is the service it performs for all of us. [8]It keeps us in touch with what is happening around the world, we have therefore learned more about our fellow citizens and people from other places and cultures. [9]In fact, millions of people have at times worked together to aid others whose misfortunes they learned about on television news.

Word groups with run-ons: _____   _____   _____   _____   _____

Test 4: Standard English Verbs

Mistakes in each passage: 5

Passage A

¹Sal should have stayed in bed yesterday. ²He knew it when he tried to shut off his alarm and accidentally pushed the clock to the floor. ³Sal decide to brave fate anyway. ⁴He dressed and headed for the breakfast table. ⁵After putting two slices of bread into the toaster, he went out to get the paper. ⁶Rain hurtled down from a dark sky. ⁷The paper was not under the shelter of the porch but was sitting, completely soak with water, on the walk. ⁸"Thanks a lot, paperboy," Sal said to himself as he left the paper where it was and return to the kitchen. ⁹After eating quickly, he gathered his books and ran down to the bus stop. ¹⁰No one was there, which meant he had miss the bus. ¹¹As he stood for twenty minutes waiting for the next bus, his pants were splashed by two cars that went by. ¹²When the bus finally pulled up, Sal reached into his pocket for the fare. ¹³Two dimes slipped out of his fingers and fell into the water at the curb. ¹⁴After fishing out the coins and paying his fare, Sal discovered there were no empty seats on the bus. ¹⁵Standing there, he wonder what other kinds of bad luck awaited him at school.

Sentences with nonstandard verbs: _____ _____ _____ _____ _____

Passage B

¹Keeping cities clean became more difficult as cities grew larger. ²Some ancient cities solve the cleanliness problem: for example, inhabitants of ancient Rome had waterborne sewage systems and public baths. ³But during the Middle Ages, these health-supporting systems disappear from the cities of Europe. ⁴Sewage and garbage were dump in yards and streets, and bathing in the river was considered to be bad for one's health. ⁵It was not surprising that a great plague, the Black Death, rage through Europe during this period, killing about one-fourth of its inhabitants. ⁶Eventually sanitary facilities improve, and in modern cities, many social agencies take care of removing sewage, disposing of garbage, and sweeping the streets.

Sentences with nonstandard verbs: _____ _____ _____ _____ _____

Passage C

[1]The river rambles for miles around trees and bushes. [2]At one point, children throw small rocks and laugh at the splashes they make. [3]Further along, factories dump gallons of slime and pollutants into the water. [4]Away from the factories, the river seem to smile as it ripples over stones. [5]A waterfall appears near a clump of trees. [6]Romantic couples sit there in the spring. [7]Occasionally, a fisherman tries his luck at the river's edge. [8]A mile or two past the waterfall, the river roar angrily along. [9]It rush noisily. [10]Boys and girls pretend they are captains of many fleets. [11]They sail paper ships and watch them sink. [12]Where the river widen and grows calm once more, someone always seems to be paddling a canoe. [13]Where a bridge stretch across the river, old men stand and look out over the water. [14]The river never gets lonely, for someone is always there to use it.

Sentences with nonstandard verbs: _____   _____   _____   _____   _____

Test 5: Irregular Verbs

Mistakes in each passage: 10

Passage A

¹When the game show contestant learned she had chose the box with only a penny in it, she was badly shaken. ²She begun to cry, and the game show host for a minute was froze with fear. ³Then he taked her hand and said, "You have not gotten to the end of the line yet, Mrs. Waterby. Cheer up." ⁴When she learned she was going to be given one more chance, Mrs. Waterby stopped crying. ⁵At the host's signal, a tray was brang onto the stage and placed in front of Mrs. Waterby. ⁶On the tray sat three shells. ⁷One shell, the host told her, covered the key to a new Lincoln Continental. ⁸Mrs. Waterby was to choose the shell she thinked had the key under it. ⁹There was a long pause, and she gived her answer, "Number three." ¹⁰The host lifted up the third shell; the key was underneath. ¹¹Mrs. Waterby danced about the stage, just as she had been instructed to do if she winned. ¹²Her husband run up on stage and embraced her. ¹³They had realized the great American dream: they had gotten something for nothing.

Sentences with irregular verbs (write down the number of a sentence twice if it contains two irregular verbs):

_____ _____ _____ _____ _____

_____ _____ _____ _____

Passage B

¹Occasionally when I have drove to work, I have gotten behind a slow driver. ²This usually occurs when I have leaved the house late. ³I have tried to pass such drivers, but traffic always seems too heavy in the opposite direction. ⁴At this point, I have spoke to myself or sung to myself, trying to forget how slow I was traveling. ⁵I have never understood the reason for going 25 miles per hour in a 50-mile-per-hour zone. ⁶Once past the stage of trying to keep calm, I have always expressed my anger to the fullest. ⁷I have shook the steering wheel and sayed the foulest words I know. ⁸I have imagined stealing a bazooka from an Army depot and blasting the slow driver with it. ⁹After I have wore myself out, I have gritted my teeth and waited for my sanity to return. ¹⁰Usually about

a mile from my office, the driver in front of me has turned off and has rode out of sight. [11]Then I have forgetted all about it and have went on with my day.

Sentences with irregular verbs (write down the number of a sentence twice if it contains two irregular verbs):

_____ _____ _____ _____ _____

_____ _____ _____ _____ _____

Passage C

[1]Pete Jenkins had knew the meaning of fear before, like the time he got a cramp while swimming. [2]Luckily, he had been saved from drowning then by a friend he always swum with. [3]But Pete admits that his first job interview brang an even greater fear. [4]On the morning of the interview, his stomach felt as if he had ate a block of cement the night before. [5]In his throat, a lump had grew to the size of a football, and he wondered if he would be able to speak at all. [6]His mother realized Pete was nervous. [7]She drived him to the interview office and then burst out laughing. [8]"Pete," she said, "this is just an interview for a job at McDonald's." [9]At first, Pete was angry with his mother for laughing, but when she apologized he forgived her. [10]He also knowed his mother was right. [11]He was just going to be interviewed for a job making hamburgers. [12]He kepted his composure during the interview and came through it with ease.

Sentences with irregular verbs (write down the number of a sentence twice if it contains two irregular verbs):

_____ _____ _____ _____ _____

_____ _____ _____ _____ _____

Test 6: Misplaced and Dangling Modifiers

Mistakes in each passage: 5

Passage A

¹The best vacation I ever had was when my friends and I rented a big old beach house in Ocean City. ²Having twelve rooms, each of us had plenty of room to ourselves. ³The house was nearly located right on the beach, so all we had to do in the morning was fall forward to be right in the middle of the action. ⁴Playing volleyball and lying in the sun, the days passed by in a blur of contentment. ⁵For lunch we strolled up to the boardwalk to buy hot dogs from a vendor with sauerkraut heaped on top. ⁶After lunch we returned to our spot on the beach to read or take a nap. ⁷When the sun got too hot in the afternoon, we retreated to the house, where we sat in comfortable old rocking chairs on the shady wraparound porch. ⁸Sitting there, we could relax and watch the action on the beach. ⁹With a cool drink in hand, the summer felt as if it just might last forever.

Sentences with misplaced modifiers: _____   _____

Sentences with dangling modifiers: _____   _____   _____

Passage B

¹Last Saturday I tried to be a good friend and agreed to help my friend Lamar move into his new apartment. ²What was supposed to take only an hour or two ended up lasting the entire day. ³Lamar's idea was to save money by doing the job himself, but I think he almost spent as much as it would have cost to hire professionals. ⁴Robert and Curt and I arrived at Lamar's apartment at eight o'clock, but he was still sound asleep. ⁵After pounding on the door, he finally let us in. ⁶Stumbling around with his eyes half closed, a half hour was wasted before Lamar finally got ready. ⁷Then he and I drove to the truck-rental agency. ⁸Before he knew what had happened to him, Lamar agreed to buy packing cartons, tape, and twine. ⁹He also paid extra for a hand truck to use in moving the refrigerator. ¹⁰Finally seated behind the wheel of the rental truck, it wouldn't start, so the attendant had to come out and start it for us. ¹¹On the way back to the apartment, Lamar stopped to borrow money to pay for the truck at his parents' house. ¹²By the time we returned to his apartment, the curb was lined with packing boxes, and Robert and Curt were

sitting on the front step. [13]The rest of the day moved a little faster than the morning. [14]But it was dark by the time we finished, and I was left wondering where my Saturday had gone.

Sentences with misplaced modifiers: _____ _____

Sentences with dangling modifiers: _____ _____ _____

Passage C

[1]One of the best jobs I ever had was as a stock expediter in a naval shipyard. [2]There were always some materials that had been ordered and paid for but never received by the shipyard, which it was my job to find. [3]Using the original invoice as a starting point, my work in finding lost items would begin. [4]Most items were found very quickly, but there were always a few that seemed to have disappeared. [5]Those were the cases I liked the most. [6]Several items had been missing for several years, and I devoted my attention to these whenever I had a spare moment. [7]Wandering through some of the old warehouses, luck would often come my way. [8]Sitting in a damp corner covered with mouse droppings, I once found a box of sheet metal screws. [9]I wrote down the number of the box on a note pad and checked it against my lists. [10]Sure enough, the box was one of the items I had been searching for. [11]It had been ordered three years earlier! [12]I felt like a very shrewd detective who had just cracked a difficult case at moments like that.

Sentences with misplaced modifiers: _____ _____

Sentences with dangling modifiers: _____ _____ _____

Test 7: Parallelism

Mistakes in each passage: 5

Passage A

¹People who do not want to pay for air conditioning can find other ways to keep a house cool during the hot weather. ²One way is to plant trees and shrubs and the use of awnings. ³As a result, outside walls and windows are kept cool. ⁴Another method is to get rid of the hot air that builds up in attic spaces by installing attic vents and power fans. ⁵In addition, window fans can be used at night to push out the hot daytime air and pull in the air that is cool in the evening. ⁶In the morning, when the house is still cool, the windows should be closed and draw the drapes. ⁷The windows and drapes can be opened if a breeze begins or a sudden drop in temperature. ⁸A final method of keeping the house cool is to water areas outside, such as concrete driveways and patios, that tend to collect heat and reflecting it against the house. ⁹Wet these every hour or so with a sprinkler or hose to prevent heat buildup.

Sentences with faulty parallelism: _____ _____ _____ _____ _____

Passage B

¹Human beings attempt to protect themselves psychologically as well as in physical ways. ²If someone harms you physically, you may want to fight back. ³To guard yourself psychologically, you may use defense mechanisms. ⁴You may be unaware of your real motives in adjusting to a situation that is undesirable or a threat. ⁵Three common defense mechanisms are regression, rationalization, and trying to compensate. ⁶Regression means returning to an earlier form of behavior. ⁷A person who regresses temporarily rejects the "hard cruel world" and is seeking the greater security of childhood. ⁸Rationalization is making excuses. ⁹A student not wanting to study for a test decides that she doesn't know what to study. ¹⁰Compensation is a form of substitution. ¹¹If a person wants a better education but cannot attend school, she may try studying on her own or to learn more through experience.

Sentences with faulty parallelism: __1__ __4__ __5__ __7__ __11__

Passage C

[handwritten: suspicious]

[1]In shopping for a good used car, be cautious and have suspicion. [2]Remember that the previous owner had some reason for getting rid of the car. [3]The reason may have been that he or she wanted to buy a new car or the [handwritten: avoiding] avoidance of costly repairs. [4]A car that appears to have a "dirt-cheap" price may turn out to have "sky-high" costs. [5]Remember, too, that the [handwritten: the better the chances are] older a car is, the chances are better that it will soon require major repairs. [6]If you buy an older car, be sure that repair parts and service facilities are available in your area. [7]Try to pick a used car with the lowest mileage on the odometer, the best overall condition, and [handwritten: a long time guarantee] that the dealer guarantees for the longest time. [8]There are several ways to protect yourself from a falsified odometer. [9]You should ask for a mileage disclosure statement, examine closely the condition of the vehicle, and contacting the previous owner.

Sentences with faulty parallelism: [handwritten: 1] [handwritten: 3] [handwritten: 5] [handwritten: 7] [handwritten: 9]

Test 8: Capital Letters

Mistakes in each passage: 10

Passage A

¹Red Riding Hood decided to visit her grandmother in brooklyn. ²Old Mrs. Hood had just been released from bayshore hospital, where she had spent the entire month of september recovering from a broken hip. ³Red Riding Hood's mother gave her daughter a container of vegetable soup to bring to Grandma Hood. ⁴Red entered the subway entrance on third avenue, and when the train roared in, she boarded a car. ⁵Suddenly, a young man approached Red. ⁶He resembled a wolf with his long, greasy hair and beard, and he said, "what a foxy face you've got, little girl. ⁷I'd like to eat you up." ⁸"Take off," said Red. ⁹"I'm a part-time Guardian angel and I know how to defend myself." ¹⁰When he tried to touch Red, she flipped the copy of *people* she was reading into his face to distract him. ¹¹Then she delivered a quick karate chop with her hand. ¹²The man staggered backward and an elderly woman then batted him with a large box of reynolds aluminum foil from her shopping bag. ¹³The train entered the station and Red Riding Hood stepped over the wolf-like man, who lay groaning on the floor. ¹⁴"Maybe this will teach you to let decent people ride the subway in peace," she said as she stepped through the doors.

Sentences with missing capitals (write the number of a sentence as many times as it contains capitalization mistakes):

——— ——— ——— ——— ———

——— ——— ——— ———

Passage B

¹Although I'm much older now, I still remember the day I found out santa claus was a fake. ²I was seven years old, and my brother Neil was five. ³That evening, Mother told us, "be sure you go to bed early, and don't try any tricks, or you won't get your christmas present till *next* december." ⁴So we quickly put on our pajamas, brushed our teeth with colgate toothpaste, and got under the covers. ⁵I didn't even finish the Wonder Woman comic book I was halfway through. ⁶We whispered for a while about whether we'd get the irish setter puppy we wanted so badly, or if we'd just get another boring game like tinkertoys that was supposed to be "educational." ⁷Then we went to sleep, but in the middle of the

night I woke up with a horrible thought. [8]What if Santa didn't know that we lived at 7201 springfield avenue? [9]He might bring our puppy to the wrong house! [10]I ran into my parents' bedroom to ask them if he knew where we lived, but they weren't there. [11]Then I heard noises coming from the living room. [12]I tiptoed downstairs—and there were my parents, putting something wrapped in green paper and tied with red ribbon under the tree. [13]To this day, I don't know what hurt more—getting a Scrabble set the next morning or finding out that the jolly fat man in a red suit and white beard was only Mom and Dad.

Sentences with missing capitals (write the number of a sentence as many times as it contains capitalization mistakes):

_____   _____   _____   _____   _____

_____   _____   _____   _____   _____

Passage C

[1]Credit cards have been abused by both the people that own them and the companies that issue them. [2]Some people fall into the habit of using their visa charge card for hotels and meals, their texaco card for gasoline, and other cards for department store purchases. [3]The danger in this, as was pointed out recently on the television program *Sixty minutes,* is that people can quickly reach a point where they cannot meet the monthly payments on their charge cards. [4]Such people can appreciate the warning in a texas newspaper, "it isn't buying on time that's difficult, it's paying on time." [5]Organizations such as consumers union have published articles alerting people to the high interest charges involved. [6]And magazines such as *time* and *newsweek* have also pointed out how quickly people lose a sense of their financial resources with charge cards. [7]Perhaps charge cards should carry the message, "excessive use of this card may be hazardous to your economic health."

Sentences with missing capitals (write the number of a sentence as many times as it contains capitalization mistakes):

_____   _____   _____   _____   _____

_____   _____   _____   _____   _____

Test 9: Apostrophes

Mistakes in each passage: 10

Passage A

¹Working as a house packer for Jerrys moving service was an enjoyable job for me. ²First of all, almost no other job allows you to go into peoples houses and see at close range how they live. ³I encountered a lot of interesting surprises. ⁴For example, one womans house was as neat as a display room in a museum, but her basement was as littered as our towns dump. ⁵Another person had converted a bedroom into a small library. ⁶The rooms four walls contained storage shelves, all filled with books and magazines like *Reader's Digest* and *Time.* ⁷I also liked the job because people would give me things they didnt want anymore. ⁸For instance, I received a lot of childrens toys and a complete set of tools. ⁹In fact, my mothers cellar started filling with items I received from customers cellars. ¹⁰Im planning to work again for Jerry next year.

Sentences with missing apostrophes (write down the number of a sentence twice if it contains two missing apostrophes):

——— ——— ——— ——— ———

——— ——— ——— ——— ———

Passage B

¹Mrs. Bartlett is our towns strangest person. ²She has lived in the big house on Pine Street, without once setting foot outside, for more years than most people remember. ³In her yard she keeps several cocker spaniels thatll rip your pants in a second. ⁴While the regular mailmans face is familiar to the dogs, they treat a substitute mailman like a juicy bone. ⁵In addition to the dogs, there are dozens of tame blackbirds perched in the trees. ⁶Hitchcocks movie *The Birds* could have been made using her yard and house as a setting. ⁷If you are on her good side, Mrs. B. (everyones name for her) will invite you in for tea. ⁸Her gardener, Willy, watches the dogs while you hurry to the porch. ⁹Willys job, by the way, is also to serve as night watchman. ¹⁰Since he's almost seven feet tall, its not surprising that no prowlers have troubled the property. ¹¹Inside the house, a maid named Tina will take your coat. ¹²A curiosity-seekers question will get only a scowl from the

close-mouthed Tina and a short, "Thats not your business." [13]People in general seem to respect this answer, and no ones challenged the right of Mrs. B. to live life her own way.

Sentences with missing apostrophes (write down the number of a sentence twice if it contains two missing apostrophes):

———   ———   ———   ———   ———

———   ———   ———   ———   ———

Passage C

[1]In a small park near the center of Millville, a group of bronze statues stand in a circle. [2]Most of them are models of the individual rich men who provided money for the towns beginning. [3]The center of the circle is occupied by a nameless man. [4]Citizens call him Joe because hes a symbol of the common man. [5]Joes clothes appear tattered, but his body seems strong. [6]His face looks tired, but his eyes look proud. [7]Each person Joe represents couldnt give money to the town but gave strength and sweat instead. [8]A farmers back worked to keep the town in food. [9]A womans hands wove, knitted, and sewed clothes. [10]A blacksmiths arms struggled to provide horseshoes and tools. [11]Joes eyes must talk to passersby. [12]People seem to realize that without the ordinary persons help, that circle of rich men wouldnt exist.

Sentences with missing apostrophes (write down the number of a sentence twice if it contains two missing apostrophes):

———   ———   ———   ———   ———

———   ———   ———   ———   ———

Test 10: Quotation Marks

Quotation marks needed in each passage: 10 pairs

Passage A

[1]When my friend Brad asked me what I wanted to drink at the party, I said, "Pepsi, if there is any. I don't drink."

[2]"Very funny, Joe. Now what do you want?" he asked. [3]He was truly shocked when I repeated my words. [4]I think he was even a little embarrassed that he had brought me to the party. [5]Later the subject of drinking came up when I was talking to a young woman I met.

[6]"You must be in training," she assumed. [7]"Or is it that you're on medication?"

[8]"Neither—I just don't like to drink," I answered patiently.

[9]"Oh, I see. You're the type who proves himself different by playing the role of Mr. Nonconformist."

[10]"That's partly it," I agreed. [11]"I don't want to be an average Joe."

[12]"But you can drink and still be yourself, an individual. Just be comfortable with yourself," she asserted.

[13]I responded, "I do feel comfortable with myself. But I wouldn't if I drank just to be like everyone else here."

Sentences or sentence groups with missing quotation marks:

_____ _____ _____ _____ _____

_____ _____ _____ _____ _____

Passage B

[1]Tony and Lola were standing in the express line at the Safeway supermarket. [2]Lola pointed to a sign above the checkout counter that read, Express line—ten items or less. [3]She then said to Tony, Look at that guy in front of us. He has at least seventeen items in his cart. He shouldn't be in the express lane.

[4]Be quiet, said Tony. [5]If you're not, he'll hear you.

[6]I don't mind if he does hear me, Lola replied. [7]People like that think the world owes them a favor. I hope the cashier makes him go to another lane.

[8]The man in front of them suddenly turned around. [9]Stop acting as if I've committed a federal crime, he said. [10]See those five cans of Alpo—that counts as one item. See those four packs of Twinkies—that's one item.

[11]Let's just say this, Lola replied. [12]You have an interesting way of counting.

Sentences or sentence groups with missing quotation marks:

_____ _____ _____ _____ _____

_____ _____ _____ _____ _____

Passage C

[1]Once when I was walking down a lonely street, three boys came up to me. [2]Hey, Mister! one of them said. [3]Will you give us a nickel?

[4]I'm sorry, fellows, I replied. [5]I don't have any change to spare.

[6]All we want are three nickels, Mister, they said and suddenly surrounded me.

[7]Get out of my way, will you? I asked, trying to be polite. [8]I'm in a hurry.

[9]At this point the boy in front of me said, Stop trying to walk over me, Mister.

[10]As I raised my arm to move him aside, I felt a hand going into my back pocket. [11]I spun around and yelled, Give me that wallet! to the boy who had taken it. [12]I grabbed the wallet and the coin purse snapped open, with change spilling out over the sidewalk. [13]The boys scooped up the coins, chanting, Thanks for the change, Mister. [14]I wanted to belt one of them but decided it would be safer to walk quickly away.

Sentences or sentence groups with missing quotation marks:

_____ _____ _____ _____ _____

_____ _____ _____ _____ _____

Test 11: Commas

Mistakes in each passage: 10

Passage A

¹Going to a big arena for a sporting event or musical performance means being bombarded by hard selling. ²The pitches begin on the road into the parking areas. ³As lines of cars wait to enter the lot salespeople will walk past the crawling cars. ⁴They will hawk programs souvenirs pennants and even droopy carnations. ⁵The ticketholder may pass up these items but they are only the first assault on his or her sales resistance. ⁶Near the arena's ticket gates are more vendors. ⁷In addition to the same programs and souvenir items they hawk T-shirts and different kinds of snacks. ⁸Inside the enormous building is a chain of concessionaires' booths with everything from hot dogs to cheap jewelry. ⁹People who continue to resist the hard sell have one last hurdle for there are still the hawkers who roam the aisles. ¹⁰Their voices can be heard crying out all across the rows of seats "Beer here!" or "Peanuts while they last!" ¹¹The last holdouts especially if they have children with them usually give in at this point. ¹²They fork over several dollars for a tiny bag of chips and a watery soda.

Sentences with missing commas (write down the number of a sentence as many times as it contains comma mistakes):

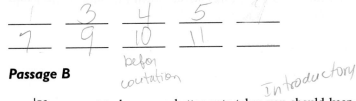

Passage B

¹If you want to become a better note-taker you should keep in mind the following hints. ²Most important you should attend class on a regular basis. ³The instructor will probably develop in class all the main ideas of the course and you want to be there to write the ideas down. ⁴Students often ask "How much should I write down?" ⁵By paying close attention in class you will probably develop an instinct for the material that you must write down. ⁶You should record your notes in outline form. ⁷Start main points at the margin indent major supporting details and further indent more subordinate material. ⁸When the speaker moves from one aspect of a topic to another show this shift on your

paper by skipping a line or two. [9]A last hint but by no means the least is to write down any points your instructor repeats or takes the time to put on the board.

Sentences with missing commas (write down the number of a sentence as many times as it contains comma mistakes):

_1 7 3 _ 4 578 _ 9_

_____ _____ _____ _____ _____

Passage C

Interrupting.

[1]Studies have found that people have a psychological need for plants. [2]People who grew up in urban areas one survey revealed often mentioned the presence or absence of lawns in their neighborhood. [3]One person observed "I realized how much I missed lawns and trees after living in a city where concrete covered everything." [4]Unfortunately the city is a difficult environment for plants. [5]The soil of the city is covered mostly with buildings and pavements so there is little space for plants to grow. [6]Plants that are present are often hurt by haze smog and air pollution. [7]Some plants are more sensitive to pollution than others; snapdragons for example do poorly in polluted air. [8]When planners choose what kind of plants to place in urban areas they must consider the plants' chances for survival under the difficult growing conditions of city streets.

Quotations
Introductory
joining word
series

Introductory

Introductory

series

Sentences with missing commas (write down the number of a sentence as many times as it contains comma mistakes):

_2 2 3 4 5_

_6 6 7 7 8_

Test 12: Commonly Confused Words

Mistakes in each passage: 10

Passage A

¹Recently, I was driving across town in heavy city traffic. ²Cars followed one another bumper-to-bumper, and their were bicyclists and pedestrians darting threw the streets. ³Beside the heavy traffic, it had begun to rain, making the traffic situation even worse. ⁴I was driving cautiously, keeping ten feet or so from the rear of the car in front of me. ⁵Than, in my rearview mirror, I noticed the woman behind me. ⁶Her car was so close our bumpers were almost locked. ⁷Her face was red and angry, and she tapped impatiently on her steering wheel. ⁸Suddenly, she saw a five-second brake in the traffic. ⁹She past me with a roar and squeezed in ahead of me. ¹⁰I though angrily, "Your a complete idiot!" and honked my horn. ¹¹She honked back at me and lifted her hand in an obscene gesture. ¹²I am a little ashamed at the affect this had on me—I was so enraged I wanted to drag her out of her car and punch her. ¹³It took me more than an hour to calm down completely and except the fact that the incident had been a very minor one.

Sentences with commonly confused words (write down the number of a sentence twice if it contains two commonly confused words):

____ ____ ____ ____ ____

____ ____ ____ ____ ____

Passage B

¹Anyone whose stayed up all night studying for a test knows the dizzy, foggy feeling you're head gets. ²Although I have had this terrible experience more than once, I can't seem to discipline myself enough to avoid it. ³As a result, I always have to cram at exam time, and I am up righting notes and studying all through the night.

⁴Hear are some of the techniques I use to stay awake. ⁵I drink large doses of coffee. ⁶I take No-Doz, to, if I feel that the coffee begins to lose its affect on me. ⁷And I eat candy bars, though the fewer the better, for they can upset my stomach. ⁸There are also two study methods that really help me. ⁹First, I take regular little brakes—about ten minutes an hour, I lie down for a few minutes' peace. ¹⁰Second, I pace back and forth when I'm studying. ¹¹The principle value of this study method is that I don't get sleepy if I am physically

moving about. [12]Its probably a strange sight to see me walking up and down the hallway reciting notes to myself, but the plane fact is that the technique works.

Sentences with commonly confused words (write down the number of a sentence twice if it contains two commonly confused words):

_____ _____ _____ _____ _____

_____ _____ _____ _____ _____

Passage C

[1]If at all possible, try to take you're summer vacation any time accept during the summer. [2]First, by scheduling your vacation at another time of the year, you will avoid the crowds. [3]You will not have to fight the traffic around resort areas or drive passed dozens of motels with "No Vacancy" signs. [4]Beaches and campsites will be quite, to. [5]By vacationing out of season, you will also see many areas at there most beautiful, without the bother of summer's heat, thunderstorms, and insects. [6]Weather you go in spring or fall, you can travel by car without feeling stuck to your seat or to exhausted to explore the city or park. [7]Finally, an off-season trip can save you money. [8]Before and after the summer, prices at resorts drop, for fewer people are demanding reservations. [9]Its possible to stay too weeks for the price of one; or you might stay in a luxury hotel you might not otherwise be able to afford.

Sentences with commonly confused words (write down the number of a sentence twice if it contains two commonly confused words):

_____ _____ _____ _____ _____

_____ _____ _____ _____ _____

Combined Editing Tests

EDITING FOR
SENTENCE-SKILLS MISTAKES

The twelve editing tests in this section will give you practice in finding a variety of sentence-skills mistakes. People often find it hard to edit a paper carefully. They have put so much work into their writing, or so little, that it's almost painful for them to look at the paper one more time. You may have to simply *force* yourself to edit. Remember that eliminating sentence-skills mistakes will improve an average paper and help ensure a strong grade on a good paper. Further, as you get into the habit of editing your papers, you will get into the habit of using the sentence skills consistently. They are a basic part of clear and effective writing.

Tests 1 and 2 check your understanding of the correct format to use when writing and handing in a paper. The remaining tests check your ability to identify a variety of sentence-skills mistakes, especially sentence fragments and run-ons. In tests 3 through 8, the spots where errors occur have been underlined; your job is to identify each error. In tests 9 through 12, you must locate as well as identify the errors. Use the progress chart on page 536 to keep track of your performance on these tests.

Combined Editing Test I

Identify the five mistakes in paper format in the student paper that follows. From the box below, choose the letters that describe the five mistakes and write those letters in the spaces provided.

---

a. The title should not be underlined.

b. The title should not be set off in quotation marks.

c. There should not be a period at the end of a title.

d. All the major words in a title should be capitalized.

e. The title should just be several words and not a complete sentence.

f. The first line of a paper should stand independent of the title.

g. A line should be skipped between the title and the first line of the paper.

h. The first line of a paper should be indented.

i. The right-hand margin should not be crowded.

j. Hyphenation should occur only between syllables.

	"Nervous times"
	There are three different times that I feel nervous. First of all, if
	I'm in a classroom full of students I don't know and I'm asked to
	answer a question, I may begin to stutter. Or I may know the
	answer, but my mind will just block out. Second, if I'm going out
	on a date with a guy for the first time, I won't eat. Eating when
	I'm nervous makes my fork tremble, and I'm likely to drop food on
	my clothes. Finally if I'm going to a job interview, I will practice
	at home what I'm going to say. But as soon as I'm alone with the
	interviewer, and he asks me if there's anything I'd like to say, I
	say something dumb like "I'm a people person, you know." One day
	I hope to overcome these nervousness problems.

1. _____   2. _____   3. _____   4. _____   5. _____

Combined Editing Test 2

Identify the five mistakes in paper format in the student paper that follows. From the box below, choose the letters that describe the five mistakes and write those letters in the spaces provided.

a. The title should not be underlined.
b. The title should not be set off in quotation marks.
c. There should not be a period at the end of a title.
d. All the major words in a title should be capitalized.
e. The title should just be several words and not a complete sentence.
f. The first line of a paper should stand independent of the title.
g. A line should be skipped between the title and the first line of the paper.
h. The first line of a paper should be indented.
i. The right-hand margin should not be crowded.
j. Hyphenation should occur only between syllables.

	<u>coming down with the flu.</u>
	I could tell that I was coming down with it. For one th-
	ing, my nose and throat were shutting down. I could not breathe
	through my nose at all, while my nose was running nonstop, so
	that I soon went through a box of tissues. My throat was sore,
	and when I was brave enough to speak, my voice sounded horrible.
	Another reason I knew I had the flu was fever and chills. The
	thermometer registered 102 degrees. My chills were so bad that
	to get warm I had to put on sweat socks, flannel pajamas, and a
	heavy robe, and I then had to get under two blankets and a
	sheet. Finally, I was extremely fatigued. After I got into bed, I
	slept for eight hours straight. When I woke up I was still so tired
	that I couldn't get out of bed. My eyelids felt as if they weighed
	a hundred pounds each, and I could not lift my head off the pillow.
	Too tired to think, I drifted back to sleep with hazy thoughts of
	my mother's homemade chicken soup.

1. _____   2. _____   3. _____   4. _____   5. _____

Combined Editing Test 3

Identify the sentence-skills mistakes at the underlined spots in the selections that follow. From the box below, choose the letter that describes each mistake and write it in the space provided. The same mistake may appear more than once.

a. fragment	d. missing comma
b. run-on	e. faulty parallelism
c. missing apostrophe	f. misplaced modifier

Selection A

<u>On the day when her divorce papers came</u>. Roz tried to feel something. She wanted
₁
to be very happy or <u>feel sadness</u>. However, she felt <u>nothing a part</u> of her life had simply
₂ ₃
ended. She <u>didnt</u> care about Don anymore, and that disturbed her. She felt guilty about
₄
not caring. <u>Until she remembered that she had a right to happiness, too.</u>
₅

Selection B

When I was four years <u>old I</u> had the first traumatic experience of my life. My family
₆
was staying at my <u>aunts</u> old house at the lake. I was chasing my cousin Michelle toward
₇
the steps <u>with untied shoelaces</u>. Running too <u>quickly I</u> tripped and fell. My mouth hit the
₈ ₉
bottom of the wooden steps. I thought I would <u>die I</u> must have cried for hours. To this
₁₀
day, I still have a bump on my lower lip.

1. _____   3. _____   5. _____   7. _____   9. _____

2. _____   4. _____   6. _____   8. _____   10. _____

Combined Editing Test 4

Identify the sentence-skills mistakes at the underlined spots in the selection that follows. From the box below, choose the letter that describes each mistake and write it in the space provided. The same mistake may appear more than once. In one case, there is no mistake.

---

a. fragment	d. missing capital letter
b. run-on	e. missing comma
c. dropped verb ending	f. no mistake

The worst thing that <u>happen</u> to me recently was when I <u>decide</u> to play a quick game of
$\quad$ 1 $\qquad\qquad\qquad\qquad\qquad$ 2
touch football with some friends. I felt good physically when the game was over. The next

morning, <u>however</u> I learned that I was not in the shape I thought I was. <u>When I tried to get</u>
$\qquad$ 3 $\qquad\qquad\qquad\qquad\qquad\qquad\qquad\qquad$ 4
<u>out of bed but couldn't.</u> After my wife <u>help</u> me out of <u>bed I</u> felt a little better. But all during
$\qquad\qquad\qquad\qquad\qquad\qquad\qquad$ 5 $\qquad$ 6
the day I had to struggle whenever I got into or out of my car. I thought the <u>"monday</u>
$\qquad\qquad\qquad\qquad\qquad\qquad\qquad\qquad\qquad\qquad\qquad\qquad\qquad$ 7
<u>soreness" was the end of it. Until the next morning, when my wife had to help me put my</u>
$\qquad\qquad\qquad\qquad\qquad\qquad\qquad\qquad\qquad\qquad\qquad\qquad$ 8
<u>shoes on.</u> I could barely walk all <u>day, I</u> even needed help getting out of my car. <u>My body</u>
$\qquad\qquad\qquad\qquad\qquad$ 9 $\qquad\qquad\qquad\qquad\qquad\qquad\qquad\qquad$ 10
<u>has delivered a loud and clear message to me, forcing me to reconsider my imagined</u>

<u>physical prowess.</u>

1. _____   3. _____   5. _____   7. _____   9. _____

2. _____   4. _____   6. _____   8. _____   10. _____

Combined Editing Test 5

Identify the sentence-skills mistakes at the underlined spots in the selection that follows. From the box below, choose the letter that describes each mistake and write it in the space provided. The same mistake may appear more than once. In one case, there is no mistake.

a. fragment	e. mistake in irregular verb
b. run-on	f. missing comma
c. dangling modifier	g. no mistake
d. mistake in subject-verb agreement	

When I was a child, my brother took advantage of my fear of ghosts. I would be taking a shower, and my brother would open the <u>door turn</u> out the lights and start "wooing" until
₁
I began to cry. Then he would almost suffocate from laughing. Other times, he would make moaning sounds through the keyhole of my bedroom door. <u>Rattling the doorknob as well.</u>
₂
One night he did the worst thing of <u>all he</u> took out the main fuse in the fuse box, and all the
₃
lights in the house went out. Neither one of my parents <u>were</u> home at the <u>time, and</u> I was
₄   ₅
so petrified that at first I couldn't move. But I sure did move when my brother came running down the hall with a white sheet over his head. <u>Screaming at the top of his lungs.</u> He must
₆
have chased me around the house for almost a half hour. I finally <u>stopped grabbed</u> an apple
₇
out of the fruit basket, and <u>throwed</u> it at him as hard as I could. I missed him but not the
₈
kitchen window. <u>Telling my parents what happened later,</u> they spanked my brother. But
₉
thanks to him, I can't walk down a dark street today. <u>Without thinking there is someone</u>
₁₀
<u>behind me.</u>

1. _____	3. _____	5. _____	7. _____	9. _____
2. _____	4. _____	6. _____	8. _____	10. _____

● Combined Editing Test 6

Identify the sentence-skills mistakes at the underlined spots in the selection that follows. From the box below, choose the letter that describes each mistake and write it in the space provided. The same mistake may appear more than once.

a. fragment	e. missing capital letter
b. run-on	f. missing comma
c. mistake in irregular verb	g. faulty parallelism
d. mistake in apostrophe	

People often wonder why they have spended so much money at the supermarket.
                                          1
On things they didn't intend to buy in the first place. A recent survey indicates that 75
                                    2
percent of all grocery shoppers' make at least one impulse purchase. They might not
                              3
have ate recently and reach for a package of ritz crackers to munch on while they go up
      4   5
and down the aisles. They may be lured by an eye-catching display or a colorful package
                                                                                        6
over one-third of all impulse purchases are made because the item is temptingly wrapped.
When shoppers are waiting in the checkout line a final surge of buying fever often comes
                                                7
over them. They'll buy magazines candy, and other small items on the racks next to the
                        8
checkout counter. There are ways of avoiding impulse buying and to save money on
                                                                          9
groceries. Shoppers should make a list and stick to it buy no-frills brands, and eat well
                                                        10
before going shopping.

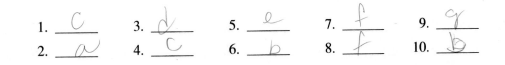

1. __C__   3. __d__   5. __e__   7. __f__   9. __g__

2. __a__   4. __C__   6. __b__   8. __f__   10. __b__

Combined Editing Test 7

Identify the sentence-skills mistakes at the underlined spots in the selection that follows. From the box below, choose the letter that describes each mistake and write it in the space provided. The same mistake may appear more than once. In one case, there is no mistake.

---

a. fragment	e. missing quotation marks
b. run-on	f. missing comma
c. dangling modifier	g. no mistake
d. faulty parallelism	

I have never understood why my parents each felt so differently about me. They are both dead <u>now, I</u> guess I will never have the answer. I am convinced that my father did
¹
not love me. <u>Although never physically cruel,</u> there was little affection for me. He used
²
to say, <u>I love all my children,</u> but I don't like them all." He once looked at me when he
³
said this, adding, "You know what I mean, Karen." He never seemed proud of me or
<u>was there an interest</u> in what I was doing. <u>My report cards, for example.</u> He skipped the
⁴   ⁵
class plays I appeared in and rarely asked anything personal. He didn't say, "Do you have a boyfriend? What's he like?" Instead, he would <u>grunt,</u> "Don't be late or you know
⁶
what'll happen." On the other <u>hand my</u> mother seemed to care for me more than anyone
⁷
else. Maybe she wanted to make it up to me for my father's behavior. She made clothes for me on her sewing machine and <u>decorating my room</u> the way I wanted it. <u>Also, driving me</u>
⁸   ⁹
<u>places in the car.</u> She asked me about school and about my friends. She would get my father out of the house so that I could have a <u>party, she</u> would save her money to buy me special
¹⁰
birthday and Christmas presents. Without my mother's special love, I think I would never have survived my father's indifference.

1. _____   3. _____   5. _____   7. _____   9. _____

2. _____   4. _____   6. _____   8. _____   10. _____

Combined Editing Test 8

Identify the sentence-skills mistakes at the underlined spots in the selections that follow. From the box below, choose the letter that describes each mistake and write it in the space provided. The same mistake may appear more than once. In one case, there is no mistake.

a.	fragment	e.	dangling modifier
b.	mistake in subject-verb agreement	f.	missing capital letter
c.	mistake in subject pronoun	g.	no mistake
d.	dropped -*ly* ending (adverb mistake)		

Selection A

Cindy had a weird but fascinating dream last night. Simply by turning the dial on her
magical television set. She could see what anyone in the world was doing at the time. On
one channel she could see her English instructor. He was sitting quiet by himself in a small
room. Watching a late movie. On another channel, she could see the president of the United
States fast asleep with his wife in a White House bedroom. Turning to another channel, the
first boyfriend Cindy ever had were on screen. Him and a young woman were having a
conversation at a singles' bar.

Selection B

My brother and I was always different when we were little boys. Once my parents took
us to see Santa Claus. Who was at the local department store instead of the North Pole.
My brother asked Santa for a red wagon and world peace. I asked Santa, "how much money
do you make?"

1. _____	3. _____	5. _____	7. _____	9. _____
2. _____	4. _____	6. _____	8. _____	10. _____

Combined Editing Test 9

See if you can locate and correct the ten sentence-skills mistakes in the following passage. The mistakes are listed in the box below. As you locate each mistake, write the number of the sentence containing that mistake. Use the spaces provided.

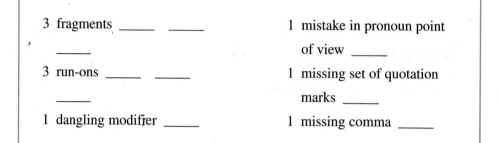

3 fragments _____ _____	1 mistake in pronoun point
_____	of view _____
3 run-ons _____ _____	1 missing set of quotation
_____	marks _____
1 dangling modifier _____	1 missing comma _____

¹The main problem in my work as a substitute mail carrier is contending with dogs. ²Who are used to the regular carrier but not to me. ³The route I was assigned to last week featured a German shepherd. ⁴The dog had been hit once while chasing a car and had lost a leg. ⁵Even though he had only three legs, he still chased cars. ⁶As I walked up the lawn of the house where the German shepherd stood guard I felt very uneasy. ⁷I could see the dog, who was sitting in the side yard, out of the corner of my eye. ⁸Giving me a hateful stare. ⁹As I opened the screen door of the house, he let out several vicious snarls and barks. ¹⁰I could see his teeth showing. ¹¹His owner appeared to get the mail, she yelled at him, You stay right where you are, Rex. ¹²I felt like asking the woman to stand there and watch Rex until I was back on the sidewalk; however, I didn't want to seem afraid. ¹³I headed back away from the house. ¹⁴Walking slowly but eagerly, I heard the door click behind me, and you knew the owner had gone back into the house. ¹⁵I wished that I felt as confident as she did that her dog would behave. ¹⁶When I was almost at the sidewalk, Rex began to bark again. ¹⁷Then his barking became louder and closer. ¹⁸I turned around and saw Rex coming at me in full, three-legged stride. ¹⁹With only three legs, I was sure that I could outrun him at least up to my truck. ²⁰I felt foolish, but that didn't stop me from running just as fast as I could. ²¹Rex was tearing at my pants as I reached the truck, I slid the door shut, using it as a wedge to detach Rex from my trousers. ²²Rex hurled himself at the door several times then he backed off when his owner began to call. ²³After catching my breath, I resolved not to return to the dog's place again. ²⁴At least not without a can of Mace.

Combined Editing Test 10

See if you can locate and correct the ten sentence-skills mistakes in the following passage. The mistakes are listed in the box below. As you locate each mistake, write the number of the sentence containing that mistake. Use the spaces provided.

---

3 fragments _3_ _12_ _6_

1 mistake in subject-verb agreement _9_

1 mistake in verb tense _13_

1 mistake in subject pronoun _9_

1 missing apostrophe _9_

1 missing capital letter _4_

2 missing sets of quotation marks _8_ _16_

---

¹Steve Miller is a stingy friend of mine. ²When he comes to work, he never brings any money. ³But always asks me if I have a quarter or two to lend him so that he can buy cookies or a small bag of potato chips. ⁴One time he asked me to lend him a dollar so he could buy a chance from another employee for a thanksgiving turkey. ⁵I refused at first, but he practically begged me. ⁶Resulting in my giving him the money. ⁷As I expected, he never offered to return my dollar. ⁸When I'd remind him, he'd say, Oh yeah, I'll get it to you soon, but he never did. ⁹Another example of Steves stinginess were the time he and me and two of our friends decided to go out and eat during our lunch hour at the Red Rooster, a new restaurant. ¹⁰Steve suggested that we take his car, and as we were driving to the restaurant, he said his gas tank was empty. ¹¹I couldn't believe he would have the nerve to ask us for gas money. ¹²With only a total of eight miles to the restaurant and back. ¹³However, he pulls into an Exxon gas station and cheerfully said that a dollar for gas from each of us would be fine. ¹⁴I was really fuming because I could see that his gas tank was at least a quarter full. ¹⁵After we pulled into the restaurant parking lot, Steve informed us that he would wait in the car while the rest of us ate. ¹⁶I asked him in a hard voice, Don't you have any money? ¹⁷Steve's reply was, "Yeah, but I'm not going to spend it eating out when I can go home and eat for nothing."

● Combined Editing Test 11

See if you can locate and correct the ten sentence-skills mistakes in the following passage. The mistakes are listed in the box below. As you locate each mistake, write the number of the sentence containing that mistake. Use the spaces provided.

2 fragments _____ , _____	2 missing commas after introductory words _____ _____
2 run-ons _____ _____	
1 mistake in irregular verb _____	2 missing commas in a series _____ _____
1 inconsistent pronoun point of view _____	

¹While shopping one morning, I passed a weird-acting character on the street, he was sitting on a car fender, rocking violently up and down. ²I was puzzled and, along with several other people, stopped and turned after I passed him. ³In order to stare. ⁴The man reached suddenly into his back pocket. ⁵And took out a small packet containing miniature tools. ⁶With a screwdriver in his right hand he leaned over and started to unscrew the license plate on the rear of the car. ⁷Soon the license plate fell clattering to the ground. ⁸The man then put his screwdriver away and just sat on the bumper for a minute, perhaps thinking of what to do next. ⁹Then, without using his hands but getting enormous thrust from his legs, he leaped to the sidewalk. ¹⁰He ran over to the open-air fruit stand nearby grabbed a banana and started eating it with the skin still on. ¹¹A woman working at the stand shouted, "Get out of here, you wild man." ¹²However, she didn't try to take the banana away from him. ¹³She shook her head, rolled her eyes, and turned her attention to a nearby customer. ¹⁴The man suddenly seemed to become aware of the crowd watching him he heard someone laughing, and he begun to laugh also, but louder. ¹⁵At the same time, his eyes filled with tears. ¹⁶You suddenly felt ashamed and also guilty about watching him. ¹⁷As I turned and walked away I heard the man's terrible laughing and sobbing echo behind me.

Combined Editing Test 12

See if you can locate and correct the ten sentence-skills mistakes in the following passage. The mistakes are listed in the box below. As you locate each mistake, write the number of the sentence containing that mistake. Use the spaces provided.

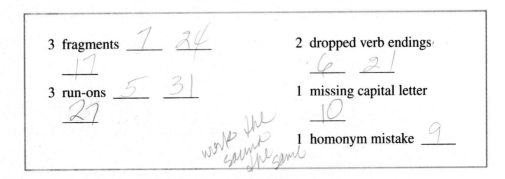

3 fragments ___1___ ___24___
___17___

3 run-ons ___5___ ___31___
___27___

2 dropped verb endings
___6___ ___21___

1 missing capital letter
___10___

1 homonym mistake ___9___

¹When I met a girl named Barbara, my life started to change. ²Our relationship began one lonely night this past winter. ³I was sitting in the Dewdrop Inn with a friend. ⁴We were having a couple of beers and shooting a game of darts. ⁵The place was almost empty, I guess there were about four people at the bar. ⁶Then Barbara and her friend walk in. ⁷Passing in front of us. ⁸At the jukebox they played some records. ⁹On there way to the bar, I asked Barbara if she and her friend would like to play some darts. ¹⁰To my surprise, she said, "yes, we would." ¹¹I still can't believe what happened then. ¹²They beat us.

¹³The night went on until Barbara and her friend said they had to go home. ¹⁴I felt sort of sad. ¹⁵I walked with her to her car, kissed her good-night, and made a date to go bowling on Saturday afternoon. ¹⁶However, I didn't show up for our date. ¹⁷Because I was afraid she wouldn't be there. ¹⁸I went to the auto races with a buddy instead. ¹⁹A couple of days went by before I saw her again. ²⁰I didn't think that she would talk to me. ²¹But she fooled me. ²²We made another date, and this time I kept it.

²³We started to see each other several nights a week. ²⁴Becoming closer and closer to one another. ²⁵It's hard to explain what I felt about her. ²⁶When she met me, I was often drinking from early in the morning to late at night. ²⁷I did not have a job, I felt as though I had nothing to work for. ²⁸She changed me. ²⁹I went out and got a job and did well at it.

³⁰Then I applied to college, and I am now in school trying to learn and do well in life. ³¹Barbara is helping me out as I try to achieve these goals, we are married and are happy. ³²In this strange world of ours, if a man has something to work for, he will do his best in order to achieve. ³³I can honestly say that I now have meaning in my life.

Sentence Variety Through Combining Activities

Part
Four

INTRODUCTION

Part Two of this book gives you practice in skills needed to write clear sentences. Part Three helps you work on reinforcing those skills. The purpose of this part of the book—Part Four—is to provide you with methods for writing varied and interesting sentences. Through the technique of sentence combining, you will learn about the many different options open to you for expressing a given idea. At the same time, you will develop a natural instinct and an "ear" for choosing the option that sounds best in a particular situation. By the end of Part Four, you will be able to compose sentences that bring to your writing style a greater variety and ease. You will also be able to write sentences that express more complex thoughts.

How Sentence Combining Works: The combining technique used to help you practice various sentence patterns is a simple one. Two or more short sentences are given and then combined in a particular way. You are then asked to combine other short sentences in the same way. Here is an example:

- The diesel truck chugged up the hill.
- It spewed out black smoke.

  Spewing out black smoke, the diesel truck chugged up the hill.

The content of most sentences is given to you, so that instead of focusing on *what* you will say, you can concentrate on *how* to say it.

The sentence-combining activities are presented in a sequence consisting of three sections. The first section describes the four traditional sentence patterns in English and explains two important techniques that are central to those patterns: coordination and subordination. The second section presents other patterns that can be used to add variety to writing. The third section provides a number of practice units in which you can apply the combining patterns you have learned as well as compose patterns of your own.

Four Traditional Sentence Patterns

Sentences have been traditionally described in English as simple, compound, complex, or compound-complex. This section explains and offers practice in all four sentence types. The section also describes coordination and subordination—the two central techniques you can use to achieve different kinds of emphasis in your writing.

SIMPLE SENTENCE

A simple sentence has a single <u>subject</u>-<u>verb</u> combination.

> <u>Children</u> <u>play</u>.
> The <u>game</u> <u>ended</u> early.
> My <u>car</u> <u>stalled</u> three times last week.
> The <u>lake</u> <u>has been polluted</u> by several neighboring streams.

A simple sentence may have more than one subject:

> <u>Lola</u> and <u>Tony</u> <u>drove</u> home.
> The <u>wind</u> and <u>water</u> <u>dried</u> my hair.

or more than one verb:

> The <u>children</u> <u>smiled</u> and <u>waved</u> at us.
> The <u>lawn mower</u> <u>smoked</u> and <u>sputtered</u>.

or several subjects and verbs:

> <u>Manny</u>, <u>Moe</u>, and <u>Jack</u> <u>lubricated</u> my car, <u>replaced</u> the oil filter, and <u>cleaned</u> the spark plugs.

Activity

On separate paper, write:

Three sentences, each with a single subject and verb
Three sentences, each with a single subject and a double verb
Three sentences, each with a double subject and a single verb

In each of your sentences, underline the subject once and the verb twice. (See page 84 if necessary for more information on subjects and verbs.)

COMPOUND SENTENCE

A compound, or "double," sentence is made up of two (or more) simple sentences. The two complete statements in a compound sentence are usually connected by a comma plus a joining word (*and, but, for, or, nor, so, yet*).

A compound sentence is used when you want to give equal weight to two closely related ideas. The technique of showing that ideas have equal importance is called *coordination*.

Following are some compound sentences. Each sentence contains two ideas that the writer considers equal in importance.

The rain increased, so the officials canceled the game.

Martha wanted to go shopping, but Fred refused to drive her.

Tom was watching television in the family room, and Marie was upstairs on the phone.

I had to give up wood carving, for my arthritis had become very painful.

Activity I

Combine the following pairs of simple sentences into compound sentences. Use a comma and a logical joining word (*and, but, for, so*) to connect each pair.

Note: If you are not sure what *and, but, for,* and *so* mean, review pages 115–116.

Example ● We hung up the print.
● The wall still looked bare.

We hung up the print, but the wall still looked bare.

1. ● My cold grew worse.
 ● I decided to see a doctor.

_____

_____

2. ● My uncle always ignores me.
 ● My aunt gives me kisses and presents.

_____

_____

3. ● We played softball in the afternoon.
 ● We went to a movie in the evening.

_____

_____

4. ● I invited Rico to sleep overnight.
 ● He wanted to go home.

_____

_____

5. ● Police raided the club.
 ● They had gotten a tip about illegal drugs for sale.

_____

_____

Activity 2

On separate paper, write five compound sentences of your own. Use a different joining word (*and, but, for, or, nor, so, yet*) to connect the two complete ideas in each sentence.

COMPLEX SENTENCE

A complex sentence is made up of a simple sentence (a complete statement) and a statement that begins with a dependent word.[*] Here is a list of common dependent words:

after	if, even if	when, whenever
although, though	in order that	where, wherever
as	since	whether
because	that, so that	which, whichever
before	unless	while
even though	until	who
how	what, whatever	whose

A complex sentence is used when you want to emphasize one idea over another in a sentence. Look at the following complex sentence:

Because I forgot the time, I missed the final exam.

The idea that the writer wishes to emphasize here—*I missed the final exam*—is expressed as a complete thought. The less important idea—*Because I forgot the time*—is subordinated to the complete thought. The technique of giving one idea less emphasis than another is called *subordination*.

Following are other examples of complex sentences. In each case, the part starting with the dependent word is the less emphasized part of the sentence.

While Sue was eating breakfast, she began to feel sick.
I checked my money *before* I invited Tom for lunch.
When Jerry lost his temper, he also lost his job.
Although I practiced for three months, I failed my driving test.

---

[*] The two parts of a complex sentence are sometimes called an independent clause and a dependent clause. A *clause* is simply a word group that contains a subject and a verb. An *independent clause* expresses a complete thought and can stand alone. A *dependent clause* does not express a complete thought in itself but "depends on" the independent clause to complete its meaning. Dependent clauses always begin with a dependent or subordinating word.

Activity I

Use logical dependent words to combine the following pairs of simple sentences into complex sentences. Place a comma after a dependent statement when it starts the sentence.

Examples
- I obtained a credit card.
- I began spending money recklessly.

  When I obtained a credit card, I began spending money recklessly.

- Alan dressed the turkey.
- His brother greased the roasting pot.

  Alan dressed the turkey while his brother greased the roasting pot.

1.
- The instructor announced the quiz.
- The class groaned.

  _____

  _____

2.
- Gene could not fit any more groceries into his cart.
- He decided to go to the checkout counter.

  _____

  _____

3.
- Your car is out of commission.
- You should take it to Otto's Transmission.

  _____

  _____

4.
- I finished typing the paper.
- I proofread it carefully.

  _____

  _____

5.
- We owned four cats and a dog.
- No one would rent us an apartment.

  _____

  _____

Activity 2

Rewrite the following sentences, using subordination rather than coordination. Include a comma when a dependent statement starts a sentence.

Example   The hair dryer was not working right, so I returned it to the store.

Because the hair dryer was not working right, I returned it to the

store.

1.   Ruth turned on the large window fan, but the room remained hot.

_____

_____

2.   The plumber repaired the water heater, so we can take showers again.

_____

_____

3.   I washed the sheets and towels, and I scrubbed the bathroom floor.

_____

_____

4.   You should go to a doctor, for your chest cold may get worse.

_____

_____

5.   The fish tank broke, and guppies were flopping all over the carpet.

_____

_____

Activity 3

Combine the simple sentences that follow into complex sentences. Omit repeated words. Use the dependent words *who, which,* and *that.*

Notes

a   The word *who* refers to persons.
b   The word *which* refers to things.
c   The word *that* refers to persons or things.

Use commas around the dependent statement only if it seems to interrupt the flow of thought in the sentence. (See also pages 259–260.)

Examples
- Clyde picked up a hitchhiker.
- The hitchhiker was traveling around the world.

  Clyde picked up a hitchhiker who was traveling around the world.

___

- Larry is a sleepwalker.
- Larry is my brother.

  Larry, who is my brother, is a sleepwalker.

___

1.
   - The magazine article was about abortion.
   - The article made me very angry.

___

2.
   - The woodshed has collapsed.
   - I built the woodshed myself.

___

3.
   - The power drill is missing.
   - I bought the power drill at half price.

___

4.
   - Rita Haber was indicted for bribery.
   - Rita Haber is our mayor.

___

5.
   - The chicken pies contained dangerous preservatives.
   - We ate the chicken pies.

___

Activity 4

On separate paper, write eight complex sentences, using, in turn, the dependent words *unless, if, after, because, when, who, which,* and *that.*

COMPOUND-COMPLEX SENTENCE

A compound-complex sentence is made up of two (or more) simple sentences and one (or more) dependent statements. In the following examples, a solid line is under the simple sentences and a dotted line is under the dependent statements.

When the power line snapped, Jack was listening to the stereo, and Linda was reading in bed.

After I returned to school following a long illness, the math instructor gave me makeup work, but the history instructor made me drop her course.

Activity 1

Read through each sentence to get a sense of its overall meaning. Then insert a logical joining word (*and, or, but, for,* or *so*) and a logical dependent word (*because, since, when,* or *although*).

1. _____ he suffered so much during hay fever season, Pete bought an air conditioner, _____ he swallowed allergy pills regularly.

2. _____ I put on my new flannel shirt, I discovered that a button was missing, _____ I angrily went looking for a replacement button in the sewing basket.

3. _____ the computer was just repaired, the screen keeps freezing, _____ I have to restart the program.

4. _____ I have lived all my life on the East Coast, I felt uncomfortable during a West Coast vacation, _____ I kept thinking that the ocean was on the wrong side.

5. _____ water condensation continues in your basement, either you should buy a dehumidifier, _____ you should cover the masonry walls with waterproof paint.

Activity 2

On separate paper, write five compound-complex sentences.

REVIEW OF COORDINATION AND SUBORDINATION

Remember that coordination and subordination are ways of showing the exact relationship of ideas within a sentence. Through coordination we show that ideas are of equal importance. When we coordinate, we use the words *and, but, for, or, nor, so,* and *yet.* Through subordination we show that one idea is less important than another. When we subordinate, we use dependent words like *when, although, since, while, because,* and *after.* A list of common dependent words is given on page 464.

Activity

Use coordination or subordination to combine the groups of simple sentences that follow into one or more longer sentences. Omit repeated words. Since various combinations are possible, you might want to jot several combinations on separate paper. Then read them aloud to find the combination that sounds best.

Keep in mind that very often the relationship among ideas in a sentence will be clearer when subordination rather than coordination is used.

Example
- My car is not starting on cold mornings.
- I think the battery needs to be replaced.
- I already had it recharged once.
- I don't think charging it again will help.

Because my car is not starting on cold mornings, I think the battery needs to be replaced. I already had it recharged once, so I don't think charging it again will help.

Comma Hints

a   Use a comma at the end of a word group that starts with a dependent word (as in "Because my car is not starting on cold mornings, . . .").

b   Use a comma between independent word groups connected by *and, but, for, or, nor, so,* or *yet* (as in "I already had it recharged once, so. . . .").

1. • Louise used a dandruff shampoo.
   • She still had dandruff.
   • She decided to see a dermatologist.

   _____

   _____

   _____

2. • Omar's parents want him to be a doctor.
   • Omar wants to be a salesman.
   • He impresses people with his charm.

   _____

   _____

   _____

3. • The instructor conducted a discussion period.
   • Jack sat at his desk with his head down.
   • He did not want the instructor to call on him.
   • He had not read the assignment.

   _____

   _____

   _____

4. • Lola wanted to get a quick lunch at the cafeteria.
   • All the sandwiches were gone.
   • She had to settle for a cup of yogurt.

   _____

   _____

   _____

5. • I was leaving to do some shopping in town.
   • I asked my son to water the back lawn.
   • He seemed agreeable.
   • I returned three hours later.
   • The lawn had not been watered.

   _____

   _____

   _____

   _____

   _____

6. ● I had eaten too quickly.
   ● My stomach became upset.
   ● It felt like a war combat zone.
   ● I took two Alka-Seltzer tablets.

_____

_____

_____

_____

7. ● Midge is always buying plants and flower seeds.
   ● She enjoys growing things.
   ● Not many things grow well for her.
   ● She doesn't know why.

_____

_____

_____

_____

8. ● My car was struck from behind yesterday.
   ● I slowed suddenly for a red light.
   ● The driver of the truck behind me slammed on his brakes.
   ● He didn't quite stop on time.

_____

_____

_____

_____

9. ● Ed skimmed through the help-wanted ads.
   ● Nothing was there for him.
   ● He desperately needed a job.
   ● He would have to sell his car.
   ● He could no longer keep up the payments.

_____

_____

_____

_____

10. • The meat loaf didn't taste right.
    • The mashed potatoes had too much salt in them.
    • We sent out for a pizza.
    • It was delivered late.
    • It was cold.

    _____

    _____

    _____

    _____

    _____

Other Patterns That Add Variety to Writing

This section gives you practice in other patterns or methods that can add variety and interest to your sentences. The patterns can be used with any of the four sentence types already explained. Note that you will not have to remember the grammar terms that are often used to describe the patterns. What is important is that you practice the various patterns extensively, so that you increase your sense of the many ways available to you for expressing your ideas.

-ING WORD GROUPS

Use an *-ing* word group at some point in a sentence. Here are examples:

The doctor, *hoping* for the best, examined the x-rays.
Jogging every day, I soon raised my energy level.

More information about *-ing* words, also known as *present participles,* appears on page 162.

Activity 1

Combine each pair of sentences below into one sentence by using an -*ing* word and omitting repeated words. Use a comma or commas to set off the -*ing* word group from the rest of the sentence.

Example   ● The diesel truck chugged up the hill.
　　　　　　 ● It spewed out smoke.

Spewing out smoke, the diesel truck chugged up the hill.

_or_ _The diesel truck, spewing out smoke, chugged up the hill._

1. ● Ginger refused to get out of bed.
   ● She pulled the blue blanket over her head.

   _____

   _____

2. ● Dad is able to forget the troubles of the day.
   ● He putters around in his basement workshop.

   Putting around _____

   _____

3. ● The crowd of dancers moved as one.
   ● They swayed to the music.

   _____

   _____

4. ● George tried to protect himself from the dampness of the room.
   ● He wrapped a scarf around his neck.

   Trying to _____

   _____

5. ● The woman listened intently to the earnest young man.
   ● She caressed her hair.

   Listening _____

   _____

using
ing

Activity 2

On separate paper, write five sentences of your own that contain -*ing* word groups.

-ED WORD GROUPS

Use an -ed word group at some point in a sentence. Here are examples:

Tired of studying, I took a short break.

Mary, *amused* by the joke, told it to a friend.

I opened my eyes wide, *shocked* by the red "F" on my paper.

More information about -ed words, also known as *past participles,* appears on page 162.

Activity

Combine each of the following pairs of sentences into one sentence by using an -ed word and omitting repeated words. Use a comma or commas to set off the -ed word group from the rest of the sentence.

Example ● Tim woke up with a start.
 ● He was troubled by a dream.

Troubled by a dream, Tim woke up with a start.

or *Tim, troubled by a dream, woke up with a start.*

1. ● I called an exterminator.
   ● I was bothered by roaches.

   Bothered by roaches, I called and exterminator

2. ● Sam grew silent.
   ● He was baffled by what had happened.

   baffled by

3. ● The crowd began to file slowly out of the stadium.
   ● They were stunned by the last-minute touchdown.

   Stunned by t

4. ● I tried to stifle my grin.
   ● I was amused but reluctant to show how I felt.

   am

5.   ● Cindy lay on the couch.
     ● She was exhausted from working all day.

exhausted from working all day, Cindy lay on the couch.

APPOSITIVES

Use appositives. An *appositive* is a word group that renames a noun (any person, place, or thing). Here is an example:

Rita, a good friend of mine, works as a police officer.

The word group *a good friend of mine* is an appositive that renames the word *Rita*.

Activity 1

Combine each of the following pairs of sentences into one sentence by using an appositive and omitting repeated words. Most appositives are set off by commas.

Example   ● Alan Thorn got lost during the hiking trip.
        ● He is a former Eagle Scout.
          Alan Thorn, a former Eagle Scout, got lost during the hiking trip.

1.   ● Houston is a rapidly growing city.
     ● Houston is my hometown.

2.   ● Roger refused to get involved in the argument.
     ● Roger is a gentle man.

3. ● My little brother wallpapered his room with monster pictures.
   ● My little brother is a horror movie fan.

   _____

4. ● The city park is where I go to think.
   ● The city park is a shady retreat.

   _____

5. ● The bungalow did not look safe enough to enter.
   ● The bungalow is a tilted structure with a sagging roof.

   _____

   _____

Activity 2

On separate paper, write five sentences of your own that contain appositives. Use commas as necessary to set the appositives off.

-LY OPENERS

Use an -*ly* word to open a sentence. Here are examples:

Gently, he mixed the chemicals together.
Anxiously, the contestant looked at the game clock.
Skillfully, the quarterback rifled a pass to his receiver.

More information about -*ly* words, which are also known as *adverbs,* appears on page 191.

Activity 1

Combine each pair of sentences below into one sentence by starting with an -*ly* word and omitting repeated words. Place a comma after the opening -*ly* word.

Example • I gave several yanks to the starting cord of the lawn mower.
　　　　　• I was angry.

　　　　　Angrily, I gave several yanks to the starting cord of the lawn

　　　　　mower.

1. • The burglars carried the television out of the house.
   • They were quiet.

　　　_____

　　　_____

2. • Janelle squirmed in her seat as she waited for her turn to speak.
   • She was nervous.

　　　_____

　　　_____

3. • I reinforced all the coat buttons with a strong thread.
   • I was patient.

　　　_____

　　　_____

4. • He finished answering the last question on the test.
   • He was quick.

　　　_____

　　　_____

5. • I tore the wrapping off the present.
   • I was excited.

　　　_____

　　　_____

Activity 2

On separate paper, write five sentences of your own that begin with -*ly* words.

TO OPENERS

Use a *to* word group to open a sentence. Here are examples:

To succeed in that course, you must attend every class.
To help me sleep better, I learned to quiet my mind through meditation.
To get good seats, we went to the game early.

The *to* in such a group is also known as an *infinitive,* as explained on page 162.

Activity I

Combine each of the following pairs of sentences into one sentence by starting with a *to* word group and omitting repeated words. Use a comma after the opening *to* word group.

Example   ● I fertilize the grass every spring.
        ● I want to make it greener.
        To make the grass greener, I fertilize it every spring.

1. ● Doug ran five miles a day all summer.
    ● He wanted to prepare for the track season.

    _____

    _____

2. ● You should meet Al's parents.
    ● This will help you understand him better.

    _____

    _____

3. ● She wants to get the stain off her hand.
    ● She will have to use an abrasive soap.

    _____

    _____

4. ● I left the house early.
    ● I had to get to the church on time.

    _____

    _____

5. • I punched in my code number.
    • I did this to make the automatic banking machine work.

_____

_____

Activity 2

On separate paper, write five sentences of your own that begin with *to* word groups.

PREPOSITIONAL PHRASE OPENERS

Use prepositional phrase openers. Here are examples:

From the beginning, I disliked my boss.
In spite of her work, she failed the course.
After the game, we went to a movie.

Prepositional phrases include words like *in, from, of, at, by,* and *with.* A full list is on page 87.

Activity 1

Combine each of the following groups of sentences into one sentence by omitting repeated words. Start each sentence with a suitable prepositional phrase and place the other prepositional phrases in places that sound right. Generally, you should use a comma after the opening prepositional phrase.

Example • A fire started.
        • It did this at 5 A.M.
        • It did this inside the garage.

        At 5 A.M., a fire started inside the garage.

1. • I sat napping.
    • I did this during my work break.
    • I did this in the lunchroom corner.
    • I did this with my head on my arm.

_____

_____

2.   ● We played basketball.
     ● We did this in the church gym.
     ● We did this during the winter.
     ● We did this on many evenings.

_____

_____

3.   ● Fred Grencher studies his bald spot.
     ● He does this with grave concern.
     ● He does this in the bathroom mirror.
     ● He does this before going to bed.

_____

_____

4.   ● The car skidded.
     ● It did this on an oil slick.
     ● It did this on a sharp curve.
     ● It did this during the race.

_____

_____

5.   ● The teenage driver raced his car to the busy intersection.
     ● He did this without slowing down.
     ● The intersection is in the heart of town.

_____

_____

Activity 2

On separate paper, write five sentences of your own, each beginning with a prepositional phrase and containing at least one other prepositional phrase.

SERIES OF ITEMS

Use a series of items. Following are two of the many items that can be used in a series: adjectives and verbs.

Adjectives in Series

Adjectives are descriptive words. Here are examples:

The *husky young* man sanded the *chipped, weather-worn* paint off the fence.

Husky and *young* are adjectives that describe *man; chipped* and *weather-worn* are adjectives that describe *paint.* More information about adjectives appears on page 189.

Activity 1

Combine each of the following groups of sentences into one sentence by using adjectives in a series and omitting repeated words. Use commas between adjectives only when *and* inserted between them sounds natural.

Example ● I sewed a set of buttons onto my coat.
      ● The buttons were shiny.
      ● The buttons were black.
      ● The coat was old.
      ● The coat was green.

       I sewed a set of shiny black buttons onto my old green coat.

1. ● The boy stomped on the bug.
    ● The boy was little.
    ● The boy was angry.
    ● The bug was tiny.
    ● The bug was red.

      _____

      _____

2.   • The man slowly wiped his forehead with a bandanna.
     • The man was tall.
     • The man was thin.
     • His forehead was sweaty.
     • His bandanna was dirty.
     • His bandanna was blue.

_____

_____

3.   • My sister is intelligent.
     • My sister is good-natured.
     • My sister is humorous.

_____

_____

4.   • The boy looked at the girl.
     • The boy was shy.
     • The boy was timid.
     • The girl was grinning.
     • The girl was curly-haired.

_____

_____

5.   • A man wearing work clothes strode into the tavern.
     • The man was short.
     • The man was muscular.
     • The man was bald.
     • The work clothes were wrinkled.
     • The work clothes were green.
     • The tavern was noisy.
     • The tavern was smoke-filled.

_____

_____

Activity 2

On separate paper, write five sentences of your own that contain a series of adjectives.

Verbs in Series

Verbs are words that express action. Here are examples:

In my job as a cook's helper, I *prepared* salads, *sliced* meat and cheese, and *made* all kinds of sandwiches.

Basic information about verbs appears on page 84.

Activity 1

Combine each group of sentences below into one sentence by using verbs in a series and omitting repeated words. Use a comma between verbs in a series.

Example
- In the dingy bar Sam shelled peanuts.
- He sipped a beer.
- He talked up a storm with friends.

  In the dingy bar Sam shelled peanuts, sipped a beer, and talked

  up a storm with friends.

1.
   - When the popular comedian walked from behind the curtain, the crowd applauded.
   - The crowd stomped their feet.
   - The crowd shouted, "Hi . . . oh!"

   _____

   _____

2.
   - Everywhere in the cafeteria students were pulling on their coats.
   - They were scooping up their books.
   - They were hurrying off to class.

   _____

   _____

3.
   - By 6 A.M., I had read the textbook chapter.
   - I had taken notes on it.
   - I had studied the notes.
   - I had drunk eight cups of coffee.

   _____

   _____

4. • I pressed the Rice Krispies into the bowl.
    • I poured milk on them.
    • I waited for the milk to soak the cereal.

    _____

    _____

5. • I am afraid the dentist's drill will slip off my tooth.
    • I am afraid it will bite into my gum.
    • I am afraid it will make me jump with pain.

    _____

    _____

Activity 2

On separate paper, write five sentences of your own that use verbs in a series.

Note: The section on parallelism (pages 207–212) gives you practice in some of the other kinds of items that can be used in a series.

Sentence-Combining Exercises

This section provides a series of combining exercises. The exercises are made up of a number of short sentence units, each of which can be combined into one sentence. (Occasionally, you may decide that certain sentences are more effective if they are not combined.) The patterns you have already practiced will suggest ideas for combining the units that you work on. However, do not feel limited to previous patterns. Use your own natural instinct to explore and compose a variety of sentence combinations. It will help if you write out possible combinations and then read them aloud. Choose the one that sounds best. You will gradually develop an ear for hearing the option that reads most smoothly and clearly and that sounds most appropriate in the context of surrounding sentences. As you continue to practice, you will increase your ability to write more varied, interesting, and sophisticated sentences.

Here is an example of a short sentence unit and some possible combinations:

- Martha moved in the desk chair.
- Her moving was uneasy.
- The chair was hard.
- She worked at her assignment.
- The assignment was for her English class.

> *Martha moved uneasily in the hard desk chair, working at the assignment for her English class.*
>
> *Moving uneasily in the hard desk chair, Martha worked at the assignment for her English class.*
>
> *Martha moved uneasily in the hard desk chair as she worked at the assignment for her English class.*
>
> *While she worked at the assignment for her English class, Martha moved uneasily in the hard desk chair.*

Note: In combining short sentence clusters into one sentence, omit repeated words where necessary. Use separate paper.

 I Stray Dog

- A dog trots down the street.
- The dog is a stray.
- The dog is hungry.

- He has a lovable face.
- He has a healthy coat.
- But someone has abandoned him.

- He approaches a house.
- He smells a trash can.
- The can is filled with garbage.

- The dog knocks the can over.
- Garbage spills to the ground.

- Inside the house, the owner is alerted.
- He is alerted by the sound of the falling can.

- The dog digs into his find.
- He doesn't hear the owner coming.

- The owner opens his back door.
- He yells at the dog.
- The dog is quickly scared off.

- The owner cleans up the mess.
- The dog appears out of the shadows.
- The dog is hungry.

- The owner feels sorry for the dog.
- He returns to his house.
- He gets the dog some real food.

 2 April Fool

- April Fool's Day is an occasion.
- It happens yearly.
- It brings out the worst in people.

- People play tricks.
- They play tricks on their friends.
- They send them unordered pizzas.
- They tell them their cars were stolen.

- Practical jokers also like to make phone calls.
- The calls are to the zoo.

- The zoo answers.
- The caller asks for someone.
- The someone has a name.
- The name is of an animal.

- A caller asks to speak to Mr. Lyon.
- A caller asks to speak to Mr. Bear.
- A caller asks to speak to Ms. Fish.

- One year a joker tried something.
- The something was new.
- He asked for Mr. Tad Pole.

- This year the local zoo is trying an approach.
- The approach is clever.
- The approach will discourage these calls.

- An April Fool's joker calls.
- The zoo will play a recording.
- The recording will say this.

- "Thank you for calling the zoo."
- "Mr. Lyon and his friends are busy."
- "They can't come to the phone."

- "They would prefer a visit."
- "The visit would be from you."
- "Please visit them soon."

3 Department Store Sale

- There's a sale at the large chain store.
- The sale is in all departments.

- Shoppers flood the store.
- They hurry down the aisles.

- People paw through sweaters.
- People paw through shirts.
- The sweaters and shirts are on special sales tables.
- The people do this excitedly.

- Stacks of coffeemakers are snapped up.
- The coffeemakers are reduced by 50 percent.
- This happens quickly.

- There is a long line of women.
- The women are holding piles of clothes.
- The line is in front of the fitting room.

- Some people buy things they don't need.
- Other people buy things they don't want.

- The manager smiles at the success of the sale.
- His employees don't smile.

- The shoppers mistreat the salespeople.
- The shoppers act like animals.
- The salespeople hate sales.

- The shoppers throw clothes on the floor.
- The shoppers throw dirty looks at each other.

- At the end of the day the store has made money.
- At the end of the day the manager is happy.
- At the end of the day the salespeople feel like quitting.

● 4 The Garbage Problem

- We have a garbage problem.
- The problem is severe.
- The problem is in the United States.

- This problem has been growing for a long time.
- No one ever wanted to think about it.

- No one wanted to plan ahead for the day the dumps would fill up.
- No one wanted to plan ahead for the day the chemical drums would begin to leak.

- We ignored the problem.
- We did this by covering it up with pleasant-sounding words.

- We call garbage men "sanitation engineers."
- We call garbage trucks "sanitation vehicles."
- We call garbage dumps "landfills."

- A landfill is really a pit.
- The pit is full of garbage.
- The garbage is smelly.
- The garbage is decaying.

- The euphemisms we use sound clean.
- They sound harmless.
- They help us forget about the garbage.
- The garbage is piling up in our country.

- Now, we are faced with a crisis.
- The crisis involves buried chemical poisons.
- The crisis involves overflowing garbage dumps.

- Language has helped us avoid this problem.
- The time has come to drop the cover-up.
- The time has come to face the situation honestly.

5 Cocoa and Doughnut

- A cup of cocoa sat on the high-chair tray.
- Half a doughnut sat on the high-chair tray.
- The cocoa was dark brown.
- The doughnut was a white sugar doughnut.

- A little boy was in the high chair.
- He stuck his finger into the cocoa.
- The sticking of his finger was careful.

- Then he picked up the doughnut half.
- He pushed the doughnut into the cup.
- His pushing was deep.

- Cocoa flowed over the top of the cup.
- It ran onto the tray.
- It dropped off the tray onto a tablecloth.
- The tablecloth was white linen.

- The little boy grabbed at the doughnut.
- The doughnut was spongy.
- The doughnut would not come out of the cup.

- The boy pushed at the cup.
- The cup rolled onto its side.
- It rocked back and forth on the metal tray.
- The rocking was gentle.

- The boy dug his hand into the cup.
- He pulled out a piece of doughnut.

- He pressed the doughnut against the metal tray.
- He pressed it with his fist.
- The doughnut flattened.
- The flattening was like a pancake.

- The boy shoved the pressed doughnut.
- He shoved most of it off the tray.
- It splattered onto the floor.
- It splattered onto the tablecloth.

- The boy picked up a fistful of doughnut.
- He jammed it into his mouth.

- He sat chewing the doughnut.
- His chewing was contented.

- The boy's father walked into the room.
- The boy looked up at his father.
- The boy was happy.

6 Jack Alone

- Jack entered his apartment.
- He locked the door.
- The muscles in his face began to relax.
- The muscles in his body began to relax.

- He felt happy to be at home.
- He felt happy after an exhausting day at work.
- The work was as a delivery man for United Parcel.

- He was carrying a newspaper.
- He was carrying his mail.
- He dropped both of them on the sofa.

- He walked into the kitchen.
- He opened the freezer door.
- He took out a TV dinner.
- The TV dinner was a Swanson's Hungry Man Salisbury Steak dinner.

- He placed the dinner in his toaster oven.
- He set the oven at 450°.

- Then he went into the bedroom.
- He undressed.
- He hung on a chair his heavy brown shirt.
- He hung on a chair his heavy brown pants.
- The hanging was neat.

- In the bathroom he washed his face.
- He washed his arms and hands.
- He brushed the tangles out of his hair.
- His hair was curly.
- His hair was black.

- He put on a corduroy shirt.
- The shirt was soft.
- He pulled on a pair of trousers.
- The trousers were old.
- The trousers were baggy.
- The trousers hung loosely around his waist.

- Then he put on a pair of slippers.
- The slippers were blue.
- The slippers were fleece-lined.

- Jack shuffled back to the kitchen.
- He boiled water.
- He made a large cup of tea.

- To the tea Jack added a tablespoon of honey.
- To the tea Jack added a tablespoon of bourbon.

- Jack carried the tea to the living room.
- He sat down beside his newspaper and mail.
- He flicked on the television.

- Later Jack might feel lonely.
- Now he was relaxed.
- Now he was comfortable.
- Now he was happy to be by himself.

7 A Surprise for Dracula

- Lola had a dream.
- The dream was recent.
- The dream was about Dracula.

- Dracula slipped through a window.
- The window was open.
- He approached Lola.
- Lola was sleeping.

- Dracula's lip curled back.
- His fangs were revealed.
- The fangs were long.
- The fangs were pointed.
- The pointing was cruel.

- Dracula bent over Lola.
- Lola stirred.
- She felt the shadow above her.

- Lola opened her eyes.
- Dracula grinned down at her.
- He assumed his victim was powerless.

- He bent down to her neck.
- The bending was slow.
- But then something happened.
- What happened was unexpected.

- Lola's hand flew out.
- She gave him a karate chop.
- The karate chop was quick.
- The karate chop was on the side of his head.

- Dracula was knocked backward.
- He tripped on his cape.
- He fell to the floor.

- Dracula sprang up.
- He made a cry.
- The cry was terrible.
- The cry was chilling.
- The cry was of an incensed beast.

- He leaped at Lola.
- She held up a crucifix.
- The crucifix was small.
- The crucifix was shining.

- Dracula winced.
- He came to a stop.
- The stop was abrupt.

- The crucifix radiated.
- It radiated an invisible shield.
- The shield was protective.
- Dracula could not penetrate the shield.

- Dracula drew his cape about him.
- He grew smaller in size.
- This happened rapidly.

- He disappeared.
- Only a bat remained.
- The bat was squeaking.

- It flew out of the room.
- Its going was quick.
- It was a bat returning to Hell.

8 Writing a Paper

- Martha has writer's block.
- She can think of nothing to write.

- She scribbles words on the page.
- The words do not develop the subject.
- She crosses out the words.

- Martha is sweating.
- Martha is frustrated.
- She feels bored.
- She feels stupid.

- She pulls at the collar of her blouse.
- She gets up.
- She walks around the room.
- She walks for a couple of minutes.

- She stares out the window.
- She wishes that the paper were finished.
- Her wishing is desperate.

- She thinks of what she could be watching on television.
- She thinks of calls she could make to friends.

- Then she sighs.
- She returns to the desk.

- She does two things.
- The things are to break the writer's block.

- First, she writes about her subject.
- She writes whatever comes into her head.
- She does this for twenty minutes.

- Then she reads what she has written.
- She tries to decide on her main point.
- She tries to decide on her support for that point.

- This work helps clear her confusion.
- Her confusion is now not so great.

- She senses the point of her paper.
- She senses how to support that point.
- She senses how to organize the support.

- She works hard for more than an hour.
- The result is the first rough draft of her paper.

- Martha sighs with relief.
- She gets up to take a break.

- She still has a second draft to write.
- She even has a third draft to write.
- But the worst part is over.
- Martha knows she has won the battle.

9 Victim

- The TV van hurried to the scene.
- The scene was of an auto accident.
- The lights of the TV van were flashing.

- An ambulance pulled away from the scene.
- It carried a dead boy.
- It left as the van arrived.

- The boy had backed his car out of a driveway.
- He had done so without looking.

- His car was struck by a truck.
- The truck was oncoming.
- He was killed instantly.

- The mother of the boy stood in the driveway.
- She was sobbing.
- She was talking to neighbors.

- TV lights were focused on her face.
- The focusing was cruel.
- A TV reporter approached her with a microphone.
- He asked her to speak.

- Her friends moved aside.
- Their moving was uncertain.
- Her friends did not stop the TV crew.

- Bystanders jostled in the background.
- Police moved them aside.
- The police did not stop the TV crew.

- The woman began to talk.
- The woman talked about the accident.
- The woman talked about her dead son.

- She began to cry.
- She tried to keep talking.
- The camera continued to roll.

- The reporter looked sympathetic.
- He stood to one side.
- His standing was careful.
- He wanted the camera to have a good angle.

- The woman felt obliged to the TV people.
- She felt obliged to cooperate.
- She should not have.

- The woman did not have to share her grief.
- The grief was private.

- The woman should have said something to the TV people.
- She should have said, "Get out of here."
- She should have said, "My tragedy is none of your business."

- The woman did not do this.
- The camera whirled.

10 Life in Winter

- For many people, winter is a dead season.
- It is actually full of life.
- The life is hidden.

- For instance, many insects die.
- They do this in autumn.
- They leave life behind.
- It is in the form of eggs.

- The eggs are on tree bark.
- They are on weeds.
- They are in the ground.

- The eggs will hatch.
- This will happen next spring.
- Millions of crickets will emerge.
- Millions of wasps will emerge.
- Millions of spiders will emerge.

- Woolly caterpillars are different.
- They do not die.
- Instead, they find a piece of wood.
- They attach themselves to it.
- They freeze solid during the winter.

- They will defrost.
- They will crawl away.
- This will happen in the spring.

- Other animals bury themselves alive.
- They do this to avoid winter's cold.

- Frogs dig into the mud.
- Turtles dig into the mud.
- They enter a state of hibernation.

- The pond will freeze.
- The frogs and turtles will be alive.
- They will be waiting for spring.

- Woodchucks go into a sleep too.
- The sleep is deep.
- The sleep is months-long.

- The woodchuck enters its den.
- It rolls into a ball.
- The ball is tight.
- The woodchuck's limbs grow rigid.
- This happens when it is ready to hibernate.

- A woodchuck's heart beats eighty times a minute.
- This happens normally.
- The heart slows to five beats a minute.
- This happens during hibernation.

- Life goes on.
- This happens under the deepest snows.
- This happens in the most bitter cold.

Appendixes

INTRODUCTION

Three appendixes follow. Appendix A consists of diagnostic and achievement tests that measure many of the skills in this book. The diagnostic test can be taken at the outset of your work; the achievement test can be used to measure your progress at the end of your work. Appendix B supplies answers to the introductory projects and the practice exercises in Part Two. The answers, which should be referred to only after you have worked carefully through each exercise, give you responsibility for testing yourself. (To ensure that the answer key is used as a learning tool only, answers are *not* given for the review tests in Part Two or for the reinforcement tests in Part Three. These answers appear only in the Instructor's Manual; they can be copied and handed out at the discretion of your instructor.) Finally, Appendix C provides handy progress charts that you can use to track your performance on all the tests in the book and the writing assignments as well.

Appendix A

Diagnostic and Achievement Tests

SENTENCE-SKILLS DIAGNOSTIC TEST

Part I

This test will help check your knowledge of a number of sentence skills. In each item below, certain words are underlined. Write *X* in the answer space if you think a mistake appears at the underlined part. Write *C* in the answer space if you think the underlined part is correct.

A series of headings ("Fragments," "Run-Ons," and so on) will give you clues to the mistakes to look for. However, you do not have to understand the heading to find a mistake. What you are checking is your own sense of effective written English.

Fragments

_____ 1. After I had done fifty push-ups. I felt like a worn-out rubber band. I wasn't planning to move until the middle of next week.

_____ 2. My little brother loves to go out at night, especially when the moon is full. My sister is convinced he's a werewolf.

_____ 3. Susie stood on tiptoe and craned her neck. Trying to see over the heads of the people in front of her. Finally she decided to go home and watch the parade on television.

_____ 4. Fran was excited about the job interview. She decided to have her hair done. And bought a new briefcase so she would look like an executive.

Run-Ons

_____ 5. The instructor assigned two chapters of the <u>book, he</u> also handed out a library research project.

_____ 6. Something was obviously bothering <u>Martha</u> a small muscle in her temple was throbbing.

_____ 7. The tires on my Chevy are <u>worn, but</u> the car itself is in good condition.

_____ 8. I could afford the monthly car <u>payments, I</u> did not have enough money to pay for insurance as well.

Standard English Verbs

_____ 9. Aunt Agatha <u>sees</u> much better when she puts on her bifocals.

_____ 10. The game was lost when the other team <u>score</u> a fourth-quarter touchdown.

_____ 11. At the end of the hike, we <u>was</u> covered with mosquito bites.

_____ 12. Martina <u>have</u> only three more courses to take to earn her degree.

Irregular Verbs

_____ 13. That show must be a rerun; I <u>seen</u> it at least twice.

_____ 14. If I had <u>taken</u> more notes in that class, I would have done better on the exam.

_____ 15. I accidentally <u>throwed</u> away the parking ticket when I cleaned out the glove compartment of my car.

_____ 16. At the end of the practice session, all the players <u>drank</u> Gatorade.

Subject-Verb Agreement

_____ 17. The major story on all the news programs <u>concerns</u> the proposed tax hike.

_____ 18. There <u>was</u> only two handkerchiefs left in the drawer.

_____ 19. My sister and her husband <u>take</u> my father bowling every Thursday night.

_____ 20. Each of my little boys <u>need</u> a warmer jacket for the winter.

Consistent Verb Tense

_____ 21. After I checked my bank balance, I <u>realized</u> I did not have enough money for a new stereo.

_____ 22. Upon finding a seat on the bus, Ralph unfolded his newspaper, <u>turns</u> to the sports section, and began to read.

Pronoun Reference, Agreement, and Point of View

_____ 23. All students should try their best to get good grades.

_____ 24. My first year in college I stayed in a dorm, where they chose a roommate for me.

_____ 25. Our company never gives bonuses to its employees, no matter how hard you work.

Pronoun Types

_____ 26. Paula writes much better than me.

_____ 27. My sister and I have both gotten part-time jobs.

Adjectives and Adverbs

_____ 28. The children smiled so sweet that I knew they were up to something.

_____ 29. The professor spoke honestly to me about my writing strengths and problems.

_____ 30. Weighing 350 pounds, Max the Mauler was the most heaviest of the four wrestlers in the ring.

_____ 31. Soap operas are more enjoyable to Martha than game shows.

Misplaced Modifiers

_____ 32. At the new video store, we bought a video cassette recorder that has a stop-action feature.

_____ 33. I returned the toy to the store that was broken.

Dangling Modifier

_____ 34. While playing cards, two pizzas were eaten.

_____ 35. Glancing out the window, Felipe saw a strange car pull into the driveway.

Parallelism

_____ 36. Before I can settle down to studying, I must take out the garbage, dry the dishes, and the leftovers have to be put away.

_____ 37. Three ways of treating a cold are bed rest, chicken soup, and taking vitamin C tablets.

Capital Letters

_____ 38. Daylight saving time usually ends on the last <u>sunday</u> in October.

_____ 39. Last summer I worked as a stock boy at <u>Sears</u>.

_____ 40. Most of the people who live in that neighborhood are <u>doctors</u>.

_____ 41. Vince yelled, <u>"hurry</u> up, the show's starting in ten minutes."

Numbers and Abbreviations

_____ 42. So far <u>7</u> students have dropped out of my math course.

_____ 43. The assignment starts on page <u>132</u> of the math book.

_____ 44. Norm's insurance <u>co.</u> increased his rates after he was involved in a car accident.

End Marks

_____ 45. Are you going to the church service tomorrow<u>.</u>

_____ 46. I wondered if I should give Terry a call<u>.</u>

Apostrophe

_____ 47. <u>Lucys</u> goal is to become the head nurse at the same hospital where her mother once worked.

_____ 48. I <u>wasnt</u> able to sleep at all the night after my wisdom teeth were pulled.

_____ 49. I did some careful thinking before I rejected my <u>lawyer's</u> advice in the matter.

_____ 50. Several storm <u>windows'</u> in the house are badly cracked.

Quotation Marks

_____ 51. <u>Benjamin Franklin once wrote, "Fish and visitors begin to smell after three days."</u>

_____ 52. <u>I'll be with you in just a moment, the harried salesperson said."</u>

_____ 53. <u>If that's your opinion," said Fran, "you're more narrow-minded than I thought."</u>

_____ 54. <u>Time is money, the manager said, and I don't have much."</u>

Comma

_____ 55. The dessert consisted of homemade ice cream and a choice of fresh strawberries blueberries or peaches.

_____ 56. My brother, who lifts weights, rarely loses an argument.

_____ 57. When I opened the door to my apartment I quickly sensed that something was wrong.

_____ 58. It was supposed to rain heavily all day, but we only got a light drizzle in the morning.

Spelling

_____ 59. If I had controlled my time better this semester, I would have been a successful student.

_____ 60. Maureen has alot of definitions to study for her biology test.

_____ 61. My roommate wants to hold partys in our apartment every weekend.

_____ 62. The house we just bought has two baths and a sunken liveing room.

Omitted Words and Letters

_____ 63. As a child, I always cut the crusts my bread.

_____ 64. All three record stores in the mall have sales on cassette tapes.

_____ 65. All the outside doors in our house have dead-bolt lock.

Commonly Confused Words

_____ 66. I'm very sorry to hear that your not feeling well.

_____ 67. You can't judge a book by it's cover.

_____ 68. The car was going much to fast to stop at the light.

_____ 69. The tenants decided to take their landlord to court.

Effective Word Choice

_____ 70. Our car was <u>totaled</u> in the accident; we're lucky to be alive.

_____ 71. Without financial aid, my children are going to have a lot of trouble trying <u>to make ends meet</u>.

_____ 72. Ernest <u>was promoted</u> more quickly than other employees in the company.

_____ 73. My <u>expectancy</u> is to become a doctor someday.

_____ 74. <u>In my personal opinion</u>, I think that a tax hike is ridiculous.

_____ 75. <u>Because of the fact</u> that Jennifer missed the final exam, she failed the course.

Part 2 (Optional)

Do the following at your instructor's request. This second part of the test will provide more detailed information about skills you need to know. On separate paper, number and correct all the items you have marked with an *X*. For example, suppose you had marked the word groups below with an *X*. (Note that these examples were not taken from the actual test.)

4. <u>When I picked up the tire</u>. Something in my back snapped. I could not stand up straight as a result.

7. The phone started <u>ringing, then</u> the doorbell sounded as well.

15. <u>Marks</u> goal is to save enough money to get married next year.

29. Without checking the rearview <u>mirror the</u> driver pulled out into the passing lane.

Here is how you should write your corrections on a separate sheet of paper:

4. When I picked up the tire, something in my back snapped.

7. The phone started ringing, and then the doorbell sounded as well.

15. Mark's

29. mirror, the driver

There are over forty corrections to make in all.

SENTENCE-SKILLS ACHIEVEMENT TEST

Part I

This test will help check your knowledge of a number of sentence skills. In each item below, certain words are underlined. Write *X* in the answer space if you think a mistake appears at the underlined part. Write *C* in the answer space if you think the underlined part is correct.

A series of headings ("Fragments," "Run-Ons," and so on) will give you clues to the mistakes to look for.

Fragments

_____ 1. After I finished my morning classes. I had a quick lunch in the cafeteria. Then I hurried off to my job as a supermarket cashier.

_____ 2. My family loves outdoor sports, especially touch football. We often play outside until it's dark.

_____ 3. Simone waved her hand back and forth. Trying to catch the instructor's attention. She wanted to ask a question and make a comment about the lecture.

_____ 4. The instructor handed back my term paper. She told me to rewrite the conclusion. And retype the footnotes so that the form was correct.

Run-Ons

_____ 5. Myrna was angry at herself, she had forgotten to pick up some potatoes on the way home.

_____ 6. My husband often sings in the morning our cat hides under the bed.

_____ 7. Ed is an absentminded person, so he writes notes to help remember things.

_____ 8. I kept drinking cups of coffee, I had a lot of studying to do that night.

Standard English Verbs

_____ 9. My husband thinks more clearly in the morning than at night.

_____ 10. When the pile of rags caught on fire, Theo reach for the hose.

_____ 11. At Saturday's football game, we was the only couple that brought an umbrella.

_____ 12. I don't think that Roger have thought enough about his future.

Irregular Verbs

_____ 13. My boyfriend and I <u>seen</u> the new Burt Reynolds movie at the drive-in last night.

_____ 14. We should not have <u>taken</u> the children shopping with us today.

_____ 15. The second baseman fielded the grounder, stepped on the bag, and then <u>throwed</u> to first for a double play.

_____ 16. My cotton sweater <u>shrank</u> so much in the wash that I gave it to my daughter.

Subject-Verb Agreement

_____ 17. The price of the theater tickets <u>seems</u> much too high.

_____ 18. There <u>was</u> only three pieces of wood left in the pile.

_____ 19. The new tenant and her little boy <u>make</u> a lot of noise.

_____ 20. Each of the office secretaries <u>work</u> from 9 to 5.

Consistent Verb Tense

_____ 21. My father interrupted me as I studied my accounting and <u>asked</u> me to balance his checkbook.

_____ 22. When they got back from the party, Ann lost her temper, <u>screams</u> at her husband, and then refused to talk about the cause.

Pronoun Reference, Agreement, and Point of View

_____ 23. All registered voters should do <u>their</u> civic duty at the polls.

_____ 24. Carol joined the sorority because <u>they</u> have the same interests that she does.

_____ 25. I'm going to move out of the city because <u>you</u> never feel safe there.

Pronoun Types

_____ 26. Larry had a lot more to eat than <u>me</u>.

_____ 27. My brother and <u>I</u> are getting married in the same month.

Adjectives and Adverbs

_____ 28. The dress was made <u>beautiful</u>, with a full silk lining and covered buttons.

_____ 29. The boy walked <u>timidly</u> up to the baseball player and asked for his autograph.

_____ 30. Which would you say is the <u>more harder</u> exercise—swimming or jogging?

_____ 31. General Psychology is the <u>most interesting</u> course I am taking this semester.

Misplaced Modifiers

_____ 32. At the campus bookstore, I just bought a diary <u>that has a genuine leather cover.</u>

_____ 33. Most people do not go on summer vacations <u>that are poor.</u>

Dangling Modifiers

_____ 34. <u>While carrying the packages out of the store,</u> my ankle was sprained.

_____ 35. <u>Jogging down the street,</u> Phil was almost hit by a car.

Parallelism

_____ 36. This weekend, Steve has to mow the lawn, take the dog to the vet, <u>and the family station wagon needs to be washed.</u>

_____ 37. Barbara was frightened, upset, and <u>a nervous wreck;</u> she had three exams in the next two days.

Capital Letters

_____ 38. The sale ends this coming <u>tuesday.</u>

_____ 39. I just got a call from <u>allstate</u> that my insurance is being dropped.

_____ 40. Frank's goal is to become a successful <u>accountant</u> someday.

_____ 41. Linda asked, "<u>who</u> wants to go out and get some more ice?"

Numbers and Abbreviations

_____ 42. Before the game was over, <u>four</u> players had been ejected.

_____ 43. Your doctor's appointment has been scheduled for <u>8:15</u> tomorrow evening.

_____ 44. I spent almost ten <u>hrs.</u> studying for the exam.

End Marks

_____ 45. Do you know where Bob is tonight<u>?</u>

_____ 46. Tisha wondered how long the sprain would take to heal<u>.</u>

Apostrophe

_____ 47. Sams proudest moment came when he got his first A on a paper.

_____ 48. Doesnt your bank stay open late on Fridays?

_____ 49. The doctor's advice contradicted that of the other doctor I had seen.

_____ 50. The little girl at the front door explained that she has some puppies' for sale.

Quotation Marks

_____ 51. Benjamin Franklin once wrote, "There never was a good war or a bad peace."

_____ 52. "I'd rather make a fast nickel than a slow dollar, the store owner said."

_____ 53. "Don't come back after lunch," the boss said, "because you're fired."

_____ 54. "After you finish writing the essay," said the instructor, be sure to proofread it carefully."

Comma

_____ 55. Stella has just learned that she is allergic to shrimp crabmeat and salmon.

_____ 56. My Uncle Al, who is very forgetful, always asks me my name.

_____ 57. As the vampire was about to bite his victim he saw that the sun was shining.

_____ 58. Last summer I worked in a factory, but this summer I'll have a job in a resort hotel.

Spelling

_____ 59. Through someone's mistake, my name was dropped from the list of graduating seniors.

_____ 60. It's alright with me if you skip breakfast.

_____ 61. There are three unidentified bodys in the police morgue.

_____ 62. The counselor asked how many courses I planned on takeing next semester.

Omitted Words and Letters

_____ 63. The kids in street played ball with cutoff broom handles.

_____ 64. Sharp splinters jutted out of the wooden pilings on the pier.

_____ 65. I need at least a thousand dollar to pay off my debts.

Commonly Confused Words

_____ 66. If your in the mood for some shopping, so am I.

_____ 67. The supplement helps my body get it's daily dose of potassium.

_____ 68. Caroline is to self-centered to be a good friend.

_____ 69. The players will forfeit their salaries if they go on strike.

Effective Word Choice

_____ 70. Someone broke into my car and ripped off my tape deck.

_____ 71. I need a new coat; my old corduroy one has seen better days.

_____ 72. The employee layoff was handled in a sensitive way by the company.

_____ 73. My parents are desirous of my earning a college degree.

_____ 74. Owing to the fact that we don't play cards, we weren't invited to the party.

_____ 75. Personally, my own belief is that every home will have a computer someday.

Part 2 (Optional)

Do the following at your instructor's request. This second part of the test will provide more detailed information about skills you need to know. On separate paper, number and correct all the items you have marked with an X. For example, suppose you had marked the word groups below with an X. (Note that these examples were not taken from the actual test.)

  4. When I picked up the tire. Something in my back snapped. I could not stand up straight as a result.

  7. The phone started ringing, then the doorbell sounded as well.

15. Marks goal is to save enough money to get married next year.

29. Without checking the rearview mirror the driver pulled out into the passing lane.

Here is how you should write your corrections on a separate sheet of paper:

  4. When I picked up the tire, something in my back snapped.

  7. The phone started ringing, and then the doorbell sounded as well.

15. Mark's

29. mirror, the driver

There are over forty corrections to make in all.

Appendix B

Answers to Introductory Projects and Practice Exercises in Part Two

This answer key can help you teach yourself. Use it to find out why you got some answers wrong—you want to uncover any weak spot in your understanding of a given skill. By using the answer key in an honest and thoughtful way, you will master each skill and prepare yourself for the many tests in this book that have no answer key.

SUBJECTS AND VERBS

Introductory Project

Answers will vary.

Practice 1 (page 85)

1. I ate
2. Barracuda swim
3. Sally failed
4. movie ended
5. Kerry borrowed
6. children stared
7. newspaper tumbled
8. Lola starts
9. job limits
10. windstorm blew

Practice 2 (86)

1. sister is
2. chips are
3. defendant appeared
4. Art became
5. ride . . . seems
6. building was
7. weeks . . . were

8. banana split and . . . cake . . . look
9. Jane . . . feels
10. Rooms . . . seem

Practice 3 (86)

1. clock runs
2. player . . . is
3. shoppers filled
4. trucks rumbled
5. children drew
6. picture fell
7. Chipmunks live
8. uncle monopolized
9. tomatoes were
10. company canceled

Practice (87–88)

1. For that course, you need three different books.
2. The key to the front door slipped from my hand into a puddle.
3. The checkout lines at the supermarket moved very slowly.
4. With his son, Jamal walked to the playground.
5. No quarrel between good friends lasts for a very long time.

516

6. In one weekend, Martha planted a large vegetable garden in her backyard.
7. Either of my brothers is a reliable worker.
8. The drawer of the bureau sticks on rainy days.
9. During the movie, several people walked out in protest.
10. At a single sitting, my brother reads five or more comic books.

Practice (89)

1. He has been sleeping
2. foundations were attacked
3. I have not washed
4. instructor had not warned
5. bus will be leaving
6. You should not try
7. They have just been married
8. He could make
9. Kim has decided
10. company should have purchased

Practice (90)

1. hypnotist locked and sawed
2. Connie began and finished
3. Nissans, Toyotas, and Hondas glittered
4. Tony added and got
5. car sputtered, stalled, and started
6. Whiteflies, mites, and aphids infected
7. Ruth disconnected . . . and carried
8. We walked and bought
9. Tony and Lola looked and bought
10. aunt and uncle married, divorced, and remarried

FRAGMENTS

Introductory Project

1. verb
2. subject
3. subject . . . verb
4. express a complete thought

Practice 2 (96–97)

Note: The underlined part shows the fragment (or that part of the original fragment not changed during correction).

1. Although the air conditioner was working, I still felt warm in the room.
2. When Tony got into his car this morning, he discovered that he had left the car windows open. The seats and rug were soaked, since it had rained overnight.
3. After cutting fish at the restaurant all day, Jenny smelled like a cat food factory.
4. Franco raked out the soggy leaves that were at the bottom of the cement fish pond. When two bullfrogs jumped out at him, he dropped the rake and ran.
5. Because he had eaten and drunk too much, he had to leave the party early. His stomach was like a volcano that was ready to erupt.

Practice 1 (99)

1. Eli lay in bed after the alarm rang, wishing that he had $100,000.
2. Investigating the strange, mournful cries in his neighbor's yard, George found a puppy tangled in its leash.
3. As a result, I was late for class.

Practice 2 (100)

1. Glistening with dew, the gigantic web hung between the branches of the tree.
2. Martha is pleased with the carpet of Astroturf in her kitchen, claiming that crumbs settle in the grass so she never sees them.
   Or: Martha is pleased with the carpet of Astroturf in her kitchen. She claims that crumbs settle in the grass so she never sees them.
3. Ron picked through the box of chocolates, removing the kinds he didn't like.
   Or: He removed the kinds he didn't like.
4. The grass I was walking on suddenly became squishy because I had hiked into a marsh of some kind.
   Or: The reason was that I had hiked into a marsh of some kind.
5. Steve drove quickly to the bank to cash his paycheck.
   Or: He had to cash his paycheck.

Practice 1 (102)

1. For example, he managed to cut his hand while crumbling a bar of shredded wheat.
2. All day, people complained about missing parts, rude salespeople, and errors on bills.
3. For example, she suggests using club soda on stains.

Practice 2 (102-103)

1. My little boy is constantly into mischief, such as tearing the labels off all the cans in the cupboard.
2. For example, it had a hand-carved mantel and a mahogany banister.
3. For instance, he chewed with his mouth open.
4. A half hour later, there were several explosions, with potatoes splattering all over the walls of the oven.
   Or: Potatoes splattered all over the walls of the oven.
5. Janet looked forward to seeing former classmates at the high school reunion, including the football player she had had a wild crush on.

Practice (104)

1. Fred went to the refrigerator to get milk for his breakfast cereal and discovered about one tablespoon of milk left in the carton.
   Or: He discovered about one tablespoon of milk left in the carton.
2. Then I noticed the "Out of order" sign taped over the coin slot.
3. Our neighborhood's most eligible bachelor got married this weekend but did not invite us to the wedding.
   Or: But he did not invite us to the wedding.
4. Also, he was constantly criticizing Larry's choice of friends.
5. Wanda stared at the blank page in desperation and decided that the first sentence of a paper is always the hardest to write.
   Or: And she decided that the first sentence of a paper is always the hardest to write.

RUN-ONS

Introductory Project

1. period
2. but
3. semicolon
4. although

Practice 1 (113)

1. down. He
2. station. A
3. panicked. The
4. exam. The
5. wood. One
6. hand. Guests
7. earth. Earthworms
8. party. A
9. time. Her
10. stacks. The

Practice 2 (114)

1. class. His
2. increasing. Every
3. properly. We
4. it. Half
5. places. Our
6. water. This
7. speeding. He
8. times. Nobody
9. names. For
10. floor. His

Practice 1(116)

1. , and
2. , for
3. , but
4. , for
5. , for
6. , but
7. , and
8. , so
9. , but
10. , so

Practice (118)

1. out; nobody
2. rerun; the
3. cool; everyone
4. year; an
5. stop; he

Practice 1 (119)

1. insecticide; otherwise, the
2. props; also, I (*or* in addition *or* moreover *or* furthermore)
3. basement; instead, he
4. week; consequently, I (*or* as a result *or* thus *or* therefore)
5. semester; in addition, she (*or* also *or* moreover *or* furthermore)

Practice 2 (119–120)

1. seat; however,
2. match; as a result,
3. headache; furthermore,
4. razors; consequently,
5. hair; nevertheless,

Practice I (121)

1. because
2. When
3. While *or* When
4. After *or* When
5. before

Practice 2 (121–122)

1. Because (*or* Since) Sharon didn't understand the instructor's point, she asked him to repeat it.
2. Although (*or* Even though) Fred remembered to get the hamburger, he forgot to get the hamburger rolls.
3. After Michael gulped two cups of strong coffee, his heart started to flutter.
4. When a car sped around the corner, it sprayed slush all over the pedestrians.
5. Although (*or* Even though) Lola loved the rose cashmere sweater, she had nothing to wear with it.

STANDARD ENGLISH VERBS

Introductory Project

played . . . plays
hoped . . . hopes
juggled . . . juggles

1. past time . . . -*d* or -*ed*
2. present time . . . -*s*

Practice I (128)

1. hates
2. messes
3. feels
4. covers
5. smells
6. C
7. blurs
8. thinks
9. pretends
10. seems

Practice 2 (129)

Charlotte reacts badly when she gets caught in a traffic jam. She opens the dashboard compartment and pulls out an old pack of Marlboros that she keeps for such occasions. She lights up and drags heavily, sucking the smoke deep into her lungs. She gets out of the car and looks down the highway, trying to see where the delay is. Back in the car, she drums her fingers on the steering wheel. If the jam lasts long enough, she starts talking to herself and angrily kicks off her shoes.

Practice I (130)

1. raced
2. glowed
3. walked
4. sighted
5. stared
6. decided
7. C
8. needed
9. scattered
10. decided

Practice 2 (130)

Bill's boss shouted at Bill. Feeling bad, Bill went home and cursed his wife. Then his wife screamed at their son. Angry himself, the son went out and cruelly teased a little girl who lived next door until she wailed. Bad feelings were passed on as one person wounded the next with ugly words. No one managed to break the vicious circle.

Practice I (132)

1. has
2. does
3. is
4. are
5. was . . . had
6. was
7. did . . . was
8. were
9. had
10. am

Practice 2 (133)

1. ~~be~~ is
2. ~~is~~ are
3. ~~has~~ have
4. ~~don't~~ doesn't
5. ~~is~~ are
6. ~~have~~ had
7. ~~done~~ did
8. ~~have~~ had
9. ~~has~~ had
10. ~~was~~ were

Practice 3 (133)

My mother sings alto in our church choir. She has to go to choir practice every Friday night and is expected to know all the music. If she does not know her part, the other choir members do things like glare at her and are likely to make nasty comments, she says. Last weekend, my mother had houseguests and did not have time to learn all the notes. The music was very difficult, and she thought the other people were going to make fun of her. But they were very understanding when she told them that she had laryngitis and couldn't make a sound.

IRREGULAR VERBS

Introductory Project

1. screamed . . . screamed
2. wrote . . . written
3. stole . . . stolen
4. asked . . . asked
5. kissed . . . kissed
6. chose . . . chosen
7. rode . . . ridden
8. chewed . . . chewed
9. thought . . . thought
10. danced . . . danced

Practice 1 (139)

1. ~~chose~~ chosen
2. ~~done~~ did (*or* had done)
3. ~~wore~~ worn
4. ~~wrote~~ written
5. ~~gived~~ gave
6. ~~be~~ was
7. ~~broke~~ broken
8. ~~lended~~ lent
9. ~~seen~~ saw
10. ~~knewed~~ knew

Practice 2 (139–141)

1. (a) sees
   (b) saw
   (c) seen
2. (a) chooses
   (b) chose
   (c) chosen
3. (a) takes
   (b) took
   (c) taken
4. (a) speaks
   (b) spoke
   (c) spoken
5. (a) swims
   (b) swam
   (c) swum
6. (a) drives
   (b) drove
   (c) driven
7. (a) wears
   (b) wore
   (c) worn
8. (a) blows
   (b) blew
   (c) blown
9. (a) begins
   (b) began
   (c) begun
10. (a) goes
    (b) went
    (c) gone

Practice (142)

1. lays
2. lay
3. Lying
4. laid
5. lay

Practice (143)

1. sit
2. setting
3. set
4. sat
5. set

Practice (144)

1. rise
2. raise
3. risen
4. raised
5. rises

SUBJECT-VERB AGREEMENT

Introductory Project

Correct: There <u>were</u> many applicants for the position.
Correct: The pictures in that magazine <u>are</u> very controversial.
Correct: Everybody usually <u>watches</u> the lighted numbers while riding in the elevator.

1. applicants . . . pictures
2. singular . . . singular

Practice (148)

1. stain ~~on the sheets~~ comes
2. coat, ~~along with two pairs of pants~~, sells
3. roots ~~of the apple tree~~ are
4. sisters, ~~who wanted to be at his surprise party~~, were
5. albums ~~in the attic~~ belong
6. cost ~~of personal calls made on office telephones~~ is
7. cups ~~of coffee in the morning~~ do
8. moon ~~as well as some stars~~ is
9. wiring ~~in the apartment~~ is . . . needs
10. Chapter 4 ~~of the psychology book, along with six weeks of class notes~~, is

Practice (149)

1. <u>are lines</u>
2. <u>were dogs</u>
3. <u>were dozens</u>
4. <u>are pretzels</u>
5. <u>were Janet and Maureen</u>
6. <u>are rats</u>
7. <u>were boys</u>
8. <u>is house</u>
9. <u>were fans</u>
10. <u>lies pastry</u>

Practice (150)

1. ignores
2. dances
3. deserves
4. were
5. appears
6. offers
7. owns
8. has
9. thinks
10. has

Practice (151)

1.	match	4.	plan
2.	have	5.	are
3.	are		

Practice (151–152)

1.	were	4.	give
2.	stumble	5.	appears
3.	blares		

CONSISTENT VERB TENSE

Introductory Project

Mistakes in verb tense: Alex <u>discovers</u> . . . <u>calls</u> a . . . <u>present</u> . . . <u>past</u>

Practice (155–156)

1.	causes	6.	sprinkled
2.	decided	7.	discovered
3.	picked	8.	asked
4.	hopes	9.	overcharges
5.	informs	10.	swallowed

ADDITIONAL INFORMATION ABOUT VERBS

Practice (Tense; 161)

1.	had walked	6.	had looked
2.	was feeling	7.	has studied
3.	had placed	8.	has seen
4.	was trying	9.	was watching
5.	is growing	10.	had thrown

Practice (Verbals; 162)

1.	*P*	6.	*P*
2.	*G*	7.	*P*
3.	*G*	8.	*I*
4.	*I*	9.	*P*
5.	*I*	10.	*G*

Practice (Active and Passive Verbs; 163–164)

1. Charlotte organized the surprise party.
2. The comedian offended many people.
3. The neighbors pay for the old woman's groceries.
4. The boys knocked the horse chestnuts off the trees.
5. The exorcist drove the devil out of Regan.
6. Four perspiring men loaded the huge moving van.
7. The inexperienced waiter dropped a tray of glasses.
8. My forgetful Aunt Agatha is always losing umbrellas.
9. Pete Rose finally broke Stan Musial's National League hitting record.
10. The airport security staff found a bomb in the suitcase.

PRONOUN REFERENCE, AGREEMENT, AND POINT OF VIEW

Introductory Project

1. b   2. b   3. b

Practice (167–168)

Note: The practice sentences could be rewritten to have other meanings than the ones indicated below.

1. Mario insisted that it was Harry's turn to drive.
   Or: Mario insisted to Harry, "It is my turn to drive."
2. I failed two of my courses last semester because the instructors graded unfairly.
3. Don's parents were very much pleased with the accounting job Don was offered.
   Or: The accounting job Don was offered pleased his parents very much.
4. Tony became very upset when he questioned the mechanic.
   Or: The mechanic became very upset when Tony questioned him.
5. I was very nervous about the unexpected biology exam.
6. Paul told his younger brother, "The dog chewed your new running shoes."
7. My cousin is an astrologer, but I don't believe in astrology.
8. When Liz was promoted, she told Elaine.
   Or: Liz told Elaine, "You have been promoted."
9. Whenever I start enjoying a new television show, the network takes it off the air.
10. When the center fielder heard the crack of the bat, he raced toward the fence but was unable to catch the ball.

Practice (169)

1. they . . . their
2. it
3. them
4. it
5. they

Practice (171)

1. his
2. her
3. his
4. his
5. her
6. his
7. her
8. she
9. its
10. his

Practice (172–173)

1. I always feel hungry
2. they have finished
3. they work
4. we can never be sure
5. she should register
6. he (or she) should check
    Or: If people plan . . . they should check
7. I do not get paid for all the holidays I should.
    Or: One does not get paid . . . one should.
8. you should take action
9. we had
10. we want it

PRONOUN TYPES

Introductory Project

Correct sentences:

Ali and I enrolled in a computer course.
The police officer pointed to my sister and me.
Lola prefers men who take pride in their bodies.
The players are confident that the league championship is theirs.
Those concert tickets are too expensive.
Our parents should spend some money on themselves for a change.

Practice 1 (179)

2. I (*S*)
3. they (*did* is understood) (*S*)
4. her (*O*)
5. she (*S*)
6. he (*S*)
7. She (*S*)
8. We (*S*)
9. I (*am* is understood) (*S*)
10. She and I (*S*)

Practice 2 (180)

2. me *or* him
3. me *or* her *or* him *or* them
4. me *or* her *or* him *or* them
5. me *or* her *or* him
6. I *or* he *or* she
7. I *or* he *or* she
8. them
9. him *or* her *or* them
10. us

Practice 1 (182)

1. who
2. that
3. who
4. whom
5. who

Practice (183)

1. ~~its~~ its
2. ~~him~~ his
3. ~~mines~~ mine
4. ~~they~~ their
5. ~~ours~~ ours

Practice 1 (184)

1. That dog
2. This fingernail
3. Those girls
4. those shopping bags
5. that corner house

Practice (186)

1. himself
2. themselves
3. yourselves (*or* yourself)
4. themselves
5. ourselves

ADJECTIVES AND ADVERBS

Introductory Project

Answers will vary for 1–4.

adjective . . . adverb . . ly . . . er . . . est

Practice 1 (190)

kinder . . . kindest

more ambitious . . . most ambitious

more generous . . . most generous

finer . . . finest

more likable . . . most likable

Practice 2 (191)

1. most comfortable
2. most difficult
3. easiest
4. less
5. best
6. longest
7. most memorable
8. more experienced . . . most experienced
9. worse . . . worst
10. better

Practice (192)

1. violently
2. quickly
3. angrily
4. considerable
5. gently
6. really
7. regularly . . . regular
8. quietly . . . angrily
9. carefully . . . exact
10. Slowly . . . surely

Practice (193)

1. well
2. good
3. well
4. well
5. well

MISPLACED MODIFIERS

Introductory Project

1. Intended: The farmers were wearing masks.
   Unintended: The apple trees were wearing masks.

2. Intended: The woman had a terminal disease.
   Unintended: The faith healer had a terminal disease.

Practice 1 (196–197)

Note: In each of the corrections below, the underlined part shows what was a misplaced modifier.

1. Driving around in their car, they finally found a laundromat.

2. In the library, I read that Chuck Yeager was a pilot who broke the sound barrier.
   Or: I read in the library that Chuck Yeager was a pilot who broke the sound barrier.

3. Taking the elevator, Evelyn was thinking about her lost chemistry book.

4. Lola selected a doughnut filled with banana cream from the bakery.
   Or: From the bakery, Lola selected a doughnut filled with banana cream.

5. Howard worked almost twenty hours overtime to pay some overdue bills.

6. Tickets have gone on sale in the college bookstore for next week's championship game.
   Or: In the college bookstore, tickets have gone on sale for next week's championship game.

7. I returned the orange socks that my uncle gave me to the department store.

8. Looking through the binoculars, the camper saw the black bear.

9. I earned nearly two hundred dollars last week.

10. In the refrigerator, mushrooms should be stored enclosed in a paper bag.

Practice 2 (198)

1. In our science class, we agreed to go out to dinner tonight.
   Or: We agreed in our science class to go out to dinner tonight.

2. On a rainy day in June, Bob and I decided to get married.
   Or: Bob and I, on a rainy day in June, decided to get married.

3. Weighed down with heavy packages, Suki decided to hail a taxi.
   Or: Suki, weighed down with heavy packages, decided to hail a taxi.

4. Without success, I've looked everywhere for an instruction book on how to play the guitar.
   Or: I've looked everywhere without success for an instruction book on how to play the guitar.

5. Over the phone, Mother told me to wash the car.
   Or: Mother told me over the phone to wash the car.

DANGLING MODIFIERS

Introductory Project

1. Intended: The giraffe was munching leaves from a tall tree.
   Unintended: The children were munching leaves.
2. Intended: Michael was arriving home after ten months in the service.
   Unintended: The neighbors were arriving home after ten months in the service.

Practice I (203–204)

1. Since it was folded into a tiny square, I could not read the message.
   Or: I could not read the message, which was folded into a tiny square.
2. As I waded into the lake, tadpoles swirled around my ankles.
3. *C*
4. Hanging on the wall was a photograph of my mother.
   Or: I saw a photograph of my mother hanging on the wall.
5. Settling comfortably into the chair, I let the television capture my attention for the next hour.
   Or: After I settled comfortably into the chair, the television captured my attention for the next hour.
6. As I was driving home after a tiring day at work, the white line became bleary.
   Or: Driving home after a tiring day at work, I saw the white line become bleary.
7. The batter hit the first home run of his career, which soared high over the left-field fence.
8. Since the rug was threadbare and dirty, Martha knew the time had come to replace it.
   Or: Martha knew the time had come to replace the rug, which was threadbare and dirty.
9. After we spent most of the night outdoors in a tent, the sun rose and we went into the house.
   Or: After spending most of the night outdoors in a tent, we went into the house when the sun rose.
10. While they were hot and sizzling, we bit into the apple tarts.
    Or: We bit into the apple tarts, which were hot and sizzling.

PARALLELISM

Introductory Project

Correct sentences:

> I use my TV remote control to change channels, to adjust the volume, and to turn the set on and off.
>
> One option the employees had was to take a cut in pay; the other was to work longer hours.
>
> The refrigerator has a cracked vegetable drawer, a missing shelf, and a strange freezer smell.

Practice I (209)

1. aching arms
2. freshly made soups
3. bad-tempered
4. replacing weather stripping
5. her green eyes
6. hear her sing *or* hear her songs
7. praying
8. attended
9. complaining about her strict parents
10. chased by bill collectors

PAPER FORMAT

Introductory Project

In "A," the title is capitalized and centered and has no quotation marks around it; there is a blank line between the title and the body of the paper; there are left and right margins around the body of the paper; no words are incorrectly hyphenated.

Practice I (215)

2. Don't put quotation marks around the title.
3. Capitalize the major words in the title (The Generation Gap in Our House).
4. Skip a line between the title and first line of the paper.
5. Indent the first line of the paper.
6. Keep margins on both sides of the paper.

Practice 2 (215–216)

Here are some possible titles:

1. Selfishness in Young Children
2. The Benefits of Daily Exercise *or* The Value of Daily Exercise
3. My Stubborn Son *or* My Stubborn Teenage Son
4. Essential College Study Skills
5. Drawbacks and Values of Single Life

Practice 3 (216–217)

1. The worst day of my life began when my supervisor at work gave me a message to call home.
2. Catholic church services have undergone many changes in the last few years.
3. An embarrassing incident happened to me when I was working as a waitress at the Stanton Hotel.
4. Correct
5. Many television commercials that I watch are degrading to human dignity.

CAPITAL LETTERS

Introductory Project

1–13: Answers will vary, but all should be capitalized.
14–16: On . . . "Let's . . . I

Practice (221)

1. Halloween . . . Thanksgiving
2. If . . . I'm
3. Ford . . . Connecticut . . . Florida . . . Goodyear
4. *Life* . . . World War
5. Northside Improvement Association . . . Third
6. Soundworks . . . Washington Boulevard . . . Panasonic
7. Fort Gordon . . . Germany
8. Thursday . . . Weight Watchers'
9. February . . . *Return* . . . *Dracula* . . . *Alien*
10. Gloria Vanderbilt . . . Burlington Mall

Practice (224)

1. Aunt Esther
2. Spanish . . . Aerobic Exercise

3. Dr. Purdy's
4. Hispanic . . . Southwest
5. Intermediate Math

Practice (225)

1. summer . . . sunbathe . . . magazines
2. week . . . tune . . . melody
3. high school . . . states . . . college
4. title . . . paper . . . instructor . . . grade
5. friend . . . college . . . degree . . . life

NUMBERS AND ABBREVIATIONS

Introductory Project

Correct choices:

First sentence: 8:55 . . . 65 percent
Second sentence: Nine . . . forty-five
Second sentence: brothers . . . mountain
Second sentence: hours . . . English

Practice (229)

1. five . . . three
2. Two
3. 8:30
4. nine o'clock
5. $282
6. 23
7. May 31, 1956
8. 2 . . . 5
9. 50 percent
10. five . . . twelve

Practice (230)

1. cousin . . . apartment
2. Wednesday
3. account . . . month
4. moving . . . president . . . company
5. pounds . . . weeks
6. favorite . . . especially
7. secretary . . . temporary . . . minute
8. brother . . . high school
9. gallon . . . streets
10. hospital . . . room

END MARKS

Introductory Project

1. depressed.
2. paper?
3. parked.
4. control!

Practice (234)

1. continue?
2. road!
3. arthritis.
4. visit?
5. wallet.
6. cars.
7. sunglasses!
8. Rings.
9. mess!"
10. wig?"

APOSTROPHE

Introductory Project

1. The apostrophes indicate omitted letters: *You are, he is, does not.*
2. In each case, the apostrophe indicates possession or ownership.
3. In the first sentence in each pair, the *s* in *books* and *cars* indicates plural number; in the second sentence in each pair, the *'s* indicates possession.

Apostrophe in Contractions

Practice 1 (236)

aren't	wouldn't	who's
you're	we're	doesn't
they've	hasn't	where's

Practice 2 (237)

1. I'll . . . you'll
2. It's . . . wouldn't
3. shouldn't . . . you're
4. isn't . . . weren't
5. I'd . . . who's . . . it's

Practice (238)

1. They're . . . their
2. You're . . . your
3. Who's . . . whose
4. It's . . . it's
5. you're . . . their . . . it's

Apostrophe to Show Ownership or Possession

Practice 1 (239–240)

1. Lola's sneakers
2. Veronica's lipstick
3. His brother's house
4. The car's tires
5. Jan's bicycle
6. the blue jay's nest
7. my paper's title
8. My mother's arthritis
9. My sister's boyfriend
10. anybody's game

Practice 2 (240)

2. Georgia's
3. friend's
4. teacher's
5. girlfriend's
6. Albert's
7. daughter's
8. boss's
9. night's
10. son's

Practice 3 (241)

Answers will vary, but the following possessors should be used:

2. neighbor's
3. car's
4. sister's
5. doctor's

Practice (242–243)

1. onions: simple plural meaning more than one onion
   Rons: Ron's, meaning "eyes of Ron"
   eyes: simple plural meaning more than one eye
2. mothers: mother's, meaning "recipe of my mother"
   relatives: simple plural meaning more than one relative
   friends: simple plural meaning more than one friend
3. Sailors: simple plural meaning more than one sailor
   stations: simple plural meaning more than one station
   ships: ship's, meaning "alarm of the ship"
4. kites: kite's, meaning "string of the kite"
   branches: simple plural meaning more than one branch
5. guys: simple plural meaning more than one guy
   colleges: college's, meaning "football game of my college"
   movies: simple plural meaning more than one movie
6. cuffs: simple plural meaning more than one cuff
   mens: men's, meaning "pants of men"
   pants: simple plural meaning more than one pants leg
   ashes: simple plural meaning more than one ash
7. tubes: simple plural meaning more than one inner tube
   rivers: river's, meaning "rushing currents of the river"
   currents: simple plural meaning more than one current

8. directors: director's, meaning "specialty of the director"
   films: simple plural meaning more than one film
   vampires: simple plural meaning more than one vampire

9. copies: simple plural meaning more than one copy
   companys: company's, meaning "tax returns of the company"
   returns: simple plural meaning more than one return
   years: simple plural meaning more than one year

10. Scientists: simple plural meaning more than one scientist
    Africas: Africa's, meaning "Congo region of Africa"
    relatives: simple plural meaning more than one relative
    dinosaurs: simple plural meaning more than one dinosaur

Practice (244)

1. firefighters'
2. drivers'
3. friends'
4. grandparents'
5. soldiers'

QUOTATION MARKS

Introductory Project

1. Quotation marks set off the exact words of a speaker.
2. Commas and periods following quotations go inside quotation marks.

Practice 1 (248)

1. "Have more trust in me," Lola said to her mother.
2. The instructor asked Sharon, "Why are your eyes closed?"
3. Christ said, "I come that you may have life, and have it more abundantly."
4. "I refuse to wear those itchy wool pants!" Ralph shouted at his parents.
5. His father replied, "We should give all the clothes you never wear to the Salvation Army."
6. The nervous boy whispered hoarsely over the telephone, "Is Linda home?"
7. "When I was ten," Lola said, "I spent my entire summer playing Monopoly."
8. Tony said, "When I was ten, I spent my whole summer playing basketball."
9. The critic wrote about the play, "It runs the gamut of emotions from A to B."
10. "The best way to tell if a mushroom is poisonous," the doctor solemnly explained, "is if you find it in the stomach of a dead person."

Practice 2 (248–249)

1. Fred said, "I'm going with you."
2. "Everyone passed the test," the instructor informed them.
3. My parents asked, "Where were you?"
4. "I hate that commercial," he muttered.
5. "If you don't leave soon," he warned, "you'll be late for work."

Practice 1 (250)

2. Fran replied, "I thought you were going to write them this year."
3. Nick said, "Writing invitations is a woman's job."
4. Fran exclaimed, "You're crazy!"
5. Nick replied, "You have much better handwriting than I do."

Practice 2 (251)

1. He said that as the plane went higher, his heart sank lower.
2. The designer said that shag rugs were back in style.
3. The foreman asked Jake if he had ever operated a lift truck.
4. My nosy neighbor asked if Ed and Ellen were fighting.
5. Martha complained that she married a man who eats Tweeties cereal for breakfast.

Practice (252–253)

1. The young couple opened their brand-new copy of Cooking Made Easy to the chapter titled "Meat Loaf Magic."
2. Annabelle borrowed Hawthorne's novel The Scarlet Letter from the library because she thought it was about a varsity athlete.
3. Did you know that the musical West Side Story is actually a modern version of Shakespeare's tragedy Romeo and Juliet?
4. I used to think that Richard Connell's short story "The Most Dangerous Game" was the scariest piece of suspense fiction in existence—until I began reading Bram Stoker's classic novel Dracula.
5. Every year at Easter we watch a movie like The Robe on television.
6. During the past year, Time featured an article about DNA titled "Building Blocks of the Future."
7. My father still remembers the way that Julie Andrews sang "I Could Have Danced All Night" in the original Broadway production of My Fair Lady.

8. As I stand in the supermarket checkout line, I always look at a feature titled "Life in These United States" in the <u>Reader's Digest</u>.

9. My favorite Simon and Garfunkel song is "Mrs. Robinson," which can be found in their album <u>Bookends</u>.

10. Absentmindedly munching a Dorito, Hana opened the latest issue of <u>Newsweek</u> to its cover story, "The Junk Food Explosion."

COMMA

Introductory Project

1. a. news, a movie, a *Honeymooners* rerun,
   b. check, write your account number on the back,
   (commas between items in a series)
2. a. indoors,
   b. car,
   (commas after introductory words)
3. a. opossum, an animal much like the kangaroo,
   b. Derek, who was recently arrested,
   (commas around interruptors)
4. a. preregistration, but
   b. intersection, and
   (commas between complete thoughts)
5. a. said, "Why
   b. interview," said David, "I
   (commas with direct quotations)
6. a. 1,500,000
   b. Highway, Jersey City, New Jersey, October 23, 1992,
   (commas with everyday material)

Practice I (258)

1. red, white, and blue
2. laundry, helped clean the apartment, waxed the car, and watched
3. patties, special sauce, lettuce, cheese, pickles, and onions

Practice 2 (258)

1. Cold eggs, burnt bacon, and watery orange juice are the reasons I've never returned to that diner for breakfast.
2. Bill relaxes by reading Donald Duck, Archie, and Bugs Bunny comic books.
3. Tonight I've got to work at the restaurant for three hours, finish writing a paper, and study for an exam.

Practice I (259)

1. When I didn't get my paycheck at work, . . . According to the office computer,
2. After seeing the accident, . . . Even so,
3. Once there, . . . Also,

Practice 2 (259)

1. Even though Tina had an upset stomach, she went bowling with her husband.
2. Looking back over the last ten years, I can see several decisions I made that really changed my life.
3. Instead of going with my family to the mall, I decided to relax at home and to call up some friends.

Practice I (261)

1. deadline, the absolute final deadline,
2. cow, a weird creature, . . . dish, who must also have been strange,
3. Tod, voted the most likely to succeed in our high school graduating class, . . . King Kongs, a local motorcycle gang,

Practice 2 (261)

1. My sister's cat, which she got from the animal shelter, woke her when her apartment caught on fire.
2. A bulging biology textbook, its pages stuffed with notes and handouts, lay on the path to the college parking lot.
3. A baked potato, with its crispy skin and soft inside, rates as one of my all-time favorite foods.

Practice (262–263)

1. no comma needed
2. mountain, and
3. eating, but
4. speech, and
5. no comma needed
6. car, but
7. no comma needed
8. shops, but
9. no comma needed
10. math, for

Practice I (263)

1. fries," said Lola. . . . She asked, "What
2. Coke," responded Tony.
3. grief," said Lola. . . . "In fact," she continued, "how much

Practice 2 (264)

1. "You better hurry," Thelma's mother warned, "or you're going to miss the last bus of the morning."
2. "It really worries me," said Marty, "that you haven't seen a doctor about that strange swelling under your arm."
3. The student sighed in frustration and then raised his hand. "My computer has crashed again," he called out to the teacher.

Practice (265)

1. sorry, sir,
2. 6, 1954,
3. June 30, 2000,
4. Seas, P.O. Box 760, El Paso, Texas 79972.
5. Leo, turn

Practice (266)

1. Jerome said to me that
2. must be added to
3. cat fur and dust,
4. on the corner asked,
5. tractor rumbled
6. and Atlantic City are
7. young man who
8. money and
9. reads a lot
10. invite her to

OTHER PUNCTUATION MARKS

Introductory Project

1. Artist:
2. life-size
3. (1856–1939)
4. track;
5. breathing—but alive.

Practice (271)

1. work: 2. Sears: 3. Hazlitt:

Practice (272)

1. death; in . . . death; and
2. ridiculous; for example,
3. Bank; Jay . . . Bank; and

Practice (273)

1. condition—except
2. minutes—in fact,
3. work—these

Practice (274)

1. sixty-five dollars . . . sixty-five cents
2. ten-year-old . . . self-confident
3. split-level

Practice (274)

1. charts (pages 16–20) in
2. prepare (1) a daily list of things to do and (2) a weekly study schedule.
3. drinkers (five or more cups a day) suffer

DICTIONARY USE

Introductory Project

1. fortutious (fortuitous)
2. hi/er/o/glyph/ics
3. be
4. oc/to/ge/nar'/i/an
5. (1) an identifying mark on the ear of a domestic animal (2) an identifying feature or characteristic

Answers to the activities are in your dictionary. Check with your instructor if you have any problems.

SPELLING IMPROVEMENT

Introductory Project

Misspellings:

akward . . . exercize . . . buisness . . . worryed . . . shamful . . . begining . . . partys . . . sandwichs . . . heros

Practice (288)

1. studied
2. advising
3. carries
4. stopping
5. terrified
6. compelled
7. retiring
8. hungrily
9. expelling
10. judges

Practice (290)

1. groceries
2. towns
3. supplies
4. bodies
5. lotteries

6. passes
7. tragedies
8. watches
9. suits
10. bosses

OMITTED WORDS AND LETTERS

Introductory Project

> bottles . . . in the supermarket . . . like a wind-up toy . . .
> his arms . . . an alert shopper . . . with the crying

Practice (294–295)

1. When I began eating the box of chicken I bought at the
    fast-food restaurant, I found several pieces that consisted
    of a lot of crust covering nothing but chicken bones.
2. Sally had an instructor who tried to light a piece of chalk,
    thinking it was a cigarette.
3. In his dream, Harry committed the perfect crime: he
    killed his enemy with an icicle, so the murder weapon
    was never found.
4. Dr. Yutzer told me not to worry about the sore on my foot,
    but I decided to get a second opinion.
5. As the little girl ate the vanilla sugar cone, ice cream
    dripped out of a hole at the bottom onto her pants.
6. When thick black clouds began to form and we felt
    several drops of rain, we knew the picnic would be
    canceled.
7. After spending most of her salary on new clothes, Susan
    looks like something out of a fashion magazine.
8. As wasps buzzed around the room, I ran for a can of
    Raid.
9. Sam put the pair of wet socks in the oven, for he wanted
    to dry them out quickly.
10. Because the weather got hot and stayed hot for weeks,
    my flower garden started to look like a dried flower
    arrangement.

Practice I (295–296)

1. boyfriends . . . blows
2. curses
3. paragraphs . . . events
4. windshields . . . cars
5. houses . . . highways

6. days . . . times
7. billboards
8. chairs . . . pillows
9. watchtowers . . . states
10. motorists . . . trucks

COMMONLY CONFUSED WORDS

Introductory Project

1. Incorrect: your
    Correct: you're
2. Incorrect: who's
    Correct: whose
3. Incorrect: there
    Correct: their

4. Incorrect: to
    Correct: too
5. Incorrect: Its
    Correct: It's

Homonyms (299–307)

all ready . . . already
brake . . . break
coarse . . . course
here . . . hear
hole . . . whole
It's . . . its
knew . . . new
no . . . know
pear . . . pair
past . . . passed
piece . . . peace
plain . . . plane
principal . . . principle
write . . . right
then . . . than
there . . . their . . . they're
through . . . threw
To . . . two . . . too . . . too
wear . . . where
weather . . . whether
whose . . . who's
you're . . . your

Other Words Frequently Confused (307–312)

an . . . a
Except . . . accept
advise . . . advice
affect . . . effect
Among . . . between
besides . . . beside
can . . . may
cloths . . . clothes
dessert . . . desert

Does . . . dose
fewer . . . less
former . . . latter
loose . . . lose
quite . . . quiet
Though . . . thought

Incorrect Word Forms

being that (313)

1. Since (*or* Because) she's a year older
2. because (*or* since) the bus drivers
3. Since (*or* Because) I didn't

can't hardly/couldn't hardly (313)

1. I can hardly
2. You can hardly
3. You could hardly

could of/must of/should of/would of (313–314)

1. Anita must have
2. I should have
3. they would have
4. she could have

irregardless (314)

1. regardless of the price
2. regardless of their age
3. Regardless of the risk

EFFECTIVE WORD CHOICE

Introductory Project

Correct sentences:

1. After the softball game, we ate hamburgers and drank beer.
2. Someone told me you're getting married next month.
3. Psychological tests will be given on Wednesday.
4. I think the referee made the right decision.

1 . . . 2 . . . 3 . . . 4

Note: The answers may vary for all of these word-choice practices.

Practice (319)

1. If you don't start working regularly in this course, you're going to fail the midterm exam.
2. Living with a roommate is troublesome, but the extra money helps when the rent is due.
3. We were badly beaten in the football game.
4. If people keep saying bad things about Gene, soon no one will be friends with him.
5. I got so anxious when the instructor called on me that my mind went blank.

Practice 1 (320–321)

1. Substitute reveal the reason for shed any light on.
2. Substitute was relieved for heaved a sigh of relief.
3. Substitute became a best-seller for began selling like hotcakes.
4. Substitute did not care for could not have cared less.
5. Substitute sick for feeling under the weather.

Practice (322)

1. My television is broken.
2. We went to the mall to see the new fall clothes.
3. José said he didn't like fish.
4. The fans booed when the pitcher played badly.
5. How long have you lived in that city?

Practice (324–325)

1. Because it was raining, I didn't go shopping.
2. I do not feel that prostitution should be legalized.
3. Please call me to arrange an interview.
4. While I was sick, I missed three math tests.
5. Only well-trained people get high-paying jobs.

Appendix C

Progress Charts

PROGRESS CHART FOR MASTERY TESTS

Enter Your Score for Each Test in the Space Provided

Individual Tests	1 Mastery	2 Mastery	3 Mastery	4 Mastery	5 IM	6 IM
Subjects and Verbs						░
Fragments						
Run-Ons						
Standard English Verbs						
Irregular Verbs						
Subject-Verb Agreement						
Consistent Verb Tense			░	░		░
Additional Information about Verbs	░	░	░	░		
Pronoun Reference, Agreement, and Point of View						░
Pronoun Types			░	░		░
Adjectives and Adverbs			░	░		░
Misplaced Modifiers			░	░		░
Dangling Modifiers			░	░		░
Parallelism			░	░		░

(Continues on next page)

Note to Instructors: Mastery tests are on perforated pages in this book. Tests in the Instructor's Manual are full-sized and can be reproduced on a copying machine.

PROGRESS CHART FOR MASTERY TESTS (CONCLUDED)

Individual Tests (concluded)	1 Mastery	2 Mastery	3 Mastery	4 Mastery	5 IM	6 IM
Capital Letters						
Numbers and Abbreviations						
End Marks						
Apostrophe						
Quotation Marks						
Comma						
Other Punctuation Marks						
Dictionary Use						
Spelling Improvement						
Omitted Words and Letters						
Commonly Confused Words						
Effective Word Choice						

Combined Tests	1 Mastery	2 Mastery	3 Mastery	4 Mastery	5 IM	6 IM
Fragments and Run-Ons						
Verbs						
Pronouns						
Faulty Modifiers and Parallelism						
Capital Letters and Punctuation						
Word Use						

PROGRESS CHART FOR
EDITING AND PROOFREADING TESTS

Date	Test	Step	Comments	To Do Next	Instructor's Initials
9/27	1	1a	Missed -ing frag; 3 copying mistakes	1b	JL
9/27	1	1b	No mistakes—Good job!	2a	JL

PROGRESS CHART FOR
EDITING AND PROOFREADING TESTS
(CONTINUED)

Date	Test	Step	Comments	To Do Next	Instructor's Initials

PROGRESS CHART FOR COMBINED EDITING TESTS

Enter your Score for Each Test in the Space Provided

Test 1		Test 7	
Test 2		Test 8	
Test 3		Test 9	
Test 4		Test 10	
Test 5		Test 11	
Test 6		Test 12	

PROGRESS CHART FOR
WRITING ASSIGNMENTS

Date	Paper	Comments	To Do Next
10/15	Worst job	Promising but needs more support. Also, 2 frags and 2 run-ons.	Rewrite

Date	Paper	Comments	To Do Next

INDEX